E/2017/50/Rev.1
ST/ESA/365

Department of Economic and Social Affairs

World Economic and Social Survey 2017

# Reflecting on seventy years of development policy analysis

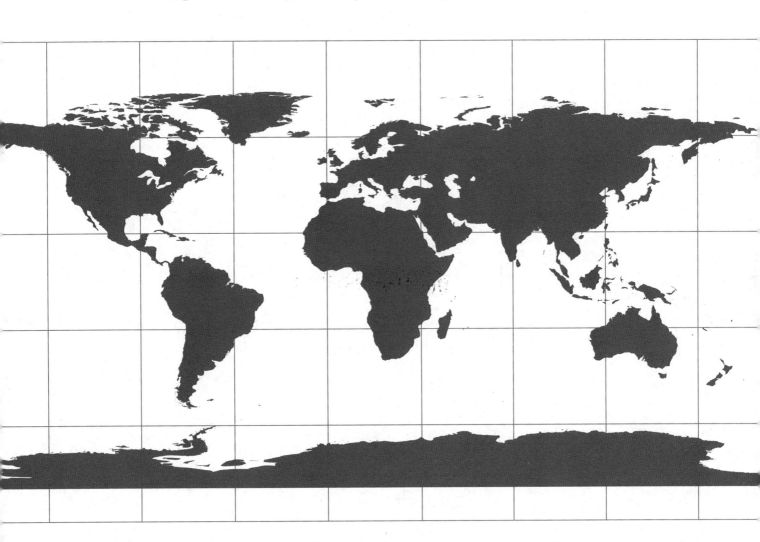

United Nations
New York, 2017

# DESA

The Department of Economic and Social Affairs of the United Nations Secretariat is a vital interface between global policies in the economic, social and environmental spheres of sustainable development and national action. The Department works in three main interlinked areas: (i) it compiles, generates and analyses a wide range of economic, social and environmental data and information on which States Members of the United Nations draw to review common problems and to take stock of policy options; (ii) it facilitates the negotiations of Member States in many intergovernmental bodies on joint courses of action to address ongoing or emerging global challenges; and (iii) it advises interested Governments on the ways and means of translating policy frameworks developed in United Nations conferences and summits into programmes at the country level and, through technical assistance, helps build national capacities.

## Note

Symbols of United Nations documents are composed of capital letters combined with figures.

E/2017/50/Rev.1
ST/ESA/365
ISBN: 978-92-1-109176-2
eISBN: 978-92-1-060598-4
Print ISSN: 1605-7910
Online ISSN: 2412-1509

United Nations publication
Sales No.: E.17.II.C.1

# Preface

The 2030 Agenda for Sustainable Development is a moral and economic imperative—and an extraordinary opportunity. The stakes are high: this is our collective chance to steer the world towards prosperity, equity, a healthy planet and peace. I am encouraged that—true to the universality of the 2030 Agenda—all regions are fully engaged in defining national priorities and action plans for implementation.

At the global level, these efforts require an enabling environment where economic and employment growth as well as financial flows support sustainable development. Yet, nearly a decade after the global financial crisis, economic growth has been disappointingly low. Experience tells us that progress requires inclusive growth with full and productive employment.

In fulfilling its mandate from the United Nations General Assembly since 1947, the *World Economic and Social Survey* has provided analysis and policy recommendations to address international economic problems and to further development. This year's *Survey* reviews 70 years of this flagship publication and draws lessons for the pursuit of sustainable development as we look ahead.

Despite significant changes in global development over the years, many parallels can be drawn between the current challenges facing the international community and those that confronted the world in the past. From this historical review, the *Survey* highlights key elements that are necessary to further development today: a stable global economy supported by coordinated global actions, well-functioning international trade and monetary systems, respect for national policy space, strengthened national capacity for development planning, and international solidarity, especially with the poor and vulnerable.

The *World Economic and Social Survey 2017* is a valuable resource for governments, scholars, development practitioners and all others engaged in the crucially important work of implementing the transformative 2030 Agenda for Sustainable Development. I commend the *Survey's* wealth of knowledge, accumulated over seven decades of development policy analysis, to a wide global audience.

ANTÓNIO GUTERRES
Secretary-General

# Acknowledgements

The *World Economic and Social Survey* is the flagship publication on major development issues prepared by the Department of Economic and Social Affairs of the United Nations Secretariat (UN/DESA).

Under the overall guidance of Lenni Montiel, Assistant Secretary-General for Economic Development at UN/DESA, the *Survey* 2017 was produced by a team led by Diana Alarcón. Core members of the team included Helena Afonso, Hoi Wai Cheng, Nicole Hunt, S. Nazrul Islam, Kenneth Iversen, Alex Julca, Hiroshi Kawamura, Marcelo LaFleur and Sérgio Vieira. Ramona Kohrs, Israel Machado and Maricela Martinez facilitated access to reference documents. Administrative support was provided by Gerard F. Reyes. Pingfan Hong, Director of the Development Policy and Analysis Division provided managerial support.

Substantive contributions in the form of background papers and draft text for sections and boxes were made by Amiya Kumar Bagchi, Anisuzzaman Chowdhury, Jayati Ghosh, John Loxley, José Antonio Ocampo, John Quiggin, Barbara Stallings, Rob Vos and Samuel Wangwe.

Comments and inputs at various stages were provided by members of the Editorial Board at UN/DESA and colleagues from other Divisions within UN/DESA. The following Expert Group Meeting participants provided valuable comments: Peride Blind, Matthias Bruckner, Maria Luisa De Jesus, Charlotte French, Navid Hanif, Ivo Havinga, Barry Herman, Dawn Holland, Robert Johnston, Richard Jolly, Seok-Ran Kim, Lisa Morrison, Eric Olson, Cristian Ossa, Mariangela Parra-Lancourt, Ingo Pitterle, Elida Reci, Marco Sánchez-Cantillo, Herman Smith, Frances Stewart and Jan Vandemoortele.

Editorial and design input at the various stages of the publication process were provided by Michael Brodsky, Leah Kennedy, Gabe Scelta, Nancy Settecasi and the Graphics Design Unit in the Department of Public Information.

# Contents

# Boxes

# Figures

# Tables

# Explanatory notes

The following symbols have been used in the tables throughout the report:

| | |
|---|---|
| .. | **Two dots** indicate that data are not available or are not separately reported. |
| – | **A dash** indicates that the amount is nil or negligible. |
| - | **A hyphen** indicates that the item is not applicable. |
| – | **A minus sign** indicates deficit or decrease, except as indicated. |
| . | **A full stop** is used to indicate decimals. |
| / | **A slash** between years indicates a crop year or financial year, for example, 2016/17. |
| - | **Use of a hyphen** between years, for example, 2016-2017, signifies the full period involved, including the beginning and end years. |

**Reference to "dollars"** ($) indicates United States dollars, unless otherwise stated.

**Reference to "billions"** indicates one thousand million.

**Reference to "tons"** indicates metric tons, unless otherwise stated.

**Annual rates** of growth or change, unless otherwise stated, refer to annual compound rates.

Details and percentages in tables do not necessarily add to totals, because of rounding.

Bibliographic information for every edition of the *World Economic and Social Survey* and of *World Economic Situation and Prospects* that is discussed in the present publication can be found on p. 199.

**The following abbreviations have been used:**

| | |
|---|---|
| CIS | Commonwealth of Independent States |
| DAC | Development Assistance Committee (OECD) |
| FDI | foreign direct investment |
| Fed | United States Federal Reserve |
| G20 | Group of Twenty |
| GATT | General Agreement on Tariffs and Trade |
| GDP | gross domestic product |
| GNI | gross national income |
| GNP | gross national product |
| ILO | International Labour Organization |
| IMF | International Monetary Fund |
| LIBOR | London Interbank Offered Rate |
| MDGs | Millennium Development Goals |
| OAPEC | Organization of Arab Petroleum Exporting Countries |
| ODA | official development assistance |
| OECD | Organization for Economic Cooperation and Development |

| | |
|---|---|
| PPP | Purchasing power parity |
| SAR | Special Administrative Region |
| SDGs | Sustainable Development Goals |
| SDRs | special drawing rights |
| UNCTAD | United Nations Conference on Trade and Development |
| UN/DESA | Department of Economic and Social Affairs of the United Nations Secretariat |
| UNDP | United Nations Development Programme |
| UNICEF | United Nations Children's Fund |
| UNIDO | United Nations Industrial Development Organization |
| UNRRA | United Nations Relief and Rehabilitation Administration |
| UN-Women | United Nations Entity for Gender Equality and the Empowerment of Women |
| USSR | Union of Soviet Socialist Republics |
| WGP | world gross product |
| WTO | World Trade Organization |
| UNICEF | United Nations Children's Fund |
| WHO | World Health Organization |

The designations employed and the presentation of the material in this publication do not imply the expression of any opinion whatsoever on the part of the United Nations Secretariat concerning the legal status of any country, territory, city or area or of its authorities, or concerning the delimitation of its frontiers or boundaries.

The term "country" as used in the text of this report also refers, as appropriate, to territories or areas.

**For analytical purposes, unless otherwise specified, the following country groupings and subgroupings have been used:**

### Developed economies (developed market economies):

Australia, Canada, European Union, Iceland, Japan, New Zealand, Norway, Switzerland, United States of America.

### Group of Eight (G8):

Canada, France, Germany, Italy, Japan, Russian Federation, United Kingdom of Great Britain and Northern Ireland, United States of America.

### Group of Twenty (G20):

Argentina, Australia, Brazil, Canada, China, France, Germany, India, Indonesia, Italy, Japan, Mexico, Republic of Korea, Russian Federation, Saudi Arabia, South Africa, Turkey, United Kingdom of Great Britain and Northern Ireland, United States of America, European Union.

### European Union (EU):

Austria, Belgium, Bulgaria, Croatia, Cyprus, Czechia, Denmark, Estonia, Finland, France, Germany, Greece, Hungary, Ireland, Italy, Latvia, Lithuania, Luxembourg, Malta, Netherlands, Poland, Portugal, Romania, Slovakia, Slovenia, Spain, Sweden, United Kingdom of Great Britain and Northern Ireland.

*EU-15:*

Austria, Belgium, Denmark, Finland, France, Germany, Greece, Ireland, Italy, Luxembourg, Netherlands, Portugal, Spain, Sweden, United Kingdom of Great Britain and Northern Ireland.

*New EU member States:*

Bulgaria, Croatia, Cyprus, Czechia, Estonia, Hungary, Latvia, Lithuania, Malta, Poland, Romania, Slovakia, Slovenia.

### Economies in transition:

*South-Eastern Europe:*

Albania, Bosnia and Herzegovina, Croatia, Montenegro, Serbia, the former Yugoslav Republic of Macedonia.

*Commonwealth of Independent States (CIS):*

Armenia, Azerbaijan, Belarus, Georgia,[a] Kazakhstan, Kyrgyzstan, Republic of Moldova, Russian Federation, Tajikistan, Turkmenistan, Ukraine, Uzbekistan.

### Developing economies:

Africa, Asia and the Pacific (excluding Australia, Japan, New Zealand and the member States of CIS in Asia), Latin America and the Caribbean.

*Subgroupings of Africa:*

*Northern Africa:*

Algeria, Egypt, Libya, Morocco, Sudan, Tunisia.

*Sub-Saharan Africa:*

All other African countries, except Nigeria and South Africa, where indicated.

*Subgroupings of Asia and the Pacific:*

*Western Asia:*

Bahrain, Iraq, Israel, Jordan, Kuwait, Lebanon, Oman, Qatar, Saudi Arabia, State of Palestine, Syrian Arab Republic, Turkey, United Arab Emirates, Yemen.

*South Asia:*

Bangladesh, Bhutan, India, Iran (Islamic Republic of), Maldives, Nepal, Pakistan, Sri Lanka.

*East Asia:*

All other developing economies in Asia and the Pacific.

*Subgroupings of Latin America and the Caribbean:*

*South America:*

Argentina, Bolivia (Plurinational State of), Brazil, Chile, Colombia, Ecuador, Paraguay, Peru, Uruguay, Venezuela (Bolivarian Republic of).

*Mexico and Central America:*

Costa Rica, El Salvador, Guatemala, Honduras, Mexico, Nicaragua, Panama.

*Caribbean:*

Barbados, Cuba, Dominican Republic, Guyana, Haiti, Jamaica, Trinidad and Tobago.

---

**a** As of 19 August 2009, Georgia officially left the Commonwealth of Independent States. However, its performance is discussed in the context of this group of countries for reasons of geographical proximity and similarities in economic structure.

### Least developed countries:

Afghanistan, Angola, Bangladesh, Benin, Bhutan, Burkina Faso, Burundi, Cambodia, Central African Republic, Chad, Comoros, Democratic Republic of the Congo, Djibouti, Equatorial Guinea, Eritrea, Ethiopia, Gambia, Guinea, Guinea-Bissau, Haiti, Kiribati, Lao People's Democratic Republic, Lesotho, Liberia, Madagascar, Malawi, Mali, Mauritania, Mozambique, Myanmar, Nepal, Niger, Rwanda, Sao Tome and Principe, Senegal, Sierra Leone, Solomon Islands, Somalia, South Sudan, Sudan, Timor-Leste, Togo, Tuvalu, Uganda, United Republic of Tanzania, Vanuatu, Yemen, Zambia.

### Small island developing States and areas:

American Samoa, Anguilla, Antigua and Barbuda, Aruba, Bahamas, Barbados, Belize, British Virgin Islands, Cabo Verde, Commonwealth of the Northern Mariana Islands, Comoros, Cook Islands, Cuba, Dominica, Dominican Republic, Fiji, French Polynesia, Grenada, Guam, Guinea-Bissau, Guyana, Haiti, Jamaica, Kiribati, Maldives, Marshall Islands, Mauritius, Micronesia (Federated States of), Montserrat, Nauru, Netherlands Antilles, New Caledonia, Niue, Palau, Papua New Guinea, Puerto Rico, Saint Kitts and Nevis, Saint Lucia, Saint Vincent and the Grenadines, Samoa, Sao Tome and Principe, Seychelles, Singapore, Solomon Islands, Suriname, Timor-Leste, Tonga, Trinidad and Tobago, Tuvalu, United States Virgin Islands, Vanuatu.

### Parties to the United Nations Framework Convention on Climate Change:

*Annex I parties:*

Australia, Austria, Belarus, Belgium, Bulgaria, Canada, Croatia, Czechia, Denmark, Estonia, European Union, Finland, France, Germany, Greece, Hungary, Iceland, Ireland, Italy, Japan, Latvia, Liechtenstein, Lithuania, Luxembourg, Monaco, Netherlands, New Zealand, Norway, Poland, Portugal, Romania, Russian Federation, Slovakia, Slovenia, Spain, Sweden, Switzerland, Turkey, Ukraine, United Kingdom of Great Britain and Northern Ireland, United States of America.

*Annex II parties:*

Annex II parties are the parties included in Annex I that are members of the Organization for Economic Cooperation and Development but not the parties included in Annex I that are economies in transition.

*Non-Annex I parties:*

Non-Annex I parties are mainly developing countries. Certain groups of developing countries are recognized by the Convention as being especially vulnerable to the adverse impacts of climate change, including countries with low-lying coastal areas and those prone to desertification and drought. Others (such as countries that rely heavily on income from fossil fuel production and commerce) experience greater vulnerability to the potential economic impacts of climate change response measures. The Convention emphasizes activities that promise to respond to the special needs and concerns of those vulnerable countries, such as investment, insurance and technology transfer.

The 48 parties classified as least developed countries by the United Nations are given special consideration under the Convention on account of their limited capacity to respond to climate change and adapt to its adverse effects. Parties are urged to take full account of the special situation of least developed countries when considering funding and technology transfer activities.

# Chapter I
# What have we learned in seventy years of development policy analysis?

## Key messages

*World Economic and Social Survey 2017* reviews the seventy-year history of a flagship publication, the oldest continuing report of its kind. A clear message from the development policy analysis carried out over seventy years is that periods of sluggish growth in the global economy pose a significant challenge to development. Anaemic growth in the current context may compromise the implementation of a transformative agenda for sustainable development. The experience of previous economic downturns attests to the urgency of expediting global policy coordination in order to accelerate economic growth, trade and financial flows for development. The objective of the present review is to draw those lessons from the past that are relevant to the implementation of the 2030 Agenda for Sustainable Development. Six messages are of particular importance.

- The *Survey* has long recognized that facilitation of global economic integration requires coordinated global actions. However, the intensification of such integration has clearly outpaced the development of effective mechanisms for global economic governance. The outbreak of the global financial crisis in 2008 was only one of the many events that illustrated the grave consequences of ineffective international policy coordination.

- Stability in the international monetary and trade systems underpins development. In that respect, the *Survey* has consistently highlighted risks associated with volatile commodity prices and warned against protectionism. Regarding the international monetary system, the *Survey* has advocated for a shift away from a single-currency system and called for effective financial regulation and supervision.

- Development, as defined by the *Survey* at its inception, is both multidimensional and context-specific and driven by the structural transformation of countries towards economic diversification, stable growth and improved living standards. The *Survey* was also an early proponent of balanced growth across the agriculture and industrial sectors as well as engagement in sustainable management of natural resources.

- Development planning and State capacity are crucial to achieving sustainable development, which requires proper coordination across various policy areas and diverse actors in bringing about structural and institutional changes.

- To accelerate development, countries need adequate policy space. During times of crisis and major adjustment, flexibility that gives countries space for adopting nationally appropriate policies is of great importance in facilitating economic recovery and development. The *Survey* has argued for a fair sharing of the adjustment burden among deficit and surplus countries during periods of economic turbulence.

- International solidarity has played an important role in supporting national development efforts. Implementation of the Marshall Plan and application of flexibility in enforcing international commitments during the post-Second World War period constitute best examples. Moving forward, it is critical to build the political will and to strengthen the governance mechanism for mobilizing international support for implementation of the 2030 Agenda for Sustainable Development.

# Key events: seventy years of development policy analysis in the *Survey*

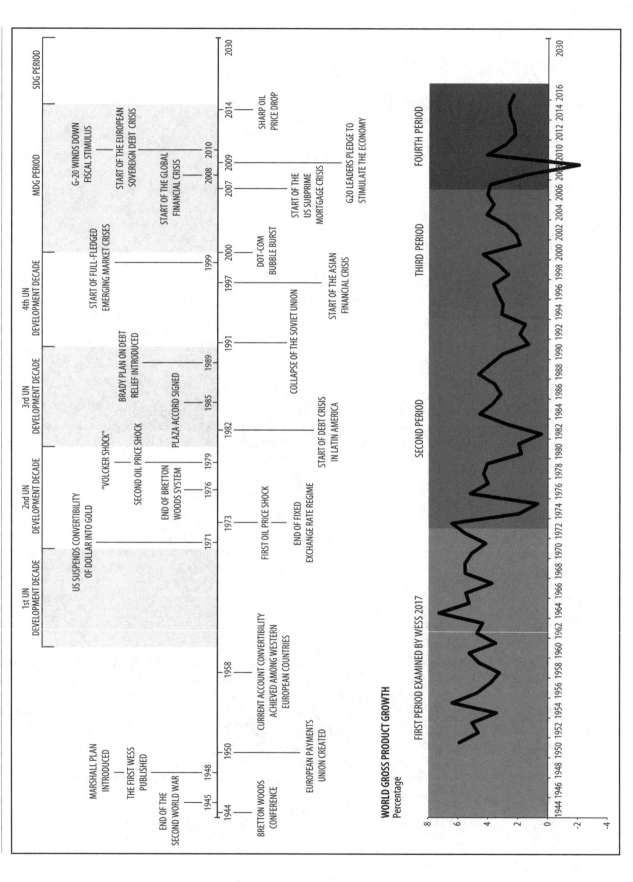

**WORLD GROSS PRODUCT GROWTH**
Percentage

## Introduction

*World Economic and Social Survey 2017* reviews the discussions on development presented in the *World Economic and Social Survey*,[1] hereinafter referred to as the *Survey*, over the past seventy years. The intention is to derive insights and lessons that can be useful for the implementation of the 2030 Agenda for Sustainable Development.[2] Such a review is particularly relevant today as countries embark, globally, upon the implementation of this ambitious agenda for "transforming our world" so as to achieve sustainable development.

Since its inception in 1947, the *Survey* had for a long time been the only publication dedicated to analysing and reporting, on an annual basis, on the evolution of the world economy and world development. It was not until 1978 that there emerged a similar effort, namely, when the World Bank published the first *World Development Report*. In accordance with its mandate of 1947, the *Survey* has provided a review of world economic conditions, as consistent with Article 55 of the Charter of the United Nations and the responsibility "to promote the solution of international economic problems, higher standards of living, full employment and conditions of economic and social progress and development" (see box I.1 and table A.1.1 in appendix A.1 for the history and evolution of the *Survey*).

**For seventy years, the *World Economic and Social Survey* has consistently reported on the global economy and development**

---

Box I.1
**Mandate of the *World Economic and Social Survey*[a]**

The *World Economic and Social Survey* is the oldest post-Second World War continuing publication dedicated to recording and analysing the performance of the global economy and global development while offering relevant policy recommendations. Publication of the *Survey* responds to General Assembly resolution 118 (II) of 31 October 1947, in which the Assembly recommended to the Economic and Social Council:

"(a) That it consider a survey of current world economic conditions and trends annually, and at such other intervals as it considers necessary, in the light of its responsibility under Article 55 of the Charter [of the United Nations] to promote the solution of international economic problems, higher standards of living, full employment and conditions of economic and social progress and development,

"(b) That such consideration include an analysis of the major dislocations of needs and supplies in the world economy,

"(c) That it make recommendations as to the appropriate measures to be taken by the General Assembly, the Members of the United Nations and the specialized agencies concerned."

The *Survey*, consistent with its mandate, has provided analysis and policy advice to both inform the international debates on development and support the efforts to meet the implementation-related challenges presented by the United Nations development agenda. Although the authors of the earlier issues of the Survey remain anonymous, some of the world's leading economists contributed to them (see appendix A.2 for a selected list of authors and contributors to the *Survey*).

a See appendix A.1 for an overview of the *Survey*'s historical evolution.

---

1    Over the 70 years under review, the *Survey* has taken on different names. In 1947, it was called the *Economic Report*; and from 1948 to 1954, the *World Economic Report*. In 1955, the publication was renamed the *World Economic Survey*. Since 1994, it has been called the *World Economic and Social Survey*. The year 1999 marked the launching of a companion publication entitled *World Economic Situation and Prospects*, which would report on macroeconomic trends. As used in the present publication, the term *Survey* may refer to any one of these reports.

2    General Assembly resolution 70/1 of 25 September 2015.

Throughout its seventy years, the *Survey* has promoted a broader understanding of development, emphasizing the importance of advancing the structural transformation of the economy, progress in social development and environmental sustainability. It has consistently documented the increasing interdependence among countries and advocated for the creation of the appropriate global institutions needed to resolve the economic and financial imbalances that often jeopardize growth and development. The *Survey* has also argued tirelessly for expediting the transfer of financial and technological resources from developed to developing countries so as to promote development.

The *Survey* played a unique role in focusing on the issue of resource transfer from developing to developed countries and has argued against over-financialization of economies. Indeed, it was ahead of the curve in predicting the possibility of what came to be known as the global financial crisis of 2008-2009. The *Survey* has put forward elaborate proposals regarding how globally coordinated policies can help accelerate growth and reverse the slow growth trajectory afflicting the global economy in the aftermath of the financial crisis. In recent years, the *Survey* has provided insightful analyses focused on how to effectively integrate the economic, social and environmental dimensions of sustainable development.

In 2015, the world community, through the General Assembly, adopted the 2030 Agenda for Sustainable Development with the aim of eradicating poverty and improving social conditions while achieving environmental sustainability. Together with the Addis Ababa Action Agenda of the Third International Conference on Financing for Development (Addis Ababa Action Agenda),[3] the Sendai Framework for Disaster Risk Reduction 2015-2030[4] and the Paris Agreement,[5] the 2030 Agenda for Sustainable Development captures the commitment of the international community to poverty eradication, human development and environmental sustainability.

Through the adoption of the Sustainable Development Goals (SDGs), the need to achieve a balance among the various dimensions of development has been placed at the core of the agenda. However, the transition towards sustainability will require deep structural changes to strengthen the links between economic growth and human development as well as the links between economic growth and the environment. Within the economic dimension itself, deep structural transformations will have to occur to facilitate economic diversification and strengthen productivity growth in the agriculture and industrial sectors in such a way as to support employment creation and improved living standards, as called for under Sustainable Development Goals 8 and 9. Accelerating the transition towards greater sustained economic growth is particularly important to least developed countries. All of these themes figured prominently in the discussions incorporated in past editions of the *Survey* and were reflected in the formulation of the International Development Strategies for the United Nations Development Decades.

The insights provided by the *Survey* over seventy years of systematic analysis of the global economy and development policy offer useful guidance for the implementation of strategies for sustainable development. Its analysis sheds light on the strategies and policies that contributed to the advancement of development in the past, as well as on those areas that

**Seventy years of policy analysis in the *Survey* offers relevant guidance for the implementation of sustainable development policies**

---

3    Adopted by the General Assembly in its resolution 69/313 of 27 July 2015, as contained in the annex thereto.

4    Adopted by the General Assembly in its resolution 69/283 of 3 June 2015, as contained in annex II thereto.

5    See FCCC/CP/2015/10/Add.1, decision 1/CP.21, annex.

continue to pose challenges. Improved international policy coordination is, in particular, an area that requires greater attention, in order to enable the creation of an environment conducive to stable growth of the world economy, a dynamic multilateral trade system and increased flows of financial resources for development. Creating an international enabling environment for development is critical for ensuring that countries have the appropriate policy space within which to "implement policies for poverty eradication and sustainable development", as called for in target 17.15 under Sustainable Development Goal 17. The review of the discussion on development available in past editions of the *Survey* will contribute to reflections on these issues.

Overall, the historical review of the analysis in the *Survey* provides food for reflection on the rich development experiences witnessed over the last seventy years. Clearly, each particular period has its own characteristics which cannot be replicated. However, looking back over the history of the *Survey*'s development policy analysis offers the opportunity to derive useful insights into the policy options available to the international community for implementation of the 2030 Agenda for Sustainable Development.

A clear message that emerges from the *Survey* concerns the urgency of strengthening national and global institutions so as to maximize the benefits from globalization by reducing the risks posed by an interdependent world. Appropriate institutions are needed to prevent the emergence of the large imbalances that almost invariably lead to global crises. In the event that imbalances—and crises—do occur, those institutions would be required to facilitate an orderly recovery that is consistent with national and global development objectives. The presence and proper functioning of such institutions can ensure that the process of globalization fulfils its promise of development of all countries, particularly the low-income countries with less resilience in the face of the dislocations associated with the operation of global markets.

In addition to managing risks and responses to crises, national and global institutions must also take a proactive role in moving human development forward. Years before the adoption of the 2030 Agenda for Sustainable Development, the 2009 *Survey* proposed a global sustainable new deal to facilitate the mobilization of the "massive investments (from the public and private sectors) in new infrastructure, new capacities and new institutions…needed to meet mitigation and adaptation challenges" (p. xviii). Based on the successful experience of the New Deal policies implemented in the United States of America to generate a recovery from the Great Depression during the 1930s, the proposed new deal would contribute to expediting stable growth of the global economy through an investment-led growth strategy. Implementation of the main components of that proposal would help turn the universal consensus reached through the adoption of the 2030 Agenda into globally coordinated policy actions to expedite investments in resilient infrastructure, employment creation and social development as a facet of the global agenda for moving towards a low-emissions, high-growth sustainable development path.

A recurrent recommendation emerging from *Survey* analyses over time has centred on the need to pay greater attention to the task of building the political will for enhanced international cooperation in designing a system of global governance that is open, transparent, participatory and responsible. Strengthening the global consensus for global collective action is of the greatest importance at the present time, when the world is facing a multiplicity of threats and a tendency to retreat behind national boundaries.

The suggestions presented above are neither new nor revolutionary. Instead, they are derived from a review of the shared experience of global development over the last seven

**Maximizing the benefits from globalization requires institutions adequately equipped …**

**…to ensure an open, transparent, participatory and responsible system of global governance**

decades. The destructive potential of crises and instability that are exported across borders, particularly to small open economies and those that are more exposed to global commodity markets, justifies rescuing forgotten lessons, engaging in new kinds of thinking and taking bold action to break the cycle of imbalances and turbulence.

## Four periods of development experience and policy analysis

In order to bring into focus the lessons derived from the past development discussion more clearly, *World Economic and Social Survey 2017* divides the seventy-year span of development experience and policy analysis into four broad periods.

The Golden Age
of Capitalism

The first period is that identified in the literature as the Golden Age of Capitalism, beginning in the post-Second World War period and ending in the 1970s, when the currency system based on the gold standard collapsed. This period witnessed unprecedented international cooperation in post-war reconstruction, establishment of an international currency system based on the gold standard, establishment of international institutions to facilitate international balance of payments (International Monetary System (IMF)) and to promote lending to developing countries (World Bank). It was also the period in which the process of decolonization entered its final phase, with a large number of countries in Africa and Asia becoming independent, and "development" emerging as a major item in the international agenda. It was also the period when several East European and Asian countries joined the (former) Union of Soviet Socialist Republics in adopting central planning as the means for allocating economic resources.

During this period, there was growing recognition of the need for the global economic system to focus also on long-term development issues. Many theories of development were formulated in response to the challenge. The United Nations responded to the development challenge by launching the First United Nations Development Decade in 1961 and the Second Development Decade in 1971. While the First Decade culminated in success, the Second faced difficult challenges. The experience and analysis of this tumultuous period can therefore provide useful insights for implementation of the 2030 Agenda, which also faces challenges arising from the current conditions in the global economy. Chapter II of this volume reviews the *Survey*'s discussion of this period.

From the collapse of the
gold standard to the
debt crisis

The second period analysed by the present *Survey* broadly comprises the 1970s and 1980s, when development in many countries experienced a setback. Beginning with the collapse of the gold standard, this period witnessed the economic upheaval caused by the oil shocks of the 1970s; the emergence of stagflation (low economic growth and high inflation); the build-up of large external debts by many developing countries, particularly those in Latin America; and the adoption of contractionary monetary policies in major developed countries leading to sharp spikes in interest rates and the resulting "debt crisis".

The response to the debt crisis by the international monetary institutions was grounded in the Washington Consensus, which was underpinned by greater faith in the market and scepticism regarding the role of the State in development. The structural adjustment policies recommended by those institutions focused on liberalization, privatization and cutting public expenditure in order to repay loans and balance the budget. This, however, meant a reduction of expenditure on health, education and the environment and neglect of issues related to income inequality. Unfortunately, the contractionary policies of structural adjustment failed by and large to produce the promised high rates of economic growth and led instead to serious deterioration as measured by important social indicators. The world witnessed a "lost decade of development", particularly in Latin America and Africa. As a result, the goals of the Second United Nations Development Decade (1971-1980) and the Third (1981-1990) were largely unmet.

At the same time, a group of East Asian economies witnessed fast economic growth, based to a large extent on rapid expansion of exports. This economic success enabled them to reduce poverty dramatically. The contrasts between experiences of the East Asian economies and those of countries acting in accordance with policies under the Washington Consensus yield significant lessons which are relevant today. Chapter III reviews the *Survey* discussion of this period.

The third period analysed by *World Economic and Social Survey 2017* begins in the 1990s, with the reaction to the development setback experienced during the previous period. Greater optimism regarding global development was generated by the ending of the cold war; and the advent of the new millennium encouraged bold long-term thinking. A recognition of the adverse social and human consequences of structural adjustment policies served to encourage a broadening of the concept of development, inspired in part by the approach of Amartya Sen to development as "freedom" and by his emphasis on "capability" and "functionings". A series of international conferences and world summits helped to build a new consensus directed towards people-centred development (for an overview of those conferences and summits, see appendix A.4).

**The new consensus towards human development and the Millennium Development Goals**

This process led to the emergence of the concept of "human development"; the launching of the *Human Development Report* in 1990 by the United Nations Development Programme (UNDP); and, ultimately, the adoption of the United Nations Millennium Declaration[6], including the formulation of the Millennium Development Goals (MDGs) and the commitment to strengthen the global partnership for development as part of the Monterrey Consensus. On the economic front, the period witnessed a surge in commodity prices which improved the export and growth performance of many developing countries. While the recovery of world growth in the early years of the new millennium provided a favourable setting for achievement of the MDGs, large underlying global imbalances eventually led to the global financial crisis in 2008. Chapter IV of this volume reviews the *Survey* discussion of this period.

The fourth period delineated by the present *Survey* begins with the development setback that resulted from the global financial crisis in 2008. The growth revival in the early years of the new millennium was accompanied by serious imbalances, which entailed large deficits and debts accumulated by many developed countries, involving a heavy reliance on debt-fuelled domestic consumption. Conditions of financial liberalization and large income gains by upper-income groups seeking investment outlets paved the way to over-financialization and greater financial integration of economies throughout the world. As a result, when the debt-fuelled bubbles burst, it resulted in the global financial crisis which led in turn to the Great Recession.

**The development setback arising from the global financial crisis**

In the absence of an adequate coordinated international response, the world economy as a whole has yet to fully overcome the challenges associated with the aftermath of the crisis and the global recession. The pace of recovery and growth across the world remains slow, with low levels of investment, limited employment expansion and slow productivity growth. Many observers wonder whether developed economies have entered a long period of secular stagnation which could act as a major constraint on growth in developing countries.

---

6　General Assembly resolution 55/2 of 8 September 2000.

At the same time, global environmental problems became acute. In particular, both atmospheric carbon concentrations and annual volumes of greenhouse gas emissions crossed crucial thresholds, creating an urgent need to reverse the process. At the same time, the experience of the decade of the 2000s led to the realization that progress in social development would not be sustainable in developing countries without economic growth, industrialization and infrastructure building. This realization exerted an impact on the elaboration of the global development agenda leading to the adoption of the 2030 Agenda for Sustainable Development, including the Sustainable Development Goals, in 2015. Implementation of the SDGs faces considerable challenges in the protracted aftermath of the global financial crisis and the great recession. Chapter V reviews the *Survey*'s discussion of this most recent period.

**Review of past experience offer important lessons for the implementation of the SDGs**

Experiences within the four periods characterized above attest to the oscillatory, cyclical nature of the development process, with considerable success having been achieved in the first period, followed by drastic setbacks in the second, and the broad revival that arose in the third, which was succeeded in turn by new setbacks in the fourth, more recent period. Although the lessons and insights to be extracted from the experiences of these periods are context-specific, they also possess features of a broader application relevant for addressing current challenges.

The following section briefly reviews the trends towards integration of the world economy and the evolution of the United Nations development agenda. This is followed by an examination of the current situation in the global economy and identification of four areas of concern—economic growth, labour markets, investment and trade, and financing for development—which need to be addressed so as to ensure support for sustainable development. The final section presents the key messages crystallized from seventy years of *Survey* policy analysis which are of the utmost relevance for the implementation of the 2030 Agenda for Sustainable Development.

## The increasingly integrated global economy and the evolution of the United Nations development agenda

In fulfilling its mandate "to promote the solution of international economic problems, higher standards of living, full employment and conditions of economic and social progress and development", the *Survey* through its policy analysis has maintained a dedicated focus on the evolution of the global economy and development trends. The present section undertakes a brief examination of the trend towards increasing integration of the world economy and the evolution of the United Nations development agenda—two processes that have provided the context for *Survey* policy analysis.

### Enhanced international policy coordination in an interdependent world

One of the major issues analysed by the *Survey* over the years has been the growing interdependence of the world economy and hence the increasing importance placed on international policy coordination for ensuring sustained growth and development.

After the Second World War, the world experienced increased economic integration, driven largely by growing cross-border trade and financial flows. Increasing interdependence resulted, in most countries, in an increase of the share of external trade in national income,

**While economic integration has contributed to growth in developing countries...**

and an improvement in the access to international capital markets through financial liberalization, which contributed to economic growth in many developing countries.

However, increasing interdependence has also brought greater uncertainty.  In the area of trade, while markets that are more open have contributed to the acceleration of economic growth and employment creation, they have also exposed countries to volatile cross-border flows of goods and services and led to the displacement of workers in less competitive sectors. Commodity price volatility has been a recurrent problem, documented by the *Survey* beginning in the 1950s. More recently, rapid shifts of production and labour across borders have had visible economic, social and political effects around the world, including in developed countries.

**...it has also exposed them to greater uncertainty**

Trade and financial globalization have been generally accompanied by the emergence and evolution of global institutions, international agreements and the creation of an extensive multilateral system for global cooperation. However global economic integration has outpaced the development of appropriate institutions for global governance. The current institutional framework has failed, at times, to foresee and stave off underlying global imbalances in cross-border flows.

**The evolution of global governance has not kept pace with economic integration**

Over time, the *Survey* has documented a troubling flow of savings from developing to developed countries. Several factors have contributed to this trend, including risk-adjusted return differentials across countries, changes in expectations regarding exchange rates, and the accumulation of precautionary foreign reserves. This long-standing disequilibrium in the flow of savings has been a factor constraining investments in infrastructure and human development, especially in low income developing countries. At several points in time, this reverse flow of resources has also contributed to the emergence of global and regional financial crises, with large economic and social costs for developing countries.

During periods when it was possible to mobilize well-coordinated global responses to crisis situations, there were highly positive results in the form of faster growth and recovery. Following the Second World War, in a remarkable effort, international support was mobilized for reconstruction in countries of Western Europe. During this period, the international community also built global institutions designed to govern the international currency and payments system. In the 1980s, by contrast, lack of adequate international mechanisms for resolving global imbalances and debt problems and the painful imposition of programmes of liberalization, privatization and fiscal retrenchment led to a lost decade of development in many countries in Latin America and Africa.

**Reconstruction after the Second World War attests to the impressive results that can be achieved through global solidarity and adequate policy coordination**

## Evolution of the United Nations development agenda

The policy analysis conducted in the *Survey* has sustained a dialectical relationship with the evolution of the United Nations development agenda and other international commitments. That is to say, the choice of topics in the *Survey* over time has been influenced by the evolution of the United Nations development agenda; and *Survey* analyses in turn influenced the evolution of that agenda. A brief overview of the evolution of the United Nations development agenda provides a fuller understanding of the institutional context within which the *Survey* conducts its development policy analysis (appendix A.3 contains a synthesis of the vision and goals set in the UN development agenda).

### Four United Nations Development Decades

The First, Second, Third and Fourth United Nations Development Decades covered the periods 1961-1970, 1971-1980, 1981-1990 and 1991-2000, respectively. Those four Decades were followed by the adoption of the United Nations Millennium Declaration by the General Assembly in its resolution 55/2 of 8 September 2000, which led to the formulation of the Millennium Development Goals for the period 2000-2015. The Sustainable Development Goals were adopted in 2015 as part of the universal commitment to sustainable development, as embodied in General Assembly resolution 70/1, with specific goals to be met by 2030. Appendix A.3 offers a synthesis of the visions and objectives set out in those international commitments.

*The concept of development adopted by the Survey has been associated with structural change...*

The concept of development as adopted by the *Survey* early on envisages a broad process of "growth plus change". The scope of that concept extends much beyond simple economic growth to encompass "structural change" or "structural transformation", which is needed to translate simple economic growth into higher standards of living, full employment and social progress and development, as called for in Article 55 of the Charter of the United Nations.

*....as reflected in the UN development agenda, including issues related to environmental sustainability...*

This expanded concept of development has been well reflected in the United Nations development agenda over time. Objectives for social development were recognized in the development agenda, as every United Nations Development Decade incorporated an increasingly comprehensive set of social goals for accelerating efforts towards addressing poverty, hunger, malnutrition, illiteracy, safe and affordable housing, and disease, among other issues. Promotion of education in general and vocational and technical training was also a consistent focus during all four Development Decades.

Environmental components entered into the development agenda starting with the International Development Strategy for the Second United Nations Development Decade (1971-1980), as adopted by the General Assembly in its resolution 2626 (XXV) of 24 October 1970. Under that Strategy, Governments pledged to "intensify national and international efforts to arrest the deterioration of the human environment" and "to take measures towards its improvement" (para. 72). The International Development Strategies for the subsequent Development Decades continued to underscore the need to ensure environmental sustainability by expanding their focus to issues such as pollution, deforestation, desertification and soil degradation.

*...economic diversification for stable and balanced growth...*

Clearly, the United Nations development agenda has adopted a comprehensive concept of development that extends beyond economic growth alone. But there has also been a recognition of the role of economic growth in facilitating the expansion of the resources available to countries for satisfying human needs. The importance of the economy has been formally acknowledged in the International Development Strategies for the United Nations Development Decades through the inclusion of quantitative goals regarding, for example, economic growth, increased saving and investment, expansion of exporting capacity and greater integration of international trade. Industrialization, economic diversification and productive agriculture have also been highlighted as crucial for achieving economic development and poverty reduction.

*... and the reduction of inequality between and within countries*

Inequality was also a recurrent theme throughout the United Nations Development Decades. Under the First United Nations Development Decade, as adopted by the General Assembly in its resolution 1710 (XVI) of 19 December 1961, concern was already expressed regarding the increasing income gap between developed and developing countries (see, for example, the fourth preambular para. of that resolution). Further, distributional imbalances *within* countries were highlighted as early as 1970, in the International Development Strategy for the Second Development Decade, where it was stated that the "ultimate purpose of development is to provide increasing opportunities to all people for a better life" (para. 18) and that it was "essential to bring about a more equitable distribution of income and wealth". Specifically, the Strategy called for a substantial reduction in "regional, sectoral and social" disparities (ibid.).

The emphasis on development as a long-term process which requires coordinated policy efforts, underpinned by strong domestic resource mobilization and supported by international commitments, prevailed in all four United Nations Development Decades. An overarching theme that was emphasized during the Development Decades, whose strategies recognized the interlinkages among different dimensions of development, was the establishment of integrated national development plans in accordance with countries' specific socioeconomic structure and stage of development. In terms of financing for development, while the Strategies for the Decades had affirmed that developing countries should bear the main responsibility in that regard, they also stressed the importance of external financial resources—both public and private—for development. Particularly, the Strategies for all of the Decades except the first included the target for developed countries of providing official development assistance (ODA) equivalent to 0.7 per cent of their gross national income (GNI) to developing countries.

As for broader international cooperation, the Strategies for the United Nations Development Decades had called consistently for strengthening international collaboration and policy coordination to support national development efforts. In its resolution 1710 (XVI), the General Assembly affirmed that it was "[c]onvinced of the need for concerted action to demonstrate the determination of Member States to give added impetus to international economic cooperation" (sixth preambular para.). This set the tone for the following Development Decades and consecutive International Development Strategies pushing for effective international cooperation in a multiplicity of areas, including trade, financing for development, environmental protection, and research and technology. The need for special assistance to least developed countries, landlocked developing countries and small island developing States in many of those areas was duly recognized, as was the need for greater international support to developing countries in accessing technology, expanding infrastructure and improving statistics.

*Policy coordination centred on integrated national development plans is key to development*

### The Millennium Development Goals

While the International Development Strategies for the four United Nations Development Decades were similar in terms of their comprehensive coverage including the various dimensions of development, the adoption of the Millennium Development Goals represented an effort to focus on human development issues, considered the most pressing problems at the time. To a great extent, such a shift in emphasis under the development agenda was driven by the experience of many developing countries, particularly in Africa and Latin America, during the lost decade of development from the 1980s to the early 1990s, when the overemphasis on policies designed to stimulate economic growth failed to translate into poverty reduction and broader human development. Formulation of the Millennium Development Goals reflected the concerns expressed at the above-mentioned series of summits and international conferences organized by the United Nations in the 1980s and 1990s, which focused on human development outcomes (see appendix A.4).

*Unlike the focus of previous United Nations development strategies, that of the MDGs was on human development…*

While the Millennium Development Goals, with their particular focus on poverty, provided, collectively, an integrated perspective for the implementation of policies aimed at advancing the social agenda, they placed less emphasis on growth-induced structural transformation and the environment. As a result, issues such as employment, productivity, investment and changes in production patterns received less attention compared with the focus during the United Nations Development Decades. Moreover, while gender equality was featured as one of the MDG goals and poverty reduction was linked with addressing inequality, economic inequalities and in many other dimensions were not explicitly incorporated within the MDG framework. The Millennium Development Goals continued the tradition of the United Nations development agenda in calling for international cooperation, with Goal 8 dedicated to strengthening the global partnership for development, including issues related to trade and finance; addressing the special needs of the least developed countries, landlocked developing countries and small island developing States; external debt sustainability; affordability of essential drugs; and new technologies.

### 2030 Agenda for Sustainable Development

On 25 September 2015, the General Assembly, by its resolution 70/1, adopted the 2030 Agenda for Sustainable Development, including the 17 Sustainable Development Goals and 169 targets. A total of 193 international Heads of State and Government and High Representatives committed themselves to sustainable development through full implementation of the Agenda by 2030. This was complemented by the welcoming of the entry into force of the Paris Agreement by the Assembly in its resolution 71/228 of 21 December 2016 and the endorsement by the Assembly of both the Addis Ababa Action Agenda of the Third International Conference on Financing for Development, on 27 July 2015, and the Sendai Framework for Disaster Risk Reduction 2015-2020, on 3 June 2015. These international agreements were the outcome of a long process of negotiations among States Members of the United Nations and consultations with civil society organizations, the private sector, academics and the larger development community. The new international consensus for sustainable development therefore reflects the aspirations of broad groups of peoples across the globe.

The 2030 Agenda for Sustainable Development revives the tradition of previous development strategies by providing a comprehensive framework for global development. The Sustainable Development Goals, as formulated, fully capture the various dimensions of development, but, most importantly, the Goals stress the interdependence across its economic, social and environmental dimensions. For example, the goal of economic growth encompasses various social and environmental dimensions, such as environmental sustainability and inclusiveness, with full and productive employment and decent work for all. A similar emphasis is observed in the articulation of all the other Goals, highlighting the interconnectivity across the various dimensions of sustainable development. This feature of the 2030 Agenda calls for policy coherence so as to ensure that the various dimensions of development are taken into account in the design of policy interventions.

In terms of the level of ambition, the 2030 Agenda surpasses previous development agendas. It calls for complete eradication of poverty, hunger, illiteracy, gender-related discrimination and other forms of social disparity. Goal 10 is to reduce inequality, both within and among countries. Further, calls, inter alia, for inclusion, elimination of discriminatory laws, social protection, and greater voice and representation of developing countries in global institutions are well reflected in the Goals. This emphasis on reduction of inequality builds upon previous commitments, as embodied in the International Development Strategies for the United Nations Development Decades, and captures the spirit of the Copenhagen Declaration on Social Development (United Nations, 1996).

The Sustainable Development Goals place special emphasis on environmental sustainability and its interlinkages with other dimensions of development. Several goals focus explicitly on the environment, such as combating climate change; protection of oceans, seas and the marine environment; and protection of terrestrial ecosystems. Issues related to the environment have also been included in the targets under Goals related to economic growth and social development.

While emphasizing social and environmental goals, the 2030 Agenda also redirects attention towards the importance of economic growth, economic diversification and industrialization, and infrastructure building, particularly within the context of the least developed countries—issues that figured prominently in the Strategies for the four United Nations Development Decades.

The 2030 Agenda has been defined as universal, applying as it does to both developed and developing countries. The role of developed countries is no longer limited to the provision of financial and technical assistance to developing countries, since it is recognized that each country has to undertake policy actions to achieve all of the Sustainable Development Goals according to its own national context.

Finally, the Sustainable Development Goals convey the importance of recognizing that countries need to define their own priorities and policies for effective progress within the various dimensions of sustainable development. In that regard, national ownership is critical to success. Countries are committed to adapting the goals and targets so that they reflect their own national reality and to defining the strategies and policies best suited to their advance along sustainable development pathways. The policy analysis conducted in the *Survey* sheds light on development experiences of the past that are still relevant to the process of forging such pathways.

**...and recognition of the importance of national ownership when defining development priorities**

## The current global situation and the challenges for sustainable development

Global conditions played an important role in facilitating (or constraining) progress towards achievement of the international development agenda. The impressive global cooperation that existed following the Second World War and the institutions that were built through that cooperation provided favourable conditions for the implementation of the First United Nations Development Decade and contributed to the achievement of the targets in advance of the deadline. However, the aspirations embodied in the International Development Strategies for the subsequent Development Decades remained largely unfulfilled owing, to a great extent, to adverse global conditions and the lack of appropriate international policy coordination and development cooperation.

More recently, progress towards achieving the Millennium Development Goals was supported by the favourable global economic conditions of the early years of the new millennium. The goal of halving extreme poverty by 2015 at the global level was achieved by 2010. However, in 2008-2009, the world suffered the most severe financial crisis since the Great Depression in 1929. Since 2009, the average annual rate of global growth has dropped by nearly one full percentage point compared with the decade before the global financial crisis, and actual growth rates have consistently disappointed

**Progress in development requires an enabling international environment for stable growth and global cooperation**

**MDG implementation was supported by favourable global economic conditions early in the new millennium**

forecasters' expectations. As a result, progress in achieving some of the Millennium Development Goals slowed down in the final years before 2015.

The aforementioned experiences during the final—and post-crisis—years of the Millennium Development Goals period strongly suggest that sustained and inclusive economic growth, full and productive employment, and macroeconomic and financial stability are key elements for the achievement of the Sustainable Development Goals. Revitalizing global economic growth is therefore of the utmost importance. However, the world continues to struggle against a prolonged economic slowdown, with weak labour markets, low levels of investment and poor productivity growth. More than eight years after the global financial crisis, policymakers around the world still face enormous challenges with regard to stimulating investment and reviving global growth.

With interest rates near zero in key developed economies, traditional monetary policy instruments have had a limited effect in bringing those economies back to full strength, with significant ramifications for the global economy. Long-term stagnation in the global economy create instability in trade and financial markets, and reduce the levels of investment and concessional finance available to developing countries.

In this context, the economic performance of the global economy is a key determinant for the achievement of the 2030 Agenda for Sustainable Development. The present section examines current global economic trends and the challenges that they pose for the implementation of the Sustainable Development Goals.

**Current slow growth in the global economy constrains investments needed to achieve the SDGs**

## Economic growth

As the rate of global economic growth slowed, in 2016, to its lowest level since the Great Recession of 2008-2009, the current international economic environment continues to be a challenging one, and a return to robust and balanced growth remains elusive. Forecasts reported in *World Economic Situation and Prospects 2017* project a modest recovery in global growth for 2017 and 2018, but growth is still expected to remain below its average rate witnessed in the period 1998-2007.

Underlying the sluggishness of the global economy are the feeble pace of global investment, dwindling world trade growth and flagging productivity growth. To a large extent, these factors have been self-reinforcing, reflecting the close linkages among aggregate demand, investment, productivity and trade. They have been exacerbated by low commodity prices since mid-2014, and by policy tightening in response to mounting fiscal and current account deficits further dampening growth prospects. In addition, conflict and geopolitical tensions continue to take a heavy toll on economic prospects in several regions.

The lack of dynamism in economic growth is likely to affect the efforts to achieve the Sustainable Development Goals in several ways. It can limit the capacity of the economy to create jobs and raise incomes and thereby reduce poverty through economic growth. Such lack of dynamism can also limit the financial resources available for essential investment needed in areas such as infrastructure, health care, education, social protection and climate change adaptation. Ultimately, the lack of sufficient resources could undermine the political will to vigorously pursue the development objectives and commitments underpinning the 2030 Agenda for Sustainable Development.

## Labour market

The protracted period of weak global growth has impacted employment. According to estimates provided by *World Employment and Social Outlook: Trends 2016* (International Labour Organization, 2016a), there were over 27 million more unemployed people in 2016 than before the global financial crisis. *World Employment and Social Outlook: Trends 2017* (International Labour Organization, 2017) expects global unemployment to increase further, by 3.4 million, in 2017, driven by rising unemployment in emerging economies. At the same time, vulnerable employment remains pervasive. Globally, 1.4 billion people (constituting 42 per cent of total employment) face vulnerable employment conditions in 2017.

The unemployment rates in some large developed countries, including Germany, Japan, the United Kingdom of Great Britain and Northern Ireland and the United States of America, have receded towards or below pre-crisis levels. However, unlike Germany and the United Kingdom, most other members of the European Union continue to struggle with high unemployment rates. At the same time, real wages have been stagnant or declining in recent years, a factor that has contributed to rising income inequality in many developed countries.

Also, in most developing regions, labour-market conditions have worsened in recent years. Most regions face the challenge of high unemployment and/or high vulnerable employment. In East and South Asia, unemployment rates are generally low, but vulnerable employment, informal employment and working poverty remain significant challenges for most countries. In Latin America and the Caribbean, labour-market conditions have deteriorated in recent years in the wake of severe economic crises in several countries. In sub-Saharan Africa, poor-quality employment remains the most significant labour-market challenge, which has been compounded by rapid growth of the working-age population. Northern Africa and Western Asia have elevated unemployment rates as well.

In many regions, both developed and developing, youth unemployment is a huge concern. As reported in *World Employment and Social Outlook: Trends for Youth 2016* (International Labour Organization, 2016b), after a number of years of improvement, the global youth unemployment rate was estimated to have increased to 13.1 per cent in 2016. High youth unemployment can have severe implications for progress towards achieving the Sustainable Development Goals, as it can exert both immediate and long-term impacts on inequality and working poverty, labour-force withdrawal, outward migration, disincentives to pursue education and social unrest.

**High levels of unemployment, vulnerable employment and stagnant wages may compromise poverty reduction and other SDG targets**

## Investment and trade

In recent years, weak investment has been the fundamental reason for the slowdown in global economic growth, through its linkages with demand, productivity and international trade. Sluggish demand conditions, compounded by high economic and policy uncertainty in the global environment, have made firms reluctant to invest in productive capital. In spite of easy global monetary conditions, capital investment growth failed to rebound after the global financial crisis and has slowed markedly since 2014.

The protracted period of weak investment explains the slowdown in productivity growth that has been observed in developed and many developing economies. Reduced investment can adversely impact the rate of innovation and the quality of infrastructure,

**One factor explaining the slowdown in global economic growth is weak investment...**

which in turn drive technological change and efficiency gains generating productivity growth in the medium term. Insufficient investments in infrastructure, such as public utilities, transportation and renewable energy projects, can undermine growth and sustainable development prospects.

...which has restrained global trade

The declining demand for capital goods associated with weak investment has also restrained global trade. In fact, capital goods account for about 39 per cent of world merchandise trade. Consequently, in many countries, the visible decline in investments has imposed a significant constraint on trade growth. Against this backdrop, world trade volumes expanded by just 1.2 per cent in 2016. The weakness in trade flows is widespread and can be witnessed across developed, developing and transition economies. Furthermore, trade growth is weak not only from a historical perspective, but also in relation to overall economic growth. Since the 1990s, the ratio of world trade growth to world gross product growth has fallen steadily, from a factor of 2.5 to 1.

As international trade has the potential to speed the rate of technological diffusion between countries and improve the efficiency of resource allocation, the slowdown in world trade growth may result in weak productivity growth. Experience from the past shows clearly that international trade has generated substantial economic gains for many countries through improved efficiency in the allocation of resources worldwide. International trade, however, has also led to major dislocations when certain economic sectors become less competitive in a larger global environment; such dislocations have been associated with widening income inequality, job losses and declining wages for workers in those sectors.

More recently, the apparent rise in the appeal of protectionism and inward-looking policies in many countries reflects growing discontent with the way in which the costs and benefits arising from deeper global economic integration have been distributed. A universal, rules-based, open, non-discriminatory and equitable multilateral trading system—as called for under Sustainable Development Goal target 17.10—can make an important contribution to the acceleration of development efforts in many countries, provided that there are proper mechanisms in place, both nationally and internationally, to manage global imbalances and prevent negative social impacts.

Unless these trends are reversed, progress towards achieving sustainable development may be compromised

Subdued trade and investment are together affecting productivity growth, which can have long-term implications for progress towards achieving the Sustainable Development Goals. Unless these trends are reversed, the progress towards these goals may be compromised, particularly with respect to the goals of eradicating extreme poverty and creating decent work for all.

## Financing for sustainable development

Sustainable development requires the mobilization of significant financial resources

Closing the financing gap so as to achieve the Sustainable Development Goals by 2030 requires the mobilization of significant financial resources, both domestic and international. However, the prolonged slowdown in global economic growth makes generating long-term investment particularly challenging.

The period of weak economic growth has negatively affected government revenues in many countries, resulting in a worsening of fiscal positions. For the commodity-dependent developing economies, the growing strains on public finances have been particularly marked since the sharp decline in commodity prices in 2014. Foreign currency-denominated debt has been gaining in importance in developing countries, which is explained partly by historically low interest rates in developed countries, leaving borrowers exposed to exchange rate risk.

With efforts to ensure fiscal and debt sustainability, there is a growing risk that countries will resort to cutting social protection expenditures, for the provision of, for example, income support, health care and education. Also, cutbacks in productive investment, such as in crucial infrastructure projects, will worsen existing structural bottlenecks and constrain productivity growth in the medium to long run, further impeding the realization of the Sustainable Development Goals. In this regard, international finance is a critical complement to domestic revenue mobilization. However, for a long time, developing countries as a whole have been experiencing large outflows of financial resources.

The monetary policies adopted in developed economies in the aftermath of the global financial crisis have had a significant effect on capital flows to and from developing countries, especially emerging markets with a high degree of financial market openness. In particular, the use by developed country central banks of unconventional monetary policy instruments—such as large-scale asset purchases under a policy known as quantitative easing—has had sizeable cross-border spill-over effects. Recent empirical studies indicate that the quantitative easing measures have amplified the procyclicality and volatility of capital flows to developing countries.

These large swings in cross-country capital flows have led to increased financial vulnerability in many countries. For central banks and Governments, managing volatile capital flows has presented a significant policy challenge in recent years. Going forward, the divergence of monetary policy stances between the United States Federal Reserve and central banks of other major countries could further intensify capital flow volatility.

ODA and other forms of international public financing are critical channels for the financing of sustainable development, especially in the least developed countries. Concessional and non-concessional international public financial flows to developing countries have risen modestly over the past few years. According to the Organization for Economic Cooperation and Development (OECD) Development Assistance Committee (DAC), development aid reached a new peak of US$ 142.6 billion in 2016, an increase of 8.9 per cent from 2015. As a share of GNI, it increased to 0.32 per cent, up from 0.30 per cent in 2015. However, only six countries met the target of keeping ODA at or above the level of 0.7 per cent of GNI.[7]

Lending by multilateral development banks and through South-South cooperation has risen notably in the past few years. Nonetheless, available domestic and international financial resources remain insufficient to fill investment financing gaps for sustainable development, particularly in the poorest countries.

Putting the global economy and the global financial system back on a dynamic path requires faster progress on the systemic issues related to policy and institutional coherence for enhanced "global macroeconomic stability", as captured in Sustainable Development Goal target 17.13.

**The global economy and financial systems need to be put on a dynamic path in order to facilitate progress towards the SDGs**

## Key messages

The current global economic situation, including its implications for sustainable development, poses a serious challenge. Within this context, the following six key messages, distilled from a careful review of analyses conducted by the *World Economic and Social Survey* over

---

7    See http://www.oecd.org/dac/development-aid-rises-again-in-2016-but-flows-to-poorest-countries-dip.htm.

the seventy years of its publication, are of the utmost relevance for the implementation of the 2030 Agenda:

(a) Development is multidimensional, context-specific, and about transformation;

(b) Development planning and State capacity are important for achieving results;

(c) Global integration requires global policy coordination;

(d) Stability in the international monetary and trade system underpins development;

(e) Countries need adequate policy space for accelerating development;

(f) International solidarity plays an important role in supporting national development efforts.

## Development is multidimensional, context-specific, and about transformation

The concept of development, which has evolved over time, has been duly reflected in the analysis of the *Survey*. In the late 1950s, the *Survey* began to recognize that "[t]he problem of economic development is not merely one of inducing marginal shifts in the allocation of resources among existing branches of economic activity; it is rather one of introducing large-scale fundamental changes into the economic structure" (*World Economic Survey 1959*, p. 7) .

Economic development was recognized as the process leading, through the structural transformation of countries, towards economic diversification, stable growth which reflects a balance between the agricultural and industrial sectors, and improved living standards. The *Survey* advanced an argument of great relevance to many developing countries today, namely, that a "rapid breaking up of the traditional sector is neither likely to happen nor wise to recommend" and that "[o]n the contrary, optimal growth of the economy requires a balance between the release of factors from the subsistence sector and the opening up of employment opportunities in the market sector" (*World Economic Survey 1969-1970*, pp. 15-16). In addition, there was a clear recognition of the need to stimulate high and stable growth, and in that regard, that "[t]oday's problem of scarcity and want [was] too immense to be tackled merely by redistributing and improving existing quantities" (*World Economic Survey, 1971*, p. 12). Accelerating economic growth, especially in the context of the least developed countries, is essential, and duly recognized under Sustainable Development Goal 8, particularly in target 8.1, which calls for annual GDP growth of at least 7 per cent per year in the least developed countries.

Early on, social and economic objectives were interlinked within the concept of development. Issues related to the management of natural resources, environmental degradation and climate change and their links with other dimensions of development were incorporated in the analysis of the *Survey* over time, with an even greater focus on these dimensions in the early 2000s.

With respect to an issue of such great significance for current discussions, *World Economic Survey 1969-1970* gave due recognition to the importance of context by affirming that "[d]evelopment is no predestined path along which all countries must go: it is a diverse and uncertain process reflecting the culture and preferences of people as well as the resources at their disposal and an ever-changing technology" (p. 1).

## Development planning and State capacity are important for achieving results

Strengthening States' capacity for strategic planning is one issue of particular relevance with respect to the challenges associated with the effort to achieve sustainable development. Strengthening the positive interrelations along the economic, social and environmental dimensions of development requires proper coordination both across various policy areas and among diverse actors, including the private sector, Governments and civil society. Effecting the transition towards sustainable development requires improved institutional capacity within Governments to make short-term policy decisions consistent with long-term development objectives.

In 1964, the *Survey* incorporated a discussion on planned development which is still relevant today. The *Survey* observed that "the acceleration of economic and social development requires a more long-sighted approach to policy formulation" and that "it has come to be understood that current policy decisions can no longer be made simply in response to the circumstances of the moment but have to contribute actively to bringing about the structural and institutional changes which underlie economic development" (*World Economic Survey 1964*, Part I, p. 2). Improved capacity of public administration for domestic resource mobilization and the quality of social services remain key to sustainable development.

The importance of strategic planning is accompanied by the recognition of the critical role of the State for development. The contrast between the experience of countries in Latin America and Africa and countries in Asia in the 1980s and 1990s provided insights into the important role of the State in the management of the economy. Countries following the market-centred policy direction of the Washington Consensus endured large development setbacks, while countries with a more active developmental State exhibited stronger growth, economic diversification and large-scale poverty reduction. According to the analysis of the *Survey*, strengthening the capacity of national States to manage the economy is critical to long-term development.

With the adoption of the 2030 Agenda, the international consensus has come back full circle to recognize the importance of development planning and the need to raise countries' capacity to manage the interlinkages across the various dimensions of sustainable development, over longer periods of time and with full account taken of the role of multiple actors. Sustainable Development Goal target 17.9 explicitly calls for strengthening capacity-building "to support national plans to implement all the Sustainable Development Goals", an issue that is well reflected in the formulation of other Sustainable Development Goals.

## Global integration requires global policy coordination

From the very first edition of the *Survey*, entitled *Economic Report: Salient Features of the World Economic Situation 1945-47*, there was explicit recognition of the need for coordinated global action to accelerate the growth of world production, to facilitate the flow of goods and services across countries and to support effective utilization of resources. An expanding and integrated world economy (p. 29) is central to the promotion of "higher standards of living, full employment, and conditions of economic and social progress and development", in line with Article 55 of the Charter of the United Nations.

In the 1970s and 1980s, the lack of effective international cooperation led to high inflation, macroeconomic instability, high unemployment in developed countries and, at least, as mentioned above, one decade of lost development in major regions of the world. Throughout the 1970s and 1980s, the *Survey* argued for international economic coordination, observing that "a greater measure of economic cooperation among countries is a shared requirement for sustained revival of the world economy" (*World Economic Survey 1983*, p. 18).

Intensification of global economic integration since the 1990s has clearly outpaced the development of global institutions and arrangements for proper governance of the global economic system. In the early years of the 2000s, the lack of effective international mechanisms for macroeconomic policy coordination and deeper flaws in the international financial architecture facilitated the growth of the major imbalances that contributed to the 2008 global financial crisis.

The *Survey* has repeatedly emphasized the need to create proper international mechanisms for policy coordination, as defined in target 17.13, under Sustainable Development Goal 17, with adequate representation from developing countries—a central requirement that is clearly recognized in target 16.8: to "broaden and strengthen the participation of developing countries in the institutions of global governance".

## Stability in the international monetary and trade system underpins development

A recurrent concern of the *Survey* has been the large fluctuations in commodity prices. The absence of mechanisms for managing these price swings and corresponding fluctuations in foreign exchange earnings has characterized the world economy since the early post-war years and continues to be a problem today. Excessive price fluctuations in commodity markets disrupt development, especially in view of their disproportionate impact on the income, health and nutritional status of poor consumers and small-scale farmers. The *Survey* has put forward several recommendations including a proposal to set up international commodity price stabilization funds for the purpose of helping low-income countries cope with large price fluctuations. Such ideas are quite relevant today in conditions where, for example, commodity prices have experienced a downward slide following the commodity boom in the early years of the present century.

With regard to trade, the *Survey* has consistently argued for multilateralism and warned of the dangers of protectionism in response to rising trade deficits. Its strong concerns with respect to the risks of protectionism were expressed throughout the 1980s. For example, in *World Economic Survey 1981-1982*, it was noted that while the world economy had avoided "trade wars of the type experienced in the 1920s and 1930s" and liberalization efforts had continued on some fronts, the slowdown in economic growth in the industrial countries since the mid-1970s had been accompanied by "growing protectionist pressures and increasing resort to special trading arrangements as a way to ease domestic tensions" (p. 80). More recently, the *Survey* has warned of the risks of protectionisms in regard to the impact it may have in slowing down productivity, economic growth and technology diffusion.

The international monetary framework which emerged after the collapse of the Bretton Woods system in the 1970s has proved volatile and prone to crises. The international monetary system continues to be centred on the United States dollar, with no mechanism in place for addressing, in an orderly manner, global imbalances which arise when crises erupt. At different times, the *Survey* has advanced proposals for two major reforms in the global financial system: one concerning the need to render the global financial system less dependent on a single currency and more reliant on common reserve pools and improved international liquidity; and the other centred on the need to ensure effective financial regulation and supervision so as to prevent speculation and financial bubbles. In addressing these issues over time, the *Survey* has come to recognize that improving global economic and financial governance requires political leadership and a shared vision of development, together with a commitment to balancing the responsibilities of adjustment among countries according to their level of development.

## Countries need adequate policy space for accelerating development

In times of crisis and major adjustment, flexibility has been of great importance in facilitating economic recovery and development. In the early 1950s, European countries were given additional time to gradually eliminate foreign exchange restrictions and ensure current account convertibility, an obligation under the Articles of Agreement of the International Monetary Fund. The flexibility shown by IMF, in granting countries the time needed to comply, was a determinant of their success; and by 1958, most countries of Western Europe had indeed eliminated foreign exchange restrictions and established current account convertibility.

In the 1950s, flexibility in debt relief (for Europe and Latin America) was important in facilitating recovery and rapid growth. In sharp contrast, the international response to the debt crises in the 1980s undermined—and even reversed—economic and social progress (in countries of Latin America and Africa). Fiscal austerity, an element of the strict conditionality of debt restructuring, as embodied in the Washington Consensus, reduced countries' policy space for carrying out a gradual resolution of their external debt and re-establishing a balance in their economies in accordance with their own national contexts and priorities. Moreover, whereas the exercise of greater flexibility by creditors could have made for a more equal distribution of the costs incurred in resolving the debt crises, the absence of a debt workout mechanism led to the imposition of the full adjustment cost on debtor countries. The result in the 1980s and early 1990s was a lost decade for development for many countries.

Similar concerns regarding the need to provide countries with the policy space required to mitigate their economic imbalances have been raised in relation to more recent problems, in Greece and other highly indebted countries. While arguing for adjustment on the part of both deficit and surplus countries, the *Survey* has also called for due attention to be paid to the social costs of polices aimed at sharp deficit reduction.

The implementation of an ambitious agenda for sustainable development thus requires both greater policy space for countries so that they can determine the policies that best reflect their own national context and sufficient flexibility in order to ensure an orderly recovery from situations of economic stress, as aimed for in target 17.15 under Sustainable Development Goal 17.

## International solidarity plays an important role in supporting national development efforts

International solidarity has played an important role in development and reconstruction. In the aftermath of the Second World War, countries of Western Europe received resources equivalent to 1 per cent of the gross national product (GNP) of the United States of America in each year of the period from 1948 to 1952 through the European Recovery Program, better known as the Marshall Plan. Generous financial support and flexibility in the enforcement of international commitments helped countries recover financial stability, achieve a more efficient allocation of resources and expedite trade liberalization. The combination of these factors buttressed the long period of economic prosperity known commonly as the Golden Age of Capitalism.

ODA has played an important role in supporting the development efforts of developing countries; it also yields high pay-offs in terms of facilitating the dynamic incorporation of countries into the world economy. The political momentum for accelerating delivery of ODA grew soon after the Millennium Development Goals were agreed on in September 2000 and continued to grow following the explicit recognition in the Monterrey Consensus of the International Conference on Financing for Development (United Nations, 2002) of the need for a "substantial" increase in ODA (para. 41). However, the long-standing target of provision by developed countries of ODA equivalent to 0.7 per cent of their GNI for developing countries has yet to be achieved. That target has been included in target 17.2 under Sustainable Development Goal 17 as part of the commitments set out in the 2030 Agenda for Sustainable Development.

On the specific issue of financing for climate change mitigation and adaptation, the *Survey* has expressed concern about the lack of additionality of financial flows, with contributions for climate change resulting in a diversion of resources away from traditional development projects. The 2012 *Survey* analysed several proposals for raising the hundreds of billions of dollars needed for climate change mitigation and adaptation and in that regard, advanced the argument that there is indeed room for mobilizing substantially larger resources from private and public sources. However, as expressed by the Secretary-General in the preface to the volume, for those resources to become viable, "strong international agreement is needed, along with adequate governance mechanisms, to manage the allocation of additional resources for development and global public goods" (p. iii).

Building the political will and governance mechanisms required to mobilize the resources needed for effective implementation of the 2030 Agenda will be critical to realizing the vision of sustainable development.

## Chapter II
# Post-war reconstruction and development in the Golden Age of Capitalism

## Key messages

- The *World Economic and Social Survey* was an early proponent of development as a process of large-scale structural and institutional change for the promotion of high standards of living, full employment and social progress. Starting from the first edition, issued in January 1948, the *Survey* recognized the need for coordinated international action to accelerate economic growth, facilitate the cross-border flow of goods and services and support effective utilization of resources in the context of an expanding and integrated world economy.

- The expansion of international trade and a functioning payments system were recognized as two critical factors for development in the post-Second World War period. However, large fluctuations in commodity prices and, correspondingly, in foreign exchange earnings were a source of economic instability for many developing countries back then and this has continued to be the case right up to the present.

- In the 1950s, the flexibility that European countries were afforded in meeting their International Monetary Fund-related obligations enabled the successful creation of the multilateral international payments system. Six years after the initial commitment, most Western Europe countries had eliminated foreign exchange restrictions and established current account convertibility. A similar flexibility in debt negotiations was important for the facilitation of a rapid recovery in Europe in the post-Second World War period as well as in Latin America in the 1930s.

- International solidarity has played an important role in development and reconstruction. Western European countries received resources equivalent to 1 per cent of the gross national product of the United States of America in the period from 1948 to 1952 through the Marshall Plan. Generous financial support and flexibility in the enforcement of international commitments assisted in the recovery of financial stability and facilitated a more efficient allocation of resources and a more rapid liberalization of trade.

- The discussion on planned development in Part I of the 1964 edition of the *Survey* (p. 2) remains of great significance today. The *Survey* observed that "the acceleration of economic and social development requires a more long-sighted approach to policy formulation" and that policy decisions "have to contribute actively to bringing about the structural and institutional changes which underlie economic development". A key determinant of successful development outcomes is an improvement in the capacity of public administration which enables the synergies across the socioeconomic, environmental and institutional dimensions of development to be maximized.

### Key events

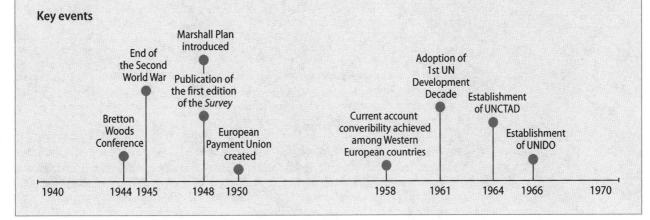

*Golden Age: a period during which something is very successful, especially in the past.*

*Oxford Advanced Learner's Dictionary, 8th edition (2010)*

## Introduction

While the Golden Age of Capitalism was a period of economic prosperity…

The present chapter examines the editions of the *Surveys*[1] published during what is identified as the "Golden Age of Capitalism", a period of economic prosperity extending from the end of the Second World War in 1945 to the early 1970s, when the Bretton Woods monetary system collapsed. The period marked the achievement of a high and sustained level of economic growth and high levels of (labour) productivity growth (particularly in Western Europe and East Asia) together with low unemployment. It was also associated with the emergence of new international institutions such as the International Monetary Fund (IMF) and the World Bank as part of the Bretton Woods monetary system, the United Nations Conference on Trade and Development (UNCTAD), the United Nations Industrial Development Organization (UNIDO) and the five Regional Commissions; the birth of many new nations as a result of decolonization; and the emergence of new mechanisms of international cooperation, such as the Marshall Plan for the reconstruction of Western Europe and in the 1960s, the strategy for the First United Nations Decade of Development.

…it was also a period during which development challenges arose that were similar to those we are facing today

The term "Golden Age" is used to describe a period in history remembered for its prosperity and happiness. A closer examination of such a period, however, often reveals hidden challenges. The Golden Age of Capitalism, the subject of this chapter, is no exception. For example, the period underwent business cycles, although they were certainly milder than those the global economy would come to experience in later decades. Some fundamental and structural problems of the post-war period also surfaced: a growing gap between industrialized and developing countries,[2] high population growth coupled with a low level of food production in developing countries, pervasive poverty and high income inequalities, high volatilities of commodity prices and a deterioration in the terms of trade of developing countries, and lack of financing for the economic development of developing countries. These problems are still part of the global landscape even though they are different in terms of their scope and depth.

The main themes taken up by the *Survey* have naturally varied from year to year, in response to the prominent economic issues discussed in the meetings of the General Assembly and the Economic and Social Council and the pressing issues confronting the

---

[1]    The *Survey* has taken on several names over the course of its history. In 1947, it was called the *Economic Report*; and from 1948 to 1954, the *World Economic Report*. In 1955, the publication was renamed the *World Economic Survey.*; and since 1994, it has been called the *World Economic and Social Survey*. The year 1999 marked the launching of a companion publication entitled *World Economic Situation and Prospects*, to present short-term economic estimates. In this chapter, all of them are referred to as the *Survey* (See appendix A.1 for the institutional history of the *Survey*.)

[2]    Countries that are now referred to as "developing" were, in the early years of the United Nations, called "underdeveloped" or "less developed". These terms were used, for example, in General Assembly resolution 1710 (XVI) of 19 December 1961, by which the Assembly designated the 1960s as the First United Nations Development Decade. The *Survey* began to employ the term "developing countries" in 1962 and, with time, it became far more common. The three terms have often been used interchangeably, however, even in the 1960s, and are used interchangeably here.

world economy. This chapter will discuss the economic and social issues of the period, with a particular focus on those that are still relevant today. The purpose is to reflect upon the lessons derived from history that may be applicable to the implementation of the 2030 Agenda for Sustainable Development.[3] It will emphasize the factors of international scope identified by the *Survey* as critical for development and the thinking on general economic development-related issues examined in the *Survey*.

Several issues and characteristics associated with international trade and finance, as observed by the *Survey* during the Golden Age, re-emerged in later decades, and continue to resurface today. For example, one of the major concerns of policymakers in the early post-war years was the critical role of trade in the recovery of the world economy. The *Survey*, which was unequivocal in its promotion of multilateralism and in its stand against protectionism, pointed out the importance of international coordination. In *World Economic Report 1953-54*, for instance, it was stated that "[t]he action of the government of one country may constitute an element disrupting the equilibrium of other countries in the absence of effective coordination" (p. 9). The *Survey* continued to advocate for what is now referred to as "common but differentiated responsibilities", a term that was elucidated as follows in the same report (p. 16):

> It is recognized that while no country is exempt from such responsibilities, not all countries are in similar position to undertake them. In general, countries with highest income levels and greatest mobility of resources are in the best position to accept such responsibilities, since they are in the best position to adjust themselves to changing conditions.

Highlighting the effectiveness of the form of aid administered by the Marshall Plan, the *Survey* promoted flexibility in the application of international rules and regulations. The *Survey's* examination of these issues yields invaluable lessons for the implementation of development policies within the context of a globalized economy.

The structure of the analytical framework employed by the *Survey* during the period was influenced by a new branch of economics, called *development economics*, which was established during the Golden Age of Capitalism. Recessions in some developed countries during the period brought an end to the traditional division of labour between developed and less developed countries that had prevailed formerly.[4] The latter group of countries which had traditionally relied on industrial imports in exchange for exports of primary goods, looked for guidance in the "catching-up" process. Demand for such guidance increased as newly independent countries emerged through decolonization. Reflecting the orientation of this new branch of economics, the *Survey* placed emphasis on issues related to savings and investment, productivity growth and industrialization, and planning as a means of coordinating policies. The Prebisch-Singer hypothesis[5] also influenced the writing of the *Survey*. In this regard, *World Economic Report 1950-51* called for "some kind of international action designed to bring about an adequate international flow of capital to underdeveloped countries" (p. 11) and for new techniques through which to stabilize the

**Development challenges related to international trade and finance, and development cooperation, received dedicated attention in the *Survey***

*Development economics*, **a new branch of economics which emerged in the Golden Age, influenced the structure of the analytical framework employed by the *Survey***

---

3       General Assembly resolution 70/1.

4       de Janvry and Sadoulet (2013), pp. 9-21.

5       The hypothesis predicts that the price of primary commodities will decline relative to the price of manufactured goods over the long run, causing the deterioration of the terms of trade of primary commodity-producing countries.

demand for (and thus the price of) primary commodities traded internationally. While most, if not all, of these ideas remain core elements of the Sustainable Development Goals, the language applied to the issues at stake evolved and has come to include such terms as "financing for development", "sustainable industrialization" and "integration of economic, social and environmental policies".

The benefits that potentially accrue to countries from their participation in the global economy have depended increasingly on (a) the level of their economic activities in global trade and finance and (b) the nature of the international trading and monetary systems. Indeed, these factors have become critical in determining the benefits to be derived from the external environment not only economically, but in the social and environmental areas as well.

The core of the chapter encompasses an overview of the global economic trends that prevailed in the period from the end of the Second World War to the collapse of the Bretton Woods monetary system; an examination of the events that unfolded during the period, focusing on trade, finance and external assistance, with a view to providing valuable lessons which are relevant to current global policymaking; and a review of some of the issues considered in the *Survey* that are relevant to the situation of the developing countries. The final section sums up the legacy of the Golden Age in the context of the challenges to be faced in implementing a strategy for sustainable development.

## Overview of the Golden Age of Capitalism: reconstruction, growth and stability

The years immediately following the Second World War were marked by an unprecedented speed of economic recovery from the most devastating conflict in the history of mankind, combined with an equally impressive strength and scale of international cooperation never before witnessed.

**The post-war period witnessed an unprecedented speed of recovery from the devastation inflicted**

In the immediate wake of the Second World War, living conditions in areas that had been theatres of war were horrendous. Several Governments ran budget deficits in an effort to rebuild both housing and industry and faced severe balance-of-payments complications in the process. In Western Europe and Japan, wartime price controls and rationing were maintained owing to high inflationary pressures and, in the case of Japan, until as late as 1948. The problem was similar in the centrally planned economies, which had to deal with, in addition to reconstruction, the impact of institutional changes as a result of the nationalization or partial collectivization of land. While rationing had been abolished in the Soviet Union by 1947, other countries maintained wartime controls—as late as 1953 in Czechoslovakia (now Czechia and Slovakia). China, immersed in a civil war which had begun before the end of the Second World War and ended in 1949, suffered hyperinflation until early 1950.

Nonetheless, the recovery in those post-war years was, to quote the introduction to *World Economic Survey 1955*, "truly impressive", in terms of both its speed and spread, as compared with the period following the First World War. The dire starting conditions in 1945 were compounded by the global economic "lethargy" of the 1930s which had included the collapse of the gold standard and large private capital flows across countries. Indeed, from that point up to the early 1970s, the world witnessed the fastest period of economic growth ever. Contributing to the commencement of this Golden Age was a better handling of the emergency situation in countries ravaged by the Second World War, supported by large aid flows from the United Nations Relief and Rehabilitation Administration (UNRRA), the United States (through the Marshall Plan) and, albeit in lesser amounts, Canada.

Various editions of the *Survey* published during this period recognized the profound changes in the structure of world economic activity, and included in-depth discussions of three main facets of reconstruction: production capacities, the trade system and international payments. Production recovered more rapidly after the Second World War than after the First: In Western Europe, it took only three years for production to return to pre-war levels and four years in the case of exports, compared with six years for both production and exports after the First World War (see table II.1). However, food consumption per capita in this region was restored to pre-war levels only in 1950. Globally, agriculture recovered more slowly than manufacturing and mining production, especially in the centrally planned economies where economic growth was also slow during the second half of the 1940s. While the process of reconstruction was fast overall, with world industrial production returning to its pre-war levels in 1947 (or 1948, if the United States is excluded), Germany and Japan recovered their pre-war levels of per capita gross domestic product (GDP) only in the mid-1950s, despite remarkable post-war growth. Countries whose production capacities were not affected by the war saw their production levels rise well above pre-war levels within two years after the war. These included the United States, Canada, the European countries that had remained neutral, Turkey, countries of the Middle East and Latin America and India. Some (notably in Latin America) benefited from increased demand for their products by belligerent nations, as trade restrictions were lifted in the post-war period. Conversely, Western Europe saw some of its markets for manufactures (e.g., textiles) shrink after the war, owing to import substitution.

The growth of the global economy in the 1960s outpaced that of the 1950s, with more people positively affected by high economic growth. At the same time, there was continuing concern with regard to economic stability and internal and external imbalances within industrialized countries. The underdeveloped countries and areas became the focus of more attention than before within the United Nations development forums and in the *Survey*.

The average annual growth rate of GDP among developed market economies was 5.0 per cent for the period 1961-1970, while that of developing countries was 5.5 per cent for the same period (see table II.2). The net material product of centrally planned economies grew by 6.7 per cent per year on average.

Growth in the major industrialized countries became more stable in the 1960s as compared with the 1950s. Low levels of inflation pressure coexisted with low levels of unemployment. The United States experienced the highest level of unemployment among those countries, with an average of about 5 per cent during the period. For the other major industrialized countries, the rate of growth ranged between 1 and 3 per cent per year. As shown in *World Economic Survey, 1972* (table 11), the average annual rate of inflation among these groups of countries for the period 1961-1970 was 3.4 per cent, with Japan experiencing the highest rate (5.7 per cent). As in the 1950s, active fiscal and monetary policies played a key role in maintaining the momentum of high and steady growth. In Northern America, where business cycles were more pronounced than in other industrialized areas, fiscal policies stimulated consumer demand and supported business investment during the first half of the 1960s. In the latter half of the decade, the general fiscal and monetary policy stance in the industrialized countries became restrictive, the aim being to bring down accelerating inflation rates.

Developing countries were producing primary commodities predominantly and their growth was largely determined by the growth of exports of agricultural and mineral

**The recovery was accompanied by profound changes in the world's economic structure**

**Economic growth in developed countries was higher and more stable in the 1960s than in the 1950s**

**Developing countries also enjoyed robust growth during the 1960s, but disparities in growth of per capita income became noticeable**

Table II.1

## Indices of mining and manufacturing production, selected countries, 1947, 1948 and 1949

| 1937 = 100 | | | | | | | |
|---|---|---|---|---|---|---|---|
| | 1947 | 1948 | 1949 | | 1947 | 1948 | 1949 |
| **Not affected by the war** | | | | **Centrally planned economies** | | | |
| United States of America | 165 | 170 | 156 | Czechoslovakia | 83 | 99 | 107 |
| Canada | 162 | 169 | 171 | German Democratic Republic | 51 | 65 | 77 |
| Ireland | 117 | 128 | 139 | Poland | 106 | 146 | 177 |
| Sweden | 141 | 150 | 156 | Union of Soviet Socialist Republics (USSR) | 93 | 118 | 141 |
| **Less devastated by the war** | | | | **Latin America and Asia** | | | |
| France | 85 | 100 | 110 | Argentina | 175 | 178 | 173 |
| Italy | 88 | 92 | 100 | Chile | 136 | 143 | 140 |
| United Kingdom of Great Britain and Northern Ireland | 98 | 110 | 118 | Mexico | 129 | 128 | 137 |
| | | | | India | 102 | 114 | 111 |
| **Devastated by the war** | | | | | | | |
| Austria | 58 | 89 | 118 | | | | |
| Federal Republic of Germany | 33 | 52 | 78 | | | | |
| Greece | 66 | 70 | 82 | **World** | 121 | 135 | 140 |
| Japan | 28 | 40 | 53 | Excluding the United States | 96 | 115 | 131 |

Source: *World Economic Report 1949-50*, statistical appendix, table I.

Table II.2

## Average annual growth rate of GDP and industrial and agricultural production, developed countries, centrally planned economies and developing countries, 1961–1970

| Percentage | Average annual rate of change |
|---|---|
| **Gross domestic product (constant 1960 prices)** | |
| World | 5.4 |
| Developed countries[a] | 5.0 |
| Centrally planned economies[b,c] | 6.7 |
| Developing countries[d] | 5.5 |
| **Industrial production** | |
| World | 6.7 |
| Developed countries[a] | 5.8 |
| Centrally planned economies[b,c] | 8.3 |
| Developing countries[d] | 7.1 |
| **Agricultural production** | |
| World | 2.6 |
| Developed countries[a] | 2.5 |
| Centrally planned economies[b,c] | 3.0 |
| Developing countries[d] | 2.8 |

Source: *World Economic Survey, 1972*, table 1.

Note: Methods of estimation differ among the production components and among the country groups. For this reason and because of the problem of assigning weights to the country groups, the aggregated changes should be interpreted with due caution. The overall figure provide no more than a rough-and-ready indicator of the magnitude of year-to-year changes.

a Northern America; Northern, Southern and Western Europe; Australia; Japan; New Zealand; and South Africa.

b Eastern Europe and the (former) USSR.

c Data refer to net material product and are not strictly comparable with those of the other country groups.

d Latin America and the Caribbean; Africa (other than South Africa); and Asia (other than China, the Democratic People's Republic of Korea, Japan, Mongolia and Viet Nam).

products. The robust growth of developed countries during the 1960s induced strong demand for these products and helped increase commodity prices. In *World Economic Survey 1967* (Part One, pp. 16-17), it was cautioned that the same period also found wider disparities in growth of per capita income between developed and developing countries, as well as among developing countries. Over the period 1955-1965, per capita output grew by $43 per year (at 1960 purchasing power) in developed countries, compared with a rise of $3 per year in the developing countries. By 1965, the average per capita income in the developed countries reached $1,725 per annum, as compared with a developing-country average of $157. Among the developing countries, there were large differences in economic performance, ranging from virtual stagnation (Democratic Republic of the Congo) to over 10 per cent growth per year (Liberia and Libya). Two thirds of the population of the developing countries lived in countries in which the average annual rise in per capita output during the period 1955-1965 was less than 2 per cent.

While the centrally planned economies continued to enjoy high economic growth of nearly 7 per cent per annum during the 1960s, this figure nevertheless signified a deceleration when compared with the average of 10 per cent in the 1950s, reflecting slower growth in agricultural production. Still, industrial production continued to be robust throughout the decade. It should be noted that the creation of the Council for Mutual Economic Assistance in 1949 led to stronger economic linkages among member countries.[6]

## Key developments in the international economy

The Golden Age of Capitalism has been characterized by unprecedented growth of international trade, in tandem with the impressive growth of the global economy as described in the previous section. The period also saw the creation of a multilateral international payments system, known as the Bretton Woods monetary system, and a United States initiative to aid Europe, known as the Marshall Plan (officially called the European Recovery Program). The negotiators shared common views on the importance of full employment and a liberal multilateral payments system which led to the creation of IMF. The flexible attitude of that institution towards member countries resulted in the successful implementation of current account convertibility[7] by the end of the 1950s. The large-scale impact exerted by the Marshall Plan in Western Europe attests to the importance of well-targeted international assistance for the recovery of productive capacity and stable economic growth. The implementation of the Marshall Plan remains significant in its exemplification of a positive experience of development cooperation, which can serve as a guide for the successful implementation of the Sustainable Development Goals. On the other hand, the high volatility of commodity prices and the declining prices of primary products (relative to manufactured goods) during that period remain unresolved issues today.

**The implementation of the Marshall Plan and the creation of the Bretton Woods monetary system were two epoch-making events of the Golden Age**

---

6   The six original members of the Council for Mutual Economic Assistance were Bulgaria, Czechoslovakia, Hungary, Poland, Romania and the Soviet Union. The final session of the Council was held in June 1991 and led to an agreement to disband within 90 days of the session.

7   Under current account convertibility, which is sometimes called Bretton Woods convertibility, individuals are allowed to engage freely in current account transactions without being subject to exchange controls, and the monetary authorities of each country are free to buy and sell foreign exchange to keep the parity fixed. The United States is free to buy and sell gold to maintain the fixed price of $35 per ounce. See Bordo (1993).

## Trade

**Global trade increased sharply during the Golden Age, but East-West trade plummeted**

The Golden Age saw an unprecedented growth of international trade. Trade volume outpaced output in the late 1940s, a phenomenon that continued into the 1950s and the 1960s, with the major exception of East-West trade, which remained significantly below pre-war levels. Trade liberalization entered a new phase with the launching of the Kennedy Round of multilateral trade negotiations in 1964, at which participating countries agreed to cut tariffs by up to 40 per cent on many items. Tariff levels, although still significantly high by today's standards, became less of a barrier to imports to developed countries; however, other forms of trade restrictions (known as non-tariff barriers) emerged.

Imports and exports reflected disparate production capacities, as discussed in the early *Surveys*. The United States emerged from the war years a more powerful and self-sufficient nation, reducing the ratio of its imports to gross national income (GNI) from 5.1 per cent in 1929 to 3.2 per cent in 1948. In the post-war years, it was the major investing nation, mainly in oil.

The impressive growth of global trade since the late 1940s had one major exception: trade between the Eastern and Western trade blocs, which remained significantly below pre-war levels. On the other hand, trade *within* each bloc continued to grow strongly. *World Economic Survey 1962* noted that trade of the developed market economies, as well as of the centrally planned economies, became increasingly concentrated within their own group. This was attested by the fact that, as noted in Part I of *World Economic Survey 1963* (p. 10), intra-group trade flows accounted for 62 per cent of world exports in 1962, as against 54 per cent in 1950. Industrialized economies led the increase in the share of trade, accompanied by a rising share of centrally planned economies, while underdeveloped countries saw, instead, a decrease in their share, except in Western Asia, which benefited from the petroleum industry. The changes in the structure of world trade reflected the changes in the structure of world production. Primary goods played a central role, even among industrialized economies. In fact, an impressive commodity boom occurred in 1950, associated with the outbreak of the Korean War. However, the biggest boom occurred in manufacturing trade (which had collapsed in the 1930s) within both the Eastern and Western trade blocs.

The volume of trade from the late 1940s grew faster despite the fact that the trade protecting barriers initially remained in place following the global depression and the war. In *World Economic Survey 1955*, it was noted "that trade ha[d] been held back much less than might have been expected by the various limitations and controls prevalent throughout most of the world" (p. 84) and postulated that the prevailing trade restrictions in the post-war era had affected the commodity composition and regional distribution of trade, rather than its total volume.

The shortage of dollars in the post-war years naturally incentivized exports to the dollar area, supporting a recovery of production in countries outside that area. However, a myriad of bilateral payments agreements inherited from the 1930s failed to support trade properly. A major step towards a multilateral system of international payments came with the creation of the European Payments Union in 1950, which used United States funds under the Marshall Plan to settle intra-European balances. Trade liberalization was stimulated, as disbursement of the funds required not only the dismantling of intra-European trade restrictions, coupled with greater coordination of national recovery plans, but also agreement on the part of recipient countries regarding how to allocate payments

(Braga de Macedo and Eichengreen, 2001). Among the centrally planned economies, a system of payments supported financially by the Soviet Union had a similar effect.

In Part I of *World Economic Survey 1962*, structural imbalance of trade between developing and industrial countries was predicted for the future. It was noted that, by 1960, the developed countries had increased their already large share in total world trade from three fifths to two thirds (p. 3) and that significant increases were also recorded by the group of centrally planned economies, whose share in the total rose from 8 to 12 per cent (p. 3 and table 1.3). In that *Survey*, it was also noted that the most significant development in world trade in the period from 1950 to 1960 was the decline of exports from the underdeveloped countries as a share of total world exports and as a share of intra-trade among underdeveloped countries themselves. At the same time, both developed countries and centrally planned economies increased their intra-area trade quite sharply.

Exports from developing countries lagged behind those of advanced countries between the late 1950s and early 1960s, owing to slower growth of export volume and the deterioration in the terms of trade. In Part I of *World Economic Survey 1962*, it was therefore cautioned that the failure of the developing countries to participate in the expansion of world trade posed a threat to their economic development. In Part I of *World Economic Survey 1963*, it was recognized that foreign trade is critical for the economic development of the developing countries because production for exports constitutes a preponderant part of their economic activity.

A critical issue identified during the Golden Age—one with relevance today—is the importance of swings in commodity prices. As pointed out in *World Economic Survey 1956*, the demand of industrialized countries for primary goods does not increase at the same rate as their increase in income, leading to the increasing difficulties of developing countries in balancing their external accounts. This creates, in the words of that *Survey*, "an inescapable dilemma—whether to accept a rate of growth consistent with external equilibrium in the full knowledge that that rate is likely to involve a widening of the gap between their levels of living and those of the industrial economies; or whether to seek to promote a more rapid rate of growth, running the risk of persistent disequilibrium in their economic relations with other countries" (p. 137). Put succinctly, "[i]nternational trade may not provide the underdeveloped countries with the external resources they require" (*World Economic Survey 1958*, p. 8) if their major exports continue to be primary products. Some of the reasons for the slow growth of demand for primary goods in industrialized countries were connected with:

(a) Increasing weight of the United States in industrial production at the global level and its reduced requirements for imported primary commodities (since it was producing a larger share of its own needs);

(b) A change in the structure of consumption entailing a shift towards industries that required fewer raw materials;

(c) Technological change which led to economies in the use of raw materials;

(d) Development of synthetic products (especially rubber and textile fibres);

(e) Food self-sufficiency policies in Western Europe and provision of price support to farmers in the United States.

The 1956 *Survey* did not explicitly refer to, but its analysis was clearly influenced by, the Prebisch-Singer hypothesis. In its simplest form, the hypothesis predicts, as noted above, that primary commodity prices tend to deteriorate relative to manufactured goods over the long run, with the result that growth dynamics of commodity producers are

**In the early 1960s, the *Survey* was already concerned with the emergence of a structural trade imbalance between developing and developed countries...**

**...largely explained by slow growth of export volume from developing countries and the deterioration in the terms of trade**

**International trade may not provide developing countries with the external resources needed for development if their major exports continue to be primary products**

dependent on global demand trends and the effects of technological innovations. Ocampo and Parra-Lancourt (2010) show that commodity prices tend to follow long-run (30- to 40-year) cycles, with the mean of each price cycle having declined significantly over the course of the twentieth century (see figure II.1). This suggests, in support of the Prebisch-Singer hypothesis, a step-wise deterioration of the terms of trade of developing countries.

Figure II.1
**Real commodity price index, 1865–2015**

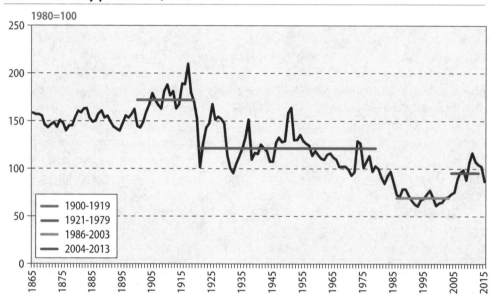

**Sources:** José Antonio Ocampo and Mariángela Parra-Lancourt (2010); and updates provided by the authors in March 2017.
**Notes:** a) Horizontal lines represent the mean price index of each price cycle.
b) Index deflated by Manufactured Unit Value.

**Economic diversification is key for enabling developing countries to benefit from trade**

The *Surveys* published in the 1950s and the 1960s argued that it was essential to make underdeveloped countries less dependent on fluctuations of earnings from a handful of primary products, which implied producing, and eventually exporting, the consumer goods and raw materials that they imported. This constituted an implicit call for industrialization. The dependence on export of primary goods was not aided by the volatility of their prices. With regard to the ability of exporting countries to manage the instability of commodity prices and the corresponding fluctuations in foreign exchange earnings, the *Survey* identified a clear need for international stabilization mechanisms connected to the underlying market realities, possibly applied commodity by commodity, and involving both consumer and producer interests. In fact, *World Economic Report 1950-51* called for "some kind of international action designed to bring about an adequate international flow of capital to underdeveloped countries" (p. 11) and for new mechanisms for stabilizing the demand for (and thus the price of) primary commodities traded internationally.

The establishment of UNCTAD in 1964, headed by Prebisch himself, led to an intensification of the debate on issues related to commodity prices at several intergovernmental conferences on commodities. Throughout the 1960s, and 1970s, several commodity agreements were achieved or renewed.[8] However, the absence of effective mechanisms

---

8    Examples include the first International Coffee Agreement of 1962; the International Sugar Agreement of 1968; and the first International Cocoa Agreement of 1972.

for managing commodity price fluctuations continues to characterize global cooperation today. Excessive price fluctuations affect poor consumers and small-scale farmers in terms of their disposable income, health and nutrition. How to smooth out price fluctuations and diversify economic activities and exports of commodity-dependent countries continues to be a major issue in the international development agenda.[9]

## International finance

In the 1930s, the world economy did not have in place a multilateral system of payments but, instead, there had existed countless bilateral agreements, protectionist policies, and import and foreign exchange controls. As a result of the "dollar shortage" which resulted from the war, European countries and Japan continued to use import and foreign exchange controls extensively, particularly with regard to the United States, despite the massive support being received from that country through the Marshall Plan.

Continuing imbalances characterized the immediate post-war years. When the United States was hit by its first post-war recession, countries had very limited reserves to manage—notably in the sterling area. In 1949, a major crisis in the level of reserves in the United Kingdom prompted the country to devalue its currency by 30.5 per cent (sterling per dollar). This was a major world economic event, given that the sterling area was the second-largest world currency area. In the early post-war years, reserve losses were massive around the world, a fact that strengthened even more the concentration of gold reserves in the United States and its dominance in the world payments system. Several Western countries (including France) followed the decision of the United Kingdom to impose controls on dollar imports. However, an increase in production of foodstuffs in Western Europe allowed for a reduction of European imports from the United States, which in turn allowed an improvement in the current account balance. The fact that reserves ultimately recovered in late 1949 helped reduce speculative capital flight. This reflected the importance of improved production capacities and an increase in food supplies rather than the importance of relative prices (exchange rates) for the restoration of payments balances. Not only is this issue of the utmost relevance nowadays, but it provides food for reflection, especially within the context of the least developed countries, which need to develop productive capacity so as to increase exports and revenue and thus balance their current account.[10]

The international community initiated the creation of a multilateral monetary system during the Second World War. Delegates representing 44 countries gathered at the United Nations Monetary and Financial Conference, held in Bretton Woods, New Hampshire, in July 1944, where they drafted Articles of Agreement for a proposed International Monetary Fund. It was the common views shared by the negotiators on the importance of full employment and a liberal multilateral payments system that led to the creation of the Fund, which became a formal entity in 1945 with 29 member countries, and having as its initial goal the reconstruction of the international payments system. The intention was to mandate each country to adopt a monetary policy that sustained its fixed exchange rate

**The post-war global economy was afflicted by an absence of a multilateral payments system, plus protectionist policies and exchange controls**

**Creation of the International Monetary Fund in 1945 had as its goal the reconstruction of the international payments system**

---

9   See chap. II of *World Economic Situation and Prospects 2017* for the latest analysis of commodity prices.

10   A discussion of outstanding challenges for building productive capacity among least developed countries can be found in the recent work of the Committee for Development Policy (United Nations, Economic and Social Council, 2016 and 2017).

to gold (with a ± 1 per cent margin). The role of IMF was to support temporary payment imbalances.

The intention in creating a multilateral payments system was to avert the mistakes of the interwar period when wildly volatile exchange rates and the collapse of the short-lived gold exchange standard had led to the transmission of deflation internationally and a resort to devaluations, and trade and exchange restrictions, along with bilateralism (Bordo, 1993).

While some difficulties were encountered in building such a multilateral international payments system immediately after the Second World War, the creation of the European Payments Union in 1950 marked a major step towards its implementation. The Marshall Plan encouraged war-battered countries in Western Europe to shift away from bilateralism in trade towards a multilateral balancing of payments. This was the starting point for the rapid growth of trade which has been witnessed by the international community over the last 70 years (Wolf, 2017). However, throughout the first half of the 1950s and with the end of the Marshall Plan, countries faced several problems, including a dollar shortage in the United Kingdom which made it difficult to restore a stable system of multilateral payments; and the extensive use of the foreign exchange and import controls imposed during the previous three decades was still an issue. Because of these obstacles, most countries were unable to comply with their obligation under the IMF Articles of Agreement to dispense with foreign exchange restrictions and current account convertibility when the agreed transition period was over at the beginning of 1952 (*World Economic Report 1951-52*, p. 8; *World Economic Survey 1955*, pp. 74-86). Foreign exchange controls were maintained for a much longer period than had originally been envisioned (de Vries, 1987, chap. 1).

**By 1958, current account convertibility had been adopted by most countries in Western Europe**

By the end of the 1950s, however, most countries were in compliance with their obligations under the Articles of Agreement as world trade and international payments became more stable and less affected by recessions in the United States. Stable trade and payments were in turn supported by an increase in the production capacities of countries, improved intra-European trade, and the accumulation of foreign reserves in most countries (which prevented capital flight from Europe and actually relaxed controls on imports from the United States). Within this new context, the United States recession of 1957-1958 did not exert the strong effects of the first post-war United States recession, in 1949 (except on commodity producing countries), thereby allowing the liberalization of trade and payments to continue. By the end of the 1950s, the Bretton Woods regime seemed to be on solid ground since "[t]he devaluations of 1949, widespread and drastic as they were, did not bring about an end to the regime of fixed exchange rates", as noted approvingly in the *World Economic Survey 1957* (p. 24). In fact, according to that *Survey*, countries were seeking to avoid exchange rate depreciations. The flexibility shown by IMF, through which countries were granted sufficient time to comply with their obligations, was a determinant of the success in moving towards a gradual reduction of foreign exchange restrictions in Western Europe and the adoption of current account convertibility by most countries in 1958.

By 1964, however, the difficulties inherent in maintaining the system of fixed exchange rates had become evident. In the United States, the payments imbalance was being redressed very slowly, and the growing gravity of the crises in sterling had raised alarm. These factors "weakened the traditional resistance to change", as described in Part II of *World Economic Survey 1964* (p. 64). The *Survey* reported that in the United Kingdom and the United States, serious doubts had arisen as to whether the role of the reserve centre did not entail "an inordinately heavy constraint on domestic policies". In the surplus countries, on the other hand, the measures taken to support these currencies had been widely questioned. The combination of "a dangerously low level of reserves at the centre and growing uncertainty about the willingness of the surplus countries to accumulate reserve currencies" had placed a considerable strain on the monetary system. An alternative source had thus to be found, for as long as the world reserve was built largely on one or two national currencies, the monetary system would remain "inherently vulnerable to crises of confidence". Various alternatives were therefore discussed, including a return to the gold standard, flexible exchange rates, a world central bank, and measures to strengthen the system.

In 1964, the international monetary system experienced, yet again, a worsening of the payments situation of the reserve currency countries, the United Kingdom and the United States, which led to a massive currency attack on both currencies and a run on gold. The United Kingdom was forced to devalue the sterling by 14.3 per cent in November 1967 and the eight countries of the gold pool[11]—established in 1961 to maintain a gold price of $35 per ounce—suspended the supply of gold to the market several months later. The crisis spurred the international monetary reforms of the 1970s.

The imbalance in the payments position of the United Kingdom and United States was not a new occurrence. The United Kingdom had experienced chronic payments difficulties in the post-war period and since the payments crisis in 1964, had most of the time remained in deficit. In 1967, imports by the United Kingdom rose while export expansion came to a halt. The imbalance was attributed partly to the hostilities in the Middle East and labour strikes in the country, but "the cumulative erosion of confidence in sterling raised serious questions about its strength" (*World Economic Survey 1967*, Part Two, p. 8). On the other hand, while the balance-of-payments deficit of the United States had been welcomed in the early post-war years (as the deficit helped European countries and Japan), dollar shortages had begun, by the late 1950s, to raise doubts about the impregnability of the dollar. Ultimately, the cumulative effect of prolonged deficits led to a decline in total reserve assets in the United States, from about $22.5 billion at the end of 1958 to about $13.8 billion in April 1968 (ibid., table 3). Under the circumstances, "a gold crisis became the logical counterpart of the crisis of the reserve currencies" (p. 8).

By 1968, it was perceived that the attempt to maintain the dollar at a fixed peg of $35 per ounce had gradually become unsustainable as gold poured out from the United States. The dollar shortage of the 1940s and 1950s became a dollar glut by the 1960s. On 15 March 1968, the London gold market was closed to combat the heavy demand for gold, while markets in other gold-pool countries remained open. The governors of the central banks of the gold-pool members decided that officially held gold should be used only for transfers among monetary authorities. The "two-tiered market system" that emerged after the agreement was reached created an opportunity for market participants to convert reserve currencies into gold and sell the gold in the private gold markets at higher rates. With accelerating inflation, the President of the United States temporarily suspended the direct convertibility of the United States dollar into gold.

*World Economic Survey 1968* (Part Two) still remained positive, suggesting that there had been "no inhibiting overall shortage of reserves" (p. 45), despite their lower gold content. It also noted that the recently created IMF special drawing rights (SDRs), a new international reserve asset defined as equivalent to 0.888671 grams of gold (equivalent in

**Maintaining the dollar at a fixed peg of $35 per ounce proved increasingly difficult**

---

11    Belgium, France, Germany, Italy, the Netherlands, Switzerland, the United Kingdom and the United States.

turn to $1 at that time) and totalling an equivalent of $9.5 billion,[12] would supplement international liquidity and help prevent an "over-hasty resort to defensive measures… setting in motion a sequence of trade-destroying policies" (p. 45). The *Survey* conceded, though, that the SDR scheme would "leave the basic problems of intercountry imbalance more or less untouched".

While there was reluctance to tamper with the regime after 25 years of growth in world trade, at the same time, the 1960s amply demonstrated how countries could "get out of line" because of domestic price movements, despite "the necessity of maintaining reasonable internal balance, with incomes rising in line with productivity" (ibid.). By July 1969, the *Survey* had admitted that there was "a prospect of the most critical examination being made of the working of the international monetary system since the Bretton Woods Conference of 1944".

**In 1971, the United States of America suspended the convertibility of the dollar into gold and in 1973, currencies began to float, marking the end of the Bretton Woods system**

With inflation accelerating in the United States, on 15 August 1971, that country suspended the convertibility of the dollar into gold or other reserve assets. As observed in *World Economic Survey 1971* (p. 2), "[t]he international monetary crisis of 1971 signalled the transition from an old era to a new one". Gold was demonetized as an international reserve asset and the link between new gold production and other sources of gold and official reserves was cut.[13] In the following years, the United States monetary authorities pressured the monetary authorities of the other countries to refrain from converting their dollar holdings into gold; and the international monetary system switched, in effect, to a de facto dollar standard.[14]

An attempt to revive the fixed exchange rates eventually failed and by March 1973, the major currencies began to float against each other, marking the collapse of the Bretton Woods monetary system. The United States monetary expansion since the late 1960s had exacerbated worldwide inflation because its monetary authorities did not maintain the price stability of the dollar against gold. Under a fixed nominal exchange rate regime, rising prices in the United States led to a real appreciation of the dollar (and a real depreciation of other currencies against the dollar). As the IMF member countries were required to maintain nominal exchange rates fixed, the impact of a higher price level in the United States directly shifted global demand to other countries and put upward pressure on domestic prices. It should be noted that the 1967 *Survey*, already expressed doubt about the sustainability of the system by posing the question "whether a widening of the gap between the two prices [that is, the official price of gold fixed at $35 per ounce which was applied to transfers among monetary authorities, and a prevailing market price of gold when market participants converted reserve currencies into gold and sold the gold in private markets] might not endanger the system" (Part Two, p. 10).

**The use of SDRs remains controverisal**

Since the creation of SDRs in 1969, some countries have been interested in establishing a link between the new reserve assets and development finance. Since the SDRs are created with minimal costs incurred by IMF under the agreement of its member countries, these resources could be transferred to member countries also at minimal cost and used to finance

---

12    After the collapse of the Bretton Woods system, the special drawing right was redefined as a basket of currencies.

13    By the announcement of 15 August 1971, the convertibility of dollars to gold ended and gold lost its status of legal tender and reserve asset. This signified the demonetization of gold. See Bordo (1993), pp. 70-72.

14    On 1 January 1975, the official price of gold was abolished as a unit of account.

development projects.[15] At the time the SDRs were created, the General Assembly (see sect. II of Assembly resolution 3202 (S-VI) of 1 May 1974 on the Programme of Action on the Establishment of a New International Economic Order) called upon members of IMF to consider the possibility of establishing that link. Although most developed countries were against the idea, calling it "premature", the few of them that were more sympathetic maintained that such a link would be useful as a means of providing additional finance to developing countries. At present, the topic of linking the SDRs to development finance still reappears in the agenda of United Nations bodies from time to time (*World Economic and Social Survey 2012*).

The Bretton Woods system was the very first fully negotiated monetary system, although its life was relatively short. It should be remembered, however, that the creation of IMF was underpinned by the views held in common by the negotiators at the Bretton Woods Conference that there was a need for the creation of a multilateral payments system to support achievement of the objective of full employment in member countries—views that might in fact have prolonged the life of the system a little longer. As already noted, the flexibility shown by IMF in granting countries the time that they needed to comply with their obligations was a determinant of their eventual success in achieving current account convertibility in 1958. Though not examined in the *Survey*, another type of flexibility was also exercised by creditor countries in debt relief negotiations in the 1950s. For example, more than half of the obligations of the then Federal Republic of Germany ("West Germany"), including those that had been derived from reparations after the First World War, were written off. The United States also exercised flexibility after the Second World War in renegotiating the foreign debts of Latin America which had accumulated in the 1930s.

## Marshall Plan

The Marshall Plan (known officially as the European Recovery Program) was a United States initiative designed to assist countries in Western Europe in their post-war reconstruction efforts.[16] The Plan is considered to be an example of successful development cooperation through which international aid assisted in the socioeconomic transformation of countries in line with their own development strategy.

The Marshall Plan was in operation for four years, beginning in 1948. At its peak, United States aid, together with a similar type of aid to Japan, amounted to 40.5 per cent of United States exports in 1946-1949 (see table II.3). One of the greatest differences between the two post-war periods lay in the size of the support provided to countries, which in the post-Second World War period was massive. Government disbursements for the period 1919-1921, which amounted to 10.5 per cent of total exports, were negligible for the period 1922-1929. Aid under the Marshall Plan amounted to about 1 per cent of the gross national

**The Marshall Plan was the first post-war success story in international development cooperation: it assisted in the socioeconomic transformation of countries of Western Europe**

---

15    Since the 1940s, there were several proposals regarding how the SDRs (and other reserve mediums) could be linked to development, including those of John Maynard Keynes, Maxwell Stamp and UNCTAD. See Park (1973); and, for more recent discussions, *World Economic and Social Survey 2005*.

16    For the political background of the Marshall Plan and the Bretton Woods monetary system, see Marglin (1990). The growing cost of the Korean War was a major factor behind the Plan's not being extended to 1953, its last year as originally scheduled.

Table II.3
**Balance of payments, United States of America, 1919–1954**

| Annual average, millions of dollars | | | | | |
|---|---|---|---|---|---|
| Item | 1919-1921 | 1922-1929 | 1930-1939 | 1946-1949 | 1950-1954 |
| Export of goods and services | 8 848.3 | 6 176.6 | 3 706.5 | 16 751.5 | 17 097.6 |
| Import of goods and services | -5 345.0 | -50 932.0 | -3 139.5 | -8 175.0 | -13 242.2 |
| Balance | 3 503.3 | -44 755.4 | 567.0 | 8 576.5 | 3 855.4 |
| Private capital and remittances | -1 075.7 | -1 315.9 | 48.9 | -1 351.0 | 1 545.2 |
| Government disbursements | -928.6 | 27.1 | -5.1 | -6 790.7 | -4 433.8 |
| Foreign capital and gold | -332.7 | 344.6 | -905.7 | -1 192.5 | 1 887.8 |
| Errors and omissions | -1 166.3 | -133.2 | 294.9 | 757.8 | 235.8 |

**Source:** UN/DESA, based on *World Economic Survey 1955*, table 30.

product (GNP) of the United States in each year of the period from 1948 to 1952.[17,18] The United States GNP in 1950 was slightly larger than the total GNP of Western European countries.[19] Thus, in the four years under consideration, Western European countries received more than 1 per cent of their total GNP in the form of external aid. Interestingly, the objectives of the Plan were the restoration of multilateralism, price stability and recovery of production capacity in receiving countries.[20] Indeed, the Marshall Plan offers a good example of how international support can assist the development of productive capacities in deficit countries to gain access to dynamic world markets.

As envisaged, the Marshall Plan helped restore production capacity in Western European countries, improved domestic price stability and helped realign their currencies in the immediate post-war period. It was in this context that assistance was provided in resolving the problems of widespread poverty and hunger that were left in the wake of the Second World War.

> **Under the Marshall Plan, 1 per cent of United States GNP was disbursed each year from 1948 to 1952, making a large contribution to the reconstruction of Europe**

While it is difficult to determine the exact impact of the Marshall Plan on the reconstruction of Western Europe, there is no doubt that international solidarity played an important role in supporting economic recovery in the region.[21] Aid to Europe, together with abolition of occupational controls in the defeated Axis countries, was directed towards rebuilding productive and export capacity in receiving countries and widening the market for American products (Glyn and others, 1990). Further, the creation of the European Payments Union ushered in a new era of multilateral trade in which there was improved resource allocation and production efficiency across Western Europe.

---

17   Glyn and others (1990), p. 67.

18   In 2015, the member countries of the Organization for Economic Cooperation and Development (OECD) accounted for about 64 per cent of world gross product. If the target of 0.7 per cent of GNP for official development assistance (ODA) to developing countries is achieved, about 0.45 per cent of global income will have been transferred to developing countries.

19   About 4 per cent larger, according to Maddison (2001), table A1-b. GDP is measured in 1990 international dollars.

20   Glyn and others (1990), p. 69.

21   See, for example, De Long and Eichengreen (1991); and Wolf (2017).

The generous financial support, equivalent to 1 per cent of United States GNP, in the period 1948-1952, helped the region recover financial stability and facilitated a more efficient allocation of resources and faster trade liberalization. These facets of the Marshall Plan provide the international community with important lessons as guidance on achieving development cooperation in support of national efforts towards sustainable development.

## Development of the less developed countries

The Golden Age of Capitalism witnessed the birth and flourishing of a new discipline known as *development economics*. The recessions in European countries during the period upset the division of labour that had prevailed between them and less developed countries or areas, including their colonies (de Janvry and Sadoulet, 2013). Developing countries imported industrial goods in exchange for exports of their primary commodities. Upon the disruption of these trade patterns, developing countries looked for guidance in the catching-up process.[22] Demand for guidance on development policies increased as newly independent countries emerged from decolonization. Recognizing the need for new trade relationships among countries, the 1956 *Survey* affirmed, in fact, that what was necessary was "a continuing reorientation of the international division of labour to reduce the excessive dependence of underdeveloped countries upon imports in relation to the world's dependence upon their exports" (p. 13).

Development economics provided countries with the theoretical framework and practical guidelines for planning and implementing catching-up strategies, including for agricultural development, industrialization, economic planning, and securing development finance from both domestic and external sources, among many other areas of activity. The successes and failures of the different national strategies implemented by less developed countries were the basis for thoughtful reflection within the domain of development economics; and analysis of those successes and failures contributed to the refinement of existing theories and guidelines and the generation of new ideas and practical guidance. Not only did development economics greatly influence the themes, approaches and policy recommendations advocated by the *Survey* during the period, but its impact on the debate on sustainable development in the United Nations continues to be felt even today.[23]

The other notable event in the Golden Age was the designation by the General Assembly, in its resolution 1710 (XVI) of 19 December 1961, of the 1960s as the First United Nations Development Decade. Within the context of the strategy for the Decade as the first of the United Nations-led development processes, the Assembly called upon all Member States to intensify support for measures required to accelerate progress towards self-sustaining socioeconomic growth and social advancement in developing countries.

Under the strategy for the First United Nations Development Decade, the international community was unified, for the first time, through their call for collective actions to support the development of less developed countries. Within the context of the Decade, the *Survey* contributed policy analysis and critical reviews of global economic trends.

**Development economics was born to provide countries with the theoretical framework and practical guidelines for planning and implementing catching-up strategies**

**During the First United Nations Development Decade, progress towards self-sustaining socioeconomic development would be accelerated, with international support**

---

[22]  At the time, development efforts of countries were associated with catching up with the level of industrialization and the living standards of more advanced countries.

[23]  Appendix A.2 lists the major contributors to the publication in its early period and their contributions to economic thinking in general and to development economics in particular.

## A brief overview of the line of development thinking laid out in the *Survey* during the Golden Age

Concern for development issues at the United Nations increased over time as the voice of developing countries gained strength. The subject of stable economic growth and the long-term development challenges of developing countries were considered more frequently and with greater depth in United Nations deliberations and in the *Survey*. There were growing demands from some Member States, namely, Argentina, China, Egypt, India and Mexico, that the United Nations take action to support development efforts, even as early as the late 1940s, when the major focus of the Organization was on reconstruction rather than long-term growth or development. In 1947, the Economic and Employment Commission[24] under the Economic and Social Council, took up the issue and stated that "[t]he concern of the United Nations with the problems of economic development of underdeveloped areas stems from its basic purpose to 'promote social progress and better standards of life in larger freedom' (Charter of the United Nations, Preamble)".[25]

*World Economic Report 1949-50*, which focused its attention on the lag in development of the underdeveloped countries when compared with the rest of the world, stated that "[t] he economic development of the underdeveloped countries remains the most important single long-run economic problem confronting the world" (p. 10). *World Economic Report 1951-52* listed "the relatively slow advance of underdeveloped countries" (p. 11) among the most pressing matters of concern for the United Nations, while *World Economic Survey 1955* lamented that "the problem of mass poverty in a large part of the world remains as stubborn as ever" (p. 3).

**In the 1950s, social progress in developing countries was not sufficient to close the income gap with developed countries**

Looking back on the first decade after the Second World War, the 1955 *Survey* concluded that advances had been made in the underdeveloped economies in many different fields such as education, health, transport and communications, energy use, new industries, exports and, most importantly, in the "evolution of a social climate favourable to economic development" in which Governments saw themselves and were seen as "engines for the promotion of economic and social welfare" (p. 3). However, growth of per capita income had remained below that of industrialized countries and the group of underdeveloped economies faced many critical challenges, including: (a) a foreign exchange and a savings gap; (b) insufficient food supplies; and (c) the volatility of commodity prices and the limited opportunities created through the sale of these goods.

The concern with development in the 1950s arose in response to two different challenges: the development of centrally planned economies and the cold war, and national development in the South. As newly independent countries became more numerous, the development of those countries was recognized as a major challenge and often given high priority in the United Nations agenda. During the early history of the United Nations, colonialism prevailed in Africa. In 1960, however, 18 countries became independent; between 1961 and 1965, 10 more became independent; and in the course of the rest of the decade, 5 other countries achieved independence.

---

24    The Economic and Employment Commission was established by the Economic and Social Council in its resolution 6 (I) of 16 February 1946.

25    In this regard, see the reports of the Economic and Employment Commission on its first session (E/255), held from 20 January to 5 February 1947, and its second session (E/445), held from 2 to 17 June 1947.

In the late 1950s, the *Survey* began considering development within a broader context and in this regard stated that "[t]he problem of economic development is not merely one of inducing marginal shifts in the allocation of resources among existing branches of economic activity; it is rather one of introducing large-scale fundamental changes into the economic structure" (*World Economic Survey 1959*, p. 7). That is, development was considered "the structural transformation of the economy". The *Survey* also pointed out that "'[d]evelopment' is no predestined path along which all countries must go: it is a diverse and uncertain process reflecting the culture and preferences of people as well as the resources at their disposal and an ever-changing technology" (*World Economic Survey, 1969-1970*, p. 1). The *Survey* emphasized that in today's world, there are no "one-size-fits-all" blueprints.

Through its recognition of the nature of development, the *Survey* identified several critical elements for sustained growth and long-term development, in both the domestic and external spheres. Among the domestic challenges considered by the *Survey* were savings and investment gaps, industrialization as a means of speeding up economic development, economic planning as a coordination tool (not to be confused with the tools associated with the centrally planned economies) and the need for statistical indicators to measure development progress.

> In the 1960s, the Survey promoted the concept of development as structural transformation

## Domestic savings and investment for development and the supplementary role of external resource transfers

During the 1950s and 1960s, the *Survey* placed great emphasis on savings and investment as prime determinants of growth and long-term development, which reflected the theory predominating in macroeconomics and development economics at that time.

*World Economic Survey 1960*, for example, emphasized that most of domestic investment should be financed by domestic savings, but that a higher level of investment could be attained by increasing support for innovation both through the use of fiscal incentives for stimulating saving and through the channelling of higher public revenue into investment. Government budgets were considered to play a critical role in financing development and Governments could transfer resources from income or consumption into well-conceived investment projects. In light of this, the *Survey* urged Member States to improve public administration and to raise the quantity and quality of public service provisioning, as strengthening the public administration was essential to improving the quality of their services related to effective tax collection and public investment for development.

> Savings and investment were recognized as prime determinants of growth and development

*World Economic Survey 1965* (Part I), on the other hand, noted that if growth rates were to be accelerated, more resources would have to be devoted to investment. The same volume pointed out that the high incidence of poverty was the common principal obstacle to increasing savings for developing countries. Even in some developing countries where domestic savings increased, it had taken almost 10 years to raise the average of the domestic savings rate by about 1 per cent of total production.

That *Survey*, noting also that direct private investment and bond issuance by public authorities had proved inadequate, recognized the important role that official external resources could play in supplementing domestic investment. However, the "tying" of aid, which was a common practice of Governments in industrialized countries, became a critical issue, as strict control over the source or physical nature of the assets transferred to developing countries posed utilization problems for the recipient countries. In addition, the *Survey* warned of the rapid rise among developing countries of outstanding external debt derived from the balances and accrued interest accumulated through these resource transfers. As a

> External resources, particularly official flows, were important in supplementing domestic savings

result of that rise of external debt, the relative contribution of external resources to domestic investment in the recipient countries contracted sharply. It is interesting to observe that a sign of the burden imposed by external debt on development of recipient countries had already emerged in the middle of the Golden Age.

## Planning for development

Attesting to the recognition of the importance of long-term economic development, enthusiasm for long-term projections and economic planning increased. The enthusiasm was due partly to the achievement of independence by many African countries and the launching of the Alliance for Progress in Latin America; and also to the influence of the advances achieved by academics in the 1950s with respect to the building of quantitative models for long-run economic growth. Since the late 1950s, many developing countries had been encouraged, by national and multilateral agencies concerned with international development assistance, to introduce medium- or long-term plans for assessing growth paths which would guide policy decisions. In many countries, development and planning "were almost synonymous in the 1950s and 1960s".[26]

**Planning became an important development tool for policy coordination**

In its resolution 1708 (XVI) of 19 December 1961, entitled "Planning for economic development", the General Assembly invited the Secretary-General to prepare a special chapter on questions of development planning in a forthcoming issue of the *World Economic Survey* (sect. III, para. 3). Pursuant to that invitation, Part I of *World Economic Survey 1964* was focused on planned development.[27] In that edition of the *Survey*, it is stated that "the acceleration of economic and social development requires a more long-sighted approach to policy formulation" and that "it has come to be understood that current policy decisions can no longer be made simply in response to the circumstances of the moment but have to contribute actively to bringing about the structural and institutional changes which underlie economic development" (p. 2). The *Survey* affirmed that the core contribution that economic planning can make to economic development lies in the coordination of policies, rather than in their selection or adoption (p. 117). Ultimately, planning is merely a means of coordinating policies so as to ensure that the available resources at hand are utilized effectively and efficiently. It was argued that markets in many developing countries were undeveloped and rudimentary, making markets poor mechanisms for reflecting the "true" opportunity costs of the society. The price system was thus regarded as less reliable and less effective for addressing the development problems of those countries.

As in other editions of the *Survey* published during the 1960s, the 1964 *Survey* identified the supply of domestic savings and the supply of key goods and services as two of the three pivotal scarcities that developing countries confronted with respect to increasing economic growth, the other being the supply of human resources.[28] It was cautioned that, in some countries, the limited supply of trained manpower or the low administrative capacity of Governments had restricted the volume of other resources which could be effectively utilized for expanding investment and output. In this context, a larger development programme could not be undertaken without a considerable loss in the efficiency of resource utilization. The 1964 *Survey* also pointed out that many developing countries had focused

---

26   Rahman (2002), p. 58.

27   Not to be confused with central planning.

28   Power and transport shortages were listed as other scarcities.

only limited attention on the issue of human resources, inasmuch as efforts to consider this issue were of quite recent origin in those countries.

The *Survey* reviewed methods for planning formulation, implementation and organization, and analysed at great length the interrelationship between national plans and international policies. This reflected both developments following the proclamation of the First United Nations Development Decade and the recognition of accelerated economic and social progress among developing countries as a matter of international responsibility. The *Survey* stated that the role of the developed countries was to offer commercial and foreign aid policies conducive to high and sustainable rates of economic growth and stressed that, at their present stage of development, developing countries could not hope to achieve such economic growth without international assistance.

In Part One of *World Economic Survey 1967*, practical solutions were proposed for dealing with challenges faced by many developing countries on their road to development—solutions that are still relevant today. These included designing a development strategy for increasing productivity and bringing about the structural changes required for continued expansion of output in the face of shortages of domestic savings and foreign exchange. It went on to observe that two kinds of difficulties frequently encountered by developing countries lie in the identification of (a) the principal obstacles (or bottlenecks) to economic growth in a manner that is operationally useful and (b) the mechanisms for dealing with, and, if necessary, for circumventing, particularly recalcitrant obstacles. This perspective is very much in line with the proposal put forward by Hausmann, Rodrik and Velasco (2005) for a practical guide to developing a framework for "growth diagnostics", that is, a strategy for identifying the most binding constraints on growth and defining the policy priorities needed to resolve them.

Other issues discussed in the *Survey* included practical guidelines on how to minimize the negative short-run impacts of adjustment during the course of development. For example, it recommended maximizing the use of available domestic resources, substituting the more plentiful for the scarcer raw material, using labour instead of mechanical equipment, and choosing technologies that were best related to the existing factor endowment. Because the formulation and implementation of development policies imposed a very heavy strain on government machinery, the 1967 *Survey* recommended instituting a plan administration that cut across the traditional departmental structure of the civil service which could improve coordination within the government. The plan administration would ensure that the functioning of the public services ran smoothly and, that the focus of operations was consistent with the larger development objectives of the country. This is an issue of great relevance today within the context of sustainable development and the need to achieve balance with respect to the economic, social and environmental dimensions.

**During the First United Nations Development Decade, the Survey identified the important role of developed countries in supporting the efforts of the developing ones**

## Assessing the First United Nations Development Decade

The decade of the 1960s is often referred to as "aspirational" with regard to development. The desire to expand the transfer of resources from the developed to the developing countries was given historical global endorsement when, on 15 December 1960, the General Assembly adopted resolution 1522 (XV), in which it set a target of 1 per cent of the combined national incomes of the developed countries, to be transferred to developing countries to support their development efforts. On 19 December 1961, pursuant to the proposal launched in his address to the General Assembly by the President of the United

States, John Fitzgerald Kennedy, the Assembly, as noted above, adopted resolution 1710 (XVI) in which it designated the 1960s (1961-1970) as the decade of development (see appendix A.3). One of the targets to be achieved under the strategy for the First United Nations Development Decade was a minimum annual rate of growth of aggregate national income of 5 per cent for developing countries at the end of the Decade, as a measurable expression of the intentions of the international community (*World Economic Survey 1967*, Part One).

The goals under the First United Nations Development Decade were visionary at a time when many countries' memory of a drastic decline in their living standards, as a result of the devastation wrought by war, was still fresh; when many areas were colonies and their societies were oppressed; and when, more notably, the majority of the global population faced poverty, hunger, poor health and poor living conditions, and inadequate levels of education. As examined above, the *Survey* recognized that in the late 1940s, the economic development of the underdeveloped countries remained the world's most important long-term economic problem.

The strategy for the First United Nations Development Decade, together with the 1962 report of the Secretary-General entitled "United Nations Development Decade: proposals for action" (E/3613), offered up a new world view focused on the importance of supporting the development objectives of developing countries. The proclamation of the Decade signalled a new concern about the need to mobilize domestic and international resources for development. National resource mobilization was to be complemented by external resources derived from aid and trade, while there were concerns about the instability of the export earnings of developing countries, due to large-scale volatility of commodity prices. The First United Nations Development Decade turned out to be the first of a series of four (to be discussed in the following chapters). The motivations, thinking and practices underpinning the Development Decades constituted the foundation for a United Nations focus on development issues which led to the adoption of both the Millennium Development Goals and the Sustainable Development Goals.

### Towards the Second United Nations Development Decade

In the late 1960s, the *Survey* had advocated for improved coherence across the political, social and economic dimensions of development

According to the 1968 *Survey* (Part One, p. 1), it may have seemed optimistic, in light of the historical record, when the General Assembly set the target of a minimum annual rate of growth of national income of 5 per cent to be attained by developing countries by the end of the 1960s. However, even if the 1960s had not yet come to a close, the 1968 *Survey* had already predicted that the actual performance of the developing regions might not fall far short of that initial objective. In the end, the average annual rate of GDP in developing countries turned out to be 5.5 per cent (table II.2).

Within the context of the preparatory work for the Second United Nations Development Decade (see chap. III), the 1968 *Survey* (Part One) pointed out the major development issues that had been identified during the Decade, contending that "if there is any criticism of general validity which can be levelled against post-war discussions of development, it is the compartmentalization of political, social and economic policies" (p. 1). It went on to argue that while social thinkers had long recognized the importance of political and social changes for economic growth, social and political policies had remained matters of separate consideration in discussions of economic measures directly related to the level and composition of output, investment and trade. The *Survey*'s concluding assertion that economic development is not accomplished within an unchanging governance and social structure—reflecting an early recognition of the need for political will and policy coherence as two fundamental factors supporting effective development—encapsulates an issue of continuing relevance today.

During this period, understanding of the nature and causes of development was broadened to encompass more than just pure economic growth. The 1968 *Survey* noted the "widespread agreement" that for broad-based economic development to be achieved, "policies to alter and improve social conditions [were] of fundamental importance" (Part One, p. 1). Thus, neither social nor economic measures should be regarded as separate actions directed towards separate ends. As an example, the 1968 *Survey* examined the interactions of three key issues which had emerged during the 1960s—the economic, social and institutional dimensions—namely, problems and policies relating to the prospective growth of population, employment and educational requirements; the increase in domestic and external resources; and policies for the acceleration of agricultural and industrial growth. All three issues were eventually reflected in the International Development Strategy for the Second United Nations Development Decade.

The subject of industrialization of less developed countries was in the agenda of the General Assembly and the Economic and Social Council during the 1950s, at a time when there was a persistent call by development economists (such as Hans Singer and Raúl Prebisch) for the industrialization of underdeveloped countries. The concern over export pessimism with regard to primary products, together with the industrialization experience of developed countries, was used to make a case for industrialization. Observing that there was "almost universal agreement that industrialization [had] a major role to play in the economic development of the underdeveloped countries" (p. 3) and emphasizing that newly independent countries were unlikely to rapidly expand their economic activities based solely on primary commodity exports, *World Economic Survey 1961* then provided a detailed discussion of the necessity of promoting industrialization. It justified large-scale planned industrialization in terms of complementarity among different industries (p. 55), while pointing out the advantages of international specialization, as well as the disadvantages of small domestic markets, a characteristic feature of many developing countries.

The *Survey* did admit that there were debates regarding the proper patterns of industrial development and stated that the advantages of international specialization, based on the relative abundance of labour, should be seen in its proper light as a dynamic process, in which development amounts to a process of transforming the prevailing demand and supply conditions. A call was made for diversification of the economic activity and export structure of developing countries. In this regard, the role of the State in development was widely recognized, specifically in mobilizing private investment for the development of infrastructure through the provision of public credit, tax exemptions for machinery and raw materials, and the attraction of foreign direct investment.

The 1964 (Part I) and 1968 (Part One) editions of the *World Economic Survey* recognized that higher productivity in agriculture was the precondition for industrialization, and that strengthening the linkages between the agricultural and industrial sectors was important. This recognition by the *Survey* was based on the experience of Latin America and the Caribbean and, to some extent, Africa, where the lack of harmonization between industry and agriculture had become an obstacle to sustainable industrialization. Accordingly, adequate food supplies were perceived as being the major determinant of living standards and a very important factor in the development of a domestic market for manufactures, an idea attributable to Michał Kalecki, a prominent economist of that time and a contributor to

**The *Survey* recognized the importance of increasing productivity in agriculture**

the *Survey* (see appendix A.2). According to the 1957 *Survey*, the shortage of food supplies emerged within the broader context of underemployment of resources and insufficient production capacities (which created excess demand and inflationary pressures). Food shortages were the most worrying supply constraint, leading to unsustainable wage-price spirals, as was the case in Chile in the period 1940-1953.[29] Hence, implicit in the call for industrialization was the belief that devising "a proper production policy" (1957 *Survey*, p. 13) constituted the first step towards economic development.

On the basis of these considerations, certain goals were set under the International Development Strategy for the Second United Nations Development Decade (1971-1980), adopted by the General Assembly in its resolution 2626 (XXV) of 24 October 1970 (see appendix A.3). It was determined that achieving an average annual rate of growth in the gross product of the developing countries as a whole should be at least 6 per cent (para. 13), which implied an average annual expansion of 4 per cent in agricultural output and of 8 per cent in manufacturing output (para. 16 (a) and (b)). Through the 1980s, Member States continued to focus their discussion primarily on the speed of industrialization rather than on its pattern, and on the international context rather than on the domestic constraints that countries could face. In the early 1970s, industrialization was often discussed within the broader context of development. After being shelved as a priority in the 1990s, it is now one of the 17 Sustainable Development Goals.

### Measuring progress in the developing countries

As will be demonstrated in the discussions in chapter III, the International Development Strategy for the Second United Nations Development Decade not only encompassed assistance for economic growth and development, but also included targets for social development in such spheres as health, education and employment.

**The *Survey* advanced the importance of measuring development progress with robust statistical indicators**

The 1969-1970 *Survey* examined the possibility of monitoring the process of economic and social development in ways that could be useful not only in assessing the nature of progress and the speed at which it is achieved, but also in evaluating the efficiency of policies. This constituted one of the early attempts by the United Nations system, including the International Labour Organization and the World Health Organization, to measure progress and policy outcomes with internationally agreed yardsticks, such as well-defined targets and indicators.

The *Survey* recommended that development indicators should distinguish between:

(a) Aspects of development that are directly reflected in human welfare and those that concern the economic mechanism through which persons seek to pursue their objectives;

(b) Current status of living conditions and actions that yield fruits only in the future such as changes in the economic capacity of countries to deliver goods and services.

At the international level, indicators call for selectivity: their application should be confined to the most significant and widespread aspects of socioeconomic progress.

---

29  In 1938, Chile had linked legislatively the minimum wage to the cost of living, which created wage-price and cost-price spirals, and added to inflationary pressures. According to the 1953-54 *Survey* (chap. 3), the inflation experienced in the period 1940-1953 was due to slow growth of food production and the rise in import prices (due to increasing international prices and exchange rate depreciation), both of which were linked to a higher real wage and high inflation.

The 1969-1970 *Survey* cautioned that, while new methods of measuring the course of development could be introduced in the long run, in the shorter run it was necessary and practical to prepare indicators "from the currently available supply of socioeconomic statistics" (p. 1). Within the context of the statistics that were available at the end of the 1960s, the *Survey* noted that the "aspects of socio-economic performance that appear to be most significant for international assessment include material output per person, adequacy of nutrition, infant mortality and life expectancy, literacy, availability (or lack) of gainful employment, internal price stability and domestic and foreign savings ratios" (p. 2).

It continually recommended that, for the purpose of measuring its progress, each country should select the series of indicators that it judged to be "most appropriate in the light of its own economic and social circumstances, its own ability to carry out the necessary measuring process, the characteristics of its own development plan and the detail with which it wishes to monitor the operation of specific policies" (pp. 1-2). These recommendations are still valid today.

## Reflecting on the experience of the Golden Age of Capitalism

Development thinking in general and international cooperation in particular were built up from the foundations provided by the Golden Age of Capitalism. Development economics offered guidelines for less developed or newly independent countries to participate in the development process. The contribution of the Marshall Plan to the rebuilding of the economies of European countries and Japan after the Second World War and the successful outcomes of the First United Nations Development Decade during the 1960s were the kind of achievements to which policymakers and practitioners in the area of development of later generations aspired in their efforts to help the less developed countries help themselves. During this period, the *Survey* both responded to the debates on world economic problems and international development and provided States Members of the United Nations with policy recommendations. The formulation of the Sustainable Development Goals, which are the most comprehensive and ambitious set of development goals ever to have been adopted, attests to the inspirational impact of the traditions in development thinking and practice.

To a large extent, present-day development thinking and practices are a fruit of the legacy of the Golden Age of Capitalism. The current target of raising the level of ODA to developing countries to 0.7 per cent of the total GNI of the donor community can be traced back to the proposal, which achieved prominence in the 1960s, that 1 per cent of the national income of the developed countries be transferred to developing countries as aid. The Marshall Plan offered an early example of successful implementation of resource transfers to countries in need. The strategies for the First United Nations Development Decade in the 1960s and for the Second Decade in the 1970s were inspirational for decades to come to everyone engaged in development. At the time, and within the context of the preparatory work for the Second Development Decade, *Survey* analyses assessed the outcome of the First Decade in terms of achievement of its goals and targets and identified the major issues of development policy with which the international community was likely to be confronted in the coming decade. It criticized the compartmentalization of various policies across economic, social and governance issues and argued that the aims of an economic policy could not be accomplished within an unchanging governance and social structure.

**Development theory and practice during the Golden Age bequeathed important lessons which are applicable to the challenges of the present day**

Further, the *Surveys* of that period expanded the scope of the concept of development, including its features and the factors that generated it, beyond the economic sphere and in this regard recommended that policymakers include an integrated approach to dealing with the economic, social and institutional facets of development. Recognition of the need for a more integrated policy approach which emerged during the Golden Age of Capitalism played a crucial foundational role in the elaboration of the United Nations development agendas, and the influence of this recognition extended down to the formulation of the Sustainable Development Goals.

The aspirations associated with the First United Nations Development Decade were very much moulded by the emergence of a large number of new nation States as part of the process of decolonization. The economic prosperity achieved by the world economy, particularly by the economies of developed countries during the 1950s and 1960s, provided the enabling international environment needed to support the high aspirations inherent in development objectives.

**The analyses and policy recommendations derived from the Golden Age are shedding light on current development challenges, including implementation of the Sustainable Development Goals**

Yet, even during the Golden Age of Capitalism, countries faced high volatility of commodity prices, and in this regard, the *Surveys* identified a clear need for international stabilization mechanisms designed to manage volatility, an issue that remains relevant in the context of implementation and achievement of the Sustainable Development Goals. The Bretton Woods monetary system made a huge contribution to the growth and stability of international trade and the payments systems in the first quarter century immediately following the Second World War. The flexibility demonstrated by IMF, which enabled member countries to eliminate foreign exchange restrictions over a longer period of time, provides a valuable policy lesson that is highly relevant today.

During the Golden Age of Capitalism, industrialization was put forward as a means of facilitating the economic development of less developed countries, and the importance of longer-term economic planning was recognized as well. The *Survey* recommended the establishment of a plan administration within the Government to coordinate various economic, social and institutional policies at a higher level, so as to prevent the disruption of normal public services delivery by line ministries while at the same time keeping the focus on the overall objectives of development. It is clear, then, that the evolution of the 2030 Agenda for Sustainable Development, which covers a 15-year horizon, was guided by a deep-seated recognition of the need for a longer-term outlook and the importance of policy coordination across various line ministries.

# Chapter III

# The end of the Golden Age, the debt crisis and development setbacks

## Key messages

- The post-war economic boom ended, in 1971, with the collapse of the Bretton Woods fixed exchange rate system. While high inflation and unemployment became the norm in most developed countries, the prolonged and painful adjustment process could have been averted through more coherent international policy coordination.

- Two approaches to global coordination were advocated by the Survey, which are still relevant today: adoption of an interest rate policy designed to reduce short-term capital flows and exchange rate volatility, and expansion of demand in surplus countries. As a result of weak policy coordination at the global level, developing countries paid a high price for adjustment, which set the stage for the debt crises of the 1980s.

- In the absence of a fair debt workout mechanism, the cost of the debt crises in the 1980s was primarily absorbed by debtor countries, leading to a lost decade of development in Latin America and Africa. More judicious debt management—by debtors and creditors alike—could have reduced the social and economic cost of the debt crises.

- While countries in Africa and Latin America implemented structural adjustment reforms imposed by conditionality for financial support, most countries in Asia followed a different development strategy. The divergence of the economic performances among regions underlines the importance of national policy space and ownership in identifying the development trajectories that best respond to a country's own context.

- After the success of the First United Nations Development Decade, in 1971, the United Nations launched a Second Development Decade. However, the experience with the Second—and later the Third and Fourth Development Decades—demonstrated how quickly a global commitment can evaporate in times of economic difficulties, which highlights the importance of a stable global economic environment for upholding the commitment to ambitious development agendas.

### Key events

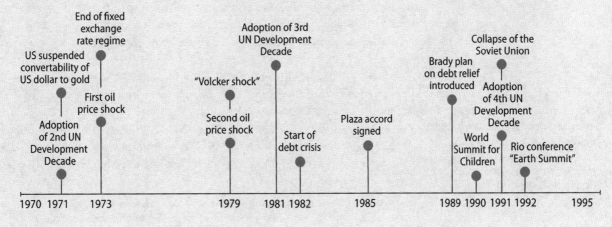

*"For many developing countries, the 1980s have been viewed as a decade lost for development. Living conditions in Africa and Latin America and the Caribbean, and in parts of Asia, have deteriorated, and economic and social infrastructure has eroded."*

*World Economic Survey 1990*

## Introduction[1]

**The 1970s began with the breakdown of the Bretton Woods system**

The decade of the 1970s began with unexpected global economic turmoil after a long stretch of economic stability and robust growth in the earlier post-war period. It also witnessed the breakdown of the post-Second World War consensus on the global economic governance architecture, as embodied in the Bretton Woods system of fixed exchange rates and gold convertibility of the United States dollar. In addition, there were two oil price shocks and the persistence of high inflation and unemployment—referred to as stagflation—in several developed countries.

As a result, a difficult global economic situation confronted the world as it entered the 1980s—a situation characterized by both internal and external imbalances; high inflation and unemployment (internal imbalance) in developed countries; and large deficits in the current account of the balance of payments (external imbalance) in both developed and developing countries. Lower demand in developed countries led to a decline in commodity prices and a deterioration of the terms of trade for many developing countries dependent on commodity exports.

**A steep increase in interest rates in the United States of America triggered sovereign debt crises**

Given the difficult economic situation, many countries in Latin America and Africa experienced an increase in debt levels. This was fostered in part by the recycling of abundant petrodollars by the financial institutions of developed countries. In this context, the steep increase in interest rates in the United States of America to combat inflation at the turn of the decade triggered debt crises in many countries of Latin America and Africa. Highly indebted countries in those regions were unable to repay the debt, as debt service payments rose sharply. The debt crisis of the 1980s is generally considered to have begun when, in August 1982, Mexico declared that it would no longer be able to service its debt. This ignited a succession of sovereign defaults around the world, with one country after another declaring a similar inability to repay.

Economic growth slowed down in all parts of the world during the second half of the 1970s and the first half of the 1980s. Before the oil price shock of 1973, the annual growth of world gross product (WGP) had been at 5.3 per cent, while during the rest of the 1970s, annual world growth reached only 2.8 per cent. In the early 1980s, annual growth decelerated even further, to only 1.4 per cent in the first four years of the decade. In particular, growth in developing countries fell dramatically. While, globally, growth recovered to some extent in the latter half of the 1980s, it was still below the levels that had marked the beginning of the 1970s (figure III.1).

**Countries were under pressure to implement policy reforms, collectively known as the Washington Consensus**

In response to the debt crisis in many developing countries, the most profound economic policy changes since the Second World War were implemented in many parts of the world. Those policy reforms, aimed at stabilization, liberalization and privatization,

---

1   The present chapter reviews the conditions in the global economy and development trends in the period between 1972 and the mid-1990s, as examined in the *World Economic Survey*. In 1993, the *World Economic Survey* changed its name to *World Economic and Social Survey*. In 1999, an additional report was launched on short term economic issues, the *World Economic Situation and Prospects*. In this chapter, all these reports are referred to as the *Survey*.

Figure III.1
**Growth of output**

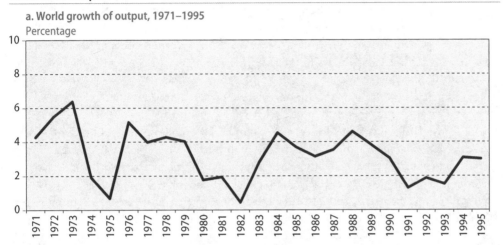

a. World growth of output, 1971–1995
Percentage

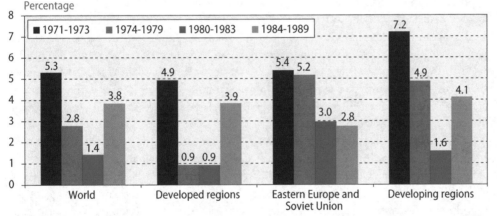

b. World and regional growth of output, 1971–1989
Percentage

Source: UN/DESA, based on data from the Statistics Division.

became known collectively as the Washington Consensus because they reflected the influence of three Washington, D.C.-based institutions, namely, the United States Treasury, the International Monetary Fund (IMF) and the World Bank. The reforms were often imposed on developing countries as conditionality for debt relief and financial support.

IMF and the World Bank, in particular, were influential in countries experiencing debt distress and, this being the case, countries in Africa and Latin America were pressured to adopt Washington Consensus-type policies. They therefore had to undertake drastic measures for fiscal consolidation, which contributed to a prolonged recession and a lost decade of development in those regions. Meanwhile, most countries in Asia, which were not under the same kind of pressure, enjoyed a larger national policy space. Contrary to what the Washington Consensus dictated, East Asia, and to a lesser extent South Asia, chose to follow a development strategy where an important role was played by the State.

The different development strategies and policies adopted by various developing regions contributed to a great economic divergence in the 1980s. While all developing regions enjoyed relative robust growth in the 1970s, the experience of the 1980s was marked by dramatic divergences. Led by China, South and East Asia grew by an annual average of 7.2 per cent in the 1980s, while developing countries in Latin America, Africa and Western Asia experienced dismal growth, of 1.5 per cent, 1.7 per cent and 1.7 per cent, respectively

**A difference in policy choices led to a great divergence in the economic performances of developing regions**

(figure III.2). Thus, a new division—between countries of East Asia and other developing countries—emerged alongside the traditional division between oil exporters and importers.

Eastern Europe and the Union of Soviet Socialist Republics (the Soviet Union) also experienced a slowdown in growth during the 1980s, compared with the post-war years, together with various other types of problems in their economies and societies. Grappling with these problems contributed to political change and by the conclusion of the decade, communism had been brought to an end in Eastern Europe, which was followed shortly thereafter, in 1991, by the dissolution of the Soviet Union and the formation of the Commonwealth of Independent States (CIS).

In the 1970s and 1980s, there were a number of economic debates on fundamental issues. There were intense discussions on the appropriate policies for tackling stagflation in developed countries, management of the growing global imbalances and the international responses to debt crises. Contractionary policies under the Washington Consensus as well as its implementation through IMF conditionality were also heavily discussed issues. The difference in policy direction among developing countries, resulting in differences in economic performance, led to a substantial debate on appropriate development strategies.

**There was less attention paid to income distribution, living standards, education, health and environmental degradation**

The frequency and depth of economic crises as well as the adjustment and austerity imposed by the Washington Consensus meant that less attention was paid to issues of income distribution, living standards, education, health and environmental degradation. This also shifted attention away from the International Development Strategies for the Second and Third United Nations Development Decades (1971-1980 and 1981-1990, respectively). When the General Assembly, by its resolution 45/199 of 21 December 1990, adopted the International Development Strategy for the Fourth United Nations Development Decade (1991-2000), as set forth in the annex thereto, the aim was to change this record of unsatisfactory progress.

While the collapse of the Soviet Union generated new hope for international cooperation and momentum for international agreements, the goals and objectives of the Fourth Development Decade were overshadowed by the economic difficulties that arose in the aftermath of that collapse. The United Nations nevertheless continued to push the development discourse towards more people-centred and rights-based approaches through

Figure III.2
**Annual average growth of GDP in developing regions, 1971–1990**

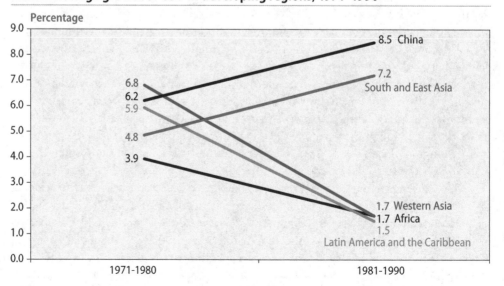

a series of world summits and international conferences on children, women and the environment in the 1990s (see appendix A.4).

## The collapse of the Bretton Woods system, oil price shocks and stagflation

The early 1970s were marked by a series of economic crises that destabilized the global economy. The first of these crises was the collapse of the Bretton Woods system in August 1971, when the United States suspended convertibility of the dollar into gold and other currencies and imposed a 10 per cent temporary surcharge on dutiable imports.[2]

This move came as the result of widespread speculative movements of capital from the United States as monetary easing reduced interest rates relative to those of its major competitors, in particular, France and the United Kingdom of Great Britain and Northern Ireland. However, the main factor underlying the collapse was the increasing reliance of the international monetary system on growing trade and fiscal deficits in the United States, in part driven by the large expenditures associated with the Vietnam War, and the consequent expansion of United States international liabilities against an inadequate value of gold reserves. The inevitable devaluation of the dollar, which had been long in the making, reached 12 per cent against major currencies in 1971.

After the collapse of the fixed exchange rate regime under the Bretton Woods system, there was a struggle to establish new foreign exchange regimes among developed and developing countries. Various approaches to exchange rate management were tried, such as establishing more flexibility around a fixed peg, often using the special drawing rights (SDRs) base and varying degrees of floating. By 1973, floating had become widespread (figure III.3) as more and more countries abandoned the fixed rate regime. Forced by high

**After the collapse of the Bretton Woods system, countries struggled to establish new foreign exchange regimes**

Figure III.3
**Exchange rate regime by share of countries, 1960–1990**

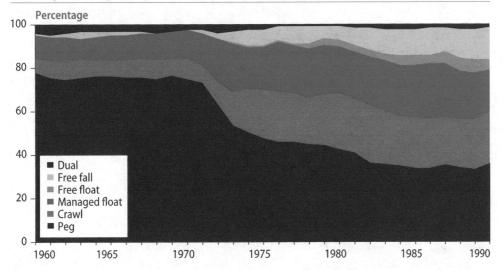

Percentage

Legend:
- Dual
- Free fall
- Free float
- Managed float
- Crawl
- Peg

**Source:** Ilzetzki, Reinhart and Rogoff (2010).

---

2    Under the Bretton Woods system, all currencies were linked to the United States dollar which was in turn linked to gold. In the end, the system turned out to be too rigid and in 1971, with the abandonment by the United States of the link between the dollar and gold, the fixed exchange rate system collapsed.

levels of inflation, floating gave rise to a new, special category of exchange rates characterized as "free falling". The size of this category increased throughout the 1970s and 1980s and peaked in the early 1990s.

**The oil price shock in 1973 contributed to a doubling of inflation in developed countries and high unemployment**

In late 1973, not too long after the collapse of the Bretton Woods system, oil prices more than doubled owing to the actions of the Organization of Arab Petroleum Exporting Countries (OAPEC) and in January 1974, they doubled again. In parallel, food prices also doubled in 1973 owing to increasing global demand and production problems in many countries (*World Economic Survey, 1974*, Part Two, p. 1-7). This contributed to a doubling of inflation in developed countries, which rose from an average of 5.1 per cent in 1971 to 10.4 per cent in 1975. All developed countries, without exception, experienced these price increases. In the United States, inflation rose from 3.3 per cent in 1971 to 11.1 per cent in 1973, and in Japan, from 4.5 per cent to 24.4 per cent over the same period (figure III.4).

The prolonged uncertainty after the collapse of the Bretton Woods system, compounded by the oil crisis in 1973, led to a stock market crash in 1973-1974 and a slowdown in growth in developed countries. In the period from 1973 to 1975, growth in the United States and in the United Kingdom fell from 5.6 to -0.2 per cent and from 6.5 to -1.5 per cent, respectively. The biggest slowdown was in Japan which grew at 9.9 per cent in 1973 and experienced negative growth in 1974. Accordingly, unemployment rates began to rise, in particular in the United States, reaching 8.3 per cent by 1975 (figure III.4).

**To deal with the problem of stagflation, countries abandoned Keynesian fiscal policy and replaced it with monetarism**

These developments meant that Governments in developed countries faced an entirely new problem of declining growth, rising unemployment and high rates of inflation, called stagflation. Hence, much of the economic debate centred around how developed country economic policies should respond to this new challenge. The Keynesian fiscal policy favoured in the 1960s seemed ill-equipped to address simultaneous problems of unemployment and inflation, and monetary policy appeared to be too blunt an instrument to deal with cost-induced inflation.

Initially, most developed country Governments attempted a blend of monetary and fiscal policies. However, as the decade wore on and with the experience of the second oil price shock of 1979, utilization of monetary policy became more prevalent. Developed countries with both progressive and conservative Governments tackled the inflation pro-

Figure III.4
**Unemployment, inflation and GDP growth in Japan, the United Kingdom and the United States, 1971–1981**

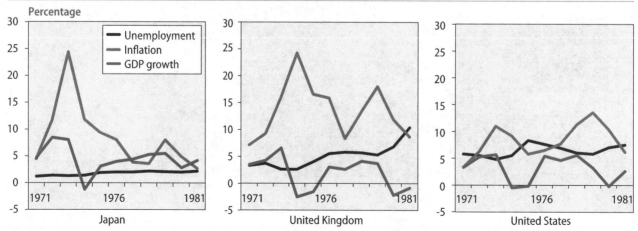

**Source:** UN/DESA, based on data from the International Labour Organization, the Statistics Division and the United Nations Conference on Trade and Development.

blem by raising interest rates and restricting credit. Eventually, contractionary monetary policy was accompanied by tight fiscal policies aimed at reducing government budgets as conservative Governments became dominant in the larger advanced economies.

The need for immediate short-term policy responses to stabilize the economy in developed countries completely overshadowed the Second United Nations Development Decade with its focus on long-run economic and social policies in the early part of the decade (*World Economic Survey, 1974*, Part One, p. 1). See below for a further discussion on the three Development Decades.

## Critical reflections in the *Survey*

One critical message of the *Survey* during this period was that managing the trade-off between unemployment and inflation required using a variety of policy measures as opposed to resorting solely to blunt monetary or fiscal instruments (*World Economic Survey, 1975*, p. 93; *World Economic Survey 1980-1981*, p. 10).

In the earlier part of the 1970s, the *Survey* argued that structural and institutional changes would be needed if unemployment was to be reduced without exacerbating inflation. These changes would involve "the selective expansion or redirection of public employment in the light of perceived social needs, the selective stimulation of private employment through new and modernizing investment that avoid[ed] freezing workers into declining industries and a much more eclectic and imaginative approach to training and retraining in facilities that [were] linked more closely to industrial and other employers and thus capable of increasing the mobility of labour not only geographically but also in terms of skills" (*World Economic Survey, 1975*, p. 93).

**The *Survey* argued for policy measures beyond monetary policy**

Beginning in 1980-1981, the *Survey* started to stress the need for coordination among developed countries in combating inflation, promoting growth, avoiding protectionism and dealing with the imbalances between trade surplus and trade deficit countries. The concern, however, was that the international coordination needed to achieve lower interest rates, as designed to stimulate investment and economic recovery, might not be feasible "as long as one or more major country [was] relying solely on monetary policies to combat inflation and those policies impl[ied] high interest rates" (*World Economic Survey 1980-1981*, p. 10). The *Survey* argued that such coordination could avoid damaging national anti-inflation programmes "only when those programmes [were] being undertaken through a wide variety of policy measures" (ibid.).

*World Economic Survey 1983* argued that a number of problematic tendencies affecting the global economy had originated in the developed countries. These included lower growth rates, unemployment, inflation, a fall in commodity prices, high real interest rates, increased protectionism and significant fluctuation in exchange rates. Since those issues were clearly interrelated, the *Survey* contended that it would be hard for any one country to tackle them alone and thus strongly recommended improved coordination among developed countries.

**The interrelated problems in the global economy led the *Survey* to argue for improved international economic coordination**

For example, the 1983 *Survey* observed that even the developed countries could not act alone: "some concordance in policies affecting current accounts and capital flows" was needed; and that more generally, a greater measure of economic cooperation among countries was "a shared requirement for sustained revival of the world economy" (p. 18). Areas for more concrete cooperation were suggested, including exchange rate policy and flows of long-term capital such as official development assistance (ODA) and multilateral bank loans to developing countries. It was also suggested that cooperation not just among developed countries but among developing countries as well could be useful.

In *World Economic Survey 1986*, a more ambitious approach to cooperation and coordination was introduced (pp. 7-10). This entailed the division of policy issues into categories according to the appropriate level of coordination required, as follows:

(a) Policy issues requiring international cooperation and action within a multilateral framework including (i) adjustments to the international trading system and the international monetary and financial systems; (ii) restoration of growth in developing countries through financing for development; (iii) resolution of commodity pricing problems; (iv) solutions to debt crises;

(b) Policy issues requiring concerted policy action within country groups including; (i) *developed countries*: pursuit of faster, non-inflationary growth and the unwinding of trade imbalances; (ii) *developing countries*: a greater voice and participation in discussions within multilateral trade and finance institutions and greater regional integration; (iii) *centrally planned economies*: greater coordination within the Council for Mutual Economic Assistance framework.

Over the decades, the *Survey* advocated for greater joint action and in doing so made a good case for international coordination; however, no guidance was provided on how that coordination might be accomplished nor was there a discussion of organizational challenges. Instead, the *Survey's* overarching recommendation centred on the use of multilateral and regional organizations. While coordination was a valuable concept, greater benefit would have been derived from closer attention to the mechanisms required for its achievement and the associated challenges.

## Growing global imbalances and increasing protectionism

**Trade imbalances started to grow in the 1970s and many countries experienced balance-of-payments difficulties**

At the same time that growth rates were falling and unemployment and inflation were rising, record trade imbalances arose in both developed and developing countries. In the 1970s, several developed countries, including the United States and the United Kingdom, were prone to balance-of-payments crises. In the 1980s, the debate focused mainly on growing trade deficits in the United States and corresponding surpluses in Japan and several European countries.[3]

In the second half of the 1970s, the balance-of-payments deficits of developing countries (except for major oil producers) more than doubled, from $46 billion in 1975 to $108 billion by 1981. It was the ability to finance such deficits through access to overseas finance that permitted imports to rise and the economy to therefore grow at the rate it did, despite rising import prices and deteriorating terms of trade. The availability of financing came as a result of ongoing liberalization of international capital markets, which led to more cross-border lending and bond issuances. As a consequence of the ongoing

---

3    Balance-of-payments difficulties arise when a country cannot obtain sufficient financing to meet international payment obligations. In the face of such difficulties, the country's currency is often forced to depreciate rapidly. Countries with deficits in their current accounts, also called external accounts, are likely to increase the level of sovereign debt, which can result in a debt crisis.

liberalization, more developing countries could finance current account deficits by tapping into international capital markets.

Economic instability gave rise to the policy debate on handling "internal imbalances" held in developed economies (see the discussion above). That debate had its counterpart in the debate on how best to manage global balance-of-payments surpluses and deficits, that is, "external imbalances". The large surpluses of oil exporters, of exporters of manufactures and, from time to time, of major developed economies, had to be reduced or recycled if global recession was to be averted.

This led to debates on the responsibility of current account surplus countries in the adjustment process. One option open to surplus countries was to expand their demand so as to increase imports and, in the process, help restore balance through growth. A second option entailed an increase of capital flows from surplus countries to countries facing deficits in the current account. A drawback in this regard, however, stemmed from the fact that international institutional arrangements were not equipped to deal with large capital imbalances. A third alternative for achieving balance entailed the restriction by developed economies of economic growth, which would result in a reduction of the exports of developing countries.

The global imbalances also led to increased protectionism. While negotiations continued on the progressive reduction of tariffs within the Tokyo Round of Multilateral Trade Negotiations, held under the auspices of the General Agreement on Tariffs and Trade (GATT), the United States and Europe complained bitterly about Japan's export juggernaut. The United States in formal terms and Europe more informally pressured Japan to agree to a set of voluntary export restraints for exports of autos, steel and other products. The pace of anti-dumping suits also picked up and protectionism was employed against developing countries as well. The renewal of the Multifibre Arrangement was of primary importance in this regard, as it resulted in a reduction of exports of textiles and clothing by developing countries.

**The global imbalances led to an increase in protectionism which affected all countries**

Another attempt to resolve the above-mentioned imbalances centred on exchange rates. With the end of the fixed-rate system in the early 1970s came the establishment of floating rates, which resulted in greater volatility than had initially been expected. In particular, the early 1980s witnessed the rise of the dollar against the major European currencies, which exacerbated the United States trade deficit (figure III.5).

The most dramatic attempt to achieve the coordination needed to address the volatility of exchange rates was represented by the 1985 Plaza Accord, under which the value of the dollar was lowered by about 50 per cent through a coordinated sale of dollars by the central banks of France, Germany, Japan and the United Kingdom. The signing of the Louvre Accord, whose goal was stabilization of the value of the dollar, occurred two years later, in February 1987.

## Critical reflections in the *Survey*

The *Survey*'s main concern was whether the trade and fiscal deficits of the United States could be financed or whether they were more likely to result in a "hard landing". While opinion on this question changed over time, the viewpoint towards the end of the period was more positively inclined. What was less discussed, however, were the implications of financing the United States deficits through a redirection of financial flows from the rest of the world.

Figure III.5

**Major exchange rates vis-à-vis the United States dollar, 1970–1995**

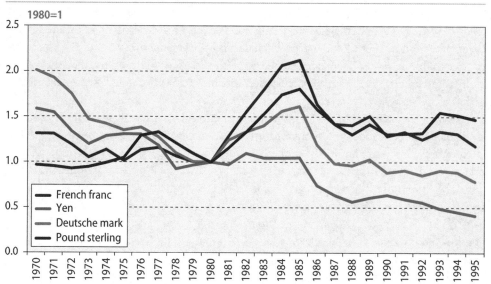

**Source:** UN/DESA, based on data from the Statistics Division.

**Protective measures introduced by developed countries were opposed by the *Survey*…**

The *Survey* consistently opposed the introduction of protective measures by developed countries and voiced opposition to the temporary surcharge on imports imposed by the United States in 1971, in general terms but more specifically on behalf of developing countries, "since the payments deficit of the United States was on the whole unrelated to trade relations with these countries" (*World Economic Survey, 1971,* p. 4). Furthermore, the surcharge ran "counter to the commitment to introduce a general preferential scheme favouring imports from developing countries" (ibid.).

**…because they ran counter to the commitment for a preferential scheme favouring imports from developing countries**

The opposition of the *Survey* to protectionism continued into the 1980s, during which protectionist tendencies were denounced in almost every issue. For example, in *World Economic Survey, 1981-1982*, it was asserted that while the world economy had "avoided trade wars of the type experienced in the 1920s and 1930s" and liberalization efforts had continued on some fronts, the slowdown in economic growth in the industrial countries since the mid-1970s had "been accompanied by growing protectionist pressures and increasing resort to special trading arrangements as a way to ease domestic tensions" (p. 80). These tensions were closely related to the increased levels of unemployment in developed countries.

The *Survey* continued to advocate for international coordination, in particular of monetary policy among developed countries, with respect to addressing exchange rate volatility and massive short-term capital flows, which at that time were already closely associated with financial instability and crisis.

Another issue highlighted by the *Survey* was that large developed economies running balance-of-payments surpluses had an obligation to expand their demand for imported goods which would, to some degree, have as its complement an increase in the exports of developing countries. Expanding effective demand in surplus countries was therefore considered an important accompaniment to any domestic adjustments required in those developing countries that were incurring external deficits (*World Economic Survey, 1971,* p. 8; *World Economic Survey, 1975,* p. 109; *World Economic Survey, 1977,* p. 3). In addition, the *Survey* critiqued the tendency towards managing imbalances through both demand compression and asymmetrical adjustments in countries experiencing external deficits versus those running surpluses.

This echoed Keynes's views on international adjustment, but ran counter to the dominant approach of IMF, which was to demand adjustment mainly from deficit countries. The dampening of economic activity in developed countries as a means of dealing with problems of inflation simply meant more balance-of-payments problems for developing countries running external deficits, which in turn increased their need for external financing (*World Economic Survey 1979-1980*, p. 12). It is because of this kind of activity that *World Economic Survey, 1971* concluded that "the major source of disequilibrium may stem from the policies of [trade] surplus countries rather than those of the deficit countries" (p. 8).

## Emergence of debt crises and reverse capital flows

By 1980, developed countries had begun to adopt restrictive monetary policies aimed at reducing inflation, which led to high nominal and real interest rates, especially in the United States. Moving from negative values in the 1970s, real rates in the United States reached 3.9 per cent in 1980-1982 and 6.7 per cent in 1983-1987 (*World Economic Survey 1988*, p. 132). For developing countries, this meant higher costs of borrowing, reduced demand for their exports and limited growth of foreign concessional assistance.

The high interest rates were especially damaging to those countries that had borrowed heavily at floating interest rates in the 1970s. Typically, loans were contracted at the London Interbank Offered Rate (LIBOR) plus a spread based on the borrower's creditworthiness. The nominal LIBOR on six-month dollar deposits reached 18.5 per cent in late 1981 and did not fall below 9 per cent until 1985 (p. 131). As a result of the pegging of the interest rate to the interbank market, the risk associated with variations in those rates was borne mainly by the borrowers (Ocampo, 2013).

Partially as a result of tendencies in the world economy, including lower growth, higher interest rates, declining terms of trade for commodity exporters and protectionism, many developing countries found themselves experiencing balance-of-payments difficulties in the early 1980s. These external problems were exacerbated by ill-conceived domestic policies which gave rise to large fiscal deficits, high inflation rates and overreliance on borrowing from international banks in the attempt to maintain growth after the oil shocks. This contributed to high levels of debt accumulated in the public sector and set the stage for the sovereign debt crises of the 1980s.

**Low growth, high interest rates, declining terms of trade and protectionism were major factors leading to the sovereign debt crises of the 1980s**

What triggered the sovereign debt crises was the decision taken by the Federal Reserve Board of the United States in October 1979 to raise interest rates steeply. That decision came to be known as the "Volcker shock," bearing the name of the then Chairman of the Federal Reserve, Paul Volcker. It had a direct impact on debt service, since much of the external debt in developing countries had been contracted at floating interest rates. The difficulties were compounded by a sharp drop in non-oil commodity prices.

While circumstances varied from region to region and from country to country, in general, large current account deficits made it impossible to continue debt service. The developing country sovereign debt crisis is considered to have begun with the announcement by Mexico in August 1982 that it would not be able to continue debt service as scheduled, unless it received help through new loans or rescheduling. That announcement marked the beginning of a decade-long process which involved most of the Latin American countries, many African countries and some countries in Asia (see figure III.6).

Figure III.6

**Tally of crises, Africa, Asia and Latin America, 1960–2010 (five-year averages)**

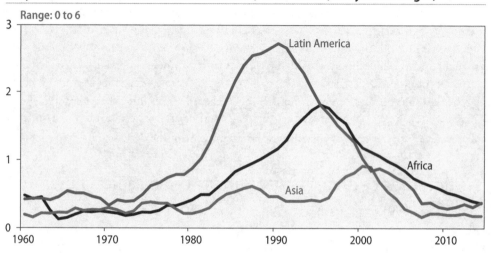

**Source:** Reinhart and Rogoff (2009).
**Note:** Each country scored one point for a crisis in any of the following six areas: currency, inflation, stock market, domestic debt, external debt, banking; and was therefore given a score ranging from 0 to 6. The regional tally is a simple average of the scores for the countries of the region.

A summary of the negotiations on the debt issue for Latin America can be separated into three phases (Stallings, 2014):[4]

(a) The austerity phase, during which policies focused heavily on lowering fiscal deficits by cutting spending and/or raising taxes and other revenues. A complementary policy entailed a large devaluation, which, in principle, would shift production towards the export sector. Debtor Governments were then expected to have more resources available for debt service, although the contraction of their economies undermined this goal;

(b) The period covered by the so-called Baker Plan, which bears the name of the United States Secretary of the Treasury, James Baker. Baker aimed towards stimulating growth in the region rather than imposing austerity. Conditionality shifted to structural adjustment programmes, through which Governments would open up their economies to increased trade, privatize State-owned firms and seek foreign investment;

(c) The period of the so-called Brady Plan, named after Baker's successor, Nicolas F. Brady. The Brady Plan, announced in 1989, also aimed towards stimulating growth, and continued to insist on structural reforms, while opening the way towards debt reduction.

The debt crisis had ended, in practical terms, by the early 1990s, when debt relief was agreed and international investors returned to the region (Ocampo and others, 2014).

It is considered that, as a result of a slow and feeble international response, the sovereign debt crisis of the 1980s was the most traumatic event in Latin America's economic history, having been responsible for the region's lost decade of development. In sub-Saharan Africa, the recovery time was even more prolonged.

In sub-Saharan Africa, poverty did not fall below the level of 1981 until 2005, while gross domestic product (GDP) per capita and investment did not return to 1981 levels until 2006-2007. In Latin America, in terms of GDP per capita and gross fixed capital formation,

**The sovereign debt crisis of the 1980s was responsible for a lost decade of development in Latin America and Africa**

---

4     As the majority of countries labelled as "highly indebted" were in Latin America, reporting on the Latin American experience gives a reasonable idea of the overall problems of this period.

the region returned to 1980 levels only in 1994. In terms of poverty, the impact was even more protracted: The poverty rate climbed sharply, from 40.5 per cent in 1980 to 48.3 per cent in 1990, and would return to 1980 levels only in 2005. Thus, as regards poverty, the lost decade in both sub-Saharan Africa and Latin America was in fact a lost quarter century.

## Critical reflections in the *Survey*

As early as the 1970s, the *Survey* was paying close attention to the forms and terms of foreign financing, in particular debt and investment, and their implications for indebted developing countries. In the mid-1970s, it had warned of the dangers of rapid growth in debt and argued that higher interest rates and shorter maturities than those of official lending implied a significant increase in the amounts required for interest and amortization payments in the period immediately ahead (*World Economic Survey, 1975*, p. 31). It concluded that this development underscored the importance not only of judicious debt management—by debtor and creditor alike—but also of more liberal trade and resource transfer policies on the part of developed countries, as envisaged under the International Development Strategy for the Third United Nations Development Decade (General Assembly resolution 35/56 of 5 December 1980, annex) and the Declaration and Programme of Action on the Establishment of a New International Economic Order (Assembly resolution 3201 (S-VI) of 1 May 1974 and Assembly resolution 3202 (S-VI) of 1 May 1974, respectively), which are discussed further below.

With respect to solutions to the sovereign debt crisis, while the Survey called repeatedly for dialogue on debt, significantly, it did not call for debt relief until this became the consensus view towards the end of the 1980s under the Brady Plan. The Survey highlighted the importance of coordination among developed countries, in particular to enable changes to be made in the regulations imposed on private banks. The efforts of the bank committees, which were formed to facilitate negotiations with individual debtor countries, constituted an example of coordination. However, those committees united banks and, informally, creditor Governments against debtor countries. Greater coordination among debtor countries, which was discussed many times but never implemented, could have ensured a more equal distribution of the costs incurred in the course of resolving the debt crisis.

**Greater coordination among debtor countries could have ensured a more equal distribution of the costs of resolving the debt crises**

A highly important focus of the recommendations in the *Survey* concerned investment. Investment was, of course, significant from two perspectives: On the supply side, it helped countries adjust to new international conditions; on the demand side, it stimulated economic growth and the creation of jobs. *World Economic Survey 1986* was where the greatest emphasis was placed on the subject, specifically in the lengthy chapter (VI), entitled "Capital formation and growth in the 1980s" (pp. 107-142). The *Survey* provided data showing that most developing countries, especially those facing major debt crises, substantially lowered their investment rates in the first half of the 1980s compared with the previous decade. In this regard, it warned that "[t]his dramatic decline in the level of investment in most debtor countries…ha(d) ominous implications for future growth and productive capacity, including capacity to export" (p. 118).

The *Survey* consistently encouraged foreign direct investment (FDI) in developing countries to help raise growth and employment and possibly enable technological progress; and highlighted policies designed to accomplish these goals, which often involved legal and institutional change (e.g., *World Economic Survey 1980-1981*, pp. 84-85). The strategies that the *Survey* noted with approval included providing investment guarantees and incentives, reducing risk and uncertainty, allowing for a higher share of foreign ownership in specific enterprises or sectors and joint ventures, promoting export processing zones, reducing red tape and speeding up investment allocations (p. 84). At the same time, the *Survey* continued to call for a code of conduct for transnational corporations (p. 83), consistent with the approaches under both the International Development Strategy for the Third United Nations Development Decade and the Declaration and Programme of Action on the Establishment of a New International Economic Order (see below for a further discussion).

**During the 1980s, many developing countries became net exporters of financial resources**

In the aftermath of the debt crises, the decline in new capital inflows and the increase in debt service meant that, during the 1980s, a number of developing countries became net exporters of financial resources. Consequently, in that decade, the *Survey* called attention to this "reverse flow" or "negative transfer" of financial resources. The problem was centred in Latin America where, from 1983 to 1989, net transfers to the rest of the world averaged $25 billion per year, compared with an inward transfer of nearly $13 billion in 1980-1981 (*World Economic Survey 1990,* p. 77).

While the *Survey* overall cautioned very early on about the dangers of developing countries' relying too heavily on short-term debt,[5] it nevertheless recognized the important role played by such debt in the recycling of the surpluses of the exporters of oil and manufactured goods. The fact, however, that the *Survey* did not call for debt write-offs until the United States Treasury took the lead in that regard is an interesting subject for reflection.

## From the Washington Consensus to adjustment beyond austerity

While in earlier decades, the role of IMF and the World Bank had not been an active one with respect to devising policies for dealing with the economic problems of developing countries, in the 1980s, they emerged as the leaders in that regard. Indeed, it was argued by the United Nations development economist Richard Jolly (1991, p. 1809) that the influence of IMF and the World Bank on the policies adopted by the countries in sub-Saharan Africa and Latin America at that time "can hardly be exaggerated".

One of the functions of IMF is to intervene when a country experiences economic difficulties. In exchange for financial support, that country must agree to implement a package of policy reforms, which became known as IMF conditionality. In the 1980s, those packages began to include a range of structural conditionalities in policy areas such as privatization of State-owned enterprises, trade and financial liberalization and economic deregulation. These policy reforms came to be referred to collectively as the "Washington Consensus"—the term for a concept first elaborated by John Williamson (1990)—because they reflected the influence of three Washington, D.C.-based institutions, the United States Treasury, IMF and the World Bank.

**Financial support to developing countries was made conditional on adopting a set of policies collectively known as the Washington Consensus**

Initially, it was stabilization, liberalization and privatization reforms that were promoted under the Washington Consensus. Later, however, the Washington Consensus came to embrace a broader set of policies underpinned by a strong belief in unfettered markets and a reduced role for government. Indeed, the term Washington Consensus has come to be used as a synonym for market fundamentalism or neoliberalism. Unfortunately, the

---

5    Short-term debt has an original maturity of one year or less. Short-term lending is often more procyclical than longer-term lending and increases the vulnerability to debt crises.

Washington Consensus was not only narrow in terms of its objectives and restrictive in terms of the set of instruments it deployed, but also limited with regard to its vision of development processes. This led Joseph Stiglitz (2016, p. 2, footnote 7) to argue that "(i)ts worst practitioners seemed to believe that if countries only let markets work on their own, there would be development". Critics have argued that by following a narrow macroeconomics agenda, IMF conditionality in the 1980s resulted in extensive "collateral damage".

Since financial support from IMF and the World Bank was conditional on implementation of the above-mentioned policy recommendations, often as part of structural adjustment programmes, the Washington Consensus exerted its influence in particular on countries in debt distress in Latin America and Africa. That influence, however, was less prevalent in most parts of Asia where countries (especially in East Asia) benefited from a more flexible national policy space. Those countries chose to pursue a different policy direction than that marked out by the market-centred Washington Consensus—one where, in particular, a more prominent role was given to the State.

**Countries with greater policy space followed a different policy direction...**

The difference in policy direction contributed to significant differences in economic performance, and a "great divergence" was manifested within the developing world. While Africa, Latin America and Western Asia witnessed significant stagnation in per capita income during the 1980s, countries of East Asia further accelerated their already fast economic growth (figure III.7).

**...thereby contributing to a "great divergence" in terms of economic performances**

As the impact of the Washington Consensus and the structural adjustment programmes became visible, there were debates on the nature and degree of the policy demands to be made upon recipient Governments in return for greater access to balance-of-payments support. It became apparent that the conditionality imposed by IMF on developing countries was often counterproductive. The debates also concerned the main reasons for the developing countries' fiscal deficit, in particular whether they were caused mainly by international problems or by inefficient domestic economic policies. Where one stood in this debate determined one's view of the balance between the financing of deficits and the adjustment of domestic policy needed to eradicate them.

Figure III.7
**Trends in GDP per capita in selected developing regions, 1970–1990**

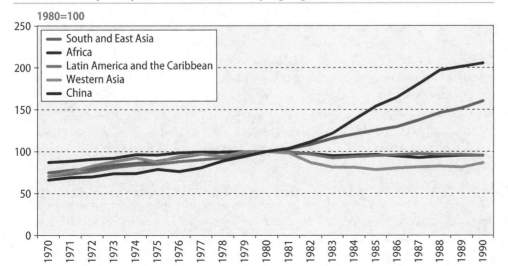

**Source:** UN/DESA, based on data from the Statistics Division.

The international financial institutions argued that domestic policies, in particular import substitution industrialization, had played a central role in creating inefficiencies and distortions in developing countries, such as overvalued exchange rates, foreign exchange shortages and distorted domestic prices (Krueger, 1978). They therefore contended that the solution was trade and market liberalization and efforts to restructure the economy towards export promotion.

**The United Nations voiced concerns over the social impact of the structural adjustment programmes led by IMF and the World Bank**

Other organizations of the United Nations system entered the debate on the adjustment process in the 1980s, but with very different stances from those of IMF and the World Bank. Perhaps the United Nations publication that was most influential in expressing concerns about the social impact—especially the impact on children—of the structural adjustment programmes led by IMF and the World Bank was a two-volume study by the United Nations Children's Fund (UNICEF) entitled *Adjustment with a Human Face: Protecting the Vulnerable and Promoting Growth* (Cornia, Jolly and Stewart, 1987), which was issued in 1987-1988.

The study called for a broader approach, one that would ensure both protection of the vulnerable and the restoration of economic growth. Such an approach, which was called "adjustment with a human face", had the following six main policy components (Cornia, Jolly and Stewart, 1987, pp. 290-291):

(a) More expansionary macroeconomic policies aimed at sustaining output, investment and living standards;

(b) Meso policies, to complement the macropolicies and to fulfil the needs of the vulnerable;

(c) Sectoral policies aimed at promoting restructuring within the productive sector to strengthen employment and income generating activities;

(d) Improving the equity and efficiency of the social sector by restructuring public expenditure both between and within sectors;

(e) Compensatory programmes designed to protect basic health and nutrition of the low-income groups during the adjustment period;

(f) Monitoring of the human situation, in particular of living standards, health and nutrition, during the adjustment process.

The study had a profound impact on how international organizations thought about the adjustment process. It was acknowledged in *World Development Report 1990* (World Bank, 1990, p. 103) that as the decade of the 1980s continued, "it became clear that macroeconomic recovery and structural change were slow in coming", that "[e]vidence of declines in income and cutbacks in social services began to mount" and that "it was UNICEF that first brought the issue into the centre of the debate on the design and effectiveness of adjustment". The report also acknowledged that "[b]y the end of the decade, the issue had become important for all agencies". Along the same lines, the Managing Director of IMF, in an address to the Economic and Social Council on 4 July 1986, affirmed that "(a)djustment that pays attention to the health, nutritional and educational requirements of the most vulnerable groups is going to protect the human condition better than adjustment that ignores them" (de Larosière, 1986).

**A series of international conferences helped to redirect the development discourse towards people-centred and rights-based development**

In the 1990s, the United Nations tried to regain its intellectual leadership of the development discourse by organizing a series of international conferences and summits at which the commitment to people-centred and rights-based development was affirmed. The principles underlying this renewed commitment of the United Nations to international development were in sharp contrast to the economic orthodoxy imposed by the Washington Consensus. The World Conference on Education for All, held in Jomtien, Thailand, from 5 to 9 March 1990, and the World Summit for Children, held in New York on 29 and 30 September 1990, were the first global conferences to be organized. As the issues to be considered at those conferences were deemed less controversial, it was believed that the chances were therefore better for arriving at a consensus on relevant global goals.

The sudden collapse of the Soviet Union in 1991 raised hopes for a peace dividend and an end to traditional divisions within the United Nations, and generated momentum for the organization of several other summits and international conferences, including on environment, nutrition, human rights, population, women, human settlements and food security (see appendix A.4). Notable among them were the United Nations Conference on Environment and Development, held in Rio de Janeiro from 3 to 14 June 1992; the World Summit for Social Development, held in Copenhagen from 6 to 12 March 1995; and the Fourth World Conference on Women, held in Beijing from 4 to 15 September 1995. Within an aspirational context of education, health and food security for all, these conferences and summits resulted in the adoption of an array of internationally agreed development goals, including the Millennium Development Goals (which will be discussed further in chap. IV), under what came to be known as the United Nations development agenda (United Nations, 2007).

## Critical reflections in the *Survey*

The *Survey* argued consistently and strenuously for IMF conditionality to be modified so as "to enable countries to sustain substantially larger deficits for periods long enough to permit structural adjustment without sacrificing economic growth" (*World Economic Survey 1980-1981*, pp. 63-64). Thus, while applauding the 1979 change in IMF guidelines, which acknowledged the need for longer-term financing so as "to alleviate the effect of corrective measures on real incomes and to contribute to a distribution of the burden of adjustment within the economy that is socially and politically more acceptable" (IMF, 1979, p. 63), the *Survey* maintained that this did not go far enough.

This is not to say that the *Survey* denied the need for developing countries to adjust domestic economic policy to meet the changing global economic conditions. On the contrary, it acknowledged the need for "adjustment" on the part of developing countries that had large and unsustainable fiscal and trade deficits. Already in *World Economic Survey, 1971*, the *Survey* had explicitly stated that "an international economic order, no matter how well conceived, cannot work if nations fail to manage their own affairs effectively", which would be all the more true if the new international economic order achieved "a degree of openness that implie[d] heightened competition among nations" (p. 11).

The *Survey*'s main concern as the decade progressed was the long-term growth and the social implications of adjustment. *World Economic Survey 1989* defined economic adjustment as "the changes needed to place an economy on a sustained path of economic growth and development" (p. 152). In particular, the *Survey* was concerned about the impact of adjustment on vulnerable groups in society, which arose from the tendency of Governments to cut back on wages and social expenditures as well as public investment. For example, *World Economic Survey 1988* (p. 147) observed that adjustment measures "often involve substantial cuts in income and these cuts are not shared equally by the different classes of society", noting by way of illustration that with real wages having fallen by 20 per

**The *Survey* was concerned about the long-term implications of adjustment and its impact on vulnerable groups**

cent or more in many countries during the 1980s, social expenditures were often "the first to be slashed".

The 1989 *Survey* contended that there was "a new consensus on the need to see people as the principal resource and potential of a country and not as a burden" (p. 5). It noted, moreover, that the translation of this understanding into programmes and policies was only beginning, and that it put social issues "high on the agenda for development cooperation". The 1989 *Survey* also offered a critique of the "one-size-fits-all" approach adopted by adjustment programmes, arguing that the models on which the policy advice was based had been "technical economic abstractions, often devoid of the political and social considerations that shape actual policymaking in developing, as well as in developed, countries" (p. 157).[6]

The Survey argued for maintaining fiscal expenditures for social services, even in times of budgetary austerity

The *Survey* strongly recommended that countries should not cut back on expenditure on social services when trying to bring their budgets back towards balance. In the 1990 *Survey* (p. 157), it was observed that the objectives of adjustment are "to change economic structures so as to regain growth momentum", but that "its short-term effects can be very harsh". The challenge, then, was "to design policies to restore sustained growth without having to pay a high social cost". The policy mentioned most often was one of maintaining fiscal expenditure for education and health, even in times of budgetary austerity.

The 1989 *Survey* highlighted several requirements for the achievement of successful development and adjustment :

(a) On the domestic policy front, the two important requirements were (i) small (or reduced) fiscal deficit and (ii) price stability and positive, but not excessive, interest rates. On the question of reducing fiscal deficits, the *Survey* emphasized that this did not mean that "government expenditures must everywhere be curtailed, especially if cutbacks ha[d] already been instituted" but it did mean that "government revenues must rise to carry the overwhelming bulk of the cost of expenditures" (p. 152);

(b) On the international front, the requirement was adequate access to finance. The *Survey* argued that the only successful adjusters had such access, noting that "not a single developing country that experienced serious debt-servicing difficulties in the early 1980s and was adjusting by mid-decade ha[d] been able to recover sufficiently to restore the confidence of its international creditors and regain normal access to international finance". It further argued that "the key question was how to find the appropriate mix of policy reforms and how much international finance to supply in support of reform" (pp. 151-152).

Interestingly, the 1989 *Survey* also maintained that successful adjustment depended on having "a robust official sector that is able to provide necessary public services and build and maintain essential infrastructure" (p. 153). Moreover, there were several other actions the government needed to take, which included ensuring a clean environment, adequate education and public health services. Indeed, the government must provide an overall perspective on "the direction in which an economy is and should be going" (ibid.). These recommendations went against the grain of much of the international advice available at the time, in particular advice provided in accordance with the Washington Consensus.

---

6     See chap. II for a related discussion on this issue.

# Three United Nations Development Decades overshadowed by economic crises

Tracking progress during the United Nations Development Decades was central to the mandate of the *Survey*, but given the unforeseen global economic and geopolitical shocks, the publication paid less attention than envisaged to issues related to income distribution, education, health, nutrition, housing and social welfare. Presented below is an overview of the achievements to which the International Development Strategies for the Second, Third and Fourth United Nations Development Decades aspired, as well as a review of the progress made and the impact of the contemporary global contexts on that progress (see appendix A.3).

## The Second United Nations Development Decade and the New International Economic Order

By its resolution 2626 (XXV) of 24 October 1970, the General Assembly launched the Second United Nations Development Decade (1971-1980) starting from 1 January 1971. The launch was accompanied by the great enthusiasm generated by the achievements of the highly successful First United Nations Development Decade (1961-1970). By the end of the Decade (the 1960s), it was found that well over 60 countries had exceeded the minimum 5 per cent growth target and that during that Decade, the growth rate for developing countries as a group averaged 5.6 per cent. In the 1969-1970 *Survey*, it was noted that by 1968, nearly half of the developing countries had exceeded the minimum target growth rate and another 12 per cent of developing countries had been within 1 percentage point of achieving that target (p. 9).

Besides aggregate and per capita growth targets for developing countries, the International Development Strategy for the Second United Nations Development Decade contained targets for employment, education and health. There was also a strong emphasis on equity in development—among different socioeconomic groups, and between the North and the South, as well as between the present and future generations. There was greater awareness of the inequity between men and women, and of the problems associated with rapid urbanization, in particular rural-urban migration. The Strategy for the Second Development Decade also emphasized structural change, entailing a move from agriculture to industry and from traditional to non-traditional exports.

The International Development Strategy for the Second United Nations Development Decade was designed to promote "a more just and rational world economic and social order" (article 12) in which countries would cooperate to raise living standards and reduce global inequities. For the developing countries, the Strategy set a target of at least 6 per cent for the annual rate of growth of GDP and a target of about 3.5 per cent for per capita income, based on an assumed average annual increase of 2.5 per cent in the population of those countries (articles 13-15).

Universal primary school education was set as a goal, as were a substantial reduction in illiteracy, improvement in the quality of education at all levels, reorientation of programmes to serve development needs and, as appropriate, establishment and expansion of scientific and technological institutions (article 18 (b)). The Strategy also called for fostering the well-being of children, ensuring the full participation of youth in the development process

**The International Development Strategy for the Second United Nations Development Decade incorporated targets for employment, education and health and placed a strong emphasis on equity**

and encouraging the full integration of women in the total development effort (article 18 (f) to (h)).

Also during the 1970s, on 1 May 1974, the General Assembly, by its resolutions 3201 (S-VI) and 3202 (S-VI), adopted, respectively, the Declaration and the Programme of Action on the Establishment of a New International Economic Order and called for greater cooperation and integration among countries and greater involvement of developing countries in decisions that affect them. Stressed in Assembly resolution 3201 (S-VI) was the line of continuity between the Declaration and the Strategy for the Second Development Decade: Accelerated implementation of obligations and commitments assumed within the framework of the Strategy would contribute significantly to fulfilment of the aims and objectives of the Declaration (article 5). Hence, commitments under the Declaration were not to be thought of as replacing those under the Strategy. Further, the Declaration reasserted the sovereign rights of developing countries, including the right to territorial integrity, to establish control over their natural resources and to adopt their own economic and social system (article 4).

The Declaration asserted that one of the main aims of reforming the international monetary system should be to promote the development of poorer countries and to increase the flow of resources to them (article 4 (l)); and called for an expanded flow of financial resources to developing countries on favourable terms and for "preferential and non-reciprocal treatment for developing countries" in all their dealings with developed countries (article 4 (n)).

**The early 1970s were marked by global economic turmoil which completely overshadowed the Second United Nations Development Decade**

The early 1970s were unfortunately marked by global economic turmoil which completely overshadowed the Second United Nations Development Decade (*World Economic Survey, 1974*, Part One, p. 1). Real growth rates in developing countries averaged 5.7 per cent per annum, a figure that was somewhat lower than the International Development Strategy target, but still respectable. The level of ODA from member countries of the Organization for Economic Cooperation and Development (OECD) Development Assistance Committee (DAC) reached only 0.35 per cent of GDP in 1981, up slightly from the 1971-1973 average of 0.33 per cent, but still only one half of the Strategy target of 0.7 per cent (Loxley, 1986, pp. 163-165). By the end of the 1970s, the *Survey* had concluded that "the prospects for early movement towards the objectives of the new International Development Strategy [had] been dimmed" (*World Economic Survey 1980-1981*, p. 2).

**The International Development Strategy for the Third United Nations Development Decade was a reaffirmation of the need for collective action for international development**

Along similar lines, while the New International Economic Order had significant support among developing countries and liberal academics and policymakers, it failed to gain traction as the larger advanced economies moved towards monetarist and neoliberal policies. The vision of multilateralism and long-term structural change, as embedded in the Declaration and Programme of Action on the Establishment of a New International Economic Order, was replaced by a focus on short-term economic management. At the International Meeting on Cooperation and Development (North-South Summit), held in Cancún, Mexico, on 22 and 23 October 1981, the President of the United States, Ronald Reagan, unilaterally declared the New International Economic Order to be dead.

## The Third United Nations Development Decade

During a global economic slowdown and within a highly inflationary environment, the General Assembly, by its resolution 35/56 of 5 December 1980, proclaimed the Third United Nations Development Decade (1981-1990), starting on 1 January 1981, and adopted the International Development Strategy for the Decade, as contained in the annex to that resolution. However, according to the report of the Secretary-General on the review and appraisal of the Strategy (United Nations, General Assembly and Economic and Social Council, 1984), the adoption of the Strategy in the worsening global economic conditions "appeared as a salutary reaffirmation of the need for collective action to create an international environment distinctly more supportive of national development efforts" (p. 4, para. 1).

In the International Development Strategy for the Third United Nations Development Decade, States Members of the United Nations acknowledged that in the extraordinary circumstances characterizing the decade of the 1970s, many of the goals and objectives of the Strategy for the Second Development Decade had remained largely unfulfilled (para. 3). They also noted that the international economy at the start of the Third United Nations Development Decade remained in a "state of structural disequilibrium" (para. 4).

However, the strategy conveyed the expectation that the global economic turmoil would not continue and deepen during the course of the 1980s. The Strategy aimed at promoting the economic and social development of developing countries, with a view to significantly reducing the existing disparities between developing and developed countries, eradicating poverty and ending dependency (para. 7). Hindsight suggests, however, that these ambitious efforts under the Strategy to accelerate the development of developing countries and establish a new international economic order were somewhat divorced from the existing reality.

The target of a minimum average annual rate of growth of GDP of 7 per cent was set for the developing countries, which would lead to an average annual rate of growth of about 4.5 per cent in per capita GDP, assuming that the average annual rate of population growth in those countries was to remain at 2.5 per cent (para. 21). It was asserted in the Strategy that hunger and malnutrition must be eliminated as soon as possible and certainly by the end of the twentieth century (para. 28). It was also determined that agricultural production in developing countries as a whole should expand at an average annual rate of at least 4 per cent so that the nutritional needs of populations could be met.

However, given the difficulties experienced during the 1980s, overall growth in the developing countries fell well short of the targeted rate: the average annual rate of overall growth was 3 per cent and that of per capita growth was 1 per cent. The 1990 *Survey* assessed the decade of the 1980s in the following terms:

> For many developing countries, the 1980s have been viewed as a decade lost for development. Living conditions in Africa and Latin America and the Caribbean, and in parts of Asia, have deteriorated, and economic and social infrastructure has eroded (p. 8, box I.1).

*The growth rate of developing countries fell well short of the target, and the 1980s was a lost decade for development for many countries*

## The Fourth United Nations Development Decade

In the preamble to the International Development Strategy for the Fourth United Nations Development Decade (1991-2000), adopted by the General Assembly by its resolution 45/199 of 21 December 1990 and contained in the annex to that resolution, States Members of the United Nations recognized that the goals and objectives of the International Development Strategy for the Third United Nations Development Decade had been for the most part unattained (para. 2). It was clearly recognized that adverse and unanticipated developments in the world economy had wiped out the premises upon which the expectation of growth had been based.

*The International Development Strategy for the Fourth United Nations Development Decade aimed at ensuring that the 1990s would be a decade of improvement in the human condition*

The principal aim of the International Development Strategy for the Fourth Development Decade was to ensure that the 1990s would be a decade of accelerated development and a significant improvement in the human condition, as well as of a reduction in the gap between rich and poor countries. The Strategy also sought to enhance the participation of all men and women in economic and political life, protect cultural identities and assure to all the necessary means of survival (para. 13).

The Fourth Development Decade was unfortunately overshadowed by the sudden, unanticipated collapse of the Soviet Union, on 25 December 1991, and its aftermath, which dominated developments during the 1990s. Another shadow was cast by the tumultuous situation in Eastern Europe and the successor States of the former Soviet Union and by further financial crises—in Mexico in 1994-1995, the fast growing Asian economies in 1997-1998 and the Russian Federation in 1998.[7]

## Reflecting on the experience of the time period

The analysis of the experience of the period from 1972 to the mid-1990s and the policy recommendations on issues related to development cooperation and international policy coordination, as presented in the *Survey*, still resonate in 2017. Today, as policymakers attempt to grapple with a global economic slowdown—a slowdown that, although its causes are different, shares a surprising number of characteristics with the slowdowns of the 1970s and 1980s. There are a number of important implications to be drawn from the experience of this period covered by the *Survey*—implications for the implementation of the 2030 Agenda for Sustainable Development[8] and other agreements, in particular the Addis Ababa Action Agenda of the Third International Conference on Financing for Development.[9]

**The prolonged global economic turmoil could have been mitigated through more coherent and internationally coordinated policy action**

In the early 1970s, the lack of international coordination meant that high inflation and monetary instability would become the norm in most developed countries throughout the 1970s and 1980s, with severe consequences for unemployment and other social indicators. Such a prolonged and painful adjustment process could have been averted through more coherent and internationally coordinated action on both monetary and fiscal policy. This highlights the importance of international economic policy coordination and coherence, and the application of a variety of policy measures designed to maintain economic stability and curtail the duration of economic crises.

The international monetary framework, which emerged after the collapse of the Bretton Woods system in the early 1970s, has proved to be volatile and prone to crises. The lack of a global mechanism for addressing global imbalances contributed to the high cost of adjustment in the 1970s and 1980s. This underlines the need to address the underlying causes of those imbalances, in particular the reliance on a single reserve currency, and to establish a coordination mechanism through which to confront global imbalances when they occur.

**More responsible lending and borrowing play an important role in reducing the likelihood of a debt crisis**

During the 1980s, countries in Latin America faced strong pressures to avoid default, which only exacerbated the cost and the duration of the sovereign debt crisis. Solutions such as those under the Brady Plan were provided relatively late in the process. While coordination among creditors towards guaranteeing debt repayment did exist, there could

---

7    See the related discussion on this issue in chap. IV.

8    General Assembly resolution 70/1 of 25 September 2015.

9    General Assembly resolution 69/313 of 27 July 2015, annex.

have been greater coordination among debtors, so as to enable a fairer distribution of the costs of debt crises. Further, it is important that more responsible lending and borrowing be promoted in order to reduce the likelihood of debt crises, and that a debt workout mechanism be in place to ensure a faster and fairer resolution of such crises. The importance of ensuring that debtors and creditors work together to prevent and resolve unsustainable debt situations is highlighted in both the 2030 Agenda for Sustainable Development (para. 69) and the Addis Ababa Action Agenda (para. 97).

Another fundamental lesson to be derived from Latin America's sovereign debt crisis is that focusing too narrowly on austerity and rapid budget adjustment entails high social and economic costs. Fiscal reform alone cannot resolve a debt crisis: austerity must constitute one component of a larger strategy—not the strategy itself.[10] The experience of Latin America also underlined the importance of economic growth for recovery. Countries capable of growth are more likely to pay their debts. On the other hand, the pressure to act in accord with the Washington Consensus contributed to a prolonged recession and a lost decade of development in that region. Debt relief for Latin America under the Brady Plan demonstrated the potential of a market-friendly default, which can reduce debt levels without excluding countries from international capital markets. The need to attain long-term debt sustainability through coordinated policies such as debt relief, debt restructuring and sound debt management is also recognized in the Addis Ababa Action Agenda (see sect. II.E).

Forcing Governments to cut back on social spending and infrastructure investment as part of the adjustment process can have long-term implications, as was the case in Latin America, where the economy took more than a decade to recover. Processes of adjustment and recovery from crisis require a broader and longer-term perspective. There should be more emphasis on long-term debt sustainability as well as an intertemporal perspective on budget deficits rather than a strict focus on short-term balancing of current budget deficits. In addition, there should be a move away from adjustment policies aimed at bringing economies into balance as fast as possible without sufficient consideration of the social cost, towards an adjustment process that minimizes that cost by protecting social spending and productive investment.

**Protecting social spending and productive investment plays an important role in minimizing the social cost incurred during processes of adjustment**

In the 1980s, the implementation of different development policies and strategies by the various developing regions contributed to a great divergence in economic performances. A new division between countries of East Asia and other developing countries emerged alongside the traditional division between oil exporters and importers. The success in this period of several developing countries, in particular in Asia, served to reinforce confidence in development narratives that were alternative to the one disseminated under the Washington Consensus. The bitter experience associated with the Washington Consensus also helped re-energize demonstrations of solidarity among developing countries, which had begun in the 1950s. This led to the emergence of South-South cooperation as a viable complement to long-standing North-South cooperation.

The failure of the "one-size fits all" approach to development promoted by the Washington Consensus demonstrates the danger of adherence to a single prescriptive model for producing stable growth and development. The experience with the lost decade in Latin America and Africa attests to the potential long-term consequences of the imposition by international organizations of a specific development narrative upon countries, and high-

**Experience with the lost decade illustrates the importance of country ownership in decision-making**

---

10    See the related discussion on this issue in chap. V.

lights the importance of the recognized principles of country ownership and home-grown national strategies for implementation of the 2030 Agenda for Sustainable Development (see, e.g., para. 66).

During the 1980s, countries with adequate national policy space for adopting alternative development strategies, especially in Asia, performed relatively well. The success of some subregions in Asia, in particular East Asia, in reducing poverty in this period highlights the potential importance of a developmental State whose role extends beyond the minimal role promoted by the Washington Consensus.[11] This also highlights the importance of maintaining national policy space for sustained, inclusive economic growth as well as for provision of more untied ODA and less stringent conditionality for financial support.

A stable global economic environment is crucial for upholding the commitment to ambitious development agendas, such as the 2030 Agenda for Sustainable Development

While the 2030 Agenda for Sustainable Development is accurately described as transformative, it should be remembered that the International Development Strategy for the Second United Nations Development Decade, adopted on 24 October 1970, was in its own way ambitious, with multidimensional targets for employment, education and health as well as a focus on inequality and structural transformation. However, the experience with the Strategy for the Second Decade, and, later, with the Strategies for the Third and Fourth United Nations Development Decades, demonstrates how easily the commitment to internationally agreed development goals can evaporate in times of economic difficulties. This highlights in turn the importance of a stable global economic environment for upholding the commitment to implementing ambitious development agendas, such as the 2030 Agenda for Sustainable Development, and the complementarity of national actions and a supportive international architecture for sustainable development, as highlighted in the Addis Ababa Action Agenda.

---

11    See the related discussion on this issue in chap. V.

# Chapter IV
# Globalization meets the Millennium Development Goals

## Key messages

- The adoption of the Millennium Development Goals (MDGs) at the turn of the century represented the successful inauguration of an effort to expand the focus beyond economic growth so as to encompass human development. As a result of rapid economic expansion and improved social policies in many developing countries, the MDG target of halving extreme poverty by 2015 globally had been reached by 2010.

- The growth momentum, however, proved to be unsustainable. Growth in the global economy was largely fuelled by strong consumer demand in the United States of America, as funded by easy credit. This pattern of growth led to mounting global imbalances and overleveraged financial institutions, businesses and households. In the absence of effective policy coordination mechanisms for securing an orderly unwinding of global imbalances, global growth proved unsustainable.

- In response to the episodic financial crises of the 1990s and 2000s, developing countries increased foreign reserves significantly as a form of self-insurance, a factor that increased the net transfer of financial resources from South to North.

- One of the central objectives of economic development policy is to facilitate the structural transformation of countries towards diversification of production and exports. This remains central to any strategy for achieving sustained economic growth in developing countries.

**Key events**

*We believe that the central challenge we face today is to ensure that globalization becomes a positive force for all the world's people.*

*United Nations Millennium Declaration (paragraph 5)*

## Introduction[1]

The present chapter analyses the key trends in the world economy and the major changes in the development agenda between the mid-1990s and the period immediately preceding the onset of the global financial crisis of 2008-2009. The process of global economic integration—globalization—had been gathering momentum since the 1980s, and the forces driving it became stronger and, in some ways, more entrenched towards the end of the 1990s. During that period, this entrenchment was reinforced by rapid trade liberalization and deregulation of the economy. In the 2000s, developing countries as a whole increased their share in global economic activities and the income gap between developing and developed countries (defined by the difference in average per capita income) decreased to some extent. Underlying these global trends was an increase in global imbalances leading to financial market instability, which eventually culminated in the global financial crisis of 2008-2009.

As examined in chapter III, the Washington Consensus prescribed a market-based approach for development founded on the assumption that the income gap between poor and rich countries would decrease through greater integration of global markets. In the 1990s, contrary to these predictions, trade and financial systems that were more open operated in parallel with increasing income inequality. Various editions of the *Survey* attributed this phenomenon largely to rapid globalization and technological change which favoured skilled labour and the withdrawal of the State from the public provisioning of basic services such as health care, education and social protection. In his preface to *World Economic and Social Survey 2000*, the Secretary-General pointed out that the number of people living in absolute poverty remained "virtually unchanged" from what it had been decades before, and that only a handful had achieved "successful development over a short period of time". The poorest countries and the poorest peoples appeared to be stuck in what he referred to as a "poverty trap", which signified that the decade of the 1990s had not witnessed the outcomes envisaged under the Washington Consensus.

States Members of the United Nations acknowledged that the goals of the International Development Strategy for the Third United Nations Development Decade[2] had been largely unattained. It was within that context that the Fourth United Nations Development Decade (1991-2000) was launched. Through the elaboration of a series of goals and objectives, including priority areas of development, the International Development Strategy for the Fourth United Nations Development Decade[3] reaffirmed the importance, inter alia,

---

1    The present chapter reviews the condition of the global economy and development trends in the period between the mid-1990s and 2007, as examined in the *World Economic and Social Survey*. It also reviews the analysis of short-term economic trends presented in *World Economic Situation and Prospects*, a companion publication which was issued starting in 1999. In this chapter, both reports are referred to as the *Survey*.

2    Adopted by the General Assembly in its resolution 35/56 of 5 December 1980 and contained in the annex thereto.

3    Adopted by the General Assembly in its resolution 45/199 of 21 December 1990 and contained in the annex thereto.

of growth, employment creation, poverty eradication, environmental protection, improved education, health and nutrition, and enhanced participation of men and women in political life (see appendix A.3). The objectives set forth in the Strategy for the Fourth Development Decade reflected a continuation of the practice under previous strategies of placing emphasis on the full range of issues relevant to development. That emphasis was in clear contrast to the narrow scope of the narrative under the Washington Consensus which focused on economic growth and market liberalization.

The discontent that had been brewing during the period of structural adjustment policies found its voice through the organization of a series of world summits and global conferences, including the World Summit for Children, held in New York on 29 and 30 September 1990; the United Nations Conference on Environment and Development, held in Rio de Janeiro from 3 to 14 June 1992; the World Summit for Social Development, held in Copenhagen from 6 to 12 March 1995, at which many of the recommendations associated with the implementation of the Strategy for the Fourth United Nations Development Decade were reiterated and expanded; and the Fourth World Conference on Women, held in Beijing from 4 to 15 September 1995 (see appendix A.4 for a comprehensive listing of the conferences held in the 1990s). At the same time, and building upon the concept of *development as freedom*, as formulated by development economist Amartya Sen, the United Nations, with the publication of the first issue of the *Human Development Report*,[4] contributed to the discussion an essential principle, namely, that people must be at the centre of development.[5]

The formulation of the MDGs, which emanated from the United Nations Millennium Declaration,[6] reflected the recognition by the international community that economic growth alone had not been sufficient to address human development concerns. In contrast, the goals and targets under the MDGs focused attention on the most critical requirements for human development at that time: reduction of poverty and hunger under Goal 1 (employment generation was subsequently added as an additional target under that Goal), improvements in education and health, gender equality and environmental sustainability.

This chapter focuses on the global economy and development trends in the period from the mid-1990s to the late 2000s (see figure IV.1), and, in particular, on three major issues that shaped the world economy during that period and beyond:

(a) The catch-up process of developing countries with respect to the average income of developed economies;

(b) Increased instability of the global economy which led eventually to the global financial crisis;

(c) Adoption and implementation of the MDGs.

A careful retrospective analysis of the underlying factors and policy decisions that framed these major events is particularly relevant to the current debate centred on the implementation of policies aimed towards achievement of sustainable development.

**Economic convergence between countries, the imbalances leading to the global financial crisis, and the adoption of the MDGs shaped the world economy in this period**

---

4    United Nations Development Programme, *Human Development Report 1990* (New York, Oxford University Press, 1990).

5    Although the report was published by the United Nations Development Programme, its preparation was a United Nations system-wide initiative, as noted in the foreword to the volume.

6    Adopted by the General Assembly in its resolution 55/2 of 8 September 2000 at the Millennium Summit, held in New York from 6 to 8 September 2000.

Figure IV.1
**Global growth of GDP, 1995–2008**

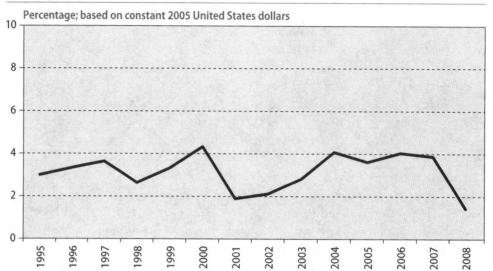

**Source:** UN/DESA, based on data
from the Statistics Division.

The period covered in this chapter encompasses the efforts of developing countries to catch up with developed countries in regard to per capita income. The catch-up process began following the burst of the dot-com bubble in 2001,[7] which marked the commencement of a new era for the world economy, with near unprecedented economic growth in developing countries and a major shift in the balance of global economic power in favour of emerging economies. The rapid expansion of trade volumes, which was associated with a rise in prices of primary commodities, resulted, for many developing countries, in improved terms of trade and more dynamic exports. The increase in income per capita in a large number of those countries narrowed the income gap with respect to developed countries. Poverty declined in most developing countries, and in some of them, the decline was substantial. The period of the global commodity boom, extending from 2002 to 2007, was therefore one during which prosperity was more widely shared across countries.

As mentioned above, this chapter will also analyse the instability of the global economy which accompanied the economic boom. The period 2002-2007 was marked by global imbalances which led to the great recession of 2008, mainly in developed countries. Most developing countries were exposed to that instability, which had originated in developed countries, and commodity-exporting countries yet again had to face volatile prices for their commodities.

**Greater economic integration increased countries' exposure to the volatility of the global economy...**

The catch-up process and global instability are, in a sense, two sides of the same coin. The increased global economic integration during the 1990s had major effects on production, investment, finance and macroeconomic policies across the world. In most economies, the share of total external trade in national income increased—in some cases, very substantially. Even relatively poor and less developed countries engaged in internal and external financial liberalization, which allowed them to access international capital markets. However, global economic integration also exposed developing countries to volatile cross-border flows to a much greater extent than had been evident in previous decades. The issue

---

7    The dot-com bubble, which is also known as the tech bubble or Internet bubble, refers to the sharp, rapid growth in equity value of the Internet sector and related fields in developed countries.

of vulnerability leads back to the discussion on the need for developing countries to diversify their economies to avoid both an over-reliance on a handful of commodity exports, and price and income volatility. Indeed, economic diversification and improved patterns of integration in the global economy for developing countries continue to be extremely pertinent issues and relevant to the success of the 2030 Agenda for Sustainable Development.[8]

The adoption of the United Nations Millennium Declaration and the formulation of the MDGs signalled recognition of an undeniable need for the development agenda to be extended beyond economic growth alone. Implementation of the goals and targets under the MDGs was considered a priority for the national Governments of developing countries in their efforts to ensure achievement of better living standards and human development. Implementation of policies towards achievement of those goals was supported by developed countries through a series of commitments towards rules-based, predictable and non-discriminatory trading and financials systems; the delivery of official development assistance (ODA); and addressing the needs of least developed countries, landlocked developing countries and small island developing States, among other goals contained under Millennium Development Goal 8, which was to develop a global partnership for development. The rapid period of globalization in previous decades had made it evident that economic growth did not always translate into sustained and social development. The series of world summits and international conferences, mentioned briefly above, as organized by the United Nations during the 1990s, generated broad support from the global community for human development goals, including improved health, education, gender equality and environmental sustainability, and helped promote a new development narrative driven by a vision of human-centred development. The major international development goals agreed at those summits and conferences were the foundation for the formulation of the MDGs.

In their attempt to capture human and social progress across different dimensions, definitions of development had themselves evolved over time. The influence exerted by the human development approach and the capability approach, as elaborated by Amartya Sen, was reflected in the integration of the different economic and social dimensions under one coherent development agenda. The United Nations Millennium Declaration and the MDGs focused attention on key social development priorities but also included references to economic and environmental goals. As observed directly above, the MDGs were shaped as objectives and targets to be achieved by developing countries with support from developed countries through a global partnership for development.

**The MDGs focused on human development priorities...**

Important features of the MDGs were the well-defined numerical targets to concretize the ambition reflected in each Goal. Such a framework, underpinned by a multiplicity of Goals and their numerical targets, facilitated the discussion on the substantive processes and policies needed to ensure that all objectives were met. The fact that different dimensions of development were integrated within that single framework led to a discussion on the need to improve policy coherence for the achievement of specific targets—a discussion that has taken centre stage with regard to the implementation of the Sustainable Development Goals (SDGs). The MDG framework, including the identification of well-defined targets, also facilitated the selection of numerical indicators to assist in the review of progress towards achievement of the MDG goals and targets and to help improve accountability.

A number of criticisms have been directed at the MDG agenda. The issues that generated considerable debate, among many others, included the risk of a disconnect between

**...but they paid less attention to the economic and environmental dimensions of development**

---

8    General Assembly resolution 70/1.

target setting and the processes that determined their achievement; and insufficient emphasis on the economic and environmental dimensions of development.

## Efforts by developing economies to catch up with developed ones

During the 1980s and 1990s, the policies associated with the Washington Consensus were imbued with the conviction that (a) free market mechanisms were essential for sustaining economic growth (see chap. III) and (b) that greater openness to the global market would lead to a closing of the income gap between poor and rich countries. In consequence, countries across the globe opened up their trade and financial systems to the global market. Empirical evidence has shown, however, that narrowing of the income gap across those countries was not achieved universally. In fact, the 1980s was characterized as a "lost decade" of development for countries in Africa and Latin America and the Caribbean. Those countries had been under pressure to adopt the policies espoused under the Washington Consensus and ended up experiencing a prolonged recession.

The 1980s witnessed the disappointing experience of developing economies and the 1990s were no more encouraging. Again, as noted by the Secretary-General in his preface to the 2000 *Survey,* while some countries had achieved successful development over a short period of time, they were far too few in number. On the other hand, the richer countries continued to make steady progress, which contributed to an ever-widening gap between what became bastions of prosperity and the rest of the world. The words of the Secretary-General bear repeating: the poorest countries and the poorest people appeared stuck in what he termed a poverty trap.

**In the period 2002-2007, rising commodity prices led to faster growth and poverty reduction in most developing countries**

Within the context of the global economy's recovery from the financial crisis in Asia (see below), fast growth in China and, to some extent, in India led, in the period 2002-2007, to a global economic boom which generated high growth rates and a shift in global economic power. As a result, some developing countries, including China and India, emerged as major economic players. That period was associated with the rapid expansion of trade volumes combined with rising prices of primary commodities, signifying a pattern that was associated with improved terms of trade for many developing countries. This meant significant acceleration of the rates of income expansion in most of the developing world, leading to substantial declines in poverty.

Signs of the commodity and oil boom were far from visible at the beginning of the decade (see figures IV.2 and IV.3). Energy (including crude oil) and metal prices increased at the beginning of the decade, but it was an increase from the lows reached at the end of the 1990s. Food and other agricultural commodity prices remained at historic lows until the latter half of the decade when food prices, in particular, spiked, marking the onset of the so-called food crisis of 2007-2008.

The "shock" to the global economy from this commodity price boom was as big as the first oil shock, in the 1970s. However, in contrast with that episode, it was induced mainly by the rapid rise in global demand for commodities rather than by supply-side shocks. As a result, the impact on global economic growth was benign, at least during 2004-2007, and commodity-exporting developing countries were among the main beneficiaries of these trends. Nonetheless, rising prices and inflation caused monetary authorities to tighten policy from mid-2004 to June 2006.

Figure IV.2
**Nominal and real Brent crude oil prices, 1980–2007**

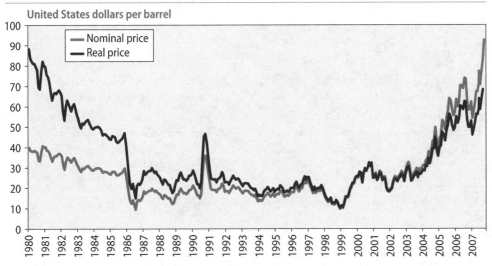

**Source:** *World Economic Situation and Prospects 2008*, p. 58, figure II.6.

Figure IV.3
**Monthly averages of free market price indices of non-oil commodities, January 2000 to September 2007**

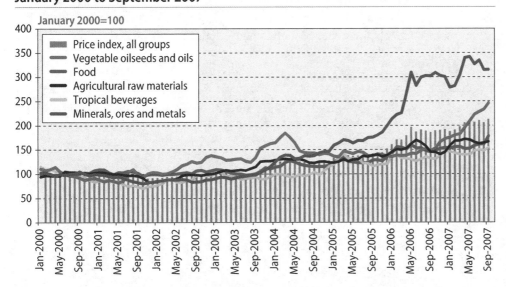

**Source:** UN/DESA, adapted from *World Economic Situation and Prospects 2008*, p. 56, figure II.5.

*World Economic Situation and Prospects 2005* assessed the 2004 oil price shock in the following terms:

> Although prices had subsided by year's end, the surge in oil prices in 2004 triggered two main concerns: first, the risk of another global oil crisis which, according to some analysts, would dwarf the crises of the 1970s (both of which wreaked havoc on the world economy), and, second, the possibility of permanently higher oil prices in the long run. Despite their surge in 2004, oil prices in inflation-adjusted terms remained far below the record levels they reached in the late 1970s; even the volatility in prices was less than in previous oil crises (p. 11).

*World Economic Situation and Prospects* emphasized that "the rise in oil prices was driven mainly by strong global oil demand, not by reductions in supply, as was the case in past oil crises" and that "[o]n this occasion, the increased oil prices [would] lead to slower global economic growth in 2005 and beyond, but not necessarily to a substantial downturn or a recession" (ibid.).

**Commodity exporting developing countries had important gains in their terms of trade**

The rise in commodity prices proved to be a bonanza for primary goods-exporting developing countries. *World Economic Situation and Prospects 2007* provided estimates of the terms-of-trade gains. During the height of the boom (2004-2006), the gains for oil exporters averaged no less than 8.0 per cent of GDP per year, while that for exporters of minerals and mining products averaged 5.4 per cent per year (table I.3, p. 12). Those gains were offset by losses incurred by exporters of manufactures from deteriorating terms of trade of about 1 per cent of their GDP. On the other hand, developing countries with more diversified export structures and countries dependent mainly on exports of food and other agricultural products witnessed little change in their terms of trade during this period.

**Fast growth in developing countries helped to narrow the gap between their income level and that of developed countries...**

Faster growth in a greater number of developing countries accelerated income convergence with developed countries. GDP per capita in developing countries grew on average more than 4 per cent per year between 2000 and 2008, while in developed countries it grew on average about 2 per cent per year during the same period. Prior to 2002, income convergence with developed economies had been ascribed mainly to growth in Asian countries, in particular in China. After 2002, this trend was extended to other developing regions such as Africa and Latin America and the Caribbean. As a result, the ratio of per capita income of developing countries to that of developed countries increased considerably during this period, thereby reducing inequalities between countries (see figure IV.4).

**....leading to formulation of the concept of "decoupling"**

The boom led several analysts, particularly those at the International Monetary Fund (IMF), to advance the concept of "decoupling" growth to account for the fact that large developing countries like China and India were no longer dependent upon economic growth in the core economies and could even provide alternative "growth poles" for the global economy (see box IV.1).

Figure IV.4

**GDP per capita of non high income countries[a] as a share of the OECD average, by region, 1990–2015**

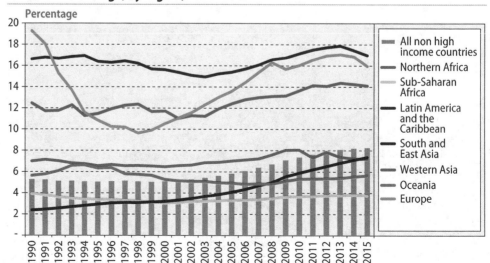

**Source:** UN/DESA, based on data from the Population and Statistics Divisions.
a A total of 132 countries comprising: developing low-income countries, middle-income countries and economies in transition, with data for all years.

However, in 2007, the economic boom ended. The financial collapse in the United States resulted in the transmission of shocks globally and on a scale that was unprecedented, with economies in all regions of the world being adversely affected. Some in fact ended up suffering much more than did the epicentre of the crisis, namely, the United States itself. As indicated in *World Economic Situation and Prospects 2007* (box I.2, p. 3) and

**Further evidence showed that growth cycles in developing countries remained correlated with those of the developed countries**

---

Box IV.1

## The thesis of growth decoupling

The argument for growth "decoupling" was founded upon the observation that, for several years, the rate of economic growth in many developing countries had been higher than that of the United States of America and other developed countries. This signified the presence of strong domestic sources of growth and a decoupling of business cycles.

Globalization played some role in the observed decoupling. Extended trade and financial networks had made the world economy more complex. In such a world, the impact of a single economy on business cycles in the rest of the world would necessarily diminish. For instance, more integrated financial markets would allow countries to find the necessary financing to absorb trade shocks emanating from a slowdown in the United States. Also, increasing South-South trade and investment flows strengthened economic ties among developing countries, thereby reducing their reliance on United States markets. At the same time, as countries became more deeply embedded in global networks, they were also exposed to new vulnerabilities.

While recognizing that the world was becoming less reliant on the state of demand in the United States, the *Survey* argued at the same time that it was premature or misguided to speak of decoupling. The *Survey* also warned that the terms-of-trade gains could not offer a stable source of long-term growth even in a period of prosperity in many developing countries, first, because the volatility of primary commodity prices and pro-cyclical responses of capital flows could be a source of major macroeconomic instability, hampering long-term growth and offsetting the short-term welfare gains; and, second, because some of the gains could easily seep out of their domestic economies. As analysed in *World Economic Situation and Prospects 2007*, the terms-of-trade gains of exporters of minerals and metals were almost entirely offset by increased net profit remittances abroad by foreign mining companies during 2004-2006, leaving only a small net income gain for those economies (table I.3, p. 12). However, such offsetting effects were much smaller for net oil exporters during that period.

As had been the case in the 1990s, growth records in developing countries were driven by rising import demand mainly from the United States economy, as the result of a particular combination of forces which could not be sustained over a longer period of time. Until 2008, the United States economy had remained the primary engine of global growth, generating demand directly for exports of manufactured goods from different regions and creating demand indirectly for primary and intermediate goods. In this process, the United States economy reversed the traditionally "expected" pattern of international capital flow by drawing in savings from the rest of the world, including from the poorest regions. This enabled it to embark on a domestic credit-fuelled boom with shaky foundations, as became only too evident during the 2008-2009 global financial crisis.

The impact of the crisis refuted the thesis of decoupling. Instead, as convincingly argued in various editions of the *Survey*, all of the developing regions remained critically dependent upon the external growth stimulus provided by the North, with the business cycles moving broadly in tandem, albeit with higher average growth rates for most of the developing world. In fact, aggregate GDP growth of developed and developing countries moved in a synchronized fashion throughout the 2000s.

As the *Survey* argued, deeper trade and financial linkages could explain why international transmission of economic cycles in the major economies to developing regions remained (and remains) strong despite strengthened domestic sources of growth. For example, much of the rapid increase in intraregional trade in developing Asia (the most dynamic region of the world in the past decade) could be attributed to the emergence of a multi-location multi-country export production platform, organized increasingly around China as the final processor. Reduced demand from the North therefore translated into reduced demand for the raw materials and intermediates required for processing, a phenomenon that has become particularly evident in the past five years.

*World Economic Situation and Prospects 2008* (p. 26; and chap. I, pp. 40-43, appendix 2), growth cycles in developing countries remained closely correlated with those of developed economies, particularly with the cycles of the United States economy.

Despite the growth-related success of some large developing countries and some degree of shifting of the balance of economic power towards the developing region, the *Survey* has suggested that it would be both premature and over-optimistic to expect a flatter world in the near future. A number of countries have experienced economic convergence towards the living standards of developed economies, but many countries are still lagging behind, especially in Africa.

More significantly, and well before the hype surrounding the growth of emerging markets had faded, the *Survey* had noted the difficulties associated with a pattern of integration that was inherently fragile. In a starkly prescient warning, the 2010 *Survey* pointed out that the pattern of uneven development brought about by globalization had so far not been sustainable. Since this time around, i.e., at the beginning of the crisis period 2007-2008, developing countries were much more integrated into the world economy, the global crisis had more profound implications and more serious consequences for development.

## A surge in global imbalances as the prelude to the global financial crisis

**Globalization since the 1990s has been accompanied by the emergence of a number of global imbalances**

Globalization in the 1990s and at the beginning of the twenty-first century was accompanied by the emergence of a number of global imbalances, which led eventually to several episodes of crisis. This chapter examines these episodes and analyses the macroeconomic policy responses that were taken at the time of each crisis.

Although the Asian crisis caused economic downturns in many developing countries, in most cases, signs of recovery had already become visible by 1999. The recovery, however, did not put an end to the turmoil in global financial markets. Financial resources flowed out of Asia and other emerging markets into dot-com stocks in the United States which drove equity prices upward, and with the Nasdaq stock exchange experiencing a boom over the period 1998-2000. When the bubble burst in 2001, the United States Federal Reserve Board (the Fed), in order to avert both an economic downturn and deflation, implemented an expansionary monetary policy during the period 2001-2004. This was perceived by many, a posteriori, as one of the major factors leading to the housing market bubble in the United States. That period witnessed the build-up of global imbalances, and financial market instability, which was imminent, led to several crises and culminated in the global financial crisis of 2008-2009.

**The end of the twentieth century was marked by the Asian financial crisis of 1997-1998**

The end of the twentieth century was marked by the Asian financial crisis of 1997-1998. Before the crisis erupted, economic performance in developing countries as a whole had been relatively strong, with aggregate GDP growth of over 5 per cent in 1995. The robust performance was due largely to fast growth in China and other countries in East and South-East Asia and, to a lesser extent, in South Asia. It was domestic demand, rather than exports, that drove growth in East and South-East Asia, although the countries of those subregions had often been held up as examples of successful export-led growth (*World Economic Survey 1991*, pp. 39-43).

At the beginning of June 1997, however, a series of currency devaluations spread throughout Asian markets. After months of speculative downward pressure on the baht, the central bank of Thailand was forced to freely float its currency, owing to the lack of the foreign currency needed to support its currency peg to the dollar. After the announcement, the baht immediately lost 18 per cent of its value against the dollar; following its devaluation, waves of speculation spread rapidly throughout Asia (exemplifying the so-called contagion effect). As a result, there was a sharp loss in value in the region of national currencies against the dollar, causing surges in dollar-denominated external debt burdens, stock market declines and reduced import revenues.

In debates on the causes of the Asian financial crisis, several interpretations were put forward. Some experts looked for root causes in market fundamentals: in the presence of the currency peg, large current account deficits created downward pressure on the currencies in East Asia, encouraging speculative attacks. High domestic interest rates prevailing before the crisis encouraged domestic companies to borrow dollars offshore at lower interest rates, in order to fund inadequately evaluated, hence, risky investments; and with weak oversight of domestic lending, rapid credit growth led to a significant increase in financial leverage. Other analysts attributed the crisis to the sudden shift in market confidence in the region's economies and the financial panic that ensued. The entire region experienced the withdrawal of many investors, who perceived the financial crisis in one economy as a sign of underlying problems in other economies of the region. It should certainly be emphasized that the vulnerability of the region's financial systems was exacerbated by their closer integration with global financial markets, which led to a massive influx of foreign capital from investors, many of whom were seeking a short-term return. That influx widened the scale of risky lending in the region, exposing it to significant capital flow risks during periods of uncertainty.

Despite policy and financial interventions on the part of IMF and the World Bank, shockwaves were felt throughout the global economy. By 1999, the Asian crisis had spread and turned into a full-fledged emerging market crisis, engulfing the Russian Federation in mid-1998. This significantly affected the countries of Central Asia, and led to currency and banking crises in Argentina and Brazil in early 1999. The financial crises in emerging economies caused economic downturns, which were sometimes severe. While signs of recovery had already become visible by the end of 1999, it was those emerging economies that shouldered most of the burden imposed by the adjustment costs required to end the crisis. For this, *World Economic and Social Survey 1999* blamed the ill-conceived contractionary macroeconomic policies implemented by national Governments, which aggravated the welfare losses incurred during the financial crises. Austerity measures and restrictive monetary policy were among the conditions imposed by IMF for injections of liquidity. The monetary policy aimed at increasing domestic interest rates so as to stem capital outflows and stabilize exchange rates and inflation, while the fiscal policy, with the aim of rebuilding international reserves, focused on reducing current account imbalances. The IMF-supported programmes failed, however, to stop the panic and capital outflows, the depreciation of exchange rates and the deterioration of financial markets. As a consequence of the contractionary policies, the slowdown of economic activity in the emerging economies was much sharper than anticipated, resulting in higher unemployment rates and political stress.

The lack of adequate mechanisms for achieving improved international macroeconomic policy coordination and the deeper flaws in the international financial architecture impeded containment of the Asian crisis (*World Economic Situation and Prospects 1999*, pp. 15-19). These deficiencies would remain a source of recurring concern within the United

**Shockwaves were felt throughout the global economy which ultimately resulted in a full-fledged emerging market crisis**

Nations from then on. However, inasmuch as the global economy started to improve during 1999, all proposals to address those deficiencies were shelved. Such proposals did not have much resonance among the world community's major players until the global crisis erupted in 2008, when the G20 emerged as a platform for achieving such coordination (see chap. V).

During 1998-2000, while some countries in South-East and East Asia were suffering from the impact of the Asian financial crisis, the dot-com bubble was forming in developed economies, particularly in the United States. The total equity value of stock markets rose rapidly in the second half of the 1990s owing largely to growth in the Internet sector and related technological areas, but in March 2000, the bubble burst. As a result, between 2000 and 2002, the stock market experienced a loss of $5 trillion in the market value of companies.

> **It was in 2000, shortly after the Asian financial crisis, that the dot-com bubble in developed economies burst**

The burst of the dot-com bubble and the Asian crisis, which were both bound up with the logic underpinning global financial markets, unintentionally created an economic environment in the late 2000s that turned out to be fertile ground for another global economic crisis. Capital flowed out of emerging markets in Asia and other regions for investment in United States dot-com stocks, which drove up equity prices. As the stock market bubble burst, the Fed adopted an expansionary monetary policy in a series of steps over the course of a period beginning in 2001 and extending well into 2004, in order to avert a downturn and possible deflation. Risk premiums hit low levels and leveraged deals became common as investors chased yields in an environment of lax regulatory oversight. This ushered in a period characterized by large-scale growth in credit and leveraged loans and a sharp increase in home prices in the United States.

The immediate effect of the dot-com crisis was, as it turned out, relatively mild owing to the fact that many developing countries had accumulated international reserves as a form of self-insurance against sudden capital outflows which would put their whole economy in jeopardy and result in costly financial crisis. High international reserves enabled central banks to intervene in the foreign exchange market to defend their national currencies in instances of speculative attack and helped cushion economies from external shocks. It should be noted, however, that as those reserves were kept in the form of highly liquid low-risk government bonds denominated by major currencies (such as United States Treasury bonds), the accumulation of reserves in developing economies translated into a net transfer of financial resources from South to North. By the end of 2007, these transfers out of developing countries as a whole, as measured by changes in foreign reserves, bordered on US$ 1 trillion. While the major current account surplus countries in East Asia and the Middle East were the biggest contributors, Africa and Latin America and the Caribbean also saw large outflows of financial resources (see *World Economic Situation and Prospects 2011*, table III.2, pp. 72-73).

> **Loose monetary policy in the US fuelled an expansion of global liquidity and imbalances...**

The major challenge of the burst of the dot-com bubble lay in the area of policy response. The shift towards loose monetary policies (especially in the United States) fuelled a massive expansion of global liquidity and global imbalances. The economy of the United States and of some other developed countries ran current account deficits, while countries of East Asia and commodity exporting countries ran massive surpluses. Low interest rates in developed economies, combined with large amounts of money flowing out of countries directly affected by the Asian crisis, triggered more risk taking within the financial markets of developed countries, the build-up of household debt and high leverage ratios of non-financial firms. The so-called yield spreads dropped to historically low levels, signifying another episode of irrational exuberance in financial markets. Speculative investment in commodity markets also helped fuel the ensuing commodity price boom. Ultimately, this led to the creation of a housing market bubble in developed countries with large current account deficits, especially the United States.

New financial instruments also played a crucial role in creating a housing bubble in the United States. Once the mortgages of individual homeowners with low credit ratings (so-called sub-prime mortgages) had been securitized—that is, repackaged into a multiplicity of new financial instruments and sold to domestic and international financial investors as "diversified", low-risk and highly liquid financial securities—markets worldwide became blinded to the underlying risks in play. It should be mentioned that housing and real estate bubbles were found also in other economies running major external deficits.

The abundance of financial capital available in the global economy did not translate into higher productive investment. Indeed, the Fed's expansionary monetary policy did not induce a boom of any strength in productive investments, but led instead to the overleveraging of households and non-bank financial firms, which extended into real estate booms; and lax monetary policy and innovative but poorly regulated financial instruments fuelled a bubble.

In response to these developments, *World Economic Situation and Prospects 2008* maintained that the ongoing downturn in housing prices in the United States had become much more serious in the third quarter of 2007 with the sub-prime mortgage meltdown, which triggered "a full-scale credit crunch" with reverberations throughout the global financial system (p. iii). The debacle in the sub-prime mortgage loan sector triggered full-blown global financial turmoil. Although sub-prime mortgages made up a relatively small fraction of the total mortgage market and an even smaller fraction of the total credit market, complex financial instruments with overstretched leverage, lack of transparency and inadequate regulation served to spread and multiply the risk beyond the sub-prime market. This was a development that most observers came to understand only after the crisis had erupted, less than a year later.

A major preoccupation during this period centred on the global imbalances and ensuing financial market instability that culminated in the global financial crisis of 2008-2009. On the other hand, the *Survey* had warned as early as 2005 against the dangers of the unsustainable pattern of global growth that had emerged about a decade before. Rapid growth was supported by strong consumer demand in the United States, which benefited from both easy access to credit and the positive wealth effects accruing from booming house prices. As mentioned above, far-reaching financial deregulation facilitated a massive and what was now an unfettered expansion of new financial instruments, such as securitizations of sub-prime mortgage lending, in global financial markets. This pattern of growth led in turn to strong export growth in developing countries and to high commodity prices. Unfortunately, it also led to a situation characterized by mounting global financial imbalances and overleveraged financial institutions, businesses and households.

Debates focused on the possible sources of those global imbalances. According to one argument put forward, especially by the Fed, the deficit was caused mainly by external factors. Hence, the fiscal adjustment policies of the United States Government would not be effective in dealing with the country's current account deficit. Emphasis was placed instead on the "savings glut", which was used to explain the global imbalances: countries with high savings rates, mainly in Asia, had significantly increased their savings above (the

**...at a time when new financial instruments were feeding a housing bubble in the United States**

**The global imbalances and ensuing financial market instability culminated in the global financial crisis of 2008-2009**

desired level of) domestic investment,[9] which thus accounted for the exceptionally low long-term interest rates worldwide. Put simply, from this perspective, as global imbalances could be attributed to excess savings outside the United States, adjusting those imbalances through a reduction in the fiscal deficit of the United States and a concomitant increase in domestic savings would not be the first relevant or the first necessary step to be taken. The logic of this argument hinged on the contention that effective global adjustment should be carried out elsewhere, specifically in emerging market economies, which were to become net borrowers once again.

From another perspective, domestic investment demand was too low relative to savings. The global investment rate, which had been on a long-term declining trend, reached a historic low in 2002 (*World Economic Situation and Prospects 2006*). It experienced a very slight recovery thereafter but remained below 22 per cent of world gross product (WGP) (ibid.). Focusing on trends at the global level and for major economies, the *Survey* argued on several occasions that investment demand had been "anaemic" in most countries having current account surpluses, with China being the notable exception among the largest economies. More specifically, since 2001, the growth of non-residential business investment had been remarkably weak in many countries, irrespective of their current account balance position, and the low level of investment had prevailed despite generally buoyant corporate profits and low interest rates worldwide. The *Survey* cautioned that these conditions posed the serious risk of a disorderly adjustment of the major economies' macroeconomic imbalances.

**Excess savings in Europe and in many countries in Asia were attributable primarily to a weakening of investment growth**

In fact, the analysis of the 2006 *Survey* showed that the increased excess savings in most major economies in Europe and many countries in Asia were attributable primarily to a weakening of investment growth. Fixed investment rates were down in almost all large developed and developing economies, and this held for both total and (non-residential) business investment. Booming oil prices were a cyclical part of the story, driving up savings surpluses in the economies of oil exporters with typically low domestic absorptive capacity. Even in China, where investment growth was robust, remarkably rapid growth in per capita income had pushed up savings rates above domestic investment.

Much capital outflow from current surplus countries were held in dollar-denominated assets, particularly United States government bonds, leading to further downward pressure on already low interest rates. In other words, the excess liquidity was large enough to exert an impact on financial markets, pumping dollar liquidity back mainly to the financial markets of the major deficit country, the United States. As no portfolio adjustment took place towards productive assets, investors, attracted by the low risk premiums, continued to pile into more liquid assets. Eventually, these conditions increased the economy-wide risk, hurting economic growth, and led to the financial crisis.

**The ever-widening deficit of the United States, financed partially by trade surpluses in developing countries, proved unsustainable**

The *Survey* insisted, throughout the 1999-2007 period, on the problem posed by exchange rate volatility related to significant financial flows from developing to developed countries. The ever-widening global imbalances—with the country issuing the world's major reserve currency, namely, the United States, accumulating increasing deficits financed in no small part by trade surpluses in developing countries—would eventually prove unsustainable. Such concerns prompted insistent calls for international coordination of macroeconomic policies to facilitate an orderly adjustment of the global imbalances

---

9    It is to be noted that a country with excess savings over investment runs a current account surplus by the national income accounts identity.

while minimizing economic growth costs. A coordinated strategy would have helped avert the negative growth effects and create confidence in the stability of financial markets (see chap. V). A growth stimulus in Europe and Asia, for instance, would have helped offset the initially contractionary effect of adjustment policies in the United States. No such coordination would come about, however, until after the crisis (ibid.).

## The need for improved global policy coordination

A coordinated strategy among countries for introducing the policy corrections needed to stem the exuberance in housing and financial markets would have helped avert the accumulation of global imbalances. *World Economic Situation and Prospects 2007* laid down the foundations and set out the required policy directions for such international coordination. The feasible corrective actions proposed by the *Survey* were adopted only once the crisis had erupted. At that point, corrective actions were too little and too late and the required efforts lacked consistency (see the discussion in chap. V).

While economic arguments for coordination remained strong, *World Economic Situation and Prospects 2007* recognized that achieving it would require strong and long-lasting political will (pp. 24-34). One of the obstacles at the time, but one that is certainly still of relevance today, was the absence of a consensus on the risks posed by the constellation of global imbalances. Even if Governments agreed that eventual adjustments were necessary, they did not agree on the matter of their urgency. Another problem stemmed from the fact that the Governments of the major economies preferred not to bear the main burden of adjustment and were therefore reluctant to follow through on their commitments.

Reforms in the global financial system constitute an area requiring international policy coordination. In particular, changing the pattern of global imbalances would remain difficult without reforming the global reserve system, which continued to rely on the dollar. Under such a system, countries were willing to maintain strong reserve positions as self-insurance against possible global market instability, thereby helping to sustain rather than minimize the pattern of global imbalances. As argued at greater length in *World Economic Situation and Prospects 2005*, a system less reliant on one national currency would likely have been a solution to the prevailing unsustainable pattern. For instance, common reserve pools and true international liquidity, including special drawing rights (SDRs), had been suggested. Such reforms could also serve as the basis for innovative climate and development financing through the issuance of SDRs.

Reforms would have also required more urgent coordinated efforts to improve financial regulation and supervision. Some emerging market countries were already responding to the return of speculative capital flows by introducing capital controls. This represented a logical means of protecting their macroeconomic policy space against short-term capital flows, which can have a devastating impact on growth and poverty reduction. Surprisingly, however, a serious discussion on capital account regulations worldwide has still not been conducted, despite the acknowledgement of its importance both in the Addis Ababa Action Agenda of the Third International Conference on Financing for Development[10] and for the success of the 2030 Agenda for Sustainable Development.[11]

> Effective global policy coordination aimed at stemming exuberance in housing and financial markets would have helped avert the accumulation of global imbalances

---

10   General Assembly resolution 69/313, annex.

11   General Assembly resolution 70/1.

## The human development approach and the emergence of the Millennium Development Goals

**The aim of the International Development Strategy for the Fourth United Nations Development Decade was to ensure accelerated development and stronger international cooperation**

The principal aim of the International Development Strategy for the Fourth United Nations Development Decade was to ensure that the 1990s would be a decade of accelerated development and stronger international cooperation. The Strategy set ambitious goals for the economic growth of countries. This would lead to a transformation through which those countries could foster productive employment, poverty eradication and environmental protection. As noted in the introduction to this chapter, the Strategy was focused on ensuring that the 1990s were a decade of, inter alia, accelerated industrialization; an increase in agricultural production and productivity to enable food self-reliance; improvement and modernization of infrastructure; and enhancement "of the participation of all men and women in economic and political life". As regards the last-mentioned goal, *World Economic Survey 1990* (chap. IX.A), *World Economic Survey 1991* (chap. IX.A) and *World Economic and Social Survey 1995* (chap. IX) all devoted separate sections to problems faced by women. The aim was that by the time it ended, the Fourth Development Decade should have witnessed a significant improvement in the human condition in developing countries and a reduction in the gap between rich and poor countries.

Under the International Development Strategy for the Fourth United Nations Development Decade, States Members of the United Nations pledged, among other things, to take effective action to provide an international environment that ensured full, equitable and effective participation of developing countries in the adoption and application of decisions in the areas of economic cooperation for development; reform of the international monetary system so as to render it responsive to the interest of developing countries; and greater market access to the exports from developing countries. It was also recognized that the international community had a special responsibility towards developing countries, which were threatened with soil erosion and soil degradation due to overgrazing and the cultivation of marginal land, as carried out by their inhabitants in their effort to make a living.

During the Fourth United Nations Development Decade, as already mentioned, the United Nations further sought to promote an overall change of perspective on global development through the organization of a series of world conferences and summits, including the World Summit for Children, the United Nations Conference on Environment and Development, the World Summit for Social Development and the Fourth World Conference on Women, at all of which specific objectives and targets were agreed. On 30 September 1990, the World Summit for Children adopted the World Declaration on the Survival, Protection and Development of Children.[12] Shortly before, the General Assembly, by its resolution 44/25 of 20 November 1989, had adopted and opened for signature, ratification and accession, the Convention on the Rights of the Child,[13] which came into force on 2 September 1990. On 14 June 1992, the United Nations Conference on Environment and Development ("Earth Summit") adopted the Rio Declaration on Environment and Development[14] and Agenda 21[15]; and in Beijing, on 15 September

---

12    Document A/45/625, annex.

13    United Nations, *Treaty Series*, vol. 1577, No. 27531.

14    *Report of the United Nations Conference on Environment and Development, Rio de Janeiro, 3-14 June 1992*, vol. I, *Resolutions Adopted by the Conference* (United Nations publication, Sales No. E.93.I.8 and corrigendum), resolution 1, annex I.

15    Ibid., annex II.

1995, the Fourth World Conference on Women adopted the key global policy documents on gender equality, namely, the Beijing Declaration and Platform for Action.[16] In the Copenhagen Declaration on Social Development and Programme of Action of the World Summit for Social Development,[17] adopted by the Summit on 12 March 1995, many of the commitments, objectives and priorities for action set out in the Strategy for the Fourth Development Decade were reiterated and expanded.

As noted in the introduction, the publication of the first issue of the *Human Development Report* broadened the discussion on development and put forward the essential idea that people must be at the centre of all development. In the foreword to the volume, the Administrator of the United Nations Development Programme (UNDP) cautioned that "(p)eople cannot be reduced to a single dimension as economic creatures" (p. iii). It was forcefully asserted that the purpose of development is "to offer people more options", one being "access to income—not as an end in itself but as a means to acquiring human well-being". Other important dimensions of development were also mentioned, including "long life, knowledge, political freedom, personal security, community participation and guaranteed human rights". Emerging as an alternative to the narrow focus on economic growth that had characterized the structural adjustment programmes of the 1980s and led to an acceleration of the globalization of economic activities during the 1990s, this change in perspective set the stage for a new paradigm in development thinking whose role in facilitating the adoption of the United Nations Millennium Declaration at the dawn of the twenty-first century was a determinant one.

The globalization process that unfolded during the 1990s revealed that economic growth did not always translate into sustained economic and social development and that different strategies were therefore required to ensure a broader concept of development. This inevitably raised questions centring on the definition and measurement of development. As shown in chapter II, definitions of development have evolved over time, reflecting the efforts to encompass the various dimensions of economic and social progress considered to be important, including, more recently, the interlinkages between economic and social progress and the environment.

The issue was discussed in the 2000 *Survey* where different proposals were put forth, evidencing a shift away from a sole focus on per capita income towards the integration of perspectives on human development as constituting a multidimensional process, including the progressive realization of human rights and capability, as conceptualized by Amartya Sen. However, as indicated in several editions of the *Survey*, economic growth and human development are often interlinked, which implies that improvement in one dimension cannot be achieved without simultaneous improvements in all the others. In other words, not only is economic growth a necessary condition for human development, but, conversely, human development is a necessary condition for economic growth.

The formulation of the MDGs reflected the international community's recognition that income expansion alone had not been sufficient to enable human development concerns to be addressed—in particular those reflected in the International Development Strategy for the Fourth United Nations Development Decade and the international development goals agreed at the summits and international conferences organized by the United Nations

*The Human Development Report broadened the discussion on development and placed people at the centre of development*

*The formulation of the MDGs reflected the recognition that achievement of human development requires more than just economic growth*

---

16    *Report of the Fourth World Conference on Women, Beijing, 4-15 September 1995* (United Nations publication, Sales No. E.96.IV.13), chap. I, resolution 1, annexes I and II.

17    *Report of the World Summit for Social Development, Copenhagen, 6-12 March 1995* (United Nations publication, Sales No. E.96.IV.8), chap. I, resolution 1, annexes I and II.

in the 1990s. The focus of the targets included under the MDGs was on some of the development concerns that were perceived at the time to be the most critical, including (under Goal 1) reduction of poverty and hunger and, subsequently, employment generation; improvements in education and health; gender equality; and environmental sustainability.

The MDGs focused on the human development objectives that were to be achieved by developing countries with support from developed countries within the framework of a global partnership. This attested to the importance of recognizing that the disjunction between economic expansion and social progress had clearly been the result of the impact of global economic and financial processes, with market dynamics jeopardizing countries' development efforts. Within the framework of the MDGs, developed countries committed, inter alia, to an open, rules-based, predictable and non-discriminatory trading and financial system, support for addressing the debt problems of developing countries, delivery of the ODA target, and expediting their access to new technology.

The *Survey* had been explicit in emphasizing that the need to address poverty reduction and other development goals should not imply subsuming them in the category of income growth alone. The focus—some would say the obsessional focus—on income growth was perceived as symptomatic of the failure of both the discipline of development economics and policy discussions to have evolved in the course of the 1980s and 1990s. In the view of *World Economic and Social Survey 2000*, "(b)y 1980, most ideas of the 1940s and 1950s, such as those concerning externalities and poverty traps, had been forgotten" (p. 126), which led to the greater prominence in policy circles of various versions of the Washington Consensus. According to the logic of the Consensus, stabilization, liberalization and privatization would automatically stimulate economic growth whose trickle-down effects should improve living standards.

The 2000 *Survey* countered these arguments by bringing to the fore several of the factors that fostered the persistence of poverty traps, including weak aggregate demand, which was perceived as reducing linkages across sectors within the economy. The absence of good-quality education and training at all levels, the lack of research and development and the failure to improve technological capabilities were also flagged as constraints on broader development and poverty reduction. In addition, the *Survey* identified institutional constraints, such as the prevalence of highly unequal asset holdings (especially landholdings), as structural factors that could contribute to a perpetuation of poverty and the creation of poverty traps.

This discussion of poverty traps remains highly pertinent within the context of the implementation of the 2030 Agenda and the Sustainable Development Goals. It was concluded at the end of the 1990s that macroeconomic policies alone were not sufficient for addressing the problems of the poor and therefore that complementary measures were necessary. In any case, there was no easy determination of which specific macroeconomic policies would work in particular contexts. According to *World Economic and Social Survey 2003*, because of "the sensitivity of poverty outcomes to the composition of fiscal expenditure and taxes", it was not possible to establish "a single general linkage between fiscal policy and poverty" (p. 146).

As observed in *World Economic and Social Survey 2006*, "the links between growth and human development are complex and they probably stand in a two-way relationship, implying that both must be promoted to sustain progress in either" (p. 19). However, the *Survey* also noted "that not all countries with relatively higher levels of human development managed to reach higher levels of long-term economic growth" which suggested that "human development is a necessary but not a sufficient condition for economic growth" (p. 20).

Taking specifically into account Goal 1: Eradicate extreme poverty and hunger, one could argue that achievement of the MDGs was relatively successful, as target 1.A, namely, to halve, between 1990 and 2015, the proportion of people whose income is less than $1 a day, had been achieved by 2010, five years prior to the 2015 deadline. Further, the proportion of people living on less than $1.25 a day had fallen globally from 36 per cent in 1990 to 12 per cent in 2015 (see figure IV.5). However, the global picture hides different regional trends. The world's most populous countries have played an important role in the global trend. By contrast, in sub-Saharan Africa, extreme poverty declined only to 41 per cent in 2015, from 57 per cent in 1990. Progress in reducing the proportion of people who suffer from hunger has been significant as well, although efforts have not been as successful to reduce extreme poverty. Globally, the proportion of undernourished people declined from 23.3 per cent in 1990 only to 13.7 per cent in 2011.

*World Economic and Social Survey 2014/2015* provided a comprehensive assessment of the period of MDGs implementation. A major concern of the *Survey* is the need for substantive coordination and integration of policy interventions for consistent progress across the multiple dimensions of development. This is an issue of great importance for the implementation of the SDGs, which are to be achieved under a much more comprehensive and ambitious agenda. The challenge lies in determining how to coordinate and integrate multisectoral policies in accordance with a single overarching vision—a vision that remains consistent with long-term objectives without losing sight of short-term priorities. An integrated approach can facilitate the design of coherent policies and help avert some of the unintended consequences of single-minded policies. Further, the huge potential for generating co-benefits through the design and implementation of a multisectoral approach, not to mention the advantages in terms of cost effectiveness, should encourage policymakers to move in this direction.

A case in point concerns the challenge of achieving food security, an objective included under both the MDGs and the SDGs. Experience has shown that achieving such a

**Figure IV.5**

**Proportion of people living on less than $1.25 a day, by region, 1990, 2008 and 2015**

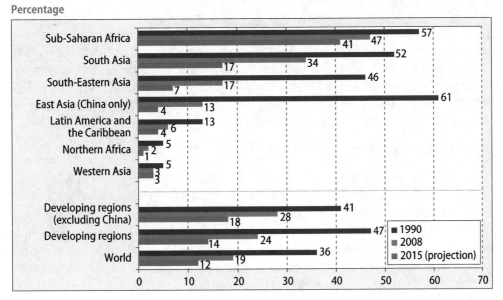

Percentage

**Source:** *The Millennium Development Goals Report* for the years 2012 and 2015. Available at http://www.un.org/millennium goals/reports.shtml.

goal requires a multisectoral approach, given the multiple interrelated dimensions that need to be focused on simultaneously. Instead of being designed in parallel with environmental policies or being driven mainly by technological and economic objectives, policies aimed at stimulating agricultural productivity should integrate goals, e.g., encompassing ecosystem preservation.

Achieving resilience in the face of climate change is another issue that entails difficult choices and trade-offs. Policymakers must seek more holistic and inclusive institutional responses which incorporate adaptation measures in the wider development planning and budgeting processes. This should start with an assessment of local vulnerabilities and a quest both for synergies between adaptation and mitigation challenges and for economies of scale which can lead to cost savings.

**The adoption of the goals and numerical targets under the MDGs brought with it the challenge of identifying the processes that would enable them to be achieved substantively**

As was made clear in several editions of the *Survey* issued during this period, another major issue that emerged through adoption of the goals and numerical targets under the MDGs was the challenge of identifying the processes and policies that would enable them to be met substantively. The fact that sustained poverty reduction, for example, was usually associated with broader economic processes (such as productive diversification into higher value added activities) was of clear-cut relevance in this regard. There was also the risk of a failure to recognize that, once numerical targets had been set, global, regional, national or local processes could work against or prevent their achievement. In addition, the tendency to focus on national-level results had led to a neglect of the question how specific social groups were being affected by, or excluded from consideration under, the new strategies being implemented. Addressing these issues, which were discussed both explicitly and implicitly in the *Survey*, could be extremely important for a successful implementation of the current 2030 Agenda, including the Sustainable Development Goals.

For example, MDG 1, whose original focus was reduction of poverty and hunger, had subsequently expanded its reach to include improvement in the conditions of employment and livelihoods, which was increasingly recognized as a precondition for meeting other goals. The fact that the *Survey* was directly or indirectly concerned with the limitations of Goal 1 contributed to a more thorough and nuanced understanding of the combination of policies that could be useful in ensuring that the Goal was successfully met. The *Survey* thereby made an important contribution to the discussion, since the elaboration of the MDGs, which were largely stand-alone in themselves, entailed little reference to the global and national policies and processes that could result in the desired outcomes. *Survey* analyses paved the way towards a greater recognition of the role played by processes in the framing of global goals. This in turn facilitated in no small measure a broader understanding of the challenges that informed the discussion leading up to the adoption of the Sustainable Development Goals and the 2030 Agenda.

## Reflecting on the experience of the period

The success enjoyed by developing economies in achieving economic growth during the first several years of the new millennium was followed by severe economic downturns as a result of the global financial crisis. This reminder—that economic booms have been transient and can create a false sense of complacency about the future—is a timely one within the context of implementation of the 2030 Agenda. Yet, it is always difficult to exercise caution in the midst of a global boom, especially for economies that are experiencing faster growth in such periods. The experience of developing countries in the areas of global production and trade during the boom-and-bust cycles of the 1990s and 2000s provides some important lessons with respect to the implementation of policies for sustainable development. For example, there is a need: (a) for national and international mechanisms with the capacity to maximize the benefits of globalization for developing countries, while minimizing the adverse impacts of increasing exposure to global economic shocks; (b) for support for economic diversification in developing countries and the building of resilience to global economic shocks; and (c) for a strong, reinvigorated and effective global partnership with the capacity to advance progress towards achievement of the SDGs.

As the *Survey* has demonstrated, despite some shift in the balance of economic power in favour of economies of the global South (China in particular but also Brazil, India and the Russian Federation, among others), it would be premature and overly optimistic to expect a flatter world in the near future. While a number of countries have undergone a significant convergence towards the advanced economies in terms of their living standards, other countries, especially in Africa, have fallen further behind.

More significantly, the experience during the late 1990s and the 2000s demonstrated that, in a world where developing countries play a much more significant role and are much better integrated, global crises have more profound implications and more serious consequences for the development of those countries. Integration of economic activities at the global level increases the exposure of developing (and developed countries) to the volatility of global markets, thereby making them inherently vulnerable to economic turmoil.

A key challenge for policymakers is thus to establish the mechanisms needed to prevent or reduce the extent and effects of economic shocks within a much more integrated world economy. This is particularly important given that once such shocks arise, protection of the poor rarely becomes a policy priority. Negative shocks have immediate and long-lasting impacts on poverty, while the impacts of positive shocks, which tend to be gradual, can be easily cancelled out when a negative shock is inflicted. Therefore, the best kind of macroeconomic policy is one that can counter boom-and-bust cycles in such a way as to prevent or soften negative shocks and provide greater economic stability.

**A key challenge for policymakers is to establish the mechanisms needed to reduce the effects of economic shocks**

In this regard, securing an orderly unwinding of global imbalances and preventing the eruption of financial turmoil continue to strongly require improved international macroeconomic policy coordination. And according to a principle that remains still relevant today, moving beyond an excessive reliance on monetary policies to support national economies requires an improved *mix* of policies (see chap. V for further details). The argument often advanced for the application of a coordinated short-term stimulus by economies with reasonably large fiscal space is consistent with benign global rebalancing.

**Securing an orderly unwinding of global imbalances remains a challenge**

The second important lesson to be derived from the experiences of this period takes the form of a continued reminder that the essence of development is structural transformation. That lesson constitutes a potent antidote to the argument that simple expansion of economic activity automatically generates socially desirable forms of economic diversification. The counterargument was focused particularly on the linkages among agriculture, the rural non-agricultural sector, the distribution of land, infrastructure and technological progress in agriculture. The main thrust was that successful development policies are those capable of taking into account and integrating all of the relevant dimensions. In the agricultural sector, for instance, this would entail dealing simultaneously with agricultural research and extension services, seed and fertilizer delivery systems, marketing and transportation, and access to finance, so as to reduce the traditional constraints faced by smallholder agriculture.

**The essence of development is structural transformation**

**Developing countries continue to advocate for the need for greater economic diversification**

The need for greater economic diversification has been urged repeatedly by a number of developing countries. This issue is particularly relevant for the implementation of the 2030 Agenda, as diversification in rural economies, for example, can help facilitate the process of adaptation to the effects of climate change. *World Economic and Social Survey 2001* provides a nuanced perspective on the implications of different attempts at economic diversification. While noting that "(d)iversification is often seen as an appropriate policy to be pursued in the face of the type of vulnerability that comes from relying heavily on the production and export of one commodity or industrial sector", the *Survey* cautions that "inappropriate diversification, directed at reducing vulnerability, but resulting in the creation of industries that are not in line with a country's true comparative advantage... could itself have adverse economic consequences" (p. 130).

**The implementation of the MDGs was supported by a reinvigorated global partnership**

The third important lesson to be derived is that the successful implementation of the MDGs was dependent largely on a strong, reinvigorated and effective global partnership, which was taken into consideration in the design of the SDGs, especially SDG 17 (Strengthen the means of implementation and revitalize the Global Partnership for Sustainable Development). It was during this period that the question of the effectiveness of development assistance, primarily ODA, received greater attention. Soon after the MDGs were agreed, ODA accelerated increasingly up until the global financial crisis in 2008-2009. Political momentum for increasing ODA grew in the early 2000s, notably through an explicit recognition of the need for a "substantial increase in ODA" (see para. 41 of the 2002 Monterrey Consensus of the International Conference on Financing for Development (United Nations, 2002) and para. 25 of the Gleneagles communiqué, adopted at the Summit of the Group of Eight held at Gleneagles from 6 to 8 July 2005).

Efforts, led mostly by the Organization for Economic Cooperation and Development (OECD) Development Assistance Committee (DAC), gave rise to the establishment of a set of principles promoting the effectiveness of development assistance. As discussions were expanding to encompass the full scope of development assistance, it was decided by the General Assembly, in its resolution 61/16 of 20 November 2006 and pursuant to the World Summit Outcome,[18] that a biennial high-level Development Cooperation Forum would be held within the framework of the high-level segment of the Economic and Social Council as an open, inclusive and balanced platform for reviewing trends and progress in international development cooperation, including strategies, policies and financing. Additionally, the Forum constitutes a space within which all stakeholders can engage and promote greater coherence among their activities, as well as strengthen the normative and operational links within the work of the United Nations.

The above commitments notwithstanding, since 2010, total ODA for developing countries has stagnated at about 0.3 per cent of gross national income (GNI) of developed countries. The target of 0.7 per cent of developed countries' GNI has yet to be achieved. As a result, developing countries continue to face a major shortfall in much-needed financial and technical resources. The issue of ODA and the other facets of the global partnership for development will need continued review, including through agreed mechanisms within the context of the Addis Ababa Action Agenda.

Market access and multilateral trade agreements are another important focus of the global partnership for development as envisaged under the MDGs. The Doha Development

---

18      General Assembly resolution 60/1.

Agenda,[19] officially launched at the Fourth Ministerial Conference of the World Trade Organization, held at Doha from 9 to 13 November 2001, gained more attention when MDG 8 was formulated; unfortunately, however, negotiations of World Trade Organization members on the Agenda have been stalled. The Doha Development Agenda places development at its centre and seeks to place developing countries' needs and interests at the heart of the Doha Work Programme. A strengthened global partnership for sustainable development requires continuous efforts to ensure that trade supports countries' development efforts, with special attention to the least developed countries. Within the framework of the Addis Ababa Action Agenda, several important initiatives have also been undertaken to prevent a future debt crisis. In the future, any cooperation framework encompassing ODA, multilateral trade and debt crisis prevention will need to include consideration of credible monitoring reports on progress in realizing cooperation targets and policy coherence, including monitoring efforts and follow-up review processes.

---

**19**    See document A/C.2/56/7, annex.

# Chapter V
# A new context for the 2030 Agenda for Sustainable Development

## Key messages

- The turbulence of the present decade, which began with the spillover effects of the 2008-2009 global financial crisis, has demonstrated that global mechanisms designed to resolve trade and financial imbalances remain, as in the past, ill suited to preventing the eruption of large-scale economic and financial turmoil.

- Long-term stagnation in developed countries could act as a major constraint on growth in developing countries, create instability in trade and financial markets, and reduce the availability of investments and concessional finance to the least developed countries.

- Periods of difficulty present a rare opportunity to restructure the global economy. Coherent and internationally coordinated policy actions, with the adequate representation of developing countries, are needed for stable growth and employment creation. Policy coordination is particularly important in the areas of monetary and fiscal policy, international trade and the global financial system. In addition, effective financial regulation and supervision are needed to prevent financial bubbles driven by speculation and short-term destabilizing flows.

- An international countercyclical response comprising public works programmes, social protection, financial support and investment incentives for employment creation is needed to reactivate economic growth. As part of a global new deal, such a response would speed up economic recovery and address sustainable development, climate change and food security challenges.

- Policies must pay particular attention to reducing the social cost of the disruptions and displacements caused by globalization and technology which increase inequalities and result in political unrest.

## Key events

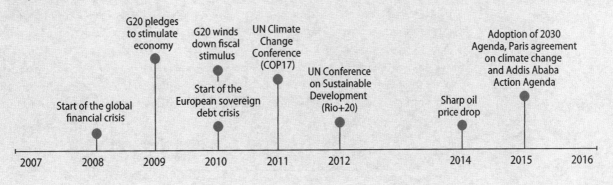

*We resolve to build a better future for all people, including the millions who have been denied the chance to lead decent, dignified and rewarding lives and to achieve their full human potential. We can be the first generation to succeed in ending poverty; just as we may be the last to have a chance of saving the planet. The world will be a better place in 2030 if we succeed in our objectives.*

General Assembly resolution 70/1 (paragraph 50)

## Introduction

**Rapid growth since the start of the new millennium has proved unsustainable**

In the early years of the new millennium, which began in 2001, the world witnessed rapid growth and income convergence among countries, reversing the trend of previous decades. That rapid growth in the first years of the decade proved unsustainable, however, because it was based on a build-up of global and domestic imbalances, resulting in the global financial crisis of 2008-2009, followed by the European sovereign debt crisis which began in late 2009 and the adoption of contractionary policies in 2011 which extended the global economic downturn.

**Since the global financial crisis, a return to robust and balanced growth has remained elusive**

As a result, the average annual rate of global growth in the period from 2008 to 2015 dropped by over a full percentage point compared with the period 1998-2007 preceding the global financial crisis (see figure V.1). A return to robust and balanced growth remains an elusive goal, and in 2016 global economic growth was at its lowest level since the great recession of 2009. While forecasts reported in *World Economic Situation and Prospects 2017* project a modest recovery in global growth for 2017 and 2018, that growth is nevertheless expected to remain below the average annual rate during 1998-2007. The sluggishness of the global economy is bound up with the feeble pace of global investment, flagging productivity growth, dwindling world trade growth and high levels of debt. In 2016, world trade volumes expanded by just 1.2 per cent, the third lowest rate of the past 30 years (see chap. I for an extensive discussion of the current global economic context).

Figure V.1
**Global growth, 2007–2015**

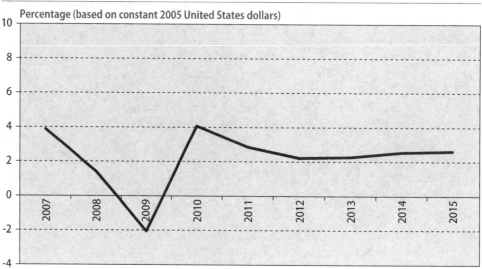

Percentage (based on constant 2005 United States dollars)

**Source:** UN/DESA, based on data from the Statistics Division.

To a large extent, the impacts of the aforementioned factors have been self-reinforcing, reflecting the close linkages among demand, investment, productivity and trade. For example, the slowdown in world trade growth may compound weak productivity growth. For commodity-exporting countries, low commodity prices since mid-2014 have exacerbated these difficulties. In addition, conflict and geopolitical tensions continue to take a heavy toll in several regions.

This is not to say, however, that there has not been significant progress in many areas of human development, most notably the rapid progress in poverty reduction. The proportion of the world's population living in extreme poverty, as measured by the international poverty line of $1.90 a day, declined from 44.3 per cent in 1981 to 10.7 per cent in 2013.[1] Still, the dramatic declines at the global level are largely a reflection of sustained rapid economic growth in a few large countries, most notably China and India.

The 2008 crisis exposed the weaknesses of the global economic and financial architecture. These weaknesses and the continued weakness in the global economic context have important implications for the ability of Governments to implement the 2030 Agenda for Sustainable Development.[2] Such context presents difficult challenges to Governments in their efforts towards eradication of poverty, achievement of environmental sustainability and creation of more equitable and inclusive societies.

The 2030 Agenda, together with three other agreements—the Addis Ababa Action Agenda of the Third International Conference on Financing for Development,[3] the Sendai Framework for Disaster Risk Reduction 2015-2030[4] and the Paris Agreement[5] adopted under the United Nations Framework Convention on Climate Change[6]—constitute a new agenda. This agenda recognizes the intrinsic connection between the global challenges of improving human development and achieving environmental sustainability. The agenda is driven by an overarching vision attesting to a more complete understanding of multidimensional development, including the various interrelationships among economic, social, political and environmental issues.

Addressing these challenges will require ambitious reforms and bold action. World leaders must agree on effective strategies for mobilizing financing for development and for ensuring both a stable global financial system and a fair multilateral trading regime—a regime that grants countries the space needed to build domestic production capacity and pursue sustainable development goals.

**Bold action and political commitment are required to achieve sustainable development**

World leaders will need to redouble efforts to improve national and international macroprudential regulation and coordination, so as to prevent the imbalances that lead to the kind of crises witnessed in the past. Development will require the mobilization of financing and a global trading system that is aligned with development objectives. Policies specifically tailored to those who are being left behind will be required, and those policies will need to be aligned with policies that reduce insecurity and the vulnerability of communities and countries to economic, financial and environmental shocks. The fact that

---

1   Based on the latest data released from the World Bank PovcalNet database, released in October 2016, which are based on 2011 purchasing power parity (PPP) data.

2   General Assembly resolution 70/1.

3   General Assembly resolution 69/313 of 27 July 2015, annex.

4   General Assembly resolution 69/283 of 3 June 2015, annex II.

5   See FCCC/CP/2015/10/Add.1, decision 1/CP.21, annex.

6   United Nations, *Treaty Series*, vol. 1771, No. 30822.

these challenges are all interconnected presents policymakers with an opportunity to make rapid gains across the multiple dimensions of development.

Global trends and their implications for human development have been tracked in *World Economic Situation and Prospects* and *World Economic and Social Survey* reports, issued annually by the Department of Economic and Social Affairs of the United Nations Secretariat. Through their analytical lens, the present chapter examines the objectives set out in the global development agenda, as reflected in the 2030 Agenda for Sustainable Development, in relation to the new global context. The chapter then focuses on how that context evolved in the aftermath of three significant global economic events; discusses the main weaknesses of the global economic architecture and why addressing them is necessary for creating an enabling environment appropriate for the achievement of the goals under the 2030 Agenda; and elaborates on the difficult challenge of implementing an ambitious agenda at a time of rising inequality, continued environmental degradation, and persistent insecurity and vulnerability. The chapter concludes with a presentation of the critical reflections to be found in both the *World Economic Situation and Prospects* and *World Economic and Social Survey* reports followed by some final considerations.

## Crisis, turbulence and a new global context for development

Momentous changes had occurred in the global economy in the aftermath of the Second World War, as described in the previous chapters, and the international context continued to evolve rapidly during the first one and a half decades of the new millennium with the expansion of global value chains and more deeply integrated global financial systems. Increased globalization was facilitated by policy changes (in particular the liberalization of trade regimes and rules regarding cross-border capital flows) in countries across the world as well as by technological changes which enabled much greater global integration of both production and distribution. The increased global economic integration through cross-border trade and financial flows had very major effects on production, investment, finance and macroeconomic policies across the world.

**The period 2002-2007 was one of rapid economic growth and deeper global interlinkages, with large poverty reduction...**

As explained in chapter IV, the period 2002-2007 was one of rapid economic growth during which prosperity seemed to be shared among countries more widely than before. The more rapid growth of some developing countries, led by China and India, inaugurated a period of convergence of the per capita incomes of developed and developing countries which continues today (Julca, Hunt and Alarcón, 2015). Trade expanded rapidly and prices of primary commodities increased, strengthening the export revenue of developing countries. As many of them (increasingly referred to as "emerging markets") found it easier to access international financial markets, private flows dwarfed various forms of official and multilateral financing. The combination of rapid aggregate income growth led by trade expansion and greater access to global capital facilitated substantial declines in poverty. While this was often associated with greater inequality within countries, the belief in "a rising tide that would lift all boats" generally helped to obscure that phenomenon.

**...but there were growing global imbalances which culminated in the 2008-2009 global financial crisis**

The global financial crisis of 2008-2009 exposed the imbalances that had emerged in the period 1998-2007, and made evident the downside of a globally interconnected economic and financial system where trade and balance sheet effects spread across borders. The collapse of the boom in the United States of America resulted in the global transmission of the shocks on a scale that was unprecedented. This began with financial retrenchment which spread like wildfire though the financial sector and from the financial sector into the real economy. The situation continued to worsen, with government debt-related problems in Greece and other European countries (2010) and the austerity response (2011) following fairly close on the heels of the crisis.

In 2017, the global economic context remains challenging. Economic performance has been disappointing, with subdued growth, weak labour markets, low levels of investment and poor productivity growth, as discussed in chap. 1. With interest rates near zero in many developed countries, traditional policy instruments have had a limited effect in bringing the economies back to full strength. This has ignited a debate over the fundamental causes in developed economies of what some refer to as "secular stagnation"—that is, a combination of poor performance and constrained policy options (LaFleur and Pitterle, 2017).

In fact, the importance of this debate can hardly be overstated, as the economic performance of developed countries is a key determinant of an enabling environment for the 2030 Agenda for Sustainable Development. Long-term stagnation in those countries could constrain growth in developing countries, create instability in trade and financial markets, and reduce the amounts of investment and concessional finance available to the least developed countries. The fact that the world economy is so interconnected also refutes the argument that there has been a "decoupling" of developing countries from developed economies. Moreover, the post-crisis experience, in particular the financial market volatility in developing countries, has demonstrated how strongly the macroeconomic conditions and policy space of developing countries depend on the measures implemented in developed economies.

**In the aftermath of the global financial crisis, growth globally has been slow**

## The 2008–2009 global financial crisis

The 2008-2009 global financial crisis resulted in what *World Economic Situation and Prospects 2009* called "the worst financial crisis since the Great Depression" (p. 1). The end of the global boom period was made evident first in the United States through the collapse of the market for sub-prime mortgages in late 2006 and, more broadly, of the housing finance market in mid-2007. The complexity and opaqueness that characterized financial markets and financial instruments led to the collapse of major banking institutions, with widespread consequences for a deeply globalized financial system. As institutions attempted to protect themselves from the unknown risks of the even more poorly understood financial assets and liabilities appearing on balance sheets, the world experienced a credit freeze. The financial crisis led to large-scale recessions in the developed countries.

In their initial response, policymakers failed to recognize the systemic factors responsible for the crisis and the risks brought on by globalized financial operations. Governments embarked on a course of liquidity support for the financial system and specific financial institutions; however, it was only as the crisis intensified, in the second half of 2008, that policymakers improved their international coordination. Governments recapitalized ailing financial institutions and strengthened the guarantees on bank deposits and financial assets. *World Economic Situation and Prospects 2010* reported that the total amount of publicly guaranteed funding for financial sector rescue operations had reached about $20 trillion, or some 30 per cent of total world gross product (WGP) (pp. xii-xiii).

In the immediate aftermath of the crisis, a consensus rapidly emerged on the need for strongly countercyclical policy responses. This entailed both a return to Keynesian macroeconomic policies, including large-scale fiscal stimulus, and a restructuring of national and

**Recognition of the need for effective global policy coordination has been slow as well**

**The crisis called for a strong countercyclical response, fiscal stimulus and a restructuring of financial systems**

global financial systems so as to reduce the danger of future crises. *World Economic Situation and Prospects 2009* strongly recommended building on the liquidity and recapitalization measures that were already in place, with massive fiscal stimulus packages coordinated across the major economies (p. iv). *World Economic Situation and Prospects* has also argued in favour of directing fiscal stimulus towards strengthening the productive capacity of countries, pointing to the opportunities for additional spending on infrastructure, education, research and development, and expanding social protection systems.

Most major economies embarked on a course of adopting countercyclical fiscal and monetary policies. On the fiscal side, Governments announced massive liquidity injections and fiscal stimulus packages, estimated at $2.6 trillion (or 4.3 per cent of WGP) during 2008-2010 (*World Economic Situation and Prospects 2010*, p. xiii). Monetary policy responses to the crisis were bold and unprecedented; and the magnitude and pace of easing policy interest rates was impressive, with some Governments cutting their interest rates to near zero.

Central banks of major developed countries were also forced to take unconventional measures to ensure that the crisis did not deepen. Measures were put in place to ensure that market interest rates would come down along with the policy rate and that interbank market spreads would decline; and monetary authorities also provided liquidity to financial institutions and in specific financial markets. Central banks purchased public sector securities to influence benchmark yields more generally and intervened in the foreign exchange market to contain upward pressure on their currencies (see *World Economic Situation and Prospects 2010* for a complete description of the monetary policy measures taken).

The coordination of policy responses, in particular at the level of the G20, was an important feature of the global response to the crisis. At the London and Pittsburgh summits, held in April and September 2009, respectively, the leaders of the G20 countries pledged to continue the stimulus and other measures as long as necessary for recovery. It was also notable that leaders pledged to deliver on all aid and other international development commitments despite the large expenditures on stabilization and recovery. In fact, world leaders called for an increase in support for countries with external financing needs and expanded lending operations by the International Monetary Fund (IMF) and the World Bank to that effect. The combined fiscal and monetary interventions were effective in stabilizing national and global financial markets and alleviating the initial economic and social impact of the crisis.

**Pressures to reduce fiscal expenditures led to premature reduction in stimulus measures, undermining a still nascent recovery...**

The recovery in 2010 was fragile. Credit conditions remained tight in major developed economies as financial institutions continued to rebuild their balance sheets. Domestic demand was rebounding owing mainly to the strong fiscal stimulus in place, while unemployment and underemployment continued to rise. Nonetheless, the pressure to wind back fiscal stimulus started to mount by late 2009, undermining the benefits of the strong and coordinated fiscal stimulus that was in place.

*World Economic Situation and Prospects 2009* cautioned repeatedly that removing the fiscal stimulus policies would have devastating short- and long-term social consequences by, for example, raising long-term unemployment. Models generated by the Department of Economic and Social Affairs of the United Nations Secretariat demonstrated the benefits of coordinated stimulus by countries with large external surpluses (*World Economic Situation and Prospects as of mid-2009*, p. 16). *World Economic Situation and Prospects 2010*, warned—accurately—that the premature withdrawal of fiscal stimulus might lead to a "double-dip" recession (p. xi).[7]

---

7　　Farrell and Quiggin (2011) discuss the strong response to the threat of systemic failure, and the subsequent return to contractionary fiscal policy.

The policy of surplus countries, most notably Germany, was in contrast to that recommended by *World Economic Situation and Prospects*. They sought rapid reductions in fiscal stimulus and a return to "normal" (and contractionary) monetary policies; and rather than a quick recovery, output in the eurozone returned to its pre-crisis level only in the third quarter of 2013. While the performance of the United Kingdom of Great Britain and Northern Ireland, which pursued similarly contractionary policies but had the benefit of its own currency, was significantly better, it returned to the pre-crisis level only in the third quarter of 2013 (see figure V.2).

**...and contributing to a prolonged period of slow growth**

Figure V.2
**Real gross domestic product, euro area and the United Kingdom, 2008 Q1–2016 Q4**

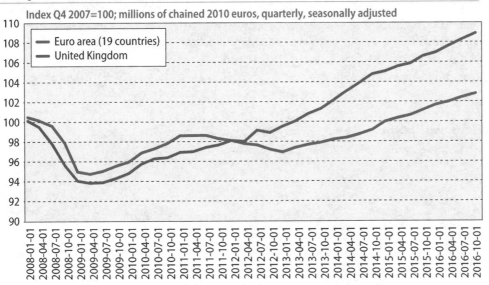

**Source:** Federal Reserve Bank of St. Louis.

# European sovereign debt management

The emergence of sovereign debt problems in Greece and other European countries in 2010 gave impetus to a reaction against Keynesian policies of fiscal stimulus, a reaction that was strongest within the central institutions of the European Union, including the European Central Bank and the European Commission. The European Central Bank, the European Commission and IMF constitute what is known as the "troika", which negotiated bailout packages with member countries of the European Union that were grappling with financial sector breakdown.

**Concerns over unsustainable government debt in Europe undermined support for continued fiscal stimulus**

The works of Alesina (2010), Alesina and Ardagna (2010)[8] and Reinhart and Rogoff (2010) were influential in promoting a shift away from fiscal stimulus. The key conclusion of Reinhart and Rogoff (2010) was that when debt levels exceed a given threshold, average annual growth of gross domestic product (GDP) declines significantly. Alesina and Ardagna

---

8    At a European Union meeting of ministers for economic and financial affairs, held in Madrid in April 2010, Alberto Alesina stated that "large, credible and decisive" spending cuts to rescue budget deficits had frequently been followed by economic growth. He was influential enough to be cited in the official communiqué of the meeting. Christina Romer—who, in her capacity as Chair of the President's Council of Economic Advisors, led the design of the United States Government's fiscal stimulus package devised to cope with the great recession of 2008-2009—acknowledged that the 2010 paper of Alesina and Ardagna had become "very influential" and that "everyone ha[d] been citing it".

(2010) argued that fiscal consolidation could, in some cases, boost economic growth, even in the short run.

Issued just before the G20 Toronto Summit, held on 26 and 27 June 2010, the *Fiscal Monitor* of 14 May 2010 (International Monetary Fund, 2010) provided the arguments for those who wished to embark on a course of rapid fiscal consolidation. Taking a contrary position, *World Economic Situation and Prospects 2010* (p. xi) argued that while concerns regarding public debt were justified, the effect of withdrawing fiscal stimulus prematurely would prove counterproductive.

European policymakers persisted in their efforts towards achieving fiscal consolidation and the debt crisis in Europe continued to drag on. Drastic measures to cut government spending made things only worse. Government debt in the eurozone reached nearly 92 per cent of GDP at the end of 2014, the highest level since the single currency had been introduced in 1999. While the proportion dropped marginally to 90.1 per cent in the third quarter of 2016, it is still well above the maximum allowed level of 60 per cent of GDP set by the Stability and Growth Pact rules designed to ensure that members of the European Union "pursue sound public finances and coordinate their fiscal policies" (figure V.3).

**Figure V.3**
**Government debt in the eurozone, 2000 Q4–2016 Q3**

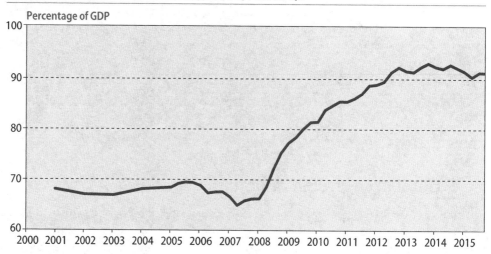

Percentage of GDP

**Source:** European Central Bank, Statistical Data Warehouse. Available at https://sdw.ecb.europa. eu/home.do?chart=t1.11.

Ex post, it is clear that aggressive fiscal consolidation measures in 2010-2014 had severe negative impacts on growth. The analysis of Reinhart and Rogoff (2010) was later found to be flawed, and subsequent analysis yielded a much more nuanced picture, demonstrating that there existed no consistent relationship between growth and public debt-to-GDP ratios (Herndon, Ash and Pollin, 2014; Pescatori, Sandri and Simon, 2014; and Chudik and others, 2015). Alesina and Ardagna also came under heavy criticism, and IMF itself later admitted that its fiscal consolidation advice in 2010 had been based on an ad hoc exercise (see Chowdhury and Islam, 2012).

## Austerity and the lesser depression

The winding back of fiscal stimulus, which had already begun by 2010, evolved into a full-blown programme of austerity in 2011. The causes of the reversal were many, involving a complex interaction between policy debates and the perspective of economic interest groups. The interests of creditors, notably banks and the financial system more generally, prevailed over those of debtors, including national Governments on the European Union periphery, where the crisis was most acute.

At the core of the policy debate lay the differences between analysts who adopted a broadly Keynesian analysis of macroeconomic policy, reinforced by experience of the crisis, and those who viewed the problem as one of public profligacy, to be remedied by cutting back the public sector and making room for private investment. The resurgent anti-Keynesians sought to rehabilitate the policies of austerity which had contributed to the Great Depression (Blyth, 2013), using the idea of "expansionary austerity". This idea was popularized during the 1990s within the context of the fiscal criteria for convergence in the eurozone.

The Keynesian argument was that the shift from fiscal stimulus to austerity placed the recovery process in jeopardy (*World Economic Situation and Prospects 2011*, p. 1). By 2012, recovery from the crisis was evidently at risk of being derailed and there were continued concerns about the failure of policymakers to address the jobs crisis and avert a renewed global recession (*World Economic and Social Survey 2012*, p. xiii). Such fears were borne out to some extent in Europe, where numerous economies experienced double-dip recessions following the adoption of austerity policy stances. A clear-cut feedback loop between fiscal consolidation and economic weakness remained a risk (*World Economic Situation and Prospects 2014*, p. 26). Declines in public investment since 2010 have also put long-term growth prospects at risk in many countries.

The evidence extracted from this period, as presented in reports issued by the Department of Economic Affairs of the United Nations Secretariat, leads to three clear-cut conclusions: (a) other things being equal, countries that had experienced less austerity fared better than others (Quiggin, 2017); (b) the premature end to monetary stimulus brought about by the European Central Bank, the Central Bank of Sweden and other institutions was misguided, as the recovery remained fragile; and (c) the appropriateness of lowering interest rates, as fiscal stimulus was wound down, was excessive.

> **The shift from fiscal stimulus to austerity in many cases resulted in "double-dip" recessions**

## A brittle global financial architecture for sustainable development

The need for a more stable and equitable global financial architecture has become both obvious—and urgent—since the global financial crisis, but in fact the problems had been building for decades. *World Economic Situation and Prospects 2010* observed that the deficiencies of the global financial system had been mounting ever since its emergence in the wake of the 1971 breakdown of the Bretton Woods system; and that, in many ways, the developing country debt crises in the 1980s and the Asian financial crisis in the late 1990s could be regarded as "dress rehearsals" for the global financial crisis (pp. 91-92).

Open capital markets increased the risk of contagion from shocks arising in external financial markets, such as shifts in international rates (driven by United States prime rate changes), variations in the exchange rates between key reserve currencies, and shocks impacting foreign debt or equity markets. The contagion generated by financial crises caused widespread economic collateral damage. Financial market liberalization in past decades led to increased volatility and uncertainty, which has negatively impacted long-term investment. The negative consequences of the deficiencies of the global financial system have been clearly illustrated by the history of the last decade and a half and the staggering costs of financial crises. This has been documented in the *World Economic and Social Surveys* for 1999, 2001, 2006, 2010 and 2014/2015 (see the discussion in chap. IV).

The global financial crisis was the latest proof of the risks associated with the interconnectedness and vulnerability of the global architecture. The momentous changes in the global economic and financial context described above had its roots in domestic and global imbalances which were transmitted through an increasingly interconnected world. Economic conditions spread quickly not only through trade and capital flows, but also as a consequence of the globalization of both the balance sheets of multinational organizations and financial and commercial interconnectedness. Given that volatility and income fluctuations were understood to worsen growth prospects over time, not only were the costs of the currency and banking crises massive in themselves, but they were responsible for a lowering of future growth potential.

Following the fiscal stimulus measures introduced in the immediate aftermath of the global financial crisis, many countries entered a period of fiscal retrenchment. This period of austerity was driven, in large measure, by the cost incurred by national Governments in accepting the bailout of financial markets, which led to debt levels deemed unsustainable by those same financial markets. The sovereign debt problems in Europe and the widespread fiscal retrenchment that followed recall the debt problems of previous decades in Latin America and other regions, as discussed in chap. III. Policies of those decades that were designed, in accordance with the Washington Consensus, to manage national debt through the use of drastic structural reforms and fiscal austerity found their echo in the most recent responses.

**Prior to the 2008-2009 global financial crisis, insufficient attention had been paid to systemic risks**

In the period before the crisis, insufficient attention had been paid to the systemic risks inherent in the operation and structure of the global financial system. There was a confident belief that the leading financial institutions were operating in an efficient market and that financial regulators would be able to correct large imbalances before they exerted large-scale macroeconomic impacts. The events of the present decade provide a strong argument for the kind of macroeconomic management that extends beyond simply preserving price stability and sustainable fiscal balances. Indeed, the *Survey* has continued to argue for the adoption of policies that do not generate large swings in economic activity and employment; that maintain sustainable external accounts and steer clear of exchange rate overvaluation; and that assure well-regulated domestic financial sectors, sound balance sheets within the banking system and sound external debt structures.

## A more ambitious global development agenda

**Implementation of the 2030 Agenda for Sustainable Development requires political will and bold policy action**

When the deadline for the Millennium Development Goals (MDGs) was reached in 2015, significant progress and encouraging results had been achieved in many areas. For one thing, the global targets for both poverty reduction and access to safe drinking water had been reached five years ahead of schedule. Significant, albeit, uneven progress was also achieved in education, health, reducing hunger and child and maternal mortality, and improving gender equality and environmental sustainability.

The vision of the 2030 Agenda for Sustainable Development attests to a more complete understanding of development. Together with the Addis Ababa Action Agenda, the Sendai Framework for Disaster Risk Reduction and the Paris Agreement, the 2030

Agenda focuses globally and more ambitiously on improving human development, ensuring environmental sustainability and advancing the structural transformations needed for sustained economic growth. Building on the achievements of the MDGs, the 2030 Agenda embodies the commitment to eradicate all forms of poverty, reduce inequalities and reverse climate change, while ensuring that no one is left behind. It recognizes the importance of improving social and environmental conditions including with respect to education, health and those in vulnerable situations, and environmental protection and sustainability. Further, derived from previous United Nations development agendas and re-established at the core of the present one is the affirmation of the need to undertake major structural changes on the path towards sustained economic growth, economic diversification and employment creation. In essence, the 2030 Agenda addresses all of the issues encompassed by the evolving United Nations vision of development, as documented by the Survey starting from its earliest days of publication (see chap. I).

The current global environment of slow growth poses significant risks with respect to the achievement of Sustainable Development Goal (SDG) 1 (End poverty in all its forms everywhere), one of whose targets (1.1) is to "eradicate extreme poverty for all people everywhere" by 2030. In order to achieve this goal, the world would collectively need to lift more than 800 million people above the extreme poverty line within a time frame of 15 years. The challenge is particularly daunting in the least developed countries, where close to 40 per cent of the population live below that line. *World Economic Situation and Prospects 2017* warns that under the current growth trajectory, without a decline in income inequality, nearly 35 per cent of the population in the least developed countries may still remain in extreme poverty in 2030 (p. vi).

> **The continued weakness of the global economy will present a challenge to progress in implementing the 2030 Agenda**

In the past decade, three issues have gained central importance in the discussion on how to realize the vision of the 2030 Agenda: (a) the rise in already high levels of inequality in many dimensions, recognized as a mounting problem which threatens progress under the broader agenda; (b) the growing urgency of reversing environmental degradation and the need to integrate environmental concerns and sustainability into all of the development objectives of the 2030 Agenda; and (c) the increasingly recognized fact that development status can be reversed by adverse shocks and that development requires resilient economies and societies with the capacity to adapt to changing circumstances.

## Rising inequality

The importance of the impact of inequality on development is reflected in the proliferation of publications on this issue in the academic literature as well as among multilateral organizations.[9] Inequalities between countries are a result of differences in growth rates across countries. The improved performance of some prominent developing countries (most notably China and other East Asian economies) has helped reduce global inequalities, even if inequalities have increased within most countries.

---

9    See, for example, Milanovic (2007; 2012a; 2012b); Cornia (2011; 2014); Galbraith (2012); Chudik and others (2015); Lim (2014); Piketty (2014); United Nations (2013); United Nations Conference on Trade and Development (2012); United Nations Children's Fund and United Nations Entity for Gender Equality and the Empowerment of Women (UN-Women) (2013); Organization for Economic Cooperation and Development (2008); World Bank (2005); International Institute for Labour Studies (2008); and International Monetary Fund (2007).

Rising inequality
between and within
countries continues to
be a problem

Inequality within countries has not seen much improvement in many regions for the past 30 years, with the exception of Latin America and the Caribbean (ibid., p. 26). Much of the inequality is a result of a rapid rise in the wage premium between high- and low-skilled workers, as shown by Autor (2014). According to that study, the factors that have contributed to the disproportionate erosion of the earnings of less educated workers and a widening skill gap include a declining minimum wage; a less progressive tax structure; growing automation in low-skilled jobs; a long-term decline in the size and power of labour unions; and the globalization of production, which demonstrates how changes in the production structure brought on by technological change and global value chains can lead to job losses and declining wages for workers in certain categories.

## Mounting environmental concerns

The world has a long way to go to achieve a sustained decoupling between economic growth and the growth of carbon emissions and ensuring sustainable consumption and production patterns (SDG 12). Nonetheless, some progress has been made along the environmental dimension of sustainable development. For one thing, the level of global carbon emissions did not increase for two consecutive years (2014-2015). Since this phenomenon reflects, to some extent, slower economic growth in major emitters, it will not be sustained if growth accelerates. However, it also reflects declining energy intensity of economic activities and a rising share of renewables in the overall energy structure, which may have lasting impacts. Developing countries, in particular, have made significant advances in renewable energy use. However, the share of renewables in global power generation remains small.

It is recognized that
the environment plays
an integral role in
many facets of human
development

The significance of the natural environment and the challenges of developing alternative "greener" strategies for development were identified many decades ago, but such concerns became an integral part of the global agenda only in 2015. Given that climate change is associated with a greater risk of natural disasters, disaster preparedness and adaptation were given priority in development discussions. Preventive measures for dealing with food vulnerability in the event of disasters, as well as linking medium-term relief activities to development strategies, were perceived as being necessary. While establishment of a global disaster mechanism for mobilizing the resources required for an integrated risk management approach was also recommended, such a mechanism has yet to be developed despite the greater prevalence of climate change related events and other natural disasters. The 2030 Agenda reflects the goals included in the Sendai Framework for Disaster Risk Reduction, which has four priorities for action: (a) understanding disaster risk; (b) strengthening disaster risk governance to manage disaster risk; (c) investing in disaster risk reduction for resilience; and (d) enhancing disaster preparedness for effective response and to improve infrastructure in the aftermath of disasters.

Switching to low-emissions and high-growth pathways to meet development and climate challenges is both necessary and feasible. Such a switch, through necessitating a major overhaul of existing production systems, technologies and supporting infrastructure and entailing very costly socioeconomic adjustments in developing countries, would therefore require a significant level of international support and solidarity. The 2009 *World Economic and Social Survey* advocated for a global new deal capable of raising investment levels and channelling resources towards lowering the carbon content of economic activities and building resilience with respect to unavoidable climate changes.

## Persistent insecurity and vulnerability

According to *World Economic and Social Survey 2008*, economic insecurity arises from the exposure of individuals, communities and countries to adverse events and from their inability "to cope with and recover from the costly consequences of those events" (p. vi). Various types of economic insecurity impact the achievement of a resilient development path and are of particular importance for vulnerable groups, such as women, informal workers, those in locations greatly affected by climate change or environmental degradation, ageing populations and migrants.

It is worth noting the insecurities arising from medium-term processes that can be very damaging. For example, while globalization has brought many benefits, it has also greatly increased the exposure of domestic economies to shocks from external sources. For example, greater liberalization of trade, income effects of terms-of-trade changes, movements of capital and volatile behaviour of financial markets pose threats to job security and income in certain sectors and for certain groups of workers.

Violence and conflict also generate insecurity and economic, social and environmental stresses are often among the root causes of violence and conflict. In fact, high unemployment, particularly youth unemployment, and food and energy price shocks can increase the risk of violence significantly (see the 2014/2015 *Survey*). Greatly increased economic inequalities across the world (as related to opportunity and to assets and income) have not only reinforced existing social inequalities but also generated counter-responses which can lead to social turbulence. Moreover, conflict itself exacts enormous socioeconomic costs—including human suffering—thereby undermining progress towards achieving development objectives.

In a more globally integrated world, external shocks can cause or compound domestic economic volatility and insecurity. To combat these external vulnerabilities, many countries have chosen expensive forms of self-insurance, which may include, for example, maintaining high levels of foreign exchange reserves, entailing a large cost to development in the form of forgone investments. However, mitigating risks in a global economy is only partly the responsibility of individual countries: such risks could be mitigated through appropriate capital management, including countercyclical measures at the global level. The international economic system must take a leading role in ensuring global financial stability, through improved international financial regulation designed to stem capital flow volatility and enhanced provision of emergency financing in response to external shocks so as to ease the burdens of adjustment.

**Persistent economic insecurity continues to threaten progress along sustainable development pathways**

## Difficulties in mobilizing sufficient development financing

Closing the investment gap so as to ensure the achievement of the SDGs by 2030 requires the mobilization of significant financial resources. However, the prolonged slowdown in global economic growth makes the goal of generating long-term investment and increasing capital formation a particularly challenging one. There is a need to strengthen development cooperation, augment trade and official development assistance (ODA) flows, facilitate public-private partnerships as a complement to public investment, and enhance international tax cooperation to enable scarce financial resources to be redirected towards sustainable development in countries and regions that are facing challenging economic situations (LaFleur, Hong and Kawamura, 2015).

**A prolonged global economic slowdown makes it difficult to mobilize the financial resources needed to achieve the SDGs by 2030**

The period of weak economic growth has negatively affected government revenues in many countries, resulting in a worsening of fiscal positions. For the commodity-dependent developing economies, the growing strains on public finances have been particularly marked since the sharp decline in commodity prices in 2014. Foreign currency-denominated debt has been gaining in importance in pockets of the developing countries, leaving borrowers exposed to exchange rate risk. Higher financing costs have been incurred in countries that have suffered sharp currency depreciations.

Developing countries have experienced negative net resource transfers in 2015 and 2016

International finance is a critical complement to domestic revenue mobilization. However, for more than a decade, developing countries as a whole have experienced negative net resource transfers. After peaking at $800 billion in 2008, yearly net transfers from developing to developed countries are estimated to have amounted to about $500 billion in both 2015 and 2016 (*World Economic Situation and Prospects 2017*, p. 74 and figure III.1). Private sector international capital flows have also remained volatile amid major global uncertainties and risks. The macroeconomic policies adopted in developed economies in the aftermath of the global financial crisis have exerted a significant effect on capital flows, especially among emerging markets that have a high degree of financial market openness. In particular, the use of unconventional monetary policy instruments by the central banks of developed countries has had sizeable effects on cross-border flows. New empirical studies[10] indicate that the quantitative easing has amplified the procyclicality and volatility of capital flows to developing countries, with strong impacts on exchange rates and asset prices. In some cases, the large swings in cross-capital flows have led to increased financial vulnerability. For central banks and Governments of developing countries, managing volatile capital flows has presented a significant policy challenge in recent years.

**It is encouraging that ODA remains on its long-term increasing trend, despite some recent temporary declines...**

ODA and other forms of international public finance are critical channels for financing sustainable development, especially in the least developed countries. The austerity policies adopted in developed countries following the global financial crisis generally included reductions in overseas development aid. As noted in *World Economic Situation and Prospects 2014* (p. 88), following the emergence of the sovereign debt crisis, ODA dropped by 2 per cent in 2011, falling particularly sharply in the poorest countries. Bilateral ODA to East, West, Central and Southern Africa fell by 7.9 per cent between 2011 and 2012. Similarly, bilateral ODA to least developed countries fell by 12.8 per cent in the same period.

It is notable that, despite the decline observed during the sovereign debt crisis, ODA has been on a long-term rise and in 2015 was 82 per cent higher in real terms than in 2000 (*World Economic Situation and Prospects 2017* and Organization for Economic Cooperation and Development (OECD) Development Assistance Committee (DAC)[11]). Between 2015 and 2016, ODA increased by an additional 8.9 per cent in real terms, to $142.6 billion. Most of this increase has been a result of additional spending on refugees.

While the recent recovery of ODA flows from their post-crisis declines is welcome, those flows remain insufficient. In 2016, total ODA from DAC donors represented just 0.32 per cent of their gross national income (GNI), a figure well below the target of 0.7 per cent of GNI to which many developed countries were committed. DAC donors' total ODA provided to least developed countries was equivalent to 0.09 per cent of GNI, a figure that falls well short of the target of 0.15 to 0.20 per cent of GNI to which donors were committed.

---

10    Punzi and Chantapacdepong (2017); Tillmann (2016); Bluwstein and Canova (2016).

11    Based on OECD/DAC online database, available from http://www.oecd.org/dac/stats/idsonline.

The composition of ODA has also shifted towards environment-related transfers, notably those associated with efforts to reduce climate change and deforestation. *World Economic Situation and Prospects 2014* reported that aid having environmental sustainability as a principal objective grew more than threefold between 1997 and 2010, reaching $11.3 billion in 2010 (p. 89).

While aid in support of environmental sustainability is welcome, there is concern that rather than expand the total amount of resources, provision of such aid is causing a diversion of traditional development aid. And given the fungibility of money, it is often hard to assess whether funds for achieving one objective have come at the expense of another. However, in numerous cases, such as that of Australia, funding for climate-related aid has been patently derived from traditional foreign aid money.[12] The reallocation of funding in the United States is a more complex matter, but it appears to follow a similar pattern.[13] More generally, there is no indication of a commitment to making funding for climate change mitigation and adaptation additional to development assistance. It is therefore likely that an increase in aid for, say, environmental programmes, will come at the expense of aid for traditional development projects.

**...but there is concern that shifting ODA towards environmental projects may come at the expense of traditional development assistance**

Within this context, private international capital flows have assumed greater importance. However, capital movements have shown a high level of volatility, leading to exchange rate volatility, credit and debt bubbles, inflation and asset price bubbles. Of even greater concern is the risk of sudden stops and withdrawals of international capital as a result of heightened risk aversion, which contribute to the spread of financial crises (*World Economic Situation and Prospects 2012*, p. 67).

**While private capital flows have assumed greater importance, they are also more volatile**

Financing long-term investment for development has been further complicated by the build-up of foreign exchange reserves by developing countries for self-insurance, as discussed above. The policy of self-insurance, however, is costly and tends to exacerbate global imbalances. This being the case, capital account regulations may provide a better way of managing volatile financial flows (ibid., pp. 67-68).

## Limited progress in trade liberalization for development

Discussions regarding trade liberalization in publications of the Department of Economic and Social Affairs of the United Nations Secretariat and of other international organizations have followed a standard format: an expression of disappointment at the lack of progress in the Doha round of trade negotiations, which broke down in the mid-2000s (see, for example, *World Economic Situation and Prospects 2008*); a discussion of the development outcomes that ought to have been delivered by an agreement in that round; and some critical observations on the proliferation of bilateral and plurilateral agreements, most notably the Trans-Pacific Partnership and the Transatlantic Trade and Investment Partnership.

**The progress of multilateral trade negotiations has been disappointing and they have recently suffered setbacks...**

At its inception, the Doha round represented the best hope for a pro-development liberalization of the global trade system. There was cautious optimism that the round might be "revitalized" following commitments made at the G20 Pittsburgh Summit in September 2009, but there also remained concern that the process could be derailed through the proliferation of bilateral agreements (*World Economic Situation and Prospects 2010*, p. ix).

---

12    http://www.skynews.com.au/news/top-stories/2015/12/01/turnbull-pledges--800-million-for-climate.html.

13    http://www.brookings.edu/blogs/planetpolicy/posts/2014/11/17-green-climate-fund-roberts.

Hopes for a developmental trade round were not realized, and expectations dwindled: there existed only a very narrow window of opportunity for concluding the negotiations in 2011 (*World Economic Situation and Prospects 2011*, p. 65).

By 2012, the Doha round's failure had been recognized as negotiations reached a stalemate. From this, there emerged a more nuanced view of bilateral and regional deals. As the prospect of a global agreement receded, there was a growing incentive for countries to engage in the establishment of preferential bilateral and regional trade agreements (*World Economic Situation and Prospects 2012*, pp. 62-63). The World Trade Organization estimates that almost 300 preferential trade agreements are currently in force worldwide, half of which have come into effect since 2000 (see figure V.4). Moreover, after a delay associated with the global financial crisis, the expansion regained momentum. A particular feature of these agreements, which came to the fore after 2000, was the extension of their scope beyond trade to encompass "WTO-plus and/or WTO-extra provisions" such as those for non-tariff measures, the services sectors, intellectual property rights, and trade policy-related labour and environment issues (ibid., p. 63).

The proliferation of bilateral, regional and plurilateral agreements gave rise to many difficulties and inconsistencies (*World Economic Situation and Prospects 2014*, pp. 59-60). Many of the new and cross-cutting issues included in the agreements have been the subject of controversy. These include the extension of strong intellectual property rights, with notable implications for pharmaceuticals; investor rights under investor-State dispute settlement provisions; and the undermining of both State-owned enterprises and provisions for government procurement, perceived as advantaging multinationals over local small and medium-sized enterprises.

It now seems clear that prospects for significant progress towards a global agreement are limited in the near term. The failure to reaffirm the Doha mandate at the Tenth Ministerial Conference of the World Trade Organization, held in Nairobi from 15 to 19 December 2015, and the call by the United States to abandon the round make this clear. As noted in *World Economic Situation and Prospects 2015*, even the World Trade Organization has shifted to a plurilateral mode, as exemplified by the Trade in Services Agreement

**...which has led to the proliferation of regional trade agreements**

Figure V.4
**Number of regional trade agreements in force, 1958–2016**

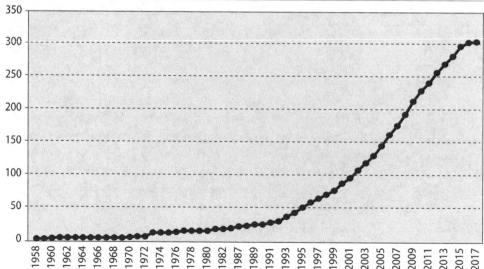

**Source:** World Trade Organization, Regional Trade Agreements Information System (RTA-IS). Available at http://rtais.wto.org/UI/PublicPreDefRepByEIF.aspx.

(pp. 54-55). The recent decision by the United States to abandon the ratification of the Trans-Pacific Partnership in favour of bilateral negotiations is further evidence of the move away from an environment where multilateral trade negotiations are conducted.

## Critical reflections on a new global context and an ambitious development agenda

The historical cyclical pattern of growth, global imbalances and crisis has had an impact on human development. A review of the critical reflections found in various publications of the Department of Economic and Social Affairs, particularly *World Economic and Social Survey* and *World Economic Situation and Prospects*, yields important insights regarding what is needed to achieve the 2030 Agenda.

Key among those insights is that the risks posed by the unsustainable build-up of global imbalances must be recognized. The *Survey* was among the first international publications to perceive the impending threat of the global financial crisis and to reject the view that liberalized financial markets had reduced the vulnerability of national and global economies to systemic risk. It is noteworthy that this note of caution was sounded in the midst of a global boom which had in fact generated a great deal of complacency across the world, especially in some of the more successful developing economies. Recognizing the global financial crisis as it emerged, the *World Economic Situation and Prospects* reports were consistent in making the case for a moderate but coordinated and sustainable fiscal stimulus (see box V.1).

Better management of the global economic and financial systems is of the utmost importance for the implementation of the 2030 Agenda for Sustainable Development. A multilateral system that is able to resolve global imbalances before they turn into full-blown crises will provide an enabling environment for sustainable development. Establishing such a system involves promoting effective macroeconomic mechanisms; a more balanced global monetary system; sufficient availability of development assistance; a multilateral trading system that is open, rules based and aligned with development objectives; and building more effective global coordination in managing imbalances and preventing crisis. Stability and growth of the global economy combined with appropriate policy coordination would also help to address the sources of global inequality.

**Better management of global economic and financial systems is needed to realize the vision of sustainable development**

### Accelerating progress in global coordination

The growing complexity and interlinkages across both economic sectors and countries call for more effective policy coordination so that the positive spillover effects of various policy interventions, at the domestic and international levels, can be maximized. Improved international policy coordination is needed to ensure consistency and complementarities among trade policy and investment policy and to better align the multilateral trading system with the 2030 Agenda, thereby ensuring inclusive growth and decent work for all. Deeper international cooperation is also needed in many other areas, entailing, e.g., expediting clean technology transfer, supporting climate finance, expanding international public finance and ODA, strengthening international tax cooperation and tackling illicit financial flows, providing a global financial safety net and coordinating policy designed to address the challenges posed by large movements of refugees and migrants.

**Deeper and more complex global interconnections require more effective policy coordination in multiple areas...**

Box V.1

**World Economic Situation and Prospects reports sounded early alarms about growing imbalances**

Starting in 2005, the *World Economic Situation and Prospects* report consistently warned of the unsustainability of the economic boom driven by credit-fuelled consumption in the United States of America. The 2005 report expressed concern about the sustainability of rising United States trade deficits and the likely impact on exchange rate instability. The report also warned about mounting global financial imbalances and overleveraged financial institutions, businesses and households; and strongly cautioned that in a highly integrated global economy without adequate regulation and global governance structures, the breakdown in one part of the system could easily lead to failure elsewhere.

The 2006 report continued to warn about the rising global imbalances, observing that "the possibility of a disorderly adjustment of the widening macroeconomic imbalances of the major economies [was] a major risk" (p. v) and the 2007 report singled out the possibility of a more severe downturn in United States housing markets as the key risk for the global economy. *World Economic Situation and Prospects 2009* noted that the near meltdown of the global economy did not come as a shock to those analysts (including those whose analyses appeared in earlier reports) who had focused on underlying imbalances in the real global economy and on the way in which they were obscured through the financialization of economic management.

The leaders of the G20 countries took initial steps towards effective policy coordination for a more balanced recovery at the Pittsburgh Summit, held on 24 and 25 September 2009. Those countries agreed to create a framework for fostering "strong, sustainable and balanced growth" of the world economy.[14] Under this framework, countries with significant external deficits, mainly the United States, would encourage private savings and undertake fiscal consolidation. Surplus countries, including China, Germany and Japan, would strengthen domestic sources of growth.

*...including macroeconomic policies and trade, tax cooperation and tackling illicit financial flows, and technology transfer*

In taking note of the absence of visible progress in building a cohesive regulatory system for international finance, *World Economic Situation and Prospects 2011* (p. 65) called attention to the suggestion set out in the communiqué of the G20 Seoul Summit (11 and 12 November 2010)[15] that "policy responses in emerging market economies with adequate reserves and increasingly overvalued flexible exchange rates m[ight] also include carefully designed macroprudential measures". *World Economic Situation and Prospects 2012*, for its part, asserted that "[f]inancial reforms are inadequate for containing systemic risks" and in that regard noted the limitations of national-level measures such as the Dodd-Frank Wall Street Reform and Consumer Protection Act (p. xii). And as observed in chapter III of *World Economic Situation and Prospects 2014*, progress towards implementing banking reforms had been "slow and uneven" (p. 81). Moreover, an excessively rigid emphasis on risk reduction may constrain lending for development.

While these sensible suggestions were followed in several advanced economies in the 1960s and 1970s, by the 2000s, they had been all but forgotten, both in developed and in developing countries, thereby enabling the build-up of financial bubbles which culminated in the global financial crisis. For developing countries, an important issue often arises from the volatility in capital flows for reasons unrelated to domestic macroeconomic policy or performance. In this regard, *World Economic and Social Survey 2005*, noting the significance

---

14   See G20 Leaders Statement: The Pittsburgh Summit. Available at www.g20.utoronto.ca/2009/2009communique0925.html.

15   Seoul Summit document, 12 November 2010, para. 6.

of capital account regulations, indicated that such regulations "potentially ha[d] a dual role: as a macroeconomic policy tool with which to provide some room for countercyclical monetary policies that smooth out debt ratios and spending; and as a 'liability policy' designed to improve private sector external debt profiles" (p. 97).

The global financial crisis, the sovereign debt problems in Europe and the fiscal retrenchment that followed led to a focusing of attention once again on the importance of fiscal spending in providing countercyclical support for economic activity. As indicated above, a key lesson extracted from the last crises has been that premature removal of fiscal support can undermine nascent recoveries and result in double-dip recessions. The challenge for policymakers, therefore, is to determine the proper timing with respect to winding down fiscal stimulus in the event of a crisis. Meaningful indicators for determining whether or when the recovery has become robust and self-supporting include (a) substantial improvements in employment conditions and (b) a reduction of output gaps. Large economies should also consider the international spillover effects of removing fiscal stimulus and should rely on a global framework for policy coordination.

**One key lesson learned in the aftermath of the global financial crisis has been that robust and sustained fiscal support is important for dynamic economic growth**

## Rebalancing the global monetary system

In *World Economic and Social Survey 2010*, it was pointed out that "the pattern of uneven development brought about by globalization" had so far been sustainable "neither economically nor environmentally", nor had it been "feasible politically" (p. xxiii). The *Survey* therefore offered a stark and, as it turned out, prescient warning to the effect that, as developing countries were that time around "much more significant and much better integrated into the world economy", the global crisis had "profounder implications and more serious consequences for development" (ibid., pp. xxiii-xxiv). While the world is becoming increasingly interconnected, those connections, by virtue of their nature and quality, need constant improvement. It has been convincingly argued in various editions of the *Survey*— particularly in a direct refutation in the 2008 *Survey* of the thesis of decoupling—that all of the developing regions remained critically dependent upon an external growth stimulus from the developed economies and that business cycles move broadly in tandem.

**Developing economies continue to gain in importance in the globalized economic and financial system...**

The continued dependence on the markets of the developed countries, even as actual production shifted to other regions, reflected the uneven pattern of economic integration. For example (and as noted in chap. IV), much of the rapid increase in intraregional trade in developing Asia (the most dynamic region of the world in the past decade) could be attributed to the emergence of a multi-location multi-country export production platform, organized increasingly around China as the final processor. Reduced demand from developed countries therefore translated into reduced demand for the raw materials and intermediates required for processing, a phenomenon that has become particularly evident in the past five years.

The highly interconnected global economic and financial system helps to accelerate growth in developing countries but also makes them more vulnerable to fluctuations within the world economy. Further, financial asymmetries between developed and developing countries affect the latter's ability to participate in and benefit from the international financial system. As explained in the 2005 *Survey*, such asymmetries account for "three basic facts", namely, "(a) the incapacity of most developing countries to issue liabilities in their own currencies, a phenomenon that has come to be referred to as the 'original sin', (b) differences in the degrees of domestic financial and capital market development, which

**...but they remain plagued by currency and maturity mismatches in the balance sheets of economic agents and are vulnerable to the changes in economic and financial conditions in developed economies**

lead to an undersupply of long-term financial instruments in developing countries; and (c) the small size of developing countries' domestic financial markets vis-à-vis the magnitude of the speculative pressures they may face" (p. 74). What this means is that developing countries are plagued by variable mixes of currency and maturity mismatches in the balance sheets of economic agents, and are affected dramatically by changes in economic and financial conditions within the core capitalist economies, which they do not have the power to influence.

The *World Economic and Social Survey* reports have continuously stressed the need for international coordination of economic policies, with no exception being made for policies related to financial regulation. Indeed, it has been argued that without such coordination, financial regulation in any one country is likely to be less effective and even counterproductive, and that, through such regulatory arbitrage, risk can be increased and disseminated throughout the global financial system.

**Recovering sustained growth requires greater private investments, productivity growth and a more balanced pattern of trade and capital flows**

A resurgence of the large global imbalances and unsustainable patterns of growth that led to the global financial crisis can be averted only if at least three conditions are met. First, Governments must ensure a timely and deliberate transition from publicly funded economic stimulus towards self-supporting economic activity generated by private demand. Second, there must be a renewed push for investment spending geared towards support of productivity growth and the transformation of energy sectors and infrastructure required to meet the challenge of climate change. Third, a more balanced pattern of international trade and capital flows across countries must be achieved. As these three objectives are highly interdependent, their fulfilment will require close policy coordination and macroprudential regulation for global stability and for mobilizing resources for investment and development.

**A global green new deal is needed to put the global economy on the path to sustainable development**

In the immediate aftermath of the global financial crisis, the *Survey* saw a rare opportunity to restructure the global economy so as to put it on the path towards sustainable consumption and production, as well as towards closing the gaps between rich and poor countries. In 2009, the Department of Economic and Social Affairs of the United Nations Secretariat took up the call for a global green new deal. Implemented through international coordination, the global green new deal would also drive balanced global development. Comprising public work programmes and social protection (especially in developing countries), it would not only hasten economic recovery and job creation, but also address sustainable development, climate change and food security challenges. Those public works programmes would be launched not only in developed countries, which can resort to deficit financing, but also in developing countries, where resources are more limited and policies more likely to be held hostage by the global financial system.

The global green new deal would be part of the broader international countercyclical response to uncertain or tepid recovery and would consist of three main elements:

(a) Financial support for developing countries to prevent economic slowdown, to be provided through an inclusive multilateral system;

(b) Public investment packages in developed and developing countries aimed at reviving and greening national economies, to be put in place by national Governments;

(c) International policy coordination to ensure that the developed countries' spending packages would not only be effective in creating jobs in developed countries, but also generate strong developmental impacts in developing countries. This would involve collaborative initiatives of Governments in both developed and developing countries.

## Mobilizing international financing for development

Improving the international financial architecture is crucial for developing countries. Over the years and since its inception, the *World Economic and Social Survey* report has been concerned with the design of the international reserve system, and, in particular, with the role of the United States dollar as the major international currency. As early as 2005, the *Survey* had highlighted the potential interaction between the macroeconomic risks associated with the current global imbalances and the potential vulnerabilities generated by the financial "innovations" and forms of consolidation that were being carried out. This could generate, accentuate and prolong global imbalances which could in turn wind down in a disorderly manner.

As was noted in *World Economic and Social Survey 2008*, "the tendency to accumulate vast amounts of foreign currency reserves in developing countries ha[d] its roots in more fundamental deficiencies of the international monetary and reserve system" (p. 48). According to the 2005 *Survey*, this in effect generated "a redistribution of income from developing economies to the major industrialized countries, a large flow of so-called reverse aid" (p. 183). This could be rectified partly through establishment of a greater role for special drawing rights (SDRs), in providing both much-needed liquidity to deficit countries and a stable counterweight to the United States dollar. The issuance of more SDRs through a permanent allocation would not only "solve the problems of adequately financing needs for extraordinary and temporary official liquidity" but also deal simultaneously with "the distributive issues associated with uneven distribution of seigniorage powers" (ibid., p. 184).[16]

> The accumulation of foreign currency reserves by developing countries generates a large flow of reverse aid; a greater role for SDRs as the basis for a renewed global reserve system is therefore needed

Among the suggestions advanced by the 2005 *Survey*, there was one regarding countercyclical cross-border financing mechanisms. Thus, "multilateral development banks and export credit agencies could introduce explicit countercyclical elements in the risk evaluations they ma[d]e for issuing guarantees for lending to developing countries" (p. 94) or provide "special stand-alone guarantee mechanisms for long-term private credit that had a strong explicit countercyclical element" (ibid., p. 95). The 2006 *Survey* suggested the adoption of financial instruments that reduced currency mismatches and linked debt-service obligations to developing countries' capacity to pay, for instance, through gross domestic product (GDP)- or commodity-linked bonds (p. xv).

The *Survey* and *World Economic Situation and Prospects* have consistently argued that domestic savings are the key to increasing domestic investment, even in open economies. Successive *Survey* reports have emphasized that three challenges associated with the domestic financial system require particular attention in developing countries: "guaranteeing an adequate supply of long-term financing in the domestic currency; making financial services available to all groups of society; and developing an adequate system of prudential regulation and supervision that guarantees the stability of the financial system" (see, e.g., the 2005 *Survey*, p. 17).

Volatile international portfolio and banking flows can ultimately undermine sustainable development. Aligning investment with the SDGs, including the goals of building sustainable and resilient infrastructure, requires policies and regulatory frameworks that incentivize changes in investment patterns. This can be addressed through the financial governance architecture and supported through various policy mixes including

> International private flows can be volatile and ultimately undermine sustainable development

---

16    In fact, the *Survey* has been making this argument consistently for over four decades, i.e., since the late 1960s.

pricing externalities, effective regulatory frameworks, blended finance and guarantees, and leveraging private investment through public intermediaries, such as development banks.

**Encouraging long-term finance calls for a greater role of development banks**

Long-term finance tends to be scarce in developing countries, as creditors prefer to offer short-term financing so as to reduce risk. *Survey* reports have argued that development banks should be the vehicle for addressing some of the unmet demand for long-term financing. The experience with development banks, however, has been mixed. As pointed out in the 2005 *Survey*, successful banks "fostered the acquisition and dissemination of expertise in long-term industrial financing" with success being "less dependent on the quantity of credit they supplied" (p. 23). Another common action of successful banks was to set clear time limits on the preferential treatment provided to borrowers. Interest rate subsidies were seen to be less important for success and in some cases, even counterproductive. Recognizing problems of inefficiencies and lack of accountability in the management of many development banks, the *Survey* therefore argued that "the institutional design should avoid excessive public sector risks and badly targeted interest rate subsidies, and should incorporate a view of the activities of development banks as complementary to those of the private sector and, indeed, a view of the banks themselves as agents of innovation that should in the long run encourage rather than limit private sector financial development" (ibid., p. 24). The role of development banks has been explicitly recognized in the Addis Ababa Action Agenda adopted at the Third International Conference on Financing for Development, held in Addis Ababa from 13 to 16 July 2015.

The 2012 *Survey* recognized the need for innovative thinking on the subject of international financing for development. It confirmed the potential of a number of mechanisms, even as it noted that realizing that potential would require international agreement and the corresponding political will to tap sources, as well as the design of appropriate governance of uses and allocation mechanisms. Some of these sources include taxes levied on international transactions and/or taxes that are internationally concerted, such as the air-ticket solidarity levy, financial or currency transaction taxes and carbon taxes; and revenues from global resources, such as SDR allocations and proceeds derived from the extraction of resources from the global commons, through, for example, seabed mining in international waters. Significantly, it was argued that international reserve asset creation—with IMF issuing more SDRs—could sharply boost finance for development and global public goods provision.

## Expanding the benefits of trade

**A rules-based multilateral trading system remains a key mechanism for growth and development but...**

The assessments of preferential trade agreements often present the trade agenda as implicitly beneficial with respect to various issues, with the notable exception of those issues related to labour, State-owned enterprises and the investor-State dispute system. With the collapse of the Trans-Pacific Partnership in 2017, the most obvious question is whether, in the absence of a global agreement clearly linked to a development agenda, plurilateral agreements should be regarded as second-best alternatives, or as harmful distortions of the global system. Opaque negotiating procedures, in which corporate interests have free access while others are excluded, are a particular concern.

In retrospect, the continued focus on the Doha round, long after its prospects had faded, is perceived to have been an overly optimistic one and meant that plurilateral agreements like the Trans-Pacific Partnership, the Transatlantic Trade and Investment Partnership, and the Trade in Services Agreement received insufficient attention. Moreover, those agreements were viewed, in large measure, as second-best substitutes for Doha round outcomes rather than as embodying a radically different mode of international governance, largely divorced from traditional concerns about trade liberalization and focused on protecting the interests of multinational corporations.

Further progress towards revitalizing the Global Partnership for Sustainable Development (under Sustainable Development Goal 17) may be constrained by the apparent increase in many countries in the appeal of protectionism and inward-looking policies, reflecting in part growing discontent with the manner in which the costs incurred, and the benefits accruing, from deeper global economic integration have been distributed. While an open, rules-based multilateral trading system has generated substantial economic gains for many countries through improved efficiency in allocating resources worldwide, it has also been associated with widening income inequality, together with job losses and declining wages for workers in certain sectors and categories.

Greater concerted international efforts to improve global governance are therefore needed, along with more effective domestic redistribution policies, so as to ensure that the gains from global economic integration are inclusive. Trade adjustment policies—entailing, for example, training and job search assistance for workers directly impacted by trade liberalization—can also help to redress the imbalance. In the absence of such efforts, protectionist tendencies may escalate, which could prolong the slow growth in the world economy.

**...uneven benefits from trade have led to social discontent and protectionist risks**

## Strengthening national ownership, policy coherence and integration

One of the more enduring and relevant lessons to be derived from the *Survey* for application to the 2030 Agenda in general and SDG 17 in particular, is the importance of policy coherence and integration that is appropriate for each country's context. Progress in multiple dimensions of development requires policy interventions that are specific to each particular context and that are able to build on the synergies and the co-benefits generated through addressing social, economic and environmental issues simultaneously. Balanced achievement of the SDGs requires a macroeconomic policy that is fully integrated with structural reforms and policies that target, for example, poverty, inequality and climate change. Fiscal policy can be made more effective through identification of key areas (such as sustainable infrastructure, education and green technology) for targeted investment, which can serve to stimulate growth in the short term, promote social and environmental progress and, at the same time, support productivity growth in the medium term.

**Policy interventions must be relevant to the social, economic and political realities of each country**

In the 2008 *Survey*, it was noted that policies which lower disaster risk could both prevent natural hazards from turning into disasters and dramatically reduce the danger to lives and the eventual costs of natural disasters. With the publication of the 2013 *Survey* began the effort to synthesize all of these issues and distil an understanding of the fact that social, economic, environmental and vulnerability issues are fundamentally interconnected. The *Survey* noted the link between inequality and environmental degradation, a link which is in fact examined inadequately in the general discussion on both of these issues.

**Protecting lives and livelihoods from the effects of climate change is fundamental to a sustainable human development path**

The 2014/2015 *Survey* expanded the argument that coherent policies should make use of the interconnections both among various environmental goals themselves and among economic, environmental and human development goals in order to accelerate progress. The *Survey* identified six overarching lessons on how to achieve effective policy integration and coordination:

(a) A coherent and comprehensive policy framework which integrates economic, social and environmental interventions is critical to the minimization of trade-offs. Critical, also, is the need to identify positive synergies and trade-offs and to focus greater attention on policy consistency so as to facilitate the simultaneous attainment of multiple development objectives;

(b) Policies must be situated appropriately within the broader development policy framework of each country and so designed as to enable specific constraints to be overcome and positive synergies to be enhanced consistent with the context of each country;

(c) Careful consideration of starting conditions and constraints is important for determining which interventions and strategies can produce the best possible outcomes. When best practices are no longer producing sound improvements in outcomes, new practices and new solutions become necessary;

(d) If they are to be fully exploitable and effective, policies must integrate communities and be properly tailored to the needs of the poorest, the underserved and the most vulnerable populations, including those groups that have been traditionally overlooked such as indigenous people, people with disabilities and those living with HIV/AIDS;

(e) Improving the quantity and quality of human resources for the provision of social service delivery will be critical for the achievement of the SDGs. This will require efforts to retain effective civil servants, and an increase in investments in quality education;

(f) It is important that programmes be monitored and evaluated effectively so as to ensure policy coherence and efficacy, and adequate outreach to targeted populations. Such assessments should be supported by greater statistical capacity and data availability.

**Efforts to improve the conditions of the most vulnerable must focus on the inequalities that define and perpetuate vulnerability**

*World Economic and Social Survey 2016* further elaborated on the links among economic status, inequality and the environment and highlighted the particular vulnerability of the livelihoods of disadvantaged population groups to the effects of climate change (see figure V.5). Focusing on inequalities across multiple dimensions as part of processes that undermine resilience, the 2016 *Survey* argued that there was an underlying structural basis for the existence of those inequalities and that, often, policies fail to understand, let alone resolve, such deeper issues.

The 2016 *Survey* contended that greater resilience of lives and livelihoods to the effects of climate change is fundamentally a development objective and noted that, in addition to investment aimed at improving infrastructure resilience, traditional development interventions would go a long way towards building resilience among people and communities, including, for example, through more diversified and secure livelihoods and better access to health services. The *Survey* argued that development policy must consider the range of options for addressing long-term human development, strengthening the adaptive capacity of individuals, and confronting the immediate vulnerabilities that threaten lives and livelihoods.

**Without addressing underlying inequalities, interventions will have only a temporary impact**

The 2016 *Survey* also maintained that multidimensional and intersecting inequalities are fundamentally connected to the vulnerability to climate change and put forth the bold argument that without addressing the particular conditions that result in inequalities, development interventions will have only a temporary effect on the disadvantaged segments of the population. On the basis of this argument, one may assert that improving the

Figure V.5
**Human interface with the climate**

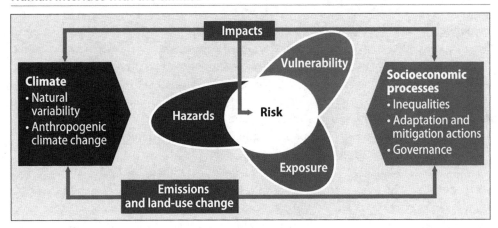

**Source:** *World Economic and Social Survey 2016*, based on Intergovernmental Panel on Climate Change (2014), p. 3.

resilience of livelihoods to the effects of climate change offers policymakers the opportunity to tackle the structural inequalities that result in vulnerability.

Through the approach they took, the 2009, 2014/2015 and 2016 *Surveys* were able to suggest ways in which confronting the challenge of climate change might be perceived as offering an opportunity to resolve long-standing development issues which are at the root of persistent inequality. Sadly, the political economy-related conditions at both global and national levels that would foster the adoption of a green new deal were not present when those reports were issued.

**Tackling climate change is an opportunity to address persistent inequality**

## Expanding opportunities and leaving no one behind

Ending poverty in all its forms in the current economic environment will require that countries tackle inequality issues more rigorously, which would include their commitments to sharing prosperity both within and across national borders. Policies aimed at reducing inequality, such as through investing in education, health and infrastructure, building stronger social safety nets, and mobilizing more inclusive financing, can play a crucial role. Reducing inequality may also have a positive feedback on growth, as a more equal distribution of wealth can lead to a more efficient allocation of resources and support aggregate demand.

**Eradicating poverty will require greater efforts to combat inequality**

The growing problem of inequality, particularly within countries, was recognized as a central issue for development well before it became the focus of international concern. The 2006 *Survey*, which was devoted entirely to the subject of the income divergence between countries, found that both external factors and domestic policies played important roles in determining the differences in growth performance among countries. The focus of part of this analysis was on domestic policies and processes, with the international community perceived as a facilitator of more conducive policies. Part of the observed growth divergence in laggard countries was attributed to gaps in public investment in, and spending on, infrastructure and human development.

In its 2005 edition entitled *The Inequality Predicament*, the *Report on the World Social Situation* (United Nations, 2005) traced trends and patterns in the economic and non-economic dimensions of inequality and examined their causes and consequences. The report focused on inequalities not only in income and wealth distribution, but also in the areas of health, education and opportunities for social and political participation. Analysed as well was how structural adjustment, market reforms, globalization and privatization affect economic and social indicators. *Report on the World Social Situation 2016* (United Nations, 2016), entitled *Leaving No One Behind: The Imperative of Inclusive Development*, examined how conditions of high inequalities and social exclusion will impact the commitment to a successful implementation of the 2030 Agenda for Sustainable Development and the key pledge of countries and stakeholders that "no one will be left behind" (preamble). The report demonstrates, in particular, that ethnicity, age, disability and migrant status affect access to opportunities, including health and education services, jobs, income and participation in political and civic life.

**Reducing inequality requires policies designed to foster economic growth and increase investment in human development and in economic, social and environmental infrastructure**

Reducing inequality requires policies designed to facilitate the easing of constraints on economic activity, the promotion of growth and increased spending on infrastructure and human development. The 2006 *Survey* argued that this can be achieved in many ways, and that several quite different forms of governance are compatible with more dynamic economic activity. The *Survey* also argued that accelerated economic growth does not always require immediate large-scale and comprehensive institutional reforms, as are often proposed in "big bang reform" packages. Incremental and relatively minor institutional changes can have profound results if there is a conviction that such changes are sustained. Additional spending on infrastructure and human development are essential as well to narrowing the gap between developed and developing countries. This requires establishing additional fiscal capacity through higher tax revenues, public-private partnerships, increased foreign aid, and other innovative financing mechanisms.

The 2008 *Survey* was entitled *Overcoming Economic Insecurity*. The issue of insecurity was a remarkably apt topic given the outbreak of the global financial crisis, which dramatically increased economic insecurity across the world. The *Survey* pointed out that through the use of average aggregates, countries could appear to be successful in terms of having assured higher per capita incomes, even when the majority of citizens did not experience rising standards of living (p. x). The combination of insecurity and inequality was seen as part of the downside of what some had described as "the new gilded age". Citing the domestic impact of various economic and other shocks upon food security, employment, livelihood, displacement and other forms of insecurity, the *Survey* argued that markets cannot be left to their own devices (ibid.).

Obviously, the nature and extent of regulation, mitigation, protection and relief depend on the kind of threats being faced and on capacities, resources and social choices at the local level. But the international community also has a role to play, one that so far has not been adequately recognized. In fact, it has become increasingly clear that global factors like trade-related treaties and the behaviour of global finance exert a huge effect on countries' performance, as was observed in the aftermath of the global financial crisis.

## Protecting livelihoods and building resilience

The significance of the natural environment and the challenges of, as well as the opportunities for, developing alternative greener strategies for development were discussed in several *Survey* reports, namely, the 2008, 2009, 2011, 2014/2015 and 2016 editions. The 2014/2015 *Survey* focused, in particular, on environmental sustainability, and in that regard, noted that despite some progress in particular indicators (such as the near elimination of ozone-depleting substances and the global increase in terrestrial and marine protected areas), concerns about environmental damage and ecological imbalances remained pressing (pp. xv-xvi).

The analysis in the 2014/2015 *Survey* consistently argued that switching to low-emissions, high-growth pathways in order to meet the development and climate challenge is necessary, since combating global warming requires eventual emissions reductions by developing countries too. Such a switch is feasible because technological solutions are available that can enable a shift in that direction. The concept of a green economy has emerged as a key underpinning of structural transformation; and progress has been made in understanding the possible pathways to achieving a more climate-friendly and efficient economy within the current global context and given different national conditions. The analysis noted the central role that would have to be played by Governments and the international community in both coordinating and financing these changes.

**Low-emissions, high-growth economic pathways are necessary for sustainable development**

Recent progress could easily be reversed without concerted efforts by both the private and public sectors to continue to improve energy efficiency and promote renewable energy, supported through international cooperation on clean technology transfer and climate finance. Any backtracking in energy and environmental policy may endanger the environmental targets under the SDGs and the Paris Agreement on climate change.

Combating economic insecurity caused by global crises, conflicts and environmental shocks is of paramount importance for preventing large reversals in the development gains of countries and for implementing a global development agenda. In the aftermath of the global financial crisis, it has become evident that policies devised to protect the most vulnerable from the effects of economic shocks are of continuing relevance. Three main reforms aimed at protecting the more vulnerable countries and populations from global economic shocks were identified:

**Insecurity arising from economic shocks, conflicts and environmental shocks threaten to undo hard-won development gains in many countries**

(a) Building a renewed Bretton Woods framework, which would provide an international financial and monetary system ensuring the application of countercyclical measures and financial regulation, as well as a healthy balance between wages and productivity growth;

(b) Revisiting Marshall Plan principles as applicable to the creation of a more effective aid architecture;

(c) Designing a global new deal, encompassing, in particular, mechanisms to enable expansion and better management of markets and redistributive measures in the face of shocks.

## Final considerations

Since 2007, it has been continuously demonstrated that global imbalances can, as in the past, destabilize even the largest economies despite the emergence of many agreements and institutions designed to manage the global economic and financial system. The global financial crisis reinforced the lesson that liberalized financial markets are not self-regulating and that globalized economic and financial systems create vulnerabilities for national and global economies. The premature return to tighter fiscal policies highlighted the limits of excessive dependence on monetary policy for stimulus; and the debt difficulties in Europe once again demonstrated that internal fiscal imbalances will lead to external crises having significant economic and social consequences.

The last ten years also offer a reminder that the causes of national and global crises are not new. As illustrated in previous chapters, instability of global capital and trade flows has, in many cases, led to economic and social difficulties, ranging from the collapse of the Bretton Woods system and the Latin American debt crisis of the 1980s to the most recent challenges. Global institutions can build on the collective global knowledge of this history and on the shared experience of recovering from turbulent times. Through this process, global institutions can find ways to be more effective in fulfilling their mission to ensure a stable global financial system, to mobilize financing for development, and to ensure a fair multilateral trading regime which allows countries space for building domestic production capacity and pursuing sustainable development goals.

A review of the critical reflections to be found in various publications of the Department of Economic and Social Affairs issued during the 2007-2016 period have yielded a variety of insights applicable to determining what is needed to achieve the goals under the 2030 Agenda within a context of slower global growth and narrow policy space. Lying at the core of those insights is a recognition of the need to prevent another unsustainable build-up of the global imbalances that inevitably leads to crisis. For emerging market economies, the accumulation of adequate—but not excessive—foreign reserves and increasingly overvalued flexible exchange rates require macroprudential measures carefully designed to prevent domestic instability. Financial reforms must be enacted to contain systemic risks and to counter an excessively rigid emphasis on limiting risk at the expense of financing development initiatives. For developing countries, volatility in capital flows justifies capital account regulations as a means of empowering monetary policies and improving private sector external debt profiles.

The above-mentioned suggestions are not new. Indeed, they were applied in several advanced economies in the 1960s and 1970s. However, their loss of importance in subsequent decades enabled the build-up of instability in the 2000s which culminated in the global financial crisis. The destructive potential of crises and instability that are exported across borders, particularly to small open economies and those exposed to global commodity markets, justifies recalling forgotten lessons, fostering innovative thinking and taking bold action to break the cycle of imbalances and turbulence.

There is a need for more effective macroeconomic mechanisms, geared towards such goals as balancing fiscal and monetary policy, providing appropriate support to both the financial and the non-financial sectors of affected economies, preventing premature removal of support, ensuring robust social safety nets and longer-term adjustment programmes for affected populations, also ensuring that developing countries are better represented and providing sufficient development assistance. In this regard, an open multilateral trading system is fundamental for continued growth and development. At the same time, it is critical to ensure that such a system results in positive development outcomes; and this requires policies designed to help those who are being left behind and those who are vulnerable to economic disruption, climate shocks or conflict. It is also critical that inequality be tackled head on, particularly within the context of globalization and technological progress, which are transforming the very essence of labour demand.

# Appendix

# A.1 Institutional history of the *World Economic and Social Survey*

## Historical overview

*The World Economic and Social Survey* (WESS) is the earliest post-Second World War recurrent publication mandated to record and analyse the performance of the global economy and social development trends and offer relevant policy recommendations. The *Survey* is issued annually pursuant to General Assembly resolution 118 (II) of 31 October 1947, in which the Assembly recommended to the Economic and Social Council:

"(a) That it consider a survey of current world economic conditions and trends annually, and at such other intervals as it considers necessary, in the light of its responsibility under Article 55 of the Charter of the United Nations to promote the solution of international economic problems, higher standards of living, full employment, and conditions of economic and social progress and development,

"(b) That such consideration include an analysis of the major dislocations of needs and supplies in the world economy,

"(c) That it make recommendations as to the appropriate measures to be taken by the General Assembly, the Members of the United Nations and the specialized agencies concerned."

Over time, the WESS underwent several changes in name and several transformations in format. The first *Survey* issued was called the *Economic Report*, with the following subtitle: *Salient Features of the World Economic Situation 1945-47*. That publication was launched at Lake Success, New York, in January 1948. In the preface, the Assistant Secretary-General in charge of Economic Affairs, economist David Owen, expressed his hope that in addition to fulfilling the mandate of the General Assembly, "it [would] also serve students of economics and the general public throughout the world" (p. iii). From 1949 to 1955, the publication was referred to as The *World Economic Report* (WER). In the foreword to *World Economic Report, 1948* (p. iii), it was noted that the *Survey* had assembled "a considerable volume of post-war economic data relating to all regions of the world, not hitherto available *within the compass of a single study*" (emphasis added) and that as added information had become available, it became possible "to give more extensive treatment to economic conditions in underdeveloped countries".

Starting with the 1955 report, issued in 1956, the *Survey* became known as the *World Economic Survey (WES)* and since 1994, it has borne its present title, *World Economic and Social Survey (WESS)*. The year 1999 marked the launching of a companion volume, *World Economic Situation and Prospects* (WESP) devoted to reporting on short-term economic estimates. The *Survey* has been prepared regularly by the Department of Economic and Social Affairs of the United Nations Secretariat (UN/DESA)—which has also undergone various reforms, including changes of name (see table A.1.1)—in collaboration with organizations of the United Nations system, although the nature and extent of the collaboration have changed over time as those organizations started to publish their own analytical reports.

Although the authors of the WESS were not acknowledged by name until 2007, some of the world's leading economists have in fact contributed to the various editions of the report (for capsule biographies of those renowned contributors, see appendix A.2). In the fact sheet entitled "The World Economic and Social Survey at sixty", it was revealed that the primary author of the 1948 *Report* had been the distinguished economist Michal Kalecki, whose teaching career included an appointment at the University of Cambridge. Hans Singer, a pioneer in the field of development economics, and one of three eminent economists to have joined the new Department of Economic Affairs of the United Nations in 1947, was, for several years, a leading member of the team responsible for preparing the report. Throughout its history, the *Survey* has benefited from the written inputs, advice and encouragement of major economists from the academia as well as economists working within other bodies of the United Nations system, including the World Bank, the International Monetary Fund, the United Nations Conference on Trade and Development (UNCTAD) and the regional commissions.

Between 1951 and 1958, the *Survey* included, in response to Economic and Social Council resolution 266 (X),[a] a companion volume, which reviewed economic conditions in Africa. Between 1951 and 1964, the Secretariat also produced a review of economic conditions in the Middle East as a supplement to the *Survey*. These volumes complemented the regional surveys prepared annually by the secretariats of the Economic Commission for Europe (ECE), the Economic and Social Commission for Asia and the Pacific (ESCAP) and the Economic Commission for Latin America and the Caribbean (ECLAC).[b]

Beginning with the 1953-54 edition, the *World Economic Report* included an examination of the longer-term problems of international trade, in addition to the analysis of contemporary economic conditions. As noted above, in 1956, starting with the 1955 edition, the report came to be known as the *World Economic Survey*. With the issuance of the 1956 *Survey*, in 1957, the report would go on to regularly include analyses of longer-term issues of general interest. This was in response to Economic and Social Council resolution 614 (XXII) D of 9 August 1956, in which the Council affirmed "the desirability of continuing to focus attention in future *Surveys* upon long-term problems of general interest". The *Survey's* insightful analyses of longer-term issues offer a comprehensive account of the changing paradigms in development economics; quite often, they have questioned the dominant paradigm and provided alternative perspectives.

As mentioned above, the year 1999 marked the launching by UN/DESA of the first issue of a separate report, *World Economic Situation and Prospects*, pursuant to the Secretary-General's programme for reform inaugurated in the late 1990s. This is a joint product of UN/DESA, UNCTAD and (beginning in 2005) the five regional commissions (ECA, ECE, ECLAC, ESCAP and ESCWA). WESP functioned as a year-end update of the *World Economic and Social Survey* until 2004. Over the period beginning in 2005, however, WESP has emerged as the lead publication focused on current economic trends and prospects. Utilizing the United Nations World Economic Forecasting Model,[c] it also provides forecasts and policy analysis. In recent years, chapter I of the WESP (on the global

---

a    In which the Economic and Social Council requested the Secretary-General "to include in the world economic report, to be prepared for the twelfth session of the Council, a special section relating to economic conditions in Africa, using material readily available and such further information as may be provided by the Governments concerned".

b    The Economic Commission for Africa (ECA) was established in 1958 and the Economic and Social Commission for Western Asia (ESCWA) in 1973.

c    The World Economic Forecasting Model, introduced in 2005, succeeded the LINK modelling system, which had been developed initially by the late Professor Lawrence R. Klein of the University of Pennsylvania. Dr. Klein had been the recipient of the 1980 Sveriges Riksbank Prize in Economic Sciences in Memory of Alfred Noble. The LINK system featured a modelling approach whereby individual country models were linked together through use of trade and other macroeconomic variables.

economic outlook) has been published in December of each year, while chapters II, III and IV which focus on trade, finance for development, and regional outlooks, respectively, are typically published in January of the same year.[d] As shorter-term economic forecasting and analysis are published in the WESP, the WESS has continued to focus on longer-term development issues.

Currently, the core responsibility for the preparation of the *World Economic and Social Survey* falls upon the staff of the Development Policy and Analysis Division (DPAD) within the Department of Economic and Social Affairs. The *Survey* has typically focused on the analysis of such longer-term development issues as poverty, climate change, ageing, economic insecurity, development finance, inequalities and international migration. The preparation of the *Survey*, which draws upon background papers written by external experts, thus provides an opportunity for contact between in-house experts at the United Nations and those working in the academia. The *Survey* team also includes researchers from other Divisions of DESA, who may provide background analysis and, depending on the focus of the *Survey* in any given year, contribute to the chapters addressing particular issues. The WESS team also seeks inputs from other United Nations organizations. However, the intensity of collaboration with the wider United Nations system has diminished over time, as the system expanded, and specialized United Nations entities began producing their own analytical reports.

It was the *Survey's* analysis that provided the foundation for the establishment of many specialized organizations of the United Nations and new Secretariat entities. For example, the 1962 and 1963 *Surveys* addressed broad issues of trade as an instrument for economic development of the developing countries and provided critical analytical inputs for discussion at the session of the Preparatory Committee for the United Nations Conference on Trade and Development, which later became a permanent United Nations organization (established in 1964). Similarly, the focus of the 1961 edition of the *Survey* was industrialization and economic development, and it laid the analytical groundwork for the establishment of the United Nations Industrial Development Organization (UNIDO) in 1966.

The body of knowledge built up through the development discussions provided in the *Survey* over the last seventy years constitutes an important point of reference for the implementation of strategies for sustainable development. While it is true that history does not repeat itself, past development challenges are in many ways similar to those of the present. By shedding light through its analysis on how these challenges were once dealt with and on the effectiveness of the policies adopted to confront them, the *Survey* has also shed light on the present—and the future. On the occasion of the sixtieth anniversary of the *Survey's* first appearance in print, the claim was made that the *Survey* had "fulfilled its mandate of surveying economic conditions, providing an analysis of the source of 'dislocations' and making appropriate recommendations". On the occasion of celebrating the seventieth anniversary of the *Survey*, the truth of that claim still holds.

---

d    The latest issue, WESP 2017, is an exception in this regard, as the whole report was published in January 2017.

Table A.1.1
**Main responsibilities in the preparation of WESS/WESP/WES/WER, 1945–2017**

| Department/division/unit | Reports/years |
|---|---|
| Department of Economic and Social Affairs (DESA)<br>Development Policy and Analysis Division (DPAD)<br>Development Strategy and Policy Unit (DSP) | WESS 2007, 2008, 2009, 2010, 2011, 2012, 2013, 2014/2015, 2016, 2017 |
| DESA<br>DPAD<br>Global Economic Monitoring Unit | WESP 2007, 2008, 2009, 2010, 2011, 2012, 2013, 2014, 2015, 2016, 2017 |
| DESA<br>Development Policy and Planning Office<br>Economic Monitoring and Assessment Unit | WESS 2004, 2005, 2006<br>WESP 2004, 2005, 2006 |
| DESA<br>DPAD<br>Development Perspectives Branch | WESS 2000, 2001, 2002, 2003 |
| DESA<br>DPAD<br>Economic Assessment and Outlook Branch | WESP 1999, 2000, 2001, 2002, 2003 |
| DESA<br>Development Policy Analysis Division<br>International Economic Relations Branch | WESS 1998, 1999 |
| Department of Economic and Social Information and Policy Analysis (DESIPA)<br>Macroeconomics Division<br>International Economic Relations Branch<br>Projections and Perspectives Studies Branch | WESS 1996, 1997 |
| DESIPA<br>Macroeconomic and Social Policy Analysis Division<br>Development Analysis Branch/International Economic Relations Branch/<br>Projections and Perspectives Studies Branch | WES 1993; WESS 1994, 1995 |
| Department of Economic and Social Development (DESD)<br>Development Policy and Analysis Division(DPAD) | WES 1992 |
| Department of International Economic and Social Affairs (DIESA)<br>General Analysis and Policies Division<br>Development Analysis Branch/International Economic Relations Branch | WES 1979–1980, 1980–1981, 1981–1982, 1983, 1984, 1985, 1986, 1987, 1988, 1989, 1990, 1991 |
| DIESA<br>Centre for Development Planning, Projections and Policies<br>Review and Appraisal Branch | WES 1977, 1978 |
| DESA<br>Centre for Development Planning, Projections and Policies<br>Review and Appraisal Branch | WES 1973, 1974, 1975, 1976 |
| DESA<br>Center for Development Planning, Projections and Policies | WES 1965, 1966, 1967, 1968, 1969–1970, 1971, 1972 |
| DESA<br>Bureau of General Economic Research and Policies<br>Current Analysis and Policies Branch | WES 1964 |
| DESA<br>Bureau of General Economic Research and Policies<br>Economic Development Branch | WES 1962, 1963 |
| DESA<br>Division of General Economic Research and Policies | WES 1959, 1960, 1961, |
| DESA<br>Bureau of Economic Affairs<br>Economic Survey Branch | WES 1955, 1956, 1957, 1958 |
| DESA<br>Bureau of Economic Affairs<br>Economic Survey Branch | WER 1953–1954 |
| Department of Economic Affairs<br>Division of Economic Stability and Development | Economic Report 1945–1947; WER 1948, 1949–1950, 1950–1951,1951–1952 |

Source: UN/DESA.

## A.2    Notable economists who have contributed to the *World Economic and Social Survey*[a]

Although the authors of the earlier issues of the *Survey* remain anonymous, some of the world's leading economists contributed to them. For example, it is known that the famous economist Michal Kalecki was the primary author of the 1948 report. Hans Singer, a pioneer of development economics and one of the three economists to join the new Economics Department of the United Nations in 1947, was a leading member of the team preparing the report for more than a decade. Throughout its history, the *Survey* also benefited from written inputs, advice and encouragement from major academic economists outside the United Nations system as well as economists working in other bodies within the system, including the World Bank, the International Monetary Fund, UNCTAD, and the regional commissions. A number of notable economists who have contributed to the *Survey* are listed below.

### Kenneth Arrow
### (1921–2017)

At the time of his retirement, Kenneth Arrow was the Joan Kenney Professor of Economics and Professor of Operations Research at Stanford University. His work focused primarily on economic theory and operations research, including social choice theory, risk bearing, medical economics, general equilibrium analysis, inventory theory, and the economics of information and innovation. Invited by Professor Lawrence Klein and the Development Policy and Analysis Division (DPAD) of the then Department of Economic and Social Development of the United Nations Secretariat to participate in the LINK project, Professor Arrow actively participated in its meetings in the 1990s as an expert and keynote speaker. In 1972, for his pioneering contributions to both general equilibrium theory and welfare theory, he shared the Nobel Memorial Prize in Economic Sciences with Sir John Hicks.

Professor Arrow served on the faculties of the University of Chicago and Harvard and Stanford Universities. Prior to that, he served as a weather officer in the United States Air Corps (1942-1946) and as a research associate at the Cowles Commission for Research in Economics (1947-1949). In addition to the Nobel Prize, he received the John Bates Clark Medal of the American Economic Association and the National Medal of Science and was a member of the National Academy of Sciences and the Institute of Medicine. He earned his Bachelor of Science degree from City College in New York and his MA and PhD degrees from Columbia University. In addition, he held approximately 20 honorary degrees.

---

[a]    The *Survey* has taken on several names throughout its history. In 1948, it was called the *Economic Report*; from 1949 to 1955, the *World Economic Report*; and from 1956 to 1993, the *World Economic Survey*. Since 1994, it has borne its present title, *World Economic and Social Survey*. The year 1999 witnessed the launch of a companion volume, entitled *World Economic Situation and Prospects*, which reports on short-term economic estimates. The term *Survey* as used here may refer to a publication bearing any of these titles.

# Michał Kalecki
## (1899–1970)

Michał Kalecki was largely self-taught and his theoretical and policy contributions to the field of economics were based on actual observation of economic life and on extensive use of data. Kalecki's work at the Institute for Research on Business Cycles and Prices in Warsaw led to a deepening of his knowledge of economics and the publication in 1933 of a major work, *Essay on the Business Cycle Theory*, which anticipated the theories of John Maynard Keynes. This study portrayed a developed capitalist economy as a demand-determined system where, in the absence of government intervention, involuntary unemployment would be a likely outcome. At the end of the Second World War, Kalecki worked for a period of time at the International Labour Office in Montreal and subsequently in Geneva.

Kalecki was a member of the Department of Economic Affairs of the United Nations Secretariat in New York from 1947 to 1954, as Assistant Director of the Division of Economic Stability and Development, where he was responsible for the creation and publication of the annual *World Economic Report*. Here he studied the post-war world economy and provided advice to various Governments, including those of Israel (1950) and Mexico (1953). This international exposure bolstered his later interests, in particular in the necessity of using economic analyses to better understand patterns in underdeveloped countries. Profoundly disheartened by the intellectual intolerance that he witnessed during the McCarthyist period in the United States of America, he resigned from his position in New York at the end of 1954 and in 1955, returned to Poland, although he did continue to provide policy advice to newly formed United Nations organizations such as the United Nations Conference on Trade and Development and the Food and Agriculture Organization of the United Nations.

Kalecki was invited for relatively long stays in India (1960) and Cuba (1960), where he advised their Governments on issues related to development planning and financing for development. Frequent travel to Latin America, especially Mexico, exposed him to the development challenges experienced by different countries.

Kalecki's contributions were always grounded in relevant stylized facts, and he sought to examine issues within the context of an  entire economy and society, including the underlying political process This highlights an important feature of his analysis, entailing the fundamental conviction that economics is ultimately about politics and that any analysis of an economy seeking to abstract from the sociopolitical determinants and implications of economic phenomena would be not only inadequate but wrong. His essays attested, in particular, to a broad concern for the distributive implications of economic strategies.

# Lawrence R. Klein
## (1920–2013)

Professor Klein was awarded the Nobel Memorial Prize in Economic Sciences in 1980 for his work in the Department of Economics at the University of Pennsylvania in creating computer models, to forecast economic trends.

Project LINK, Klein's major initiative, was created at Stanford University in 1968. The project integrates the economic models of different countries within a total system in order to improve the understanding of international economic linkages and economic forecasts. Further, LINK economic projections are used in the policy analysis and forecasts produced by *World Economic Situation and Prospects*. The project went on to become an international cooperative venture, with the central coordinating facility and software located at the University of Pennsylvania.

Project LINK, which continues to encompass new countries, new economic processes and a longer time horizon, has generated a significant amount of related incremental research by enabling countries to initiate econometric model building projects, by extending "best practice" research to various centres and by demonstrating to official international bodies how to establish interrelationships among different parts of the world economy. Ongoing research activities and biannual meetings of Project LINK, which has become an important research forum for model builders from many countries, have been conducted on an enlarged scale at the United Nations and the University of Toronto.

In the last years of his life, Klein's research efforts were focused on bringing new participants into the LINK Project, introducing modern econometrics in China and expanding the activities of the Wharton Econometric Forecasting Associates, an organization for which he served as a professional consultant.

## José Antonio Ocampo
### (born 1952)

José Antonio Ocampo is an eminent Colombian economist. Since July 2007, he has been Professor of Professional Practice in International and Public Affairs and Director of the Economic and Political Development Concentration at the School of International and Public Affairs, Columbia University. Most recently, in 2017, Dr. Ocampo was appointed to the board of the Central Bank of Colombia.

From 1989 to 1997, he held several high-level posts within the Government of Colombia, including as Minister of Finance and Public Credit and, in that capacity, as Chair of the Board of the Central Bank; Director of the National Planning Department; and Minister of Agriculture and Rural Development.

Dr. Ocampo served in a number of positions in the United Nations, most notably as Executive Secretary of the Economic Commission for Latin America and the Caribbean, from 1998 to 2003. He served in 2003-2007 as Under-Secretary-General for Economic and Social Affairs. In that capacity, he chaired the Executive Committee on Economic and Social Affairs and headed the Department of Economic and Social Affairs of the Secretariat, which produces a wide range of research and analytical outputs on development issues, leads the follow-up to the major United Nations summits and conferences, and provides substantive and organizational support to the General Assembly and the Economic and Social Council. During his tenure at the Department of Economic and Social Affairs, Dr. Ocampo headed the teams responsible for the preparation of the *World Economic and Social Survey* and *World Economic and Social Prospects*, to which he was also a contributing author.

In 2008, Professor Ocampo was awarded the Leontief Prize for Advancing the Frontiers of Economic Thought, bestowed by the Global Development and Environment Institute at Tufts University in memory of Wassily Leontief (winner of the Nobel Memorial Prize in Economic Sciences, 1973). From 2008 to 2010, he was the co-director of the United Nations Development Programme/Organization of American States project entitled "Agenda for a Citizens' Democracy in Latin America", and in 2009, he was a member of the Commission of Experts of the President of the United Nations General Assembly on Reforms of the International Monetary and Financial System.

## Göran Ohlin
## (1926–1996)

Göran Ohlin was a Swedish economic historian of great distinction. In the early 1960s, Ohlin was a professor at the Wenner-Gren Centre, Institute for International Economic Studies, University of Stockholm. From 1967 to 1969, he was a member of the staff of the Pearson Commission on International Development and in the 1980s, became the secretary of its successor, the Brandt Commission, chaired by Willy Brandt.

Ohlin served as Assistant Secretary-General of the United Nations during 1986-1991 at the Office for Development Research and Policy Analysis of the Department of International Economic and Social Affairs, currently the Department of Economic and Social Affairs. He actively participated in the discussions on debt renegotiation for developing countries, advocating for an orderly debt rollover, with attention to be paid to specific situations and case-by-case solutions. Ohlin also supported a major increase both of special drawing rights by the International Monetary Fund and of lending by the World Bank as a means of improving global liquidity. In his capacity as Assistant Secretary-General, he exercised leadership and offered substantive advice related to the production and publication of the *World Economic Survey*.

## Hans Singer
## (1910–2006)

Before Hans Singer joined the United Nations in 1947, at age 37, he had already been well established in the academic world of the United Kingdom of Great Britain and Northern Ireland, having held positions in the faculty of economics at the universities of Manchester and Glasgow and engaged in a range of diverse research activities. Along with David Owen, who became the first head of the Department of Economic Affairs of the United Nations Secretariat in New York, and Walter Oakeshott, Singer engaged in a study of the painful, harsh reality of unemployment in five different cities within the United Kingdom. Living with poor families, he witnessed first-hand the psychological, moral and physical impacts of their situation.

During his 22-year career with the United Nations, Singer worked in the Department of Economic Affairs . He helped lay the foundations for the United Nations Development Programme through his work on the Special Fund and the Expanded Programme of Technical Assistance; undertook assignments for the United Nations Children's Fund; provided the intellectual rationale for the establishment of the World Food Programme; and participated in the work of the Economic Commission for Africa, the African Development Bank, the United Nations Conference on Trade and Development, the United Nations Research Institute for Social Development, and the United Nations Industrial Development Organization.

When Singer joined the Department of Economic Affairs of the United Nations Secretariat in New York as Special Adviser within the Bureau of Economic Affairs (a post he held over the period 1955-1965), he was soon engaged in analysing the terms of trade between developing and developed countries and in advising on and contributing to several editions of the *World Economic Survey*. Singer and Raúl Prebisch of the Economic Commission for Latin America and the Caribbean formulated the Prebisch-Singer thesis—which explained the consequences of the tendency, under capitalism, towards global inequality—and drew conclusions from their work for international policy. Aspects of Singer's thinking—e.g., on food aid, social development, industrial strategy and elements of development strategy—have become embodied within the framework of institutions (the World Food Programme, the United Nations Research Institute for Social Development, the United Nations Industrial Development Organization and the United Nations Development Programme, among others). Indeed, the conceptualizations of trade and technology, as set out in the Prebisch-Singer hypothesis, remain a driving force behind the work of the United Nations Conference on Trade and Development. At a memorial for Singer, former United Nations Secretary-General Kofi Annan referred to him as "a true pioneer and titan in the world of development economics"—one "whose guiding hand is felt to this day in several United Nations entities—from the Secretariat to the United Nations Children's Fund and the World Food Programme".

## Jomo Kwame Sundaram
## (born 1952)

Jomo Kwame Sundaram holds the Tun Hussein Onn Chair in International Studies at the Institute of Strategic and International Studies, Malaysia, and is Visiting Senior Fellow at the Khazanah Research Institute, Visiting Fellow at the Initiative for Policy Dialogue, Columbia University, and Adjunct Professor at the International Islamic University, Malaysia.

During the period 2005-2012, Dr. Sundaram served as Assistant Secretary-General for Economic Development in the Department of Economic and Social Affairs of the Secretariat, providing overall guidance related to the *World Economic and Social Survey* and *World Economic Situation and Prospects*. He was appointed Assistant Director-General and Coordinator for Economic and Social Development at the Food and Agriculture Organization of the United Nations during 2012-2015.

Jomo was the Research Coordinator for the Intergovernmental Group of Twenty-four on International Monetary Affairs and Development during 2006-2012. During 2008-2009, he served as adviser to Miguel d'Escoto Brockmann, President of the sixty-third session of the United Nations General Assembly, and as a member of the Commission of Experts of the President of the United Nations General Assembly on Reforms of the International Monetary and Financial System (Stiglitz Commission).

Jomo is a leading scholar and expert on the political economy of development, especially in South-East Asia, and has authored or edited over 100 books and translated 12 volumes, in addition to having written many academic papers and articles for the media. He was the founder chair of International Development Economics Associates (IDEAs); was a member of the Board of the United Nations Research Institute for Social Development; and has received several honours and awards for his work, including the 2007 Leontief Prize for Advancing the Frontiers of Economic Thought.

Before joining the United Nations, Jomo was already recognized as an outspoken intellectual, with unorthodox, non-partisan views. Before the Asian financial crisis in 1997-1998, Jomo had early on been an advocate of appropriate new capital account management measures, which were later introduced by the Prime Minister of Malaysia, Mahathir Mohamad.

**A.3 A synthesis of the key visions, objectives, goals and areas for global partnership as set forth in the International Development Strategies for the United Nations Development Decades, the United Nations Millennium Declaration and the 2030 Agenda for Sustainable Development**

| United Nations Development Decades/United Nations Millennium Declaration/2030 Agenda for Sustainable Development | Key visions | Selected objectives/goals | Selected areas for global partnership |
| --- | --- | --- | --- |
| United Nations Development Decade: a programme for international economic cooperation (I)<br><br>**First United Nations Development Decade (December 1961–December 1970)**<br><br>Resolution 1710 (XVI) adopted by the General Assembly | • "[P]romote social progress and better standards of life in larger freedom" and "employ international machinery for the advancement of the economic and social development of all peoples"<br>• Intensify "efforts to mobilize and to sustain support for the measures required on the part of both developed and developing countries to accelerate progress towards self-sustaining growth of the economy of the individual nations and their social achievement" | **Growth-oriented objectives/goals**<br>• For developing countries as a whole, a minimum annual economic growth of 5 per cent in 1970<br>• Promote economic development in developing countries through industrialization, diversification and highly productive agriculture<br>• Increase exports from developing countries at stable and remunerative prices, and ensure that developing countries obtain an equitable share of earnings from the extraction and marketing of their natural resources<br><br>**Objectives/goals more directly linked to other dimensions of development**<br>• Accelerate the elimination of illiteracy, hunger and disease in developing countries<br>• Further promote education and vocational and technical training in developing countries | **International economic and development cooperation**<br>• Increase the flow of public and private development resources, including investment capital, to developing countries on mutually acceptable terms<br>• Improve the use of international institutions and instrumentalities for furthering economic and social development<br>• Provide international assistance, where appropriate, in education and vocational and technical training<br>• Assist developing countries in establishing integrated country plans–including, where appropriate, land reform–for self-sustained growth |
| International Development Strategy for the<br><br>**Second United Nations Development Decade (January 1971–December 1980)**<br><br>Resolution 2626 (XXV) adopted by the General Assembly | "[Create] a more just and rational world economic and social order in which equality of opportunities should be as much a prerogative of nations as of individuals within a nation" | **Growth-oriented objectives/goals**<br>• For developing countries as a whole, average annual growth of GDP of at least 6 per cent and average annual growth of GDP per capita of about 3.5 per cent (assuming an average annual increase of 2.5 per cent in population)<br>• Average annual growth of 4 per cent in agricultural output and of 8 per cent in manufacturing output in developing countries<br>• Average annual growth of 0.5 per cent in the ratio of gross domestic saving to GDP, so that this ratio rises to about 20 per cent by 1980 in developing countries<br>• Average annual growth of about 7 per cent in imports and exports in developing countries | **International economic and monetary cooperation**<br>• Reduce and eliminate tariff and non-tariff barriers against exports from developing countries, and support their efforts in economic diversification, and expansion of production and exports of manufactured and semi-manufactured goods<br>• Conclude international arrangements on commodities<br>• Stimulate and make effective use of foreign private capital, in line with national development objectives<br>• Consider the possibility of establishing a link between special drawing rights allocation and provision of additional development finance for developing countries |

A.3    A synthesis of the key visions, objectives, goals and areas for global partnership as set forth in the International Development Strategies for the United Nations Development Decades, the United Nations Millennium Declaration and the 2030 Agenda for Sustainable Development *(continued)*

| United Nations Development Decades/United Nations Millennium Declaration/2030 Agenda for Sustainable Development | Key visions | Selected objectives/goals | Selected areas for global partnership |
|---|---|---|---|
| *(continued)*<br><br>International Development Strategy for the<br><br>**Second United Nations Development Decade (January 1971–December 1980)**<br><br>Resolution 2626 (XXV) adopted by the General Assembly | | *(continued)*<br><br>**Objectives/goals more directly linked to other dimensions of development**<br>• Achieve more equitable distribution of income and wealth for social justice and efficiency of production; reduce regional, sectoral and social disparities<br>• Foster well-being of children, and ensure full participation of youth and full integration of women in development<br>• Increase share of the working population in modern-type activities and significantly reduce unemployment and underemployment in developing countries<br>• Achieve enrolment of all children of primary school age, improve education quality at all levels and substantially reduce illiteracy<br>• Formulate a coherent national health programme for preventing and treating diseases, and for raising general levels of health and sanitation<br>• Improve levels of nutrition<br>• Expand and improve housing facilities<br>• Safeguard the environment | *(continued)*<br><br>**International development cooperation**<br>• Provide international support to developing countries in accessing technology, diversifying production, securing adequate food supplies and expanding infrastructure<br>• Assist in extending and improving education systems in developing countries<br>• Pursue international cooperation on health planning and establishment of health institutions in developing countries<br>• Provide international assistance in respect of strengthening planning mechanisms, including statistical services, for formulating and implementing national development plans<br>• Provide special assistance to least developed countries and landlocked developing countries<br><br>**International development assistance and external debt management**<br>• By 1972, and no later than 1975, advanced countries should transfer financial resources of a minimum net amount of 1 per cent of GNP to developing countries; ODA to developing countries should reach a minimum of 0.7 per cent of GNP of developed countries by 1975<br>• Pursue simplified, effective, untied and expeditious disbursement of ODA<br>• Provide international assistance – including rescheduling and refinancing of existing debts, on appropriate terms and conditions – in preventing debt crises |
| International Development Strategy for the<br><br>**Third United Nations Development Decade (January 1981–December 1990)**<br><br>Resolution 35/56 adopted by the General Assembly | "[E]stablish a new international economic order based on justice and equity" | **Growth-oriented objectives/goals**<br>• For developing countries as a whole, average annual growth of GDP of 7 per cent and average annual growth of GDP per capita of 4 per cent (assuming an average annual rate of growth of population of 2.5 per cent) | **International economic and monetary cooperation**<br>• Increase the responsiveness of the international monetary system to the needs and interests of the developing countries<br>• Provide assistance to countries, particularly developing countries, with respect to structural imbalance in their external accounts and consequent balance-of-payments difficulties |

**A.3    A synthesis of the key visions, objectives, goals and areas for global partnership as set forth in the International Development Strategies for the United Nations Development Decades, the United Nations Millennium Declaration and the 2030 Agenda for Sustainable Development** (*continued*)

| United Nations Development Decades/United Nations Millennium Declaration/2030 Agenda for Sustainable Development | Key visions | Selected objectives/goals | Selected areas for global partnership |
|---|---|---|---|
| (*continued*)<br><br>International Development Strategy for the<br><br>**Third United Nations Development Decade (January 1981–December 1990)**<br><br>Resolution 35/56 adopted by the General Assembly | | (*continued*)<br>• Average annual growth of at least 4 per cent in agricultural production and of at least 9 per cent in manufacturing production in developing countries<br>• Gross investment and gross domestic saving reach 28 per cent and 24 per cent of GDP, respectively, by 1990 in developing countries<br>• Average annual growth of exports and imports of goods and services of at least 7.5 per cent and 8 per cent, respectively, in developing countries<br>• Substantially reduce inflation so as to help ensure sustained growth<br>• Expand physical and institutional infrastructure in developing countries at rates that fully support the rate of economic growth<br><br>**Objectives/goals more directly linked to other dimensions of development**<br>• Reduce and eliminate poverty and ensure fair distribution of developmental benefits by the entire population in all stages of the development process<br>• Increase the opportunities for productive employment<br>• Improve living conditions of children and eliminate child labour in conformity with the relevant international labour conventions<br>• Provide universal education on the broadest possible scale, and eradicate or considerably reduce illiteracy<br>• Eliminate hunger and malnutrition | (*continued*)<br>• Facilitate and promote developing countries' production and exports of manufactured and semi-manufactured goods<br>• Reduce or eliminate restrictions on imports from developing countries; progressively reduce or abolish non-tariff barriers<br>• Prevent, with a view to eliminating, negative effects of activities of transnational corporations and promote their positive contributions to development in developing countries<br>• Encourage mutually beneficial foreign direct investment and other sources of private capital<br>• Develop special drawing rights as the principal reserve asset of the international monetary system and establish its link with development assistance<br><br>**International development cooperation**<br>• Enhance international cooperation in support of measures on reducing poverty, promoting employment opportunities and providing the right to work through enhanced growth and measures to ensure a fair distribution of the benefits of development and institutional reforms<br>• Develop human resources in developing countries, including through international assistance in the areas of extension services and teacher training<br>• Give or facilitate, as appropriate, the freest and fullest possible access of developing countries to all energy technologies<br>• Pay special attention to pressing problems of least developing countries, landlocked developing countries and developing island countries<br><br>**International development assistance and external debt management**<br>• ODA of developed countries should reach or surpass 0.7 per cent of GNP by 1985 and certainly no later than in the second half of the Decade; the target of 1 per cent should be reached as soon as possible thereafter |

**A.3    A synthesis of the key visions, objectives, goals and areas for global partnership as set forth in the International Development Strategies for the United Nations Development Decades, the United Nations Millennium Declaration and the 2030 Agenda for Sustainable Development** *(continued)*

| United Nations Development Decades/United Nations Millennium Declaration/2030 Agenda for Sustainable Development | Key visions | Selected objectives/goals | Selected areas for global partnership |
|---|---|---|---|
| *(continued)*<br><br>International Development Strategy for the<br><br>**Third United Nations Development Decade (January 1981–December 1990)**<br><br>Resolution 35/56 adopted by the General Assembly | | *(continued)*<br>• Broaden the access of the poorest groups of their populations to health facilities and ensure immunization against major infectious diseases for all children<br>• Make safe water and adequate sanitary facilities available to all by 1990<br>• Reduce infant mortality to less than 120 per 1,000 live births in the poorest countries<br>• Provide basic shelter and infrastructure to all people<br>• Enhance developing countries' capacity to improve their environment, avert environmental degradation and give future generations the benefit of a sound environment; prevent deforestation, erosion, soil degradation and desertification<br>• Encourage rational development, management and utilization of natural resources<br>• Intensify efforts towards the development and expansion of the world's energy resources in the context of a search for a long-term solution to the energy problem, with increasing reliance on new and renewable sources of energy | *(continued)*<br>• Equitable efforts to be made by donor countries in order to double the flow of ODA to the least developed countries<br>• Substantially increase concessional and non-concessional financial flows to developing countries<br>• Develop new ways and forms of lending compatible with the development priorities and longer-term debt-servicing capacity of developing countries |
| International Development Strategy for the<br><br>**Fourth United Nations Development Decade (January 1991–December 2000)**<br><br>Resolution 45/199 adopted by the General Assembly | Release "the great potential for development that exists in the developing countries and in the world economy"<br><br>"[R]everse the adverse trends of the 1980s, address the challenges of the 1990s and move into a more productive decade" | **Growth-oriented objectives/goals**<br>• A surge in the pace of economic growth in the developing countries; a growth rate of 7 per cent would provide conditions for economic transformation, an increase in productive employment, poverty eradication and environmental protection<br>• Accelerate the process of industrialization; rate of industrialization in many developing countries should grow at the rate of 8-10 per cent annually | **International economic and monetary cooperation**<br>• Change the framework of international economic relations to ensure equitable, full and effective participation of developing countries in the formulation and application of all decisions in the field of international economic cooperation for development<br>• Reform the international monetary system to improve its responsiveness to the needs and interests of the developing countries |

**A.3 A synthesis of the key visions, objectives, goals and areas for global partnership as set forth in the International Development Strategies for the United Nations Development Decades, the United Nations Millennium Declaration and the 2030 Agenda for Sustainable Development** (*continued*)

| United Nations Development Decades/United Nations Millennium Declaration/2030 Agenda for Sustainable Development | Key visions | Selected objectives/goals | Selected areas for global partnership |
|---|---|---|---|
| (*continued*)<br><br>International Development Strategy for the<br><br>**Fourth United Nations Development Decade (January 1991–December 2000)**<br><br>Resolution 45/199 adopted by the General Assembly | | (*continued*)<br>• Raise agricultural output and strengthen food security and self-reliance in food; food production should grow at the rate of 4 per cent on average annually<br>• Increase domestic savings and investments, and improve return to investments<br>• Foster setting of sound macroeconomic management, nationally and internationally<br>• Contain inflation so as to prevent its adverse economic and social consequences<br>• Improve and modernize infrastructure in areas such as communications and transport, power, and banking and finance, which are crucial for industrialization<br><br>**Objectives/goals more directly linked to other dimensions of development**<br>• Pursue a development process that is responsive to social needs, seeks a significant reduction in extreme poverty, promotes the development and utilization of human resources and skills, and is environmentally sound and sustainable<br>• Eradicate poverty by ensuring that economic progress is distributed as widely as possible<br>• Enhance participation of men and women in economic and political life, and protect cultural identities<br>• Eradicate illiteracy and build a sound base of primary and secondary education<br>• Develop an institutional base for vocational training<br>• Eliminate starvation and death caused by famine; substantially reduce malnutrition and mortality among children; considerably reduce chronic hunger; and eliminate major nutritional diseases | (*continued*)<br>• Establish conditions of openness and fairness within the international trading system, in the interest of all countries<br>• Reduce and remove tariff and non-tariff barriers<br>• Improve developing countries' access to markets for export products, and promote further structural adjustment policies in industrialized countries in view of shifting comparative advantages<br>• Encourage foreign direct investment that furthers mutual interests<br><br>**International development cooperation**<br>• Provide international assistance for poverty eradication and achieving other broad humanitarian and social goals<br>• Promote international cooperation among developing countries on human resources development<br>• Make substantial and rapid progress in transitioning from the hydrocarbon-based international economy<br>• Examine effective modalities for favourable access to, and transfer of, environmentally sound technologies, in particular to developing countries<br>• Pay attention to the special situations of the least developed countries, landlocked developing countries and developing island countries<br><br>**International development assistance and external debt management**<br>• Increase substantially concessional and non-concessional flows to developing countries<br>• Developed countries should reach or surpass the ODA target of 0.7 per cent of GNP, and improve the quality and utilization of aid<br>• All parties involved jointly produce a durable, broad and growth-oriented solution to the problems of external indebtedness; creditor countries should continue reviewing their tax policies and regulatory practices to facilitate commercial debt and debt-service reduction operations |

**A.3** A synthesis of the key visions, objectives, goals and areas for global partnership as set forth in the International Development Strategies for the United Nations Development Decades, the United Nations Millennium Declaration and the 2030 Agenda for Sustainable Development *(continued)*

| United Nations Development Decades/United Nations Millennium Declaration/2030 Agenda for Sustainable Development | Key visions | Selected objectives/goals | Selected areas for global partnership |
|---|---|---|---|
| | | • Give special attention to primary health care and the prevention of chronic diseases, as well as to general development objectives such as sanitation, safe drinking water and nutrition<br>• All countries take effective action for the protection and enhancement of the environment in accordance with their respective capacities and responsibilities, with particular consideration to the specific needs of developing countries | |
| **United Nations Millennium Declaration (September 2000– December 2015)**<br><br>Resolution 55/2 adopted by the General Assembly | "[U]phold the principles of human dignity, equality and equity at the global level"<br><br>"[E]stablish a just and lasting peace all over the world in accordance with the purposes and principles of the Charter [of the United Nations]"<br><br>"[E]nsure that globalization becomes a positive force for all the world's people" | • Eradicate extreme poverty and hunger<br>• Achieve universal primary education<br>• Promote gender equality and empower women<br>• Reduce child mortality<br>• Improve maternal health<br>• Combat HIV/AIDS, malaria and other diseases<br>• Ensure environmental sustainability<br>• Promote a global partnership for development | **International economic and monetary cooperation**<br>• Develop further an open, rules-based, predictable, non-discriminatory trading and financial system<br><br>**International development cooperation**<br>• In cooperation with developing countries, develop strategies for decent and productive work for youth<br>• Address special needs of least developed countries, landlocked developing countries and small island developing States<br>• Provide access to affordable essential drugs in developing countries, in cooperation with pharmaceutical companies<br>• Make available the benefits of new technologies, especially in information and communications, in cooperation with the private sector<br><br>**International development assistance and external debt management**<br>• Deal comprehensively with debt problems of developing countries<br>• Increase ODA from developed countries |

**A.3**    A synthesis of the key visions, objectives, goals and areas for global partnership as set forth in the International Development Strategies for the United Nations Development Decades, the United Nations Millennium Declaration and the 2030 Agenda for Sustainable Development *(continued)*

| United Nations Development Decades/United Nations Millennium Declaration/2030 Agenda for Sustainable Development | Key visions | Selected objectives/goals | Selected areas for global partnership |
|---|---|---|---|
| **2030 Agenda for Sustainable Development (September 2015– December2030)**<br><br>Resolution 70/1adopted by the General Assembly | • A world free of poverty, hunger, disease and want, where all life can thrive<br>• A world free of fear and violence<br>• A world of universal respect for human rights and human dignity, the rule of law, justice, equality and non-discrimination; of respect for race, ethnicity and cultural diversity; and of equal opportunity permitting the full realization of human potential and contributing to shared prosperity<br>• A world in which every country enjoys sustained, inclusive and sustainable economic growth and decent work for all | **Growth-oriented goals**<br>• Promote sustained, inclusive and sustainable economic growth, full and productive employment and decent work for all<br>• Build resilient infrastructure, promote inclusive and sustainable industrialization and foster innovation<br><br>**Goals more directly linked to other dimensions of development**<br>• End poverty in all its forms everywhere<br>• End hunger, achieve food security and improved nutrition and promote sustainable agriculture<br>• Ensure healthy lives and promote well-being for all at all ages<br>• Ensure inclusive and equitable quality education and promote lifelong learning opportunities for all<br>• Achieve gender equality and empower all women and girls<br>• Ensure availability and sustainable management of water and sanitation for all<br>• Ensure access to affordable, reliable, sustainable and modern energy for all<br>• Reduce inequality within and among countries<br>• Make cities and human settlements inclusive, safe, resilient and sustainable<br>• Ensure sustainable consumption and production patterns<br>• Take urgent action to combat climate change and its impacts<br>• Conserve and sustainably use the oceans, seas and marine resources for sustainable development | **International economic and monetary cooperation**<br>• Enhance global macroeconomic stability, including through policy coordination and policy coherence<br>• Promote a universal, rules-based, open, non-discriminatory and equitable multilateral trading system under the World Trade Organization, including through the conclusion of negotiations under the Doha Development Agenda<br>• Significantly increase the exports of developing countries, in particular with a view to doubling the least developed countries' share of global exports by 2020<br>• Improve the regulation and monitoring of global financial markets and institutions and strengthen the implementation of such regulations<br>• Ensure enhanced representation and voice for developing countries in decision-making in global international economic and financial institutions in order to deliver more effective, credible, accountable and legitimate institutions<br><br>**International development cooperation**<br>• Strengthen domestic resource mobilization through international support to developing countries<br>• Enhance North-South, South-South and triangular regional and international cooperation on and access to science, technology and innovation and enhance knowledge sharing on mutually agreed terms<br>• Enhance international support for implementing effective and targeted capacity-building in developing countries to support national plans to implement the Sustainable Development Goals<br>• By 2020, enhance capacity-building support to developing countries to increase significantly the availability of high-quality, timely and reliable data, disaggregated by characteristics relevant in national contexts |

**A.3    A synthesis of the key visions, objectives, goals and areas for global partnership as set forth in the International Development Strategies for the United Nations Development Decades, the United Nations Millennium Declaration and the 2030 Agenda for Sustainable Development** *(continued)*

| United Nations Development Decades/United Nations Millennium Declaration/2030 Agenda for Sustainable Development | Key visions | Selected objectives/goals | Selected areas for global partnership |
|---|---|---|---|
| *(continued)*<br>**2030 Agenda for Sustainable Development (September 2015– December 2030)**<br><br>Resolution 70/1 adopted by the General Assembly | | *(continued)*<br>• Protect, restore and promote sustainable use of terrestrial ecosystems, sustainably manage forests, combat desertification, and halt and reverse land degradation and halt biodiversity loss<br>• Promote peaceful and inclusive societies for sustainable development, provide access to justice for all and build effective, accountable and inclusive institutions at all levels<br>• Strengthen the means of implementation and revitalize the Global Partnership for Sustainable Development | *(continued)*<br>**International development assistance and external debt management**<br>• Fully implement developed countries' ODA commitments, including the commitment to achieve the target of 0.7 per cent of gross national income for official development assistance (ODA/GNI) to developing countries and 0.15 to 0.20 per cent of ODA/GNI to least developed countries<br>• Assist developing countries in attaining long-term debt sustainability through coordinated policies aimed at fostering debt financing, debt relief and debt restructuring, as appropriate, and address the external debt of highly indebted poor countries to reduce debt distress |

Source: UN/DESA, elaborated based on official United Nations documents adopted by the General Assembly.

**A.4    Major conferences and summits, 1980–2000**

| Summit/conference | Main objectives |
|---|---|
| **World Conference of the United Nations Decade for Women: Equality, Development and Peace**, Copenhagen, 14 to 30 July 1980 | To assess the disparity between women's guaranteed rights and their capacity to exercise them |
| **International Conference on Population**, 1984, Mexico City, 6-14 August 1984 | To appraise the implementation of the World Population Plan of Action, adopted at the United Nations World Population Conference, 1974, held at Bucharest from 19 to 30 August 1974, and to expand the scope of the Plan of Action to incorporate the latest research and data |
| **World Conference to Review and Appraise the Achievements of the United Nations Decade for Women: Equality, Development and Peace**, Nairobi, 15-26 July 1985 | To seek new ways to overcome obstacles to achieving gender equality, development and peace |
| **World Conference on Education for All: Meeting Basic Learning Needs**, Jomtien, Thailand, 5-9 March 1990 | To universalise basic education and adopt the World Declaration on Education for All and a Framework for Action |
| **World Summit for Children**, New York, 29 and 30 September 1990 | To adopt the World Declaration on the Survival, Protection and Development of Children and a Plan of Action for implementing the World Declaration |
| **United Nations Conference on Environment and Development**, Rio de Janeiro, 3-14 June 1992 | To adopt a global plan of action for promoting sustainable development; and define a set of principles encompassing the rights and responsibilities of States with respect to the environment and development |
| **International Conference on Nutrition** Rome, 5-11 December 1992 | To discuss ways to eradicate hunger and malnutrition |
| **World Conference on Human Rights**, Vienna, 14-25 June 1993 | To direct education towards full human development and strengthen respect for human rights and fundamental freedoms |
| **International Conference on Population and Development**, Cairo, 5-13 September 1994 | To hold discussions on and adopt a Programme of Action for national and international action on population and development during the following 20 years |
| **World Summit for Social Development**, Copenhagen, 6-12 March 1995 | To address globalization, the changing world economy, poverty, unemployment and social disintegration |
| **Fourth World Conference on Women**, Beijing, 4-15 September 1995 | To strengthen the international goal of achieving equality, development and peace for women; and, in that regard, to adopt the Beijing Declaration and Platform for Action |
| **United Nations Conference on Human Settlements** (Habitat II), Istanbul, 3-14 June 1996 | To address two themes: "Adequate shelter for all" and "Sustainable human settlements development in an urbanizing world" |
| **World Food Summit**, Rome, 13-17 November 1996 | To provide a forum for discussion on the issue of eradication of hunger; and, in that regard, to adopt the Rome Declaration on World Food Security and the World Food Summit Plan of Action |
| **Millennium Summit**, New York, 6-8 September 2000 | To affirm the collective responsibility to uphold the principles of human dignity, equality and equity. By adopting the United Nations Millennium Declaration, world leaders committed their nations to a new global partnership for reducing extreme poverty |

Source: UN/DESA, based on information available at http://www.un.org/en/events/archives/2008.shtml.

# Annex tables[a]

**a**    The seven annex tables found in this section are a subset of indicators that were prepared for the *World Economic and Social Survey 2017* using solely United Nations sources as primary data sources. For the purpose of printing, these seven tables are presented as five-year time series, including the years available before the five-year groupings begin. The complete set of indicators, presented as annual time series, are available for download as working files at http://www.un.org/development/desa/dpad/wess-report/.

## Annex table A.1
## Gross domestic product, 1970–2015

Millions of constant 2005 United States dollars

| Country/area | 1970 | 1975 | 1980 | 1985 | 1990 | 1995 | 2000 | 2005 | 2010 | 2015 |
|---|---|---|---|---|---|---|---|---|---|---|
| Afghanistan | 6 930 | 6 658 | 6 718 | 7 501 | 5 725 | 4 532 | 3 495 | 6 622 | 10 393 | 13 300 |
| Albania | 3 170 | 3 859 | 4 665 | 5 161 | 5 271 | 4 736 | 6 053 | 8 052 | 10 414 | 11 467 |
| Algeria | 28 922 | 36 648 | 50 818 | 64 280 | 66 766 | 67 626 | 80 130 | 103 198 | 116 968 | 137 845 |
| Andorra | 885 | 1 146 | 1 264 | 1 354 | 1 687 | 1 818 | 2 255 | 3 256 | 2 837 | 2 754 |
| Angola | 15 819 | 17 790 | 16 534 | 18 070 | 21 048 | 17 732 | 23 811 | 36 971 | 55 017 | 69 536 |
| Anguilla | 31 | 36 | 46 | 55 | 109 | 130 | 170 | 229 | 240 | 252 |
| Antigua and Barbuda | 235 | 288 | 344 | 449 | 617 | 685 | 887 | 1 015 | 1 024 | 1 135 |
| Argentina | 105 129 | 121 042 | 135 290 | 122 446 | 121 001 | 161 125 | 182 980 | 201 388 | 256 328 | 274 740 |
| Armenia | ... | ... | ... | ... | 4 262 | 2 251 | 2 890 | 5 226 | 6 315 | 7 808 |
| Aruba | 206 | 318 | 492 | 760 | 1 331 | 1 811 | 2 230 | 2 331 | 2 062 | 2 215 |
| Australia | 252 241 | 291 026 | 337 174 | 390 453 | 453 840 | 532 668 | 642 882 | 761 783 | 871 727 | 993 574 |
| Austria | 125 301 | 151 954 | 178 595 | 192 112 | 223 054 | 248 960 | 288 930 | 314 641 | 335 524 | 353 566 |
| Azerbaijan | ... | ... | ... | ... | 12 143 | 5 085 | 7 148 | 13 245 | 28 277 | 31 075 |
| Bahamas | 3 123 | 2 337 | 4 115 | 4 942 | 5 567 | 5 540 | 7 099 | 7 706 | 7 617 | 7 729 |
| Bahrain | 3 791 | 4 820 | 7 835 | 6 462 | 7 784 | 9 882 | 12 417 | 15 969 | 20 928 | 25 050 |
| Bangladesh | 17 646 | 15 583 | 19 126 | 22 804 | 27 881 | 34 316 | 44 235 | 57 628 | 77 343 | 105 085 |
| Barbados | 2 376 | 2 370 | 3 029 | 2 975 | 3 326 | 3 185 | 3 694 | 3 897 | 4 054 | 4 139 |
| Belarus | ... | ... | ... | ... | 23 818 | 15 516 | 21 086 | 30 210 | 42 921 | 45 503 |
| Belgium | 166 910 | 198 884 | 232 510 | 243 698 | 283 708 | 307 035 | 354 061 | 387 356 | 415 035 | 436 223 |
| Belize | 215 | 262 | 317 | 323 | 517 | 639 | 857 | 1 114 | 1 261 | 1 426 |
| Benin | 1 153 | 1 341 | 1 668 | 2 167 | 2 431 | 3 101 | 3 966 | 4 804 | 5 800 | 7 489 |
| Bermuda | 2 214 | 2 477 | 3 122 | 3 106 | 3 331 | 3 562 | 4 282 | 4 868 | 4 881 | 4 370 |
| Bhutan | 84 | 90 | 125 | 174 | 331 | 399 | 560 | 819 | 1 288 | 1 655 |
| Bolivia (Plurinational State of) | 3 804 | 5 041 | 5 579 | 5 064 | 5 665 | 6 925 | 8 201 | 9 549 | 11 954 | 15 611 |
| Bosnia and Herzegovina | ... | ... | ... | ... | 2 870 | 3 196 | 9 067 | 11 225 | 12 912 | 13 770 |
| Botswana | 413 | 940 | 1 648 | 2 773 | 5 160 | 6 454 | 8 313 | 9 931 | 12 412 | 15 549 |
| Brazil | 227 309 | 367 251 | 520 111 | 554 072 | 608 046 | 703 848 | 777 502 | 891 634 | 1 109 705 | 1 130 906 |
| British Virgin Islands | 104 | 114 | 158 | 185 | 239 | 530 | 830 | 870 | 929 | 857 |
| Brunei Darussalam | 4 176 | 6 206 | 10 066 | 8 356 | 7 639 | 8 922 | 9 532 | 10 561 | 10 914 | 10 860 |
| Bulgaria | 11 239 | 16 374 | 22 062 | 26 007 | 28 027 | 24 556 | 22 472 | 29 821 | 34 705 | 37 424 |
| Burkina Faso | 1 299 | 1 622 | 1 904 | 2 088 | 2 415 | 2 926 | 4 012 | 5 463 | 7 139 | 9 315 |
| Burundi | 605 | 625 | 787 | 1 000 | 1 191 | 1 070 | 1 006 | 1 117 | 1 393 | 1 594 |
| Cabo Verde | 246 | 229 | 265 | 365 | 442 | 569 | 851 | 1 105 | 1 413 | 1 547 |
| Cambodia | 2 573 | 1 752 | 1 229 | 1 410 | 2 086 | 2 851 | 4 027 | 6 293 | 8 693 | 12 298 |
| Cameroon | 5 439 | 7 499 | 10 223 | 14 129 | 11 706 | 10 993 | 13 827 | 16 588 | 19 147 | 24 666 |
| Canada | 402 850 | 499 485 | 599 308 | 683 438 | 777 846 | 845 915 | 1 029 948 | 1 169 393 | 1 237 610 | 1 377 908 |
| Cayman Islands | 240 | 369 | 592 | 899 | 1 491 | 1 801 | 2 713 | 3 042 | 2 953 | 3 171 |
| Central African Republic | 1 041 | 1 021 | 1 087 | 1 169 | 1 185 | 1 304 | 1 444 | 1 413 | 1 667 | 1 173 |
| Chad | 2 125 | 2 557 | 1 712 | 2 110 | 2 622 | 2 932 | 3 349 | 6 681 | 9 700 | 14 691 |
| Chile | 30 943 | 27 658 | 39 786 | 38 321 | 53 068 | 80 487 | 98 658 | 123 056 | 147 859 | 178 847 |

**Annex table A.1**
**Gross domestic product, 1970–2015** (*continued*)

Millions of constant 2005 United States dollars

| Country/area | 1970 | 1975 | 1980 | 1985 | 1990 | 1995 | 2000 | 2005 | 2010 | 2015 |
|---|---|---|---|---|---|---|---|---|---|---|
| China | 121 023 | 161 279 | 221 242 | 366 862 | 537 245 | 958 040 | 1 448 331 | 2 308 800 | 3 944 168 | 5 762 185 |
| China, Hong Kong SAR | 22 086 | 30 289 | 52 275 | 69 050 | 100 206 | 129 722 | 147 644 | 181 569 | 220 057 | 254 353 |
| China, Macao SAR | 1 222 | 1 758 | 2 529 | 3 491 | 5 337 | 7 191 | 7 054 | 12 092 | 20 579 | 24 018 |
| Colombia | 39 504 | 52 045 | 67 546 | 75 485 | 94 460 | 117 224 | 122 698 | 146 566 | 182 951 | 228 962 |
| Comoros | 279 | 351 | 444 | 546 | 576 | 644 | 699 | 782 | 935 | 1 206 |
| Congo | 1 566 | 2 052 | 2 647 | 4 437 | 4 330 | 4 428 | 4 988 | 6 087 | 7 878 | 9 444 |
| Cook Islands | 103 | 84 | 80 | 99 | 122 | 143 | 161 | 183 | 181 | 211 |
| Costa Rica | 4 531 | 6 074 | 7 842 | 7 953 | 9 952 | 12 987 | 16 519 | 19 952 | 25 173 | 29 970 |
| Côte d'Ivoire | 6 878 | 9 389 | 11 505 | 11 659 | 13 406 | 14 519 | 17 085 | 17 085 | 19 064 | 26 187 |
| Croatia | ... | ... | ... | ... | 42 545 | 30 834 | 36 454 | 45 416 | 46 492 | 45 377 |
| Cuba | 16 893 | 21 988 | 25 838 | 38 933 | 38 541 | 26 733 | 33 377 | 42 644 | 55 439 | 63 661 |
| Curaçao | ... | ... | ... | ... | ... | ... | ... | 2 345 | 2 484 | 2 455 |
| Cyprus | 3 836 | 3 197 | 5 470 | 7 189 | 10 042 | 12 952 | 15 700 | 18 694 | 21 168 | 19 365 |
| Czechoslovakia | 78 240 | 102 247 | 122 225 | 132 828 | 141 958 | ... | ... | ... | ... | ... |
| Czech Republic | ... | ... | ... | ... | 106 767 | 102 694 | 112 177 | 135 990 | 153 349 | 165 808 |
| Democratic Republic of the Congo | 15 511 | 17 450 | 16 174 | 17 720 | 17 658 | 12 119 | 9 925 | 11 965 | 15 669 | 22 784 |
| Denmark | 124 948 | 135 666 | 154 690 | 177 084 | 190 182 | 213 383 | 247 533 | 264 467 | 267 266 | 283 052 |
| Djibouti | 405 | 501 | 489 | 519 | 543 | 602 | 617 | 709 | 961 | 1 247 |
| Dominica | 108 | 149 | 170 | 218 | 286 | 309 | 342 | 370 | 443 | 466 |
| Dominican Republic | 6 567 | 10 118 | 13 069 | 14 371 | 16 598 | 21 389 | 29 861 | 35 510 | 48 067 | 61 013 |
| Ecuador | 10 645 | 16 710 | 20 735 | 23 423 | 26 804 | 31 032 | 32 753 | 41 507 | 49 036 | 61 080 |
| Egypt | 12 933 | 15 069 | 24 170 | 37 503 | 48 644 | 61 117 | 78 834 | 94 456 | 127 460 | 144 229 |
| El Salvador | 7 067 | 9 226 | 9 714 | 8 842 | 9 702 | 13 093 | 15 219 | 17 094 | 18 341 | 20 215 |
| Equatorial Guinea | 239 | 301 | 306 | 396 | 420 | 639 | 2 753 | 8 520 | 11 245 | 11 456 |
| Eritrea | ... | ... | ... | ... | 480 | 920 | 1 133 | 1 098 | 1 057 | 1 393 |
| Estonia | ... | ... | ... | ... | 10 590 | 7 398 | 9 942 | 14 003 | 13 748 | 16 322 |
| Ethiopia | ... | ... | ... | ... | 6 771 | 7 125 | 8 904 | 12 164 | 20 386 | 33 499 |
| Ethiopia (former) | 4 808 | 5 482 | 6 215 | 6 096 | 7 381 | ... | ... | ... | ... | ... |
| Fiji | 1 014 | 1 361 | 1 638 | 1 722 | 2 148 | 2 381 | 2 644 | 2 981 | 3 090 | 3 688 |
| Finland | 72 720 | 90 167 | 105 379 | 121 263 | 143 592 | 140 425 | 179 902 | 204 431 | 212 913 | 212 573 |
| France | 904 418 | 1 093 507 | 1 290 856 | 1 397 266 | 1 650 028 | 1 758 875 | 2 029 989 | 2 203 624 | 2 289 830 | 2 400 400 |
| French Polynesia | 1 474 | 1 904 | 2 413 | 3 372 | 4 127 | 4 435 | 5 137 | 5 703 | 5 466 | 5 725 |
| Gabon | 3 152 | 7 089 | 6 577 | 7 428 | 7 866 | 9 170 | 9 125 | 9 579 | 10 123 | 13 147 |
| Gambia | 201 | 248 | 253 | 328 | 389 | 431 | 531 | 624 | 784 | 879 |
| Georgia | ... | ... | ... | ... | 12 375 | 3 512 | 4 666 | 6 411 | 8 497 | 11 262 |
| Germany | 1 365 821 | 1 539 614 | 1 816 768 | 1 944 168 | 2 286 945 | 2 529 418 | 2 781 325 | 2 861 339 | 3 042 359 | 3 291 225 |
| Ghana | 6 610 | 6 721 | 7 045 | 6 895 | 8 719 | 10 740 | 13 336 | 17 199 | 23 169 | 33 477 |
| Greece | 95 873 | 122 519 | 150 285 | 151 310 | 160 923 | 171 209 | 204 771 | 247 777 | 243 731 | 198 913 |
| Greenland | 613 | 836 | 1 165 | 1 140 | 1 281 | 1 267 | 1 527 | 1 650 | 1 868 | 1 849 |
| Grenada | 130 | 178 | 229 | 282 | 392 | 408 | 561 | 701 | 669 | 740 |
| Guatemala | 8 283 | 10 870 | 14 355 | 13 566 | 15 661 | 19 313 | 23 442 | 27 211 | 32 557 | 39 287 |
| Guinea | 1 324 | 1 570 | 1 772 | 1 958 | 2 405 | 2 882 | 3 493 | 4 063 | 4 669 | 5 552 |
| Guinea-Bissau | 308 | 359 | 339 | 374 | 451 | 525 | 542 | 587 | 692 | 797 |

Annex table A.1
**Gross domestic product, 1970–2015** (*continued*)

Millions of constant 2005 United States dollars

| Country/area | 1970 | 1975 | 1980 | 1985 | 1990 | 1995 | 2000 | 2005 | 2010 | 2015 |
|---|---|---|---|---|---|---|---|---|---|---|
| Guyana | 934 | 1 131 | 1 111 | 888 | 788 | 1 110 | 1 270 | 1 315 | 1 628 | 2 024 |
| Haiti | 2 819 | 3 397 | 4 483 | 4 275 | 4 271 | 3 771 | 4 270 | 4 154 | 4 313 | 5 100 |
| Honduras | 2 617 | 3 132 | 4 427 | 4 822 | 5 625 | 6 695 | 7 773 | 9 757 | 11 648 | 13 830 |
| Hungary | 49 766 | 67 417 | 79 112 | 86 319 | 88 596 | 78 786 | 91 227 | 112 589 | 111 471 | 122 300 |
| Iceland | 4 331 | 5 908 | 8 008 | 8 977 | 10 494 | 10 633 | 13 562 | 16 691 | 17 460 | 19 981 |
| India | 143 629 | 165 327 | 192 729 | 250 308 | 340 415 | 437 551 | 579 906 | 812 059 | 1 210 644 | 1 677 339 |
| Indonesia | 40 332 | 59 393 | 86 930 | 114 371 | 159 807 | 232 971 | 241 606 | 304 372 | 402 359 | 526 206 |
| Iran (Islamic Republic of) | 96 603 | 142 496 | 98 500 | 120 226 | 122 599 | 141 577 | 168 183 | 219 846 | 279 059 | 277 792 |
| Iraq | 9 901 | 14 980 | 27 080 | 20 184 | 24 474 | 12 059 | 35 366 | 36 268 | 48 218 | 73 104 |
| Ireland | 35 662 | 45 329 | 56 640 | 64 237 | 80 842 | 101 394 | 161 552 | 211 680 | 216 595 | 296 484 |
| Israel | 29 732 | 42 941 | 49 611 | 57 901 | 71 792 | 99 530 | 128 901 | 142 462 | 176 500 | 209 555 |
| Italy | 815 392 | 952 585 | 1 184 159 | 1 287 287 | 1 501 147 | 1 601 566 | 1 768 073 | 1 852 616 | 1 823 726 | 1 766 169 |
| Jamaica | 7 629 | 8 325 | 7 073 | 7 101 | 9 017 | 10 430 | 10 405 | 11 244 | 10 974 | 11 339 |
| Japan | 1 612 699 | 2 013 740 | 2 495 511 | 3 076 677 | 3 925 860 | 4 245 270 | 4 484 303 | 4 755 410 | 4 778 705 | 5 018 510 |
| Jordan | 2 556 | 2 525 | 4 807 | 5 982 | 5 833 | 7 894 | 9 244 | 12 589 | 17 034 | 19 469 |
| Kazakhstan | ... | ... | ... | ... | 50 254 | 30 850 | 34 880 | 57 124 | 77 245 | 97 183 |
| Kenya | 5 874 | 7 224 | 9 797 | 11 339 | 14 914 | 16 134 | 17 869 | 21 506 | 27 424 | 35 786 |
| Kiribati | 109 | 221 | 77 | 76 | 82 | 89 | 109 | 112 | 109 | 130 |
| Kosovo | ... | ... | ... | ... | 6 315 | 3 417 | 2 987 | 3 680 | 4 729 | 5 531 |
| Kuwait | 50 066 | 39 710 | 40 111 | 31 211 | 30 612 | 48 626 | 54 707 | 80 798 | 85 603 | 103 599 |
| Kyrgyzstan | ... | ... | ... | ... | 3 069 | 1 555 | 2 043 | 2 460 | 3 056 | 3 849 |
| Lao People's Democratic Republic | 426 | 556 | 611 | 889 | 1 098 | 1 482 | 1 999 | 2 717 | 3 988 | 5 808 |
| Latvia | ... | ... | ... | ... | 17 905 | 8 880 | 11 413 | 16 922 | 16 539 | 19 719 |
| Lebanon | 14 562 | 13 332 | 11 532 | 16 152 | 9 189 | 16 338 | 17 541 | 21 490 | 31 042 | 34 272 |
| Lesotho | 286 | 379 | 540 | 621 | 801 | 979 | 1 187 | 1 368 | 1 763 | 2 143 |
| Liberia | 707 | 794 | 872 | 802 | 418 | 117 | 541 | 608 | 1 099 | 1 372 |
| Libya | 19 938 | 26 704 | 40 481 | 33 739 | 30 515 | 32 935 | 35 194 | 45 451 | 60 501 | 17 204 |
| Liechtenstein | 1 101 | 1 196 | 1 510 | 1 747 | 2 240 | 2 789 | 3 926 | 4 087 | 4 552 | 4 793 |
| Lithuania | ... | ... | ... | ... | 24 869 | 14 422 | 18 116 | 26 141 | 27 715 | 33 275 |
| Luxembourg | 9 003 | 10 391 | 11 624 | 13 142 | 18 845 | 22 875 | 31 224 | 36 976 | 41 811 | 48 179 |
| Madagascar | 3 225 | 3 329 | 3 560 | 3 312 | 3 792 | 3 730 | 4 502 | 5 039 | 5 796 | 6 596 |
| Malawi | 1 119 | 1 635 | 2 218 | 2 276 | 2 589 | 2 744 | 3 251 | 3 656 | 5 228 | 6 394 |
| Malaysia | 13 102 | 21 489 | 32 370 | 41 539 | 57 312 | 90 111 | 113 869 | 143 534 | 178 674 | 231 175 |
| Maldives | 78 | 83 | 140 | 253 | 416 | 577 | 861 | 1 120 | 1 691 | 2 150 |
| Mali | 1 339 | 1 575 | 1 980 | 2 273 | 2 844 | 3 364 | 4 313 | 6 245 | 10 328 | 15 363 |
| Malta | 916 | 1 360 | 2 348 | 2 554 | 3 443 | 4 496 | 5 772 | 6 393 | 7 066 | 8 490 |
| Marshall Islands | 36 | 58 | 60 | 75 | 112 | 145 | 124 | 138 | 149 | 159 |
| Mauritania | 883 | 1 056 | 1 150 | 1 145 | 1 287 | 1 504 | 1 742 | 2 184 | 2 798 | 3 531 |
| Mauritius | 1 052 | 1 452 | 1 826 | 2 293 | 3 317 | 4 193 | 5 493 | 6 489 | 8 155 | 9 679 |
| Mexico | 247 188 | 339 384 | 468 399 | 515 589 | 560 248 | 604 407 | 788 247 | 864 810 | 952 038 | 1 093 252 |
| Micronesia (Federated States of) | 80 | 128 | 132 | 160 | 196 | 245 | 243 | 251 | 251 | 244 |
| Monaco | 1 725 | 2 086 | 2 462 | 2 665 | 3 147 | 3 355 | 3 872 | 4 203 | 4 609 | 6 170 |

**Annex table A.1**
**Gross domestic product, 1970–2015** (*continued*)

Millions of constant 2005 United States dollars

| Country/area | 1970 | 1975 | 1980 | 1985 | 1990 | 1995 | 2000 | 2005 | 2010 | 2015 |
|---|---|---|---|---|---|---|---|---|---|---|
| Mongolia | 728 | 955 | 1 276 | 1 774 | 2 146 | 1 859 | 2 137 | 2 926 | 4 005 | 6 501 |
| Montenegro | ... | ... | ... | ... | 2 636 | 1 324 | 1 978 | 2 272 | 2 821 | 3 119 |
| Montserrat | 56 | 65 | 82 | 92 | 118 | 103 | 44 | 49 | 51 | 60 |
| Morocco | 15 937 | 20 278 | 26 611 | 31 288 | 38 816 | 40 658 | 49 055 | 62 545 | 79 350 | 96 329 |
| Mozambique | 1 789 | 2 289 | 2 620 | 2 083 | 2 493 | 2 926 | 5 045 | 7 724 | 11 053 | 15 577 |
| Myanmar | 1 933 | 2 181 | 2 907 | 3 669 | 3 294 | 4 374 | 6 514 | 11 931 | 20 286 | 28 884 |
| Namibia | 2 466 | 3 013 | 3 483 | 3 386 | 3 821 | 4 866 | 5 783 | 7 121 | 8 772 | 11 470 |
| Nauru | 159 | 184 | 159 | 138 | 120 | 60 | 37 | 26 | 41 | 94 |
| Nepal | 2 190 | 2 396 | 2 690 | 3 416 | 4 271 | 5 499 | 6 960 | 8 259 | 10 299 | 12 653 |
| Netherlands | 270 527 | 319 470 | 367 789 | 388 883 | 458 501 | 513 546 | 634 947 | 678 517 | 722 835 | 750 376 |
| Netherlands Antilles | 1 147 | 1 440 | 2 539 | 2 410 | 2 559 | 3 012 | 2 881 | 3 053 | 3 291 | ... |
| New Caledonia | 2 315 | 2 730 | 2 689 | 2 670 | 4 324 | 4 982 | 5 288 | 6 236 | 7 564 | 8 550 |
| New Zealand | 47 916 | 58 697 | 59 092 | 68 786 | 69 884 | 81 617 | 94 332 | 114 721 | 123 686 | 140 960 |
| Nicaragua | 4 255 | 5 576 | 4 446 | 4 589 | 3 878 | 4 236 | 5 412 | 6 321 | 7 154 | 9 204 |
| Niger | 2 141 | 1 882 | 2 428 | 2 118 | 2 143 | 2 307 | 2 702 | 3 369 | 4 334 | 5 789 |
| Nigeria | 41 717 | 60 476 | 67 686 | 67 600 | 87 796 | 94 219 | 109 828 | 180 502 | 249 671 | 314 087 |
| Norway | 94 366 | 119 754 | 149 638 | 177 363 | 192 890 | 231 758 | 276 894 | 308 722 | 323 263 | 350 776 |
| Oman | 3 075 | 4 813 | 8 544 | 16 487 | 18 993 | 25 248 | 29 461 | 31 082 | 41 164 | 50 327 |
| Pakistan | 21 574 | 25 749 | 34 400 | 47 300 | 62 685 | 78 593 | 92 254 | 117 708 | 139 224 | 170 820 |
| Palau | 86 | 89 | 91 | 102 | 133 | 147 | 160 | 180 | 152 | 176 |
| Panama | 3 523 | 4 431 | 6 020 | 7 198 | 7 643 | 9 986 | 12 524 | 15 465 | 21 961 | 32 080 |
| Papua New Guinea | 3 223 | 3 680 | 3 679 | 3 925 | 4 193 | 6 331 | 6 573 | 7 312 | 9 550 | 12 187 |
| Paraguay | 1 827 | 2 576 | 4 236 | 4 740 | 5 737 | 6 776 | 6 710 | 8 735 | 11 148 | 14 142 |
| Peru | 32 448 | 42 582 | 46 541 | 46 436 | 42 069 | 54 299 | 61 706 | 76 080 | 106 102 | 134 093 |
| Philippines | 29 571 | 39 145 | 52 545 | 49 280 | 62 103 | 69 129 | 82 358 | 103 072 | 131 138 | 174 660 |
| Poland | 119 155 | 158 389 | 188 342 | 186 629 | 182 710 | 203 463 | 262 949 | 306 127 | 386 375 | 448 747 |
| Portugal | 64 989 | 80 528 | 103 270 | 107 932 | 142 212 | 154 749 | 188 974 | 197 300 | 203 429 | 194 244 |
| Puerto Rico | 23 872 | 28 178 | 36 289 | 39 130 | 51 514 | 62 809 | 77 411 | 83 915 | 78 370 | 76 748 |
| Qatar | 7 778 | 11 811 | 13 451 | 12 711 | 15 583 | 17 483 | 29 725 | 43 998 | 100 718 | 133 968 |
| Republic of Korea | 58 742 | 94 256 | 141 593 | 221 415 | 364 276 | 545 690 | 712 756 | 898 137 | 1 098 694 | 1 271 434 |
| Republic of Moldova | ... | ... | ... | ... | 6 101 | 2 405 | 2 122 | 2 988 | 3 502 | 4 225 |
| Romania | 32 521 | 55 611 | 79 676 | 93 084 | 84 988 | 76 334 | 75 361 | 99 699 | 115 113 | 129 514 |
| Russian Federation | ... | ... | ... | ... | 844 174 | 524 113 | 567 392 | 764 016 | 909 266 | 963 665 |
| Rwanda | 832 | 862 | 1 417 | 1 612 | 1 648 | 1 057 | 1 750 | 2 581 | 3 847 | 5 405 |
| Saint Kitts and Nevis | 99 | 125 | 171 | 207 | 295 | 359 | 462 | 543 | 556 | 661 |
| Saint Lucia | 214 | 258 | 349 | 447 | 677 | 754 | 872 | 935 | 1 039 | 1 054 |
| Saint Vincent and the Grenadines | 158 | 153 | 202 | 255 | 326 | 389 | 443 | 551 | 589 | 622 |
| Samoa | 203 | 215 | 264 | 251 | 260 | 273 | 336 | 434 | 458 | 488 |
| San Marino | 544 | 636 | 790 | 859 | 1 002 | 1 305 | 1 722 | 2 027 | 1 842 | 1 496 |
| Sao Tome and Principe | 56 | 68 | 101 | 92 | 87 | 93 | 101 | 126 | 168 | 212 |
| Saudi Arabia | 91 922 | 178 987 | 253 110 | 147 670 | 209 149 | 248 623 | 269 843 | 328 461 | 374 862 | 477 713 |
| Senegal | 3 188 | 3 584 | 3 776 | 4 381 | 5 127 | 5 498 | 6 934 | 8 708 | 10 358 | 12 655 |
| Serbia | ... | ... | ... | ... | 38 104 | 18 246 | 19 425 | 26 252 | 29 943 | 30 492 |

Annex table A.1
**Gross domestic product, 1970–2015** (*continued*)

Millions of constant 2005 United States dollars

| Country/area | 1970 | 1975 | 1980 | 1985 | 1990 | 1995 | 2000 | 2005 | 2010 | 2015 |
|---|---|---|---|---|---|---|---|---|---|---|
| Seychelles | 199 | 279 | 427 | 460 | 606 | 699 | 928 | 919 | 1 138 | 1 482 |
| Sierra Leone | 1 252 | 1 359 | 1 528 | 1 724 | 1 999 | 1 548 | 907 | 1 650 | 2 130 | 2 624 |
| Singapore | 10 075 | 15 867 | 23 979 | 33 360 | 50 440 | 76 309 | 100 380 | 127 418 | 176 458 | 214 221 |
| Sint Maarten | ... | ... | ... | ... | ... | ... | ... | 708 | 788 | 830 |
| Slovakia | ... | ... | ... | ... | 35 191 | 32 178 | 38 279 | 48 965 | 61 745 | 69 757 |
| Slovenia | ... | ... | ... | ... | 25 452 | 24 719 | 30 462 | 36 345 | 39 598 | 40 478 |
| Solomon Islands | 114 | 147 | 233 | 252 | 307 | 425 | 369 | 429 | 599 | 709 |
| Somalia | 1 670 | 1 989 | 2 271 | 2 480 | 2 610 | 1 796 | 1 978 | 2 316 | 2 628 | 3 022 |
| South Africa | 110 200 | 131 820 | 153 509 | 164 194 | 178 331 | 186 154 | 213 585 | 257 772 | 300 266 | 333 831 |
| South Sudan | ... | ... | ... | ... | ... | ... | ... | ... | 10 920 | 8 429 |
| Spain | 390 236 | 505 536 | 557 186 | 597 137 | 744 040 | 801 810 | 979 526 | 1 157 248 | 1 219 911 | 1 205 656 |
| Sri Lanka | 5 957 | 6 874 | 9 088 | 11 660 | 13 758 | 17 943 | 22 940 | 27 932 | 38 058 | 51 166 |
| State of Palestine | 624 | 986 | 1 432 | 1 463 | 2 039 | 3 324 | 4 368 | 4 832 | 6 167 | 7 778 |
| Sudan | ... | ... | ... | ... | ... | ... | ... | ... | 35 904 | 39 290 |
| Sudan (former) | 7 624 | 9 603 | 10 795 | 11 109 | 14 000 | 17 707 | 24 325 | 35 183 | 46 910 | ... |
| Suriname | 1 110 | 1 312 | 1 432 | 1 578 | 1 569 | 1 561 | 1 717 | 2 193 | 2 751 | 3 005 |
| Swaziland | 441 | 846 | 1 024 | 1 154 | 1 946 | 2 263 | 2 604 | 3 107 | 3 704 | 4 264 |
| Sweden | 183 426 | 208 397 | 222 691 | 245 761 | 276 688 | 286 677 | 341 717 | 389 043 | 420 871 | 465 838 |
| Switzerland | 238 153 | 247 951 | 269 569 | 290 505 | 335 795 | 337 990 | 378 377 | 407 543 | 454 938 | 489 939 |
| Syrian Arab Republic | 4 435 | 8 269 | 11 430 | 13 198 | 12 567 | 18 570 | 22 208 | 28 397 | 36 081 | 18 758 |
| Tajikistan | ... | ... | ... | ... | 3 829 | 1 455 | 1 457 | 2 312 | 3 162 | 4 160 |
| Thailand | 22 706 | 29 814 | 43 675 | 56 940 | 92 968 | 139 809 | 145 015 | 189 318 | 227 448 | 261 840 |
| The former Yugoslav Republic of Macedonia | ... | ... | ... | ... | 5 750 | 4 905 | 5 677 | 6 259 | 7 610 | 8 587 |
| Timor-Leste | ... | ... | ... | ... | 385 | 624 | 517 | 1 850 | 3 053 | 2 260 |
| Togo | 1 224 | 1 348 | 1 578 | 1 484 | 1 815 | 1 790 | 1 989 | 2 110 | 2 462 | 3 215 |
| Tonga | 86 | 97 | 123 | 185 | 188 | 216 | 237 | 262 | 272 | 289 |
| Trinidad and Tobago | 5 350 | 6 121 | 8 943 | 7 868 | 7 025 | 7 527 | 10 834 | 15 982 | 19 358 | 19 825 |
| Tunisia | 5 708 | 8 502 | 11 558 | 14 194 | 16 428 | 19 858 | 26 040 | 32 272 | 40 182 | 43 239 |
| Turkey | 108 950 | 144 389 | 162 294 | 205 784 | 269 684 | 315 856 | 386 584 | 482 986 | 565 099 | 699 952 |
| Turkmenistan | ... | ... | ... | ... | 14 069 | 8 890 | 11 060 | 14 182 | 23 226 | 38 315 |
| Turks and Caicos Islands | 21 | 34 | 57 | 94 | 157 | 258 | 384 | 579 | 634 | 713 |
| Tuvalu | 9 | 8 | 8 | 8 | 14 | 17 | 22 | 22 | 24 | 28 |
| Uganda | 3 174 | 3 217 | 2 646 | 2 995 | 3 959 | 5 671 | 7 753 | 11 154 | 16 480 | 20 836 |
| Ukraine | ... | ... | ... | ... | 142 797 | 68 183 | 61 683 | 89 239 | 93 824 | 83 491 |
| Union of Soviet Socialist Republics | 468 915 | 587 639 | 747 611 | 935 726 | 1 181 425 | ... | ... | ... | ... | ... |
| United Arab Emirates | 21 011 | 38 362 | 79 909 | 72 917 | 81 924 | 101 625 | 139 151 | 180 617 | 203 435 | 256 021 |
| United Kingdom of Great Britain and Northern Ireland | 1 046 484 | 1 155 783 | 1 290 538 | 1 450 700 | 1 723 238 | 1 866 706 | 2 182 818 | 2 508 111 | 2 554 677 | 2 821 007 |
| United Republic of Tanzania | 4 708 | 5 856 | 6 739 | 7 120 | 8 605 | 10 467 | 12 857 | 18 072 | 24 275 | 33 797 |

Annex table A.1
**Gross domestic product, 1970–2015** (*continued*)

Millions of constant 2005 United States dollars

| Country/area | 1970 | 1975 | 1980 | 1985 | 1990 | 1995 | 2000 | 2005 | 2010 | 2015 |
|---|---|---|---|---|---|---|---|---|---|---|
| United Republic of Tanzania: Zanzibar | ... | ... | ... | ... | 173 | 225 | 312 | 438 | 570 | 799 |
| United States of America | 4 339 695 | 4 948 468 | 5 927 123 | 6 977 897 | 8 228 651 | 9 359 504 | 11 553 319 | 13 093 726 | 13 599 258 | 15 083 356 |
| Uruguay | 8 972 | 9 691 | 12 078 | 10 537 | 12 653 | 15 453 | 17 205 | 17 363 | 23 193 | 27 549 |
| Uzbekistan | ... | ... | ... | ... | 11 171 | 9 061 | 10 989 | 14 396 | 21 707 | 31 716 |
| Vanuatu | 84 | 134 | 146 | 240 | 257 | 321 | 365 | 395 | 504 | 536 |
| Venezuela (Bolivarian Republic of) | 65 432 | 83 243 | 98 026 | 91 790 | 104 316 | 123 574 | 128 279 | 145 514 | 174 551 | 175 432 |
| Viet Nam | 7 811 | 8 602 | 11 364 | 15 942 | 19 540 | 28 984 | 40 559 | 57 633 | 78 282 | 104 331 |
| Yemen | ... | ... | ... | ... | 7 542 | 9 843 | 14 707 | 19 041 | 23 604 | 13 440 |
| Yemen Arab Republic | 1 798 | 2 885 | 4 096 | 5 219 | 6 731 | ... | ... | ... | ... | ... |
| Yemen (People's Democratic Republic of) | 658 | 438 | 898 | 1 198 | 1 305 | ... | ... | ... | ... | ... |
| Yugoslavia | 73 013 | 96 174 | 128 484 | 132 348 | 123 672 | ... | ... | ... | ... | ... |
| Zambia | 4 199 | 4 766 | 4 693 | 4 880 | 5 337 | 5 164 | 6 167 | 8 332 | 12 647 | 16 321 |
| Zimbabwe | 3 648 | 4 587 | 4 791 | 5 897 | 7 372 | 7 826 | 7 749 | 6 223 | 9 573 | 12 991 |

Source: UN/DESA, based on data from the Statistics Division. Available at https://unstats.un.org/unsd/snaama/dnlList.asp.
Note: The data set was used in its entirety by UN/DESA.
Three dots (...) indicate that data are not applicable or not available.

Annex table A.2
## Gross domestic product, 1970–2015

Millions of current United States dollars

| Country/area | 1970 | 1975 | 1980 | 1985 | 1990 | 1995 | 2000 | 2005 | 2010 | 2015 |
|---|---|---|---|---|---|---|---|---|---|---|
| Afghanistan | 1 749 | 2 367 | 3 642 | 3 322 | 3 622 | 3 236 | 3 532 | 6 622 | 16 078 | 20 270 |
| Albania | 2 266 | 2 610 | 2 142 | 2 324 | 2 147 | 2 393 | 3 488 | 8 052 | 11 927 | 11 541 |
| Algeria | 5 155 | 15 556 | 42 252 | 57 866 | 61 751 | 41 971 | 54 667 | 103 198 | 161 207 | 164 779 |
| Andorra | 99 | 279 | 565 | 439 | 1 302 | 1 491 | 1 434 | 3 256 | 3 355 | 2 812 |
| Angola | 3 807 | 4 147 | 7 151 | 9 109 | 13 662 | 6 642 | 12 207 | 36 971 | 83 799 | 117 955 |
| Anguilla | 4 | 7 | 12 | 27 | 76 | 104 | 150 | 229 | 268 | 320 |
| Antigua and Barbuda | 34 | 85 | 134 | 245 | 459 | 577 | 825 | 1 015 | 1 148 | 1 356 |
| Argentina | 33 985 | 51 741 | 81 833 | 95 530 | 153 186 | 279 701 | 308 148 | 201 388 | 428 792 | 632 343 |
| Armenia | ... | ... | ... | ... | 2 306 | 1 372 | 2 039 | 5 226 | 9 875 | 10 529 |
| Aruba | 177 | 229 | 297 | 385 | 765 | 1 321 | 1 873 | 2 331 | 2 391 | 2 702 |
| Australia | 45 121 | 108 853 | 173 123 | 181 698 | 323 807 | 392 103 | 408 865 | 761 783 | 1 293 201 | 1 230 859 |
| Austria | 15 336 | 39 962 | 81 858 | 69 221 | 166 067 | 240 474 | 196 422 | 314 641 | 390 212 | 376 967 |
| Azerbaijan | ... | ... | ... | ... | 6 529 | 3 081 | 5 273 | 13 245 | 52 906 | 53 049 |
| Bahamas | 568 | 892 | 1 581 | 2 256 | 3 700 | 4 009 | 6 328 | 7 706 | 7 910 | 8 854 |
| Bahrain | 422 | 1 185 | 3 764 | 4 475 | 4 909 | 6 787 | 9 063 | 15 969 | 25 713 | 31 126 |
| Bangladesh | 6 196 | 8 476 | 16 729 | 19 169 | 28 137 | 37 866 | 45 470 | 57 628 | 114 508 | 194 466 |
| Barbados | 216 | 476 | 1 024 | 1 425 | 2 035 | 2 275 | 3 122 | 3 897 | 4 447 | 4 385 |
| Belarus | ... | ... | ... | ... | 18 875 | 13 856 | 10 418 | 30 210 | 55 221 | 54 609 |
| Belgium | 26 850 | 66 028 | 127 511 | 86 728 | 206 429 | 289 571 | 237 905 | 387 356 | 483 549 | 455 107 |
| Belize | 25 | 104 | 195 | 209 | 405 | 587 | 832 | 1 114 | 1 397 | 1 721 |
| Benin | 322 | 674 | 1 484 | 1 130 | 1 993 | 2 345 | 2 569 | 4 804 | 6 970 | 8 476 |
| Bermuda | 266 | 492 | 902 | 1 428 | 2 035 | 2 557 | 3 480 | 4 868 | 5 855 | 5 853 |
| Bhutan | 62 | 87 | 129 | 172 | 274 | 289 | 439 | 819 | 1 585 | 2 074 |
| Bolivia (Plurinational State of) | 1 010 | 2 399 | 3 520 | 4 122 | 4 868 | 6 715 | 8 398 | 9 549 | 19 650 | 32 998 |
| Bosnia and Herzegovina | ... | ... | ... | ... | 7 755 | 2 034 | 5 694 | 11 225 | 17 164 | 16 251 |
| Botswana | 67 | 274 | 852 | 838 | 3 721 | 4 731 | 5 788 | 9 931 | 12 790 | 14 391 |
| Brazil | 35 214 | 108 051 | 191 125 | 187 426 | 406 897 | 778 053 | 652 360 | 891 634 | 2 208 838 | 1 772 591 |
| British Virgin Islands | 20 | 27 | 54 | 90 | 146 | 397 | 751 | 870 | 894 | 908 |
| Brunei Darussalam | 225 | 1 467 | 6 190 | 4 425 | 3 901 | 5 245 | 6 650 | 10 561 | 13 707 | 12 930 |
| Bulgaria | 9 000 | 11 908 | 10 843 | 16 486 | 20 726 | 14 434 | 13 148 | 29 821 | 49 939 | 48 953 |
| Burkina Faso | 450 | 890 | 1 933 | 1 569 | 3 133 | 2 404 | 2 633 | 5 463 | 8 980 | 11 065 |
| Burundi | 245 | 414 | 949 | 1 168 | 1 146 | 1 000 | 709 | 1 117 | 2 032 | 2 735 |
| Cabo Verde | 73 | 134 | 162 | 157 | 350 | 558 | 613 | 1 105 | 1 664 | 1 603 |
| Cambodia | 769 | 721 | 716 | 1 059 | 1 698 | 3 309 | 3 667 | 6 293 | 11 242 | 18 050 |
| Cameroon | 1 157 | 3 187 | 8 869 | 8 436 | 11 846 | 8 913 | 9 287 | 16 588 | 23 622 | 28 416 |
| Canada | 87 895 | 173 841 | 273 850 | 364 761 | 593 942 | 604 014 | 742 288 | 1 169 393 | 1 613 463 | 1 552 808 |
| Cayman Islands | 24 | 71 | 172 | 416 | 930 | 1 296 | 2 277 | 3 042 | 3 267 | 3 726 |
| Central African Republic | 276 | 553 | 1 163 | 905 | 1 507 | 1 167 | 957 | 1 413 | 2 034 | 1 633 |
| Chad | 355 | 752 | 789 | 987 | 1 834 | 1 643 | 1 576 | 6 681 | 9 791 | 10 009 |
| Chile | 9 559 | 7 941 | 30 336 | 18 747 | 34 481 | 74 160 | 77 383 | 123 056 | 217 538 | 240 796 |

Annex table A.2
**Gross domestic product, 1970–2015** (*continued*)

Millions of current United States dollars

| Country/area | 1970 | 1975 | 1980 | 1985 | 1990 | 1995 | 2000 | 2005 | 2010 | 2015 |
|---|---|---|---|---|---|---|---|---|---|---|
| China | 89 650 | 158 641 | 305 346 | 312 617 | 398 624 | 736 869 | 1 214 915 | 2 308 800 | 6 066 351 | 11 158 457 |
| China, Hong Kong SAR | 3 812 | 10 048 | 28 862 | 35 700 | 76 929 | 144 652 | 171 669 | 181 569 | 228 639 | 309 236 |
| China, Macao SAR | 167 | 445 | 1 008 | 1 349 | 3 221 | 6 996 | 6 720 | 12 092 | 28 124 | 46 178 |
| Colombia | 10 193 | 18 508 | 47 204 | 49 322 | 56 925 | 110 292 | 99 876 | 146 566 | 287 018 | 292 080 |
| Comoros | 37 | 114 | 257 | 238 | 507 | 480 | 419 | 782 | 995 | 1 079 |
| Congo | 262 | 683 | 1 706 | 2 161 | 2 799 | 2 116 | 3 220 | 6 087 | 12 281 | 8 493 |
| Cook Islands | 10 | 16 | 26 | 28 | 67 | 106 | 92 | 183 | 255 | 294 |
| Costa Rica | 1 173 | 2 336 | 5 755 | 4 673 | 6 801 | 10 983 | 14 950 | 19 952 | 37 269 | 52 958 |
| Côte d'Ivoire | 1 501 | 3 894 | 10 176 | 6 978 | 11 893 | 11 105 | 10 682 | 17 085 | 24 884 | 32 076 |
| Croatia | ... | ... | ... | ... | 16 619 | 22 388 | 21 774 | 45 416 | 59 665 | 48 676 |
| Cuba | 5 693 | 13 027 | 19 913 | 22 921 | 28 645 | 30 428 | 30 566 | 42 644 | 64 328 | 87 206 |
| Curaçao | ... | ... | ... | ... | ... | ... | ... | 2 345 | 2 951 | 3 152 |
| Cyprus | 616 | 789 | 2 416 | 2 711 | 6 259 | 9 933 | 9 963 | 18 694 | 25 561 | 19 561 |
| Czechoslovakia | 16 294 | 27 300 | 47 822 | 45 929 | 57 092 | ... | ... | ... | ... | ... |
| Czech Republic | ... | ... | ... | ... | 40 315 | 59 536 | 61 470 | 135 990 | 207 016 | 185 156 |
| Democratic People's Republic of Korea | 4 927 | 8 081 | 9 879 | 12 075 | 14 702 | 4 849 | 10 608 | 13 031 | 13 945 | 16 283 |
| Democratic Republic of the Congo | 4 770 | 9 758 | 15 639 | 7 524 | 14 829 | 8 947 | 8 339 | 11 965 | 21 672 | 37 569 |
| Denmark | 17 075 | 40 475 | 71 127 | 62 659 | 138 248 | 185 008 | 164 158 | 264 467 | 321 995 | 301 308 |
| Djibouti | 66 | 157 | 301 | 369 | 457 | 510 | 556 | 709 | 1 067 | 1 737 |
| Dominica | 23 | 40 | 70 | 117 | 198 | 260 | 321 | 370 | 494 | 512 |
| Dominican Republic | 1 859 | 4 504 | 8 298 | 5 618 | 9 522 | 15 747 | 23 960 | 35 510 | 53 043 | 67 103 |
| Ecuador | 2 861 | 7 728 | 17 873 | 17 141 | 15 232 | 24 421 | 18 319 | 41 507 | 69 555 | 100 177 |
| Egypt | 8 143 | 12 678 | 20 119 | 23 801 | 36 014 | 65 758 | 95 684 | 94 456 | 214 630 | 315 917 |
| El Salvador | 338 | 589 | 1 173 | 1 886 | 4 801 | 9 501 | 13 134 | 17 094 | 21 418 | 25 850 |
| Equatorial Guinea | 21 | 35 | 56 | 88 | 170 | 215 | 1 511 | 8 520 | 16 299 | 13 812 |
| Eritrea | ... | ... | ... | ... | 332 | 640 | 706 | 1 098 | 2 117 | 4 783 |
| Estonia | ... | ... | ... | ... | 5 618 | 4 423 | 5 690 | 14 003 | 19 503 | 22 460 |
| Ethiopia | ... | ... | ... | ... | 11 208 | 7 587 | 8 030 | 12 164 | 26 311 | 59 917 |
| Ethiopia (former) | 2 559 | 3 828 | 5 889 | 9 615 | 11 540 | ... | ... | ... | ... | ... |
| Fiji | 221 | 685 | 1 205 | 1 143 | 1 339 | 1 993 | 1 708 | 2 981 | 3 141 | 4 391 |
| Finland | 11 366 | 29 494 | 53 689 | 55 914 | 141 525 | 134 196 | 125 540 | 204 431 | 247 800 | 231 960 |
| France | 148 943 | 362 017 | 703 542 | 555 202 | 1 275 259 | 1 609 794 | 1 368 437 | 2 203 624 | 2 646 837 | 2 418 946 |
| French Polynesia | 263 | 714 | 1 558 | 1 716 | 3 568 | 4 421 | 3 757 | 5 703 | 6 081 | 5 135 |
| Gabon | 410 | 2 733 | 5 421 | 4 639 | 6 039 | 5 519 | 5 677 | 9 579 | 12 882 | 13 735 |
| Gambia | 96 | 352 | 504 | 654 | 708 | 786 | 783 | 624 | 952 | 942 |
| Georgia | ... | ... | ... | ... | 8 454 | 2 703 | 3 058 | 6 411 | 11 638 | 13 965 |
| Germany | 215 019 | 488 770 | 946 738 | 729 751 | 1 764 944 | 2 591 447 | 1 949 952 | 2 861 339 | 3 417 095 | 3 363 600 |
| Ghana | 3 549 | 3 528 | 5 233 | 6 605 | 9 983 | 10 361 | 7 986 | 17 199 | 32 174 | 37 156 |
| Greece | 13 134 | 28 538 | 56 845 | 47 816 | 97 893 | 136 886 | 131 719 | 247 777 | 299 362 | 194 860 |
| Greenland | 68 | 208 | 468 | 406 | 1 002 | 1 189 | 1 050 | 1 650 | 2 287 | 2 078 |
| Grenada | 19 | 51 | 89 | 137 | 238 | 280 | 523 | 701 | 777 | 954 |
| Guatemala | 1 697 | 3 250 | 7 024 | 9 967 | 6 820 | 13 066 | 17 196 | 27 211 | 41 338 | 63 794 |

Annex table A.2
**Gross domestic product, 1970–2015** (*continued*)

Millions of current United States dollars

| Country/area | 1970 | 1975 | 1980 | 1985 | 1990 | 1995 | 2000 | 2005 | 2010 | 2015 |
|---|---|---|---|---|---|---|---|---|---|---|
| Guinea | 767 | 1 251 | 1 999 | 2 848 | 3 906 | 5 260 | 4 269 | 4 063 | 6 853 | 8 875 |
| Guinea-Bissau | 281 | 508 | 469 | 415 | 610 | 800 | 363 | 587 | 849 | 978 |
| Guyana | 427 | 804 | 943 | 737 | 632 | 991 | 1 137 | 1 315 | 2 259 | 3 282 |
| Haiti | 439 | 904 | 1 835 | 2 665 | 3 096 | 2 696 | 3 665 | 4 154 | 6 708 | 8 501 |
| Honduras | 824 | 1 341 | 3 061 | 4 342 | 3 637 | 4 724 | 7 187 | 9 757 | 15 839 | 20 365 |
| Hungary | 6 358 | 12 560 | 25 359 | 23 597 | 37 011 | 46 301 | 47 209 | 112 589 | 130 256 | 121 715 |
| Iceland | 531 | 1 418 | 3 409 | 3 008 | 6 522 | 7 182 | 8 946 | 16 691 | 13 255 | 16 780 |
| India | 59 603 | 97 386 | 179 148 | 219 581 | 316 869 | 358 024 | 453 578 | 812 059 | 1 650 635 | 2 116 239 |
| Indonesia | 10 440 | 35 639 | 84 791 | 102 171 | 133 858 | 236 456 | 175 702 | 304 372 | 755 094 | 861 934 |
| Iran (Islamic Republic of) | 10 976 | 52 165 | 95 617 | 76 257 | 96 364 | 114 364 | 109 592 | 219 846 | 467 790 | 398 563 |
| Iraq | 2 357 | 4 910 | 12 560 | 12 074 | 17 079 | 3 477 | 16 898 | 36 268 | 117 138 | 164 234 |
| Ireland | 4 401 | 9 494 | 21 769 | 21 291 | 49 356 | 69 210 | 99 855 | 211 680 | 221 343 | 283 716 |
| Israel | 6 078 | 14 633 | 24 195 | 27 672 | 59 369 | 100 279 | 132 328 | 142 462 | 233 756 | 299 413 |
| Italy | 113 026 | 226 966 | 475 663 | 450 706 | 1 177 387 | 1 170 824 | 1 141 759 | 1 852 616 | 2 125 058 | 1 821 580 |
| Jamaica | 1 586 | 3 242 | 3 036 | 2 380 | 4 822 | 6 544 | 9 005 | 11 244 | 13 220 | 14 262 |
| Japan | 211 514 | 518 856 | 1 099 693 | 1 400 715 | 3 139 974 | 5 449 118 | 4 887 520 | 4 755 410 | 5 700 098 | 4 383 076 |
| Jordan | 593 | 1 220 | 4 013 | 5 119 | 4 020 | 6 732 | 8 461 | 12 589 | 26 425 | 37 517 |
| Kazakhstan | ... | ... | ... | ... | 29 716 | 20 555 | 18 292 | 57 124 | 148 047 | 181 754 |
| Kenya | 2 518 | 4 827 | 10 518 | 9 110 | 12 664 | 13 428 | 14 465 | 21 506 | 40 000 | 63 399 |
| Kiribati | 20 | 78 | 62 | 30 | 40 | 56 | 75 | 112 | 153 | 162 |
| Kosovo | ... | ... | ... | ... | 4 424 | 5 304 | 1 695 | 3 680 | 5 830 | 6 440 |
| Kuwait | 2 873 | 12 016 | 28 691 | 21 446 | 18 471 | 26 554 | 37 718 | 80 798 | 115 416 | 114 054 |
| Kyrgyzstan | ... | ... | ... | ... | 2 612 | 1 492 | 1 370 | 2 460 | 4 794 | 6 572 |
| Lao People's Democratic Republic | 115 | 206 | 320 | 601 | 866 | 1 708 | 1 665 | 2 717 | 6 744 | 12 585 |
| Latvia | ... | ... | ... | ... | 9 674 | 5 407 | 7 938 | 16 922 | 23 765 | 27 004 |
| Lebanon | 1 990 | 4 355 | 5 447 | 2 275 | 2 950 | 11 506 | 16 679 | 21 490 | 38 420 | 50 149 |
| Lesotho | 67 | 138 | 351 | 248 | 545 | 859 | 771 | 1 368 | 2 187 | 2 008 |
| Liberia | 259 | 509 | 765 | 881 | 487 | 171 | 528 | 608 | 1 074 | 2 053 |
| Libya | 3 979 | 13 649 | 38 186 | 29 887 | 31 088 | 28 292 | 38 471 | 45 451 | 80 942 | 34 457 |
| Liechtenstein | 101 | 275 | 597 | 591 | 1 588 | 2 713 | 2 775 | 4 087 | 5 678 | 6 361 |
| Lithuania | ... | ... | ... | ... | 10 257 | 6 702 | 11 539 | 26 141 | 37 130 | 41 402 |
| Luxembourg | 1 505 | 3 224 | 6 215 | 4 725 | 13 192 | 21 528 | 21 375 | 36 976 | 52 906 | 56 802 |
| Madagascar | 898 | 1 844 | 3 265 | 2 858 | 3 080 | 3 160 | 3 878 | 5 039 | 8 730 | 9 739 |
| Malawi | 579 | 1 108 | 2 236 | 2 028 | 3 166 | 2 474 | 3 150 | 3 656 | 6 960 | 6 420 |
| Malaysia | 3 864 | 9 329 | 24 488 | 31 200 | 44 025 | 88 833 | 93 790 | 143 534 | 255 018 | 296 284 |
| Maldives | 42 | 53 | 92 | 165 | 278 | 562 | 879 | 1 120 | 2 323 | 3 435 |
| Mali | 350 | 766 | 1 804 | 1 377 | 2 985 | 3 168 | 2 954 | 6 245 | 10 679 | 13 100 |
| Malta | 259 | 491 | 1 293 | 1 156 | 2 635 | 3 697 | 4 053 | 6 393 | 8 741 | 9 747 |
| Marshall Islands | 8 | 17 | 27 | 44 | 79 | 121 | 111 | 138 | 164 | 183 |
| Mauritania | 324 | 759 | 1 496 | 1 085 | 1 623 | 1 681 | 1 294 | 2 184 | 4 338 | 5 023 |
| Mauritius | 197 | 581 | 1 160 | 1 103 | 2 619 | 4 092 | 4 663 | 6 489 | 9 718 | 11 511 |
| Mexico | 44 232 | 109 521 | 231 889 | 219 661 | 293 358 | 319 551 | 648 549 | 864 810 | 1 049 925 | 1 140 724 |

Annex table A.2
**Gross domestic product, 1970–2015** (*continued*)

Millions of current United States dollars

| Country/area | 1970 | 1975 | 1980 | 1985 | 1990 | 1995 | 2000 | 2005 | 2010 | 2015 |
|---|---|---|---|---|---|---|---|---|---|---|
| Micronesia (Federated States of) | 21 | 49 | 68 | 108 | 158 | 222 | 233 | 251 | 297 | 315 |
| Monaco | 284 | 690 | 1 342 | 1 059 | 2 432 | 3 070 | 2 610 | 4 203 | 5 362 | 6 258 |
| Mongolia | 199 | 359 | 679 | 1 218 | 1 718 | 1 678 | 1 318 | 2 926 | 7 189 | 11 758 |
| Montenegro | ... | ... | ... | ... | 2 147 | 1 215 | 988 | 2 272 | 4 139 | 4 020 |
| Montserrat | 8 | 14 | 28 | 44 | 75 | 69 | 36 | 49 | 56 | 59 |
| Morocco | 4 645 | 10 549 | 22 097 | 15 111 | 30 320 | 38 728 | 38 901 | 62 545 | 93 217 | 100 359 |
| Mozambique | 3 617 | 5 748 | 5 730 | 5 752 | 3 525 | 2 572 | 5 016 | 7 724 | 10 154 | 14 806 |
| Myanmar | 2 692 | 3 680 | 5 905 | 6 606 | 5 189 | 7 764 | 7 275 | 11 931 | 41 445 | 62 601 |
| Namibia | 633 | 1 169 | 2 532 | 1 537 | 2 679 | 4 011 | 3 909 | 7 121 | 11 282 | 11 491 |
| Nauru | 15 | 34 | 42 | 33 | 49 | 35 | 22 | 26 | 62 | 189 |
| Nepal | 1 041 | 1 617 | 2 089 | 2 741 | 3 780 | 4 534 | 5 730 | 8 259 | 16 281 | 20 658 |
| Netherlands | 37 678 | 99 360 | 192 668 | 142 011 | 314 265 | 446 514 | 412 807 | 678 517 | 836 390 | 750 318 |
| Netherlands Antilles | 224 | 468 | 943 | 1 190 | 1 980 | 2 571 | 2 857 | 3 053 | 3 848 | ... |
| New Caledonia | 378 | 817 | 1 182 | 855 | 2 529 | 3 628 | 3 412 | 6 236 | 9 355 | 8 937 |
| New Zealand | 6 496 | 13 824 | 23 365 | 24 108 | 45 440 | 63 151 | 54 444 | 114 721 | 146 584 | 173 417 |
| Nicaragua | 1 144 | 2 343 | 2 718 | 3 618 | 3 567 | 4 132 | 5 110 | 6 321 | 8 741 | 12 693 |
| Niger | 427 | 894 | 2 697 | 1 531 | 2 638 | 1 786 | 1 727 | 3 369 | 5 719 | 7 143 |
| Nigeria | 23 922 | 79 839 | 198 500 | 178 821 | 68 329 | 49 030 | 74 591 | 180 502 | 369 062 | 494 583 |
| Norway | 12 814 | 32 878 | 64 439 | 65 417 | 119 791 | 152 028 | 171 315 | 308 722 | 428 527 | 386 578 |
| Oman | 268 | 2 196 | 6 256 | 10 281 | 11 556 | 13 650 | 19 450 | 31 082 | 58 641 | 69 832 |
| Pakistan | 13 139 | 14 715 | 30 994 | 38 840 | 51 666 | 77 266 | 76 866 | 117 708 | 174 508 | 266 458 |
| Palau | 10 | 16 | 26 | 44 | 85 | 116 | 146 | 180 | 186 | 258 |
| Panama | 1 147 | 2 082 | 4 054 | 5 725 | 6 077 | 9 042 | 11 621 | 15 465 | 28 917 | 52 132 |
| Papua New Guinea | 1 091 | 2 308 | 4 242 | 3 682 | 4 937 | 7 273 | 5 258 | 7 312 | 14 205 | 21 315 |
| Paraguay | 525 | 1 336 | 3 931 | 4 017 | 4 653 | 8 066 | 7 095 | 8 735 | 20 048 | 27 714 |
| Peru | 5 829 | 13 272 | 16 647 | 14 529 | 29 119 | 53 371 | 51 743 | 76 080 | 147 528 | 190 428 |
| Philippines | 7 413 | 16 502 | 35 954 | 34 052 | 49 095 | 82 121 | 81 026 | 103 072 | 199 591 | 292 449 |
| Poland | 28 277 | 48 953 | 59 108 | 73 333 | 65 978 | 142 138 | 171 887 | 306 127 | 479 321 | 477 066 |
| Portugal | 8 109 | 19 356 | 32 899 | 27 118 | 78 726 | 118 132 | 118 358 | 197 300 | 238 303 | 199 122 |
| Puerto Rico | 5 106 | 8 313 | 14 639 | 20 574 | 31 034 | 43 246 | 62 569 | 83 915 | 98 381 | 102 906 |
| Qatar | 539 | 2 470 | 7 838 | 6 153 | 7 360 | 8 041 | 17 548 | 43 998 | 123 627 | 164 641 |
| Republic of Korea | 8 999 | 21 705 | 64 981 | 100 273 | 279 348 | 556 129 | 561 634 | 898 137 | 1 094 499 | 1 377 873 |
| Republic of Moldova | ... | ... | ... | ... | 3 978 | 1 767 | 1 288 | 2 988 | 5 812 | 6 475 |
| Romania | 12 720 | 22 897 | 36 469 | 50 742 | 40 591 | 37 657 | 37 439 | 99 699 | 167 998 | 177 956 |
| Russian Federation | ... | ... | ... | ... | 570 993 | 399 472 | 259 718 | 764 016 | 1 524 917 | 1 326 016 |
| Rwanda | 228 | 604 | 1 326 | 1 813 | 2 435 | 1 230 | 1 735 | 2 581 | 5 699 | 8 096 |
| Saint Kitts and Nevis | 25 | 51 | 68 | 106 | 209 | 300 | 420 | 543 | 705 | 876 |
| Saint Lucia | 34 | 79 | 151 | 249 | 465 | 617 | 782 | 935 | 1 244 | 1 450 |
| Saint Vincent and the Grenadines | 21 | 38 | 70 | 133 | 234 | 312 | 396 | 551 | 681 | 738 |
| Samoa | 40 | 83 | 112 | 85 | 112 | 196 | 231 | 434 | 679 | 774 |
| San Marino | 80 | 160 | 336 | 318 | 831 | 1 020 | 1 141 | 2 027 | 2 139 | 1 565 |
| Sao Tome and Principe | 35 | 57 | 78 | 79 | 113 | 99 | 72 | 126 | 206 | 334 |

Annex table A.2
**Gross domestic product, 1970–2015** (*continued*)

Millions of current United States dollars

| Country/area | 1970 | 1975 | 1980 | 1985 | 1990 | 1995 | 2000 | 2005 | 2010 | 2015 |
|---|---|---|---|---|---|---|---|---|---|---|
| Saudi Arabia | 5 377 | 46 773 | 164 540 | 103 894 | 117 474 | 143 152 | 189 515 | 328 461 | 526 811 | 653 219 |
| Senegal | 952 | 2 078 | 3 254 | 2 808 | 6 205 | 4 873 | 4 680 | 8 708 | 12 926 | 13 633 |
| Serbia | ... | ... | ... | ... | 40 444 | 21 823 | 9 385 | 26 252 | 39 460 | 37 160 |
| Seychelles | 22 | 58 | 178 | 204 | 445 | 614 | 747 | 919 | 970 | 1 363 |
| Sierra Leone | 456 | 751 | 1 333 | 1 376 | 879 | 1 179 | 861 | 1 650 | 2 578 | 4 483 |
| Singapore | 1 919 | 5 789 | 12 079 | 18 555 | 38 900 | 87 892 | 95 836 | 127 418 | 236 420 | 292 734 |
| Sint Maarten | ... | ... | ... | ... | ... | ... | ... | 708 | 896 | 1 094 |
| Slovakia | ... | ... | ... | ... | 16 777 | 19 959 | 20 680 | 48 965 | 89 501 | 87 268 |
| Slovenia | ... | ... | ... | ... | 18 116 | 21 274 | 20 344 | 36 345 | 48 014 | 42 777 |
| Solomon Islands | 32 | 65 | 144 | 160 | 208 | 365 | 338 | 429 | 720 | 1 075 |
| Somalia | 341 | 757 | 575 | 810 | 994 | 1 122 | 2 052 | 2 316 | 1 071 | 1 559 |
| South Africa | 18 656 | 38 493 | 83 913 | 59 648 | 116 699 | 157 434 | 138 436 | 257 772 | 375 348 | 314 571 |
| South Sudan | ... | ... | ... | ... | ... | ... | ... | ... | 15 720 | 13 167 |
| Spain | 40 881 | 114 458 | 232 115 | 180 305 | 535 071 | 612 943 | 595 402 | 1 157 248 | 1 431 588 | 1 192 955 |
| Sri Lanka | 2 815 | 4 510 | 4 891 | 6 873 | 9 390 | 15 293 | 19 132 | 27 932 | 56 726 | 82 316 |
| State of Palestine | 177 | 579 | 1 074 | 1 005 | 1 936 | 3 283 | 4 314 | 4 832 | 8 913 | 12 677 |
| Sudan | ... | ... | ... | ... | ... | ... | ... | ... | 53 944 | 79 546 |
| Sudan (former) | 1 234 | 3 242 | 6 365 | 6 624 | 12 637 | 12 847 | 13 092 | 35 183 | 69 665 | ... |
| Suriname | 356 | 638 | 1 089 | 1 196 | 753 | 844 | 1 157 | 2 193 | 4 368 | 4 879 |
| Swaziland | 155 | 396 | 806 | 539 | 1 254 | 1 902 | 1 705 | 3 107 | 4 526 | 4 133 |
| Sweden | 37 555 | 81 717 | 140 089 | 112 514 | 258 155 | 264 053 | 259 801 | 389 043 | 488 378 | 495 694 |
| Switzerland | 24 214 | 63 411 | 118 710 | 107 495 | 257 428 | 341 768 | 271 653 | 407 543 | 581 209 | 670 790 |
| Syrian Arab Republic | 1 756 | 5 311 | 13 146 | 10 050 | 11 164 | 13 547 | 19 666 | 28 397 | 60 465 | 28 393 |
| Tajikistan | ... | ... | ... | ... | 2 844 | 1 218 | 861 | 2 312 | 5 642 | 7 853 |
| Thailand | 7 374 | 15 489 | 33 467 | 40 240 | 88 299 | 168 998 | 126 148 | 189 318 | 340 923 | 395 168 |
| The former Yugoslav Republic of Macedonia | ... | ... | ... | ... | 2 913 | 4 707 | 3 773 | 6 259 | 9 407 | 10 052 |
| Timor-Leste | ... | ... | ... | ... | 209 | 451 | 453 | 1 850 | 4 274 | 2 873 |
| Togo | 265 | 599 | 1 131 | 740 | 1 789 | 1 446 | 1 294 | 2 110 | 3 173 | 4 086 |
| Tonga | 17 | 43 | 79 | 73 | 162 | 203 | 189 | 262 | 374 | 402 |
| Trinidad and Tobago | 822 | 2 443 | 6 236 | 7 376 | 5 068 | 5 329 | 8 154 | 15 982 | 22 158 | 25 927 |
| Tunisia | 1 580 | 4 753 | 9 599 | 9 234 | 13 520 | 19 795 | 21 473 | 32 272 | 44 051 | 41 199 |
| Turkey | 24 444 | 62 735 | 92 477 | 90 379 | 202 546 | 227 607 | 266 560 | 482 986 | 731 144 | 717 888 |
| Turkmenistan | ... | ... | ... | ... | 3 076 | 2 190 | 4 932 | 14 182 | 22 583 | 37 597 |
| Turks and Caicos Islands | 10 | 18 | 32 | 58 | 106 | 191 | 319 | 579 | 687 | 863 |
| Tuvalu | 3 | 4 | 4 | 4 | 10 | 12 | 12 | 22 | 32 | 33 |
| Uganda | 1 424 | 2 791 | 3 248 | 4 742 | 4 316 | 7 146 | 6 776 | 11 154 | 19 803 | 25 282 |
| Ukraine | ... | ... | ... | ... | 93 633 | 50 379 | 32 375 | 89 239 | 141 209 | 90 615 |
| Union of Soviet Socialist Republics | 433 412 | 685 972 | 940 038 | 914 118 | 783 307 | ... | ... | ... | ... | ... |
| United Arab Emirates | 1 053 | 14 721 | 43 599 | 40 604 | 50 701 | 65 744 | 104 337 | 180 617 | 286 185 | 370 296 |
| United Kingdom of Great Britain and Northern Ireland | 130 682 | 241 735 | 564 954 | 489 256 | 1 093 214 | 1 320 322 | 1 635 365 | 2 508 111 | 2 429 680 | 2 858 003 |

Annex table A.2
**Gross domestic product, 1970–2015** (*continued*)

Millions of current United States dollars

| Country/area | 1970 | 1975 | 1980 | 1985 | 1990 | 1995 | 2000 | 2005 | 2010 | 2015 |
|---|---|---|---|---|---|---|---|---|---|---|
| United Republic of Tanzania | 2 435 | 4 894 | 9 342 | 11 654 | 6 863 | 7 575 | 13 017 | 18 072 | 31 105 | 45 628 |
| United Republic of Tanzania: Zanzibar | ... | ... | ... | ... | 137 | 186 | 298 | 438 | 746 | 1 159 |
| United States of America | 1 075 900 | 1 688 900 | 2 862 500 | 4 346 700 | 5 979 600 | 7 664 060 | 10 284 779 | 13 093 726 | 14 964 372 | 18 036 648 |
| Uruguay | 2 538 | 3 825 | 10 642 | 5 226 | 9 239 | 21 312 | 22 823 | 17 363 | 40 287 | 53 442 |
| Uzbekistan | ... | ... | ... | ... | 14 742 | 13 474 | 13 759 | 14 396 | 39 526 | 69 004 |
| Vanuatu | 38 | 80 | 124 | 133 | 171 | 273 | 265 | 395 | 701 | 737 |
| Venezuela (Bolivarian Republic of) | 13 830 | 32 125 | 69 147 | 59 963 | 47 036 | 74 889 | 117 146 | 145 514 | 393 806 | 344 331 |
| Viet Nam | 2 775 | 3 896 | 2 396 | 4 797 | 6 472 | 20 736 | 31 173 | 57 633 | 115 932 | 193 241 |
| Yemen | ... | ... | ... | ... | 4 036 | 5 936 | 10 865 | 19 041 | 30 907 | 29 688 |
| Yemen Arab Republic | 398 | 924 | 1 620 | 2 324 | 3 602 | ... | ... | ... | ... | ... |
| Yemen (People's Democratic Republic of) | 154 | 140 | 355 | 534 | 699 | ... | ... | ... | ... | ... |
| Yugoslavia | 14 554 | 33 279 | 69 959 | 73 312 | 87 994 | ... | ... | ... | ... | ... |
| Zambia | 1 544 | 2 658 | 4 315 | 2 772 | 3 795 | 3 807 | 3 601 | 8 332 | 20 265 | 21 255 |
| Zimbabwe | 2 023 | 4 692 | 7 148 | 7 548 | 11 738 | 9 576 | 7 549 | 6 223 | 9 422 | 13 893 |

Source: UN/DESA, based on data from the Statistics Division. Available at https://unstats.un.org/unsd/snaama/dnlList.asp.
Note: The data set was used in its entirety by UN/DESA.
Three dots (...) indicate that data are not applicable or not available.

Annex table A.3
## Agriculture, hunting, forestry and fishing value added, 1970–2015

Millions of current United States dollars

| Country/area | 1970 | 1975 | 1980 | 1985 | 1990 | 1995 | 2000 | 2005 | 2010 | 2015 |
|---|---|---|---|---|---|---|---|---|---|---|
| Afghanistan | 878.69 | 1 188.98 | 1 831.21 | 1 701.70 | 1 294.40 | 2 125.80 | 2 013.19 | 2 266.79 | 4 462.63 | 4 482.95 |
| Albania | 864.79 | 996.63 | 835.44 | 933.66 | 894.42 | 1 353.01 | 854.99 | 1 517.44 | 2 141.59 | 2 246.43 |
| Algeria | 683.79 | 1 748.65 | 3 402.34 | 4 839.48 | 7 074.61 | 4 166.42 | 4 647.02 | 7 937.30 | 13 648.52 | 19 231.03 |
| Andorra | 0.40 | 1.11 | 2.24 | 1.74 | 5.22 | 6.66 | 6.99 | 13.19 | 16.77 | 13.22 |
| Angola | 540.87 | 589.46 | 1 014.01 | 1 223.24 | 2 442.10 | 483.15 | 691.56 | 1 870.88 | 5 179.05 | 8 131.42 |
| Anguilla | 0.18 | 0.34 | 0.57 | 1.32 | 3.13 | 3.02 | 3.06 | 5.35 | 4.87 | 6.54 |
| Antigua and Barbuda | 1.36 | 3.93 | 4.02 | 5.09 | 8.18 | 9.49 | 13.20 | 17.97 | 18.76 | 22.86 |
| Argentina | 2 637.36 | 2 956.18 | 4 503.68 | 6 322.72 | 10 788.02 | 12 976.64 | 12 502.35 | 15 917.97 | 30 409.90 | 31 807.09 |
| Armenia | ... | ... | ... | ... | 368.26 | 523.03 | 443.59 | 934.77 | 1 574.78 | 1 818.25 |
| Aruba | 0.89 | 1.15 | 1.49 | 1.93 | 3.84 | 6.70 | 7.68 | 9.01 | 10.74 | 12.26 |
| Australia | 2 630.61 | 5 822.93 | 9 767.47 | 7 717.47 | 10 388.30 | 13 383.67 | 14 331.87 | 20 880.91 | 29 722.26 | 28 311.21 |
| Austria | 1 071.13 | 2 051.16 | 3 551.71 | 2 176.46 | 5 158.13 | 5 205.84 | 3 240.57 | 3 978.54 | 4 982.30 | 4 331.32 |
| Azerbaijan | ... | ... | ... | ... | 1 769.53 | 780.85 | 848.12 | 1 211.63 | 2 933.41 | 3 304.14 |
| Bahamas | 11.37 | 17.83 | 31.45 | 42.97 | 105.95 | 147.33 | 165.67 | 157.77 | 170.02 | 143.31 |
| Bahrain | 3.47 | 10.03 | 28.56 | 41.19 | 35.92 | 49.94 | 57.76 | 51.57 | 76.54 | 98.19 |
| Bangladesh | 2 437.22 | 4 137.13 | 5 680.73 | 6 595.42 | 8 540.70 | 9 592.43 | 11 193.75 | 11 134.25 | 19 467.68 | 28 747.90 |
| Barbados | 15.34 | 40.49 | 66.57 | 60.32 | 69.70 | 71.40 | 61.05 | 60.60 | 60.50 | 64.73 |
| Belarus | ... | ... | ... | ... | 4 315.64 | 2 184.60 | 1 277.26 | 2 573.45 | 5 095.96 | 3 673.37 |
| Belgium | 983.39 | 1 982.44 | 2 875.74 | 2 055.38 | 4 116.83 | 3 765.37 | 2 778.60 | 3 242.05 | 3 686.67 | 3 044.39 |
| Belize | 6.05 | 29.07 | 46.76 | 37.35 | 73.65 | 101.35 | 121.89 | 148.27 | 160.62 | 227.44 |
| Benin | 98.11 | 172.74 | 436.80 | 337.42 | 690.66 | 502.91 | 588.10 | 1 187.17 | 1 584.81 | 1 737.43 |
| Bermuda | 2.04 | 3.78 | 6.95 | 10.99 | 15.61 | 19.21 | 23.28 | 39.03 | 42.97 | 41.38 |
| Bhutan | 26.45 | 37.15 | 57.67 | 72.93 | 101.61 | 92.59 | 117.70 | 182.91 | 266.32 | 337.70 |
| Bolivia (Plurinational State of) | 168.35 | 499.75 | 658.29 | 1 197.08 | 747.35 | 997.85 | 1 088.85 | 1 126.10 | 2 041.58 | 3 379.05 |
| Bosnia and Herzegovina | ... | ... | ... | ... | 1 465.70 | 367.36 | 517.92 | 930.20 | 1 165.76 | 1 008.91 |
| Botswana | 26.23 | 80.82 | 112.18 | 52.78 | 155.70 | 219.39 | 161.77 | 181.58 | 318.14 | 312.91 |
| Brazil | 3 672.30 | 11 089.49 | 18 849.46 | 21 395.76 | 40 637.35 | 37 791.16 | 30 518.80 | 41 471.39 | 90 910.40 | 79 145.78 |
| British Virgin Islands | 1.02 | 1.76 | 2.66 | 3.66 | 4.69 | 7.28 | 9.46 | 9.48 | 9.00 | 9.39 |
| Brunei Darussalam | 0.93 | 6.65 | 13.26 | 18.08 | 36.36 | 58.79 | 65.73 | 96.48 | 100.52 | 142.65 |
| Bulgaria | 1 474.74 | 1 950.26 | 1 640.12 | 2 052.78 | 3 983.72 | 1 740.15 | 1 451.60 | 2 160.01 | 2 142.79 | 2 149.32 |
| Burkina Faso | 181.87 | 396.04 | 767.40 | 531.84 | 875.73 | 753.00 | 810.59 | 1 927.98 | 2 915.14 | 3 436.83 |
| Burundi | 154.70 | 250.26 | 530.70 | 640.43 | 586.07 | 420.35 | 255.29 | 456.32 | 780.96 | 1 036.10 |
| Côte d'Ivoire | 407.51 | 1 121.79 | 2 916.88 | 1 903.12 | 3 511.29 | 2 720.63 | 2 546.43 | 3 860.04 | 6 104.02 | 6 773.87 |
| Cabo Verde | 13.22 | 24.77 | 35.53 | 24.08 | 59.53 | 89.87 | 93.61 | 117.95 | 132.97 | 133.15 |
| Cambodia | 365.91 | 342.95 | 340.86 | 509.10 | 864.81 | 1 634.73 | 1 317.01 | 1 932.60 | 3 808.51 | 4 797.74 |
| Cameroon | 292.35 | 865.21 | 1 963.47 | 1 570.87 | 2 453.30 | 1 984.78 | 1 900.97 | 3 157.74 | 5 118.14 | 5 957.36 |
| Canada | 3 609.32 | 8 064.58 | 10 535.47 | 11 919.53 | 15 778.54 | 16 275.31 | 15 691.41 | 20 039.92 | 21 485.92 | 26 045.79 |
| Cayman Islands | 0.06 | 0.19 | 0.45 | 1.09 | 2.45 | 3.41 | 5.98 | 8.15 | 10.88 | 12.90 |
| Central African Republic | 77.83 | 172.34 | 388.88 | 328.76 | 566.98 | 427.29 | 393.55 | 606.95 | 785.36 | 531.50 |
| Chad | 132.19 | 279.92 | 295.71 | 351.30 | 567.30 | 524.01 | 582.84 | 1 720.75 | 3 424.79 | 2 495.40 |
| Chile | 465.76 | 356.66 | 1 495.08 | 955.12 | 1 958.01 | 3 580.47 | 3 637.76 | 4 637.41 | 6 936.19 | 8 515.52 |

Annex table A.3
**Agriculture, hunting, forestry and fishing value added, 1970–2015** (*continued*)

Millions of current United States dollars

| Country/area | 1970 | 1975 | 1980 | 1985 | 1990 | 1995 | 2000 | 2005 | 2010 | 2015 |
|---|---|---|---|---|---|---|---|---|---|---|
| China | 32 512.67 | 52 683.08 | 91 537.64 | 87 320.34 | 105 824.37 | 145 305.89 | 180 510.87 | 273 557.89 | 598 646.82 | 1 010 338.25 |
| China, Hong Kong SAR | 27.04 | 71.30 | 222.66 | 156.29 | 184.83 | 188.85 | 118.72 | 109.55 | 113.14 | 190.90 |
| Colombia | 1 761.30 | 3 087.16 | 6 370.80 | 5 837.87 | 6 436.18 | 9 925.44 | 8 295.40 | 11 323.08 | 18 661.94 | 18 235.29 |
| Comoros | 11.98 | 36.58 | 82.81 | 81.52 | 199.06 | 196.28 | 151.29 | 284.60 | 336.44 | 351.98 |
| Congo | 58.15 | 105.68 | 199.39 | 161.00 | 359.94 | 221.18 | 170.79 | 276.72 | 444.76 | 390.85 |
| Cook Islands | 2.70 | 2.83 | 3.24 | 1.92 | 6.02 | 8.25 | 9.73 | 13.13 | 13.19 | 24.62 |
| Costa Rica | 203.25 | 365.59 | 788.51 | 678.42 | 826.21 | 1 482.95 | 1 388.60 | 1 728.29 | 2 454.95 | 2 483.47 |
| Croatia | ... | ... | ... | ... | 1 130.95 | 1 340.42 | 1 161.22 | 1 923.03 | 2 483.90 | 1 677.44 |
| Cuba | 690.07 | 1 578.01 | 2 392.53 | 2 565.61 | 3 735.52 | 2 094.48 | 2 166.30 | 1 962.70 | 2 658.25 | 3 623.25 |
| Curaçao | ... | ... | ... | ... | ... | ... | ... | 13.81 | 13.23 | 13.07 |
| Cyprus | 92.08 | 116.71 | 222.13 | 194.94 | 411.69 | 474.38 | 363.35 | 511.91 | 537.85 | 391.50 |
| Czechoslovakia | 1 464.43 | 2 032.89 | 3 198.59 | 2 740.30 | 3 939.89 | ... | ... | ... | ... | ... |
| Czech Republic | ... | ... | ... | ... | 2 722.13 | 2 370.25 | 1 920.05 | 3 013.26 | 3 153.01 | 4 198.14 |
| Democratic People's Republic of Korea | 1 392.86 | 2 284.29 | 2 792.58 | 3 413.28 | 4 032.37 | 1 339.42 | 3 222.36 | 3 259.27 | 2 905.35 | 3 524.37 |
| Democratic Republic of the Congo | 807.52 | 1 899.81 | 3 961.75 | 2 251.62 | 4 470.84 | 5 058.75 | 2 666.16 | 2 581.94 | 4 621.19 | 6 945.47 |
| Denmark | 791.20 | 1 806.92 | 2 830.85 | 2 542.68 | 4 526.72 | 5 276.16 | 3 532.41 | 3 029.89 | 3 870.15 | 3 215.86 |
| Djibouti | 2.84 | 6.46 | 10.87 | 10.05 | 12.09 | 14.11 | 17.06 | 22.60 | 38.37 | 52.05 |
| Dominica | 8.08 | 8.50 | 15.69 | 22.23 | 34.53 | 33.69 | 40.10 | 41.84 | 56.62 | 66.57 |
| Dominican Republic | 322.43 | 722.04 | 1 248.53 | 728.37 | 1 222.74 | 1 545.57 | 1 609.71 | 2 560.99 | 3 195.57 | 4 068.36 |
| Ecuador | 744.73 | 1 727.60 | 2 879.49 | 3 236.02 | 3 125.75 | 5 351.10 | 2 821.90 | 3 935.36 | 6 769.91 | 9 379.85 |
| Egypt | 2 058.07 | 3 652.11 | 4 036.50 | 4 146.93 | 6 499.27 | 10 557.02 | 12 432.16 | 12 895.92 | 28 632.38 | 35 749.61 |
| El Salvador | 96.18 | 135.26 | 326.31 | 343.55 | 821.10 | 1 270.30 | 1 286.10 | 1 676.97 | 2 477.89 | 2 674.88 |
| Equatorial Guinea | 2.97 | 4.94 | 7.87 | 12.46 | 21.73 | 24.28 | 84.71 | 130.52 | 172.99 | 163.33 |
| Eritrea | ... | ... | ... | ... | 77.24 | 120.34 | 99.24 | 248.24 | 389.27 | 796.44 |
| Estonia | ... | ... | ... | ... | 880.40 | 223.72 | 246.01 | 434.19 | 544.80 | 656.90 |
| Ethiopia | ... | ... | ... | ... | 5 546.88 | 3 939.44 | 3 663.64 | 5 100.13 | 11 105.04 | 22 679.27 |
| Ethiopia (former) | 1 335.13 | 1 679.13 | 2 707.02 | 2 677.16 | 3 223.32 | ... | ... | ... | ... | ... |
| Fiji | 58.79 | 166.41 | 253.88 | 194.42 | 235.85 | 332.40 | 247.01 | 355.51 | 286.62 | 404.89 |
| Finland | 1 260.80 | 2 888.04 | 4 603.45 | 3 843.01 | 7 633.73 | 5 095.17 | 3 712.91 | 4 665.97 | 5 917.53 | 5 091.73 |
| France | 9 888.62 | 17 476.69 | 25 497.34 | 18 585.35 | 40 056.53 | 39 428.52 | 28 777.39 | 37 084.02 | 42 503.43 | 37 546.35 |
| French Polynesia | 20.68 | 37.62 | 82.81 | 73.52 | 163.86 | 210.15 | 170.54 | 174.48 | 138.01 | 130.72 |
| Gabon | 52.70 | 175.93 | 290.37 | 210.37 | 407.35 | 372.26 | 294.46 | 477.48 | 556.13 | 487.42 |
| Gambia | 42.87 | 122.11 | 141.52 | 168.49 | 141.14 | 167.88 | 192.07 | 168.94 | 275.58 | 186.04 |
| Georgia | ... | ... | ... | ... | 2 527.39 | 1 132.99 | 630.01 | 946.88 | 847.12 | 1 109.68 |
| Germany | 6 071.23 | 11 882.98 | 17 582.45 | 10 904.83 | 20 431.13 | 24 530.91 | 18 586.68 | 19 646.32 | 22 117.89 | 19 243.42 |
| Ghana | 1 353.72 | 1 366.71 | 2 463.11 | 2 409.94 | 3 439.90 | 3 264.91 | 2 289.06 | 5 234.96 | 9 021.51 | 6 752.22 |
| Greece | 1 445.16 | 3 189.82 | 5 838.23 | 4 761.46 | 7 772.51 | 10 096.46 | 7 159.27 | 10 615.31 | 8 633.68 | 7 082.06 |
| Greenland | 6.85 | 20.82 | 46.94 | 40.71 | 100.47 | 119.21 | 105.13 | 163.08 | 165.18 | 200.51 |
| Grenada | 3.21 | 12.27 | 17.70 | 17.98 | 23.97 | 23.90 | 26.86 | 20.62 | 34.80 | 67.60 |
| Guatemala | 286.63 | 563.56 | 1 078.74 | 1 592.76 | 1 091.06 | 1 950.62 | 2 425.90 | 3 372.02 | 4 569.67 | 6 706.86 |
| Guinea | 149.69 | 244.30 | 390.67 | 562.98 | 841.01 | 1 451.07 | 931.68 | 586.87 | 1 198.38 | 1 573.07 |
| Guinea-Bissau | 133.29 | 242.56 | 197.87 | 193.06 | 272.17 | 414.28 | 153.44 | 260.29 | 382.82 | 432.75 |

Annex table A.3
**Agriculture, hunting, forestry and fishing value added, 1970–2015** (*continued*)

Millions of current United States dollars

| Country/area | 1970 | 1975 | 1980 | 1985 | 1990 | 1995 | 2000 | 2005 | 2010 | 2015 |
|---|---|---|---|---|---|---|---|---|---|---|
| Guyana | 44.63 | 153.19 | 132.18 | 134.61 | 189.82 | 339.08 | 288.33 | 310.97 | 359.87 | 525.40 |
| Haiti | 193.50 | 369.67 | 591.14 | 852.06 | 920.74 | 634.95 | 829.69 | 919.27 | 1 448.29 | 1 504.00 |
| Honduras | 233.96 | 338.42 | 664.00 | 859.48 | 743.67 | 906.32 | 1 033.00 | 1 216.79 | 1 835.97 | 2 580.63 |
| Hungary | 984.86 | 1 910.73 | 3 703.94 | 3 321.08 | 4 121.37 | 3 291.78 | 2 308.58 | 4 156.09 | 3 914.58 | 4 218.04 |
| Iceland | 53.84 | 130.09 | 346.81 | 292.04 | 635.46 | 683.97 | 631.06 | 805.50 | 868.35 | 939.42 |
| India | 25 127.39 | 36 174.95 | 62 332.70 | 65 597.20 | 88 837.96 | 90 794.47 | 100 265.57 | 145 011.70 | 289 155.50 | 326 269.30 |
| Indonesia | 4 192.33 | 9 315.78 | 17 390.51 | 19 577.86 | 21 450.73 | 33 456.70 | 24 987.99 | 36 419.30 | 105 178.67 | 116 539.78 |
| Iran (Islamic Republic of) | 1 425.91 | 3 480.57 | 10 575.73 | 9 738.40 | 12 036.65 | 14 421.63 | 9 938.24 | 14 724.36 | 31 706.69 | 34 425.24 |
| Iraq | 561.65 | 575.69 | 899.29 | 2 591.28 | 5 205.58 | 764.37 | 971.74 | 3 440.32 | 7 150.63 | 8 693.47 |
| Ireland | 621.03 | 1 448.17 | 2 281.71 | 1 830.22 | 3 630.18 | 4 003.13 | 2 519.33 | 2 188.88 | 2 115.40 | 2 659.55 |
| Israel | 354.96 | 757.65 | 1 176.93 | 1 072.30 | 1 524.95 | 1 726.38 | 1 674.33 | 2 226.76 | 3 515.87 | 3 362.06 |
| Italy | 9 003.02 | 16 044.38 | 26 820.64 | 19 603.42 | 37 267.86 | 34 674.37 | 29 141.61 | 37 589.61 | 37 635.73 | 36 775.17 |
| Jamaica | 101.17 | 236.67 | 247.49 | 135.80 | 308.74 | 544.19 | 561.18 | 583.13 | 696.59 | 892.11 |
| Japan | 11 888.29 | 26 158.12 | 37 208.76 | 41 105.13 | 72 462.88 | 94 162.97 | 77 420.40 | 57 639.30 | 66 788.93 | 51 990.93 |
| Jordan | 37.09 | 69.03 | 197.79 | 239.47 | 283.71 | 248.44 | 170.51 | 347.25 | 789.94 | 1 380.14 |
| Kazakhstan | ... | ... | ... | ... | 10 109.77 | 2 534.36 | 1 483.62 | 3 638.51 | 6 677.72 | 8 685.70 |
| Kenya | 802.35 | 1 413.24 | 2 808.78 | 2 522.70 | 3 062.29 | 3 426.41 | 3 660.05 | 4 491.97 | 9 931.57 | 19 016.74 |
| Kiribati | 2.52 | 8.41 | 14.55 | 12.66 | 8.48 | 14.46 | 16.06 | 22.75 | 37.57 | 38.53 |
| Kosovo | ... | ... | ... | ... | 276.98 | 334.93 | 124.46 | 531.86 | 793.12 | 665.01 |
| Kuwait | 5.60 | 20.69 | 55.49 | 129.67 | 162.94 | 113.92 | 133.66 | 243.15 | 519.88 | 788.43 |
| Kyrgyzstan | | | | | 860.42 | 606.79 | 468.29 | 700.60 | 836.53 | 921.40 |
| Lao People's Democratic Republic | 50.06 | 89.96 | 139.29 | 251.32 | 408.03 | 740.81 | 701.78 | 934.14 | 1 943.73 | 2 817.48 |
| Latvia | ... | ... | ... | ... | 2 025.22 | 427.32 | 363.52 | 644.40 | 936.44 | 755.52 |
| Lebanon | 74.91 | 164.61 | 216.74 | 84.02 | 108.91 | 604.91 | 761.07 | 765.51 | 1 477.94 | 1 553.29 |
| Lesotho | 23.20 | 41.70 | 87.43 | 52.94 | 92.01 | 105.72 | 86.22 | 113.38 | 165.50 | 138.26 |
| Liberia | 59.96 | 52.26 | 132.74 | 293.27 | 248.08 | 130.92 | 353.91 | 404.00 | 696.00 | 1 451.99 |
| Libya | 101.22 | 305.81 | 675.07 | 1 044.69 | 2 355.11 | 2 116.52 | 2 661.45 | 1 106.33 | 2 008.23 | 249.81 |
| Liechtenstein | 2.33 | 6.38 | 14.11 | 13.24 | 31.80 | 38.37 | 22.42 | 34.45 | 41.72 | 43.17 |
| Lithuania | ... | ... | ... | ... | 2 595.11 | 661.85 | 643.79 | 1 130.33 | 1 110.47 | 1 353.65 |
| Luxembourg | 40.06 | 73.80 | 108.94 | 87.32 | 169.15 | 196.96 | 132.31 | 132.76 | 131.56 | 125.24 |
| Madagascar | 265.75 | 757.77 | 1 179.01 | 894.71 | 908.26 | 963.35 | 1 026.29 | 1 294.10 | 2 249.29 | 2 288.54 |
| Malawi | 470.01 | 632.12 | 1 158.83 | 872.07 | 1 407.10 | 729.85 | 1 237.44 | 1 203.32 | 2 061.09 | 1 486.34 |
| Malaysia | 1 113.48 | 2 865.63 | 5 638.97 | 6 327.75 | 6 699.02 | 11 503.33 | 8 065.00 | 11 859.23 | 25 731.07 | 25 042.89 |
| Maldives | 8.38 | 10.11 | 15.04 | 19.31 | 26.82 | 42.03 | 50.39 | 77.71 | 92.19 | 94.96 |
| Mali | 273.48 | 627.98 | 1 024.41 | 430.36 | 1 118.77 | 1 194.51 | 957.06 | 1 959.56 | 3 451.92 | 4 806.07 |
| Malta | 16.17 | 27.74 | 44.59 | 47.87 | 82.20 | 91.93 | 80.64 | 123.91 | 127.28 | 117.78 |
| Marshall Islands | 0.75 | 1.49 | 2.39 | 3.93 | 6.96 | 11.75 | 10.78 | 11.60 | 24.20 | 29.42 |
| Mauritania | 157.86 | 335.55 | 751.94 | 359.71 | 744.90 | 698.43 | 444.58 | 615.40 | 880.28 | 980.96 |
| Mauritius | 39.96 | 171.57 | 124.54 | 142.92 | 269.02 | 351.59 | 266.06 | 322.99 | 306.62 | 294.04 |
| Mexico | 4 806.75 | 10 937.43 | 17 274.52 | 18 060.15 | 20 670.70 | 15 678.98 | 23 401.37 | 26 436.95 | 33 680.73 | 39 107.74 |
| Micronesia (Federated States of) | 4.97 | 11.53 | 16.04 | 25.47 | 37.22 | 53.00 | 56.30 | 56.13 | 73.48 | 82.14 |
| Mongolia | 22.89 | 41.29 | 80.44 | 136.87 | 213.37 | 502.59 | 296.86 | 475.72 | 843.51 | 1 607.65 |

Annex table A.3
**Agriculture, hunting, forestry and fishing value added, 1970–2015** (*continued*)

Millions of current United States dollars

| Country/area | 1970 | 1975 | 1980 | 1985 | 1990 | 1995 | 2000 | 2005 | 2010 | 2015 |
|---|---|---|---|---|---|---|---|---|---|---|
| Montenegro | ... | ... | ... | ... | 238.27 | 134.80 | 111.93 | 199.38 | 317.79 | 326.73 |
| Montserrat | 0.30 | 0.56 | 0.89 | 1.59 | 1.50 | 3.00 | 0.41 | 0.38 | 0.54 | 0.74 |
| Morocco | 861.54 | 1 758.01 | 3 788.79 | 2 334.68 | 4 995.22 | 5 266.23 | 4 615.59 | 7 366.86 | 12 065.59 | 12 515.56 |
| Mozambique | 1 193.69 | 1 897.42 | 1 942.58 | 2 738.72 | 1 202.20 | 845.91 | 1 009.04 | 1 811.93 | 2 776.57 | 3 402.75 |
| Myanmar | 1 098.76 | 1 732.29 | 2 748.49 | 3 183.89 | 2 970.99 | 4 657.40 | 4 164.30 | 5 570.17 | 15 273.73 | 16 744.88 |
| Namibia | 76.38 | 141.43 | 292.82 | 144.34 | 309.35 | 468.49 | 420.90 | 753.65 | 967.76 | 703.09 |
| Nauru | 0.92 | 2.33 | 2.52 | 2.13 | 3.48 | 2.42 | 1.23 | 2.05 | 2.68 | 5.79 |
| Nepal | 692.57 | 1 070.69 | 1 160.72 | 1 285.13 | 1 770.41 | 1 698.88 | 2 103.11 | 2 793.54 | 5 401.89 | 6 075.01 |
| Netherlands | 2 019.97 | 4 442.07 | 6 885.75 | 5 597.38 | 13 080.70 | 14 379.44 | 9 247.28 | 12 144.95 | 14 340.87 | 12 160.92 |
| Netherlands Antilles | 1.48 | 3.07 | 6.58 | 12.06 | 15.79 | 20.97 | 19.37 | 22.31 | ... | ... |
| New Caledonia | 16.27 | 24.39 | 35.39 | 15.80 | 50.83 | 65.24 | 74.70 | 96.57 | 111.06 | 115.75 |
| New Zealand | 773.43 | 1 357.67 | 2 336.66 | 1 741.15 | 2 719.24 | 4 073.82 | 4 220.98 | 5 182.80 | 9 651.01 | 10 250.42 |
| Nicaragua | 167.07 | 307.50 | 351.51 | 502.04 | 627.17 | 831.33 | 907.74 | 1 020.13 | 1 486.26 | 2 154.24 |
| Niger | 209.58 | 431.40 | 1 126.76 | 552.38 | 877.36 | 625.54 | 672.77 | 1 430.25 | 2 338.81 | 2 601.38 |
| Nigeria | 5 598.31 | 14 538.16 | 31 171.26 | 37 700.84 | 13 279.44 | 11 639.82 | 14 845.18 | 46 016.88 | 86 820.12 | 102 041.76 |
| Norway | 653.66 | 1 353.18 | 2 336.60 | 1 870.60 | 3 574.59 | 3 936.92 | 3 121.85 | 4 334.96 | 6 725.49 | 6 235.73 |
| Oman | 43.13 | 63.32 | 175.59 | 242.60 | 312.24 | 395.94 | 403.65 | 502.43 | 810.58 | 1 131.86 |
| Pakistan | 4 838.20 | 4 888.32 | 9 062.04 | 10 989.71 | 13 126.60 | 19 932.62 | 20 974.44 | 26 903.41 | 40 628.22 | 63 981.34 |
| Palau | 1.27 | 2.02 | 3.23 | 5.81 | 14.96 | 7.52 | 6.35 | 7.00 | 7.83 | 8.65 |
| Panama | 142.12 | 206.58 | 349.10 | 458.90 | 530.87 | 634.56 | 791.30 | 1 006.60 | 1 104.88 | 1 448.88 |
| Papua New Guinea | 250.83 | 435.09 | 911.01 | 783.59 | 914.57 | 1 603.97 | 1 164.89 | 1 586.01 | 2 799.99 | 4 129.11 |
| Paraguay | 146.18 | 427.65 | 1 004.79 | 1 008.14 | 1 121.32 | 1 670.90 | 1 203.26 | 1 579.20 | 4 083.94 | 4 748.66 |
| Peru | 1 096.46 | 2 191.85 | 1 714.37 | 1 378.32 | 2 134.46 | 4 290.09 | 4 175.36 | 5 214.75 | 10 073.18 | 13 133.24 |
| Philippines | 1 906.12 | 4 360.52 | 7 864.59 | 7 289.06 | 9 365.91 | 15 468.21 | 11 316.70 | 13 053.81 | 24 578.28 | 30 021.49 |
| Poland | 3 839.95 | 6 650.76 | 8 087.40 | 10 664.25 | 4 693.53 | 6 854.68 | 5 318.13 | 8 847.52 | 12 298.94 | 11 013.13 |
| Portugal | 2 055.78 | 4 352.04 | 5 442.16 | 3 461.29 | 6 076.38 | 5 658.32 | 3 678.36 | 4 528.89 | 4 586.99 | 4 052.74 |
| Puerto Rico | 202.29 | 375.28 | 526.22 | 494.37 | 601.00 | 440.36 | 732.55 | 499.30 | 822.00 | 854.50 |
| Qatar | 3.87 | 18.06 | 41.02 | 58.52 | 57.69 | 79.95 | 66.21 | 59.34 | 147.53 | 262.91 |
| Republic of Korea | 2 372.20 | 5 289.67 | 9 189.83 | 11 716.74 | 21 235.89 | 29 683.90 | 22 148.84 | 25 509.89 | 24 477.43 | 28 944.69 |
| Republic of Moldova | ... | ... | ... | ... | 1 376.50 | 517.25 | 327.36 | 490.08 | 699.92 | 758.18 |
| Romania | 1 939.82 | 3 088.87 | 4 535.95 | 7 035.15 | 8 080.85 | 6 798.39 | 4 043.49 | 8 354.98 | 9 413.67 | 7 435.99 |
| Russian Federation | ... | ... | ... | ... | 87 231.77 | 26 361.86 | 14 498.01 | 32 515.88 | 50 991.66 | 54 983.12 |
| Rwanda | 136.57 | 342.57 | 700.24 | 873.69 | 984.16 | 502.89 | 644.09 | 991.35 | 1 855.50 | 2 646.42 |
| Saint Kitts and Nevis | 2.58 | 5.09 | 5.77 | 5.47 | 7.60 | 9.08 | 6.51 | 9.09 | 9.88 | 9.07 |
| Saint Lucia | 3.70 | 8.65 | 13.46 | 26.14 | 48.00 | 42.10 | 40.31 | 27.99 | 31.56 | 33.52 |
| Saint Vincent and the Grenadines | 2.69 | 4.93 | 7.11 | 17.77 | 34.47 | 30.52 | 29.44 | 30.15 | 41.41 | 46.98 |
| Samoa | 9.08 | 18.78 | 25.32 | 19.26 | 25.12 | 39.86 | 38.87 | 54.06 | 62.46 | 72.71 |
| San Marino | 0.07 | 0.14 | 0.30 | 0.28 | 0.73 | 0.89 | 0.99 | 1.27 | 1.19 | 1.04 |
| Sao Tome and Principe | 9.77 | 15.78 | 21.44 | 21.72 | 31.32 | 26.05 | 14.53 | 23.25 | 22.24 | 38.04 |
| Saudi Arabia | 226.37 | 431.70 | 1 612.89 | 3 783.37 | 6 663.14 | 8 374.11 | 9 268.56 | 10 513.80 | 12 472.76 | 14 789.75 |
| Senegal | 195.43 | 535.49 | 530.99 | 455.19 | 1 066.99 | 851.10 | 789.03 | 1 272.23 | 1 976.41 | 1 857.30 |
| Serbia | ... | ... | ... | ... | 7 947.38 | 4 300.09 | 1 721.58 | 2 619.51 | 3 364.39 | 2 516.81 |
| Seychelles | 1.83 | 4.68 | 11.22 | 11.30 | 19.96 | 30.48 | 28.42 | 29.91 | 21.93 | 30.89 |

Annex table A.3
**Agriculture, hunting, forestry and fishing value added, 1970–2015** (*continued*)

Millions of current United States dollars

| Country/area | 1970 | 1975 | 1980 | 1985 | 1990 | 1995 | 2000 | 2005 | 2010 | 2015 |
|---|---|---|---|---|---|---|---|---|---|---|
| Sierra Leone | 120.78 | 249.67 | 400.78 | 537.72 | 401.55 | 534.38 | 396.08 | 815.20 | 1 364.88 | 2 247.22 |
| Singapore | 49.26 | 124.78 | 182.37 | 171.08 | 125.79 | 127.21 | 88.28 | 70.18 | 86.83 | 103.58 |
| Sint Maarten | ... | ... | ... | ... | ... | ... | ... | 2.02 | 1.23 | 0.98 |
| Slovakia | ... | ... | ... | ... | 1 117.40 | 1 010.07 | 815.86 | 1 576.70 | 2 286.63 | 2 884.17 |
| Slovenia | ... | ... | ... | ... | 927.87 | 783.05 | 588.75 | 830.50 | 829.09 | 880.91 |
| Solomon Islands | 14.81 | 29.96 | 66.09 | 72.53 | 82.65 | 154.19 | 112.28 | 128.53 | 207.50 | 301.75 |
| Somalia | 179.95 | 401.28 | 370.01 | 515.26 | 700.64 | 698.90 | 1 123.00 | 1 222.13 | 566.61 | 824.52 |
| South Africa | 1 230.42 | 2 739.94 | 4 789.03 | 2 789.75 | 4 806.88 | 5 436.33 | 4 037.69 | 6 159.77 | 8 960.94 | 6 667.49 |
| South Sudan | ... | ... | ... | ... | ... | ... | ... | ... | 775.86 | 582.93 |
| Spain | 3 980.67 | 10 050.02 | 15 374.47 | 9 880.98 | 26 147.25 | 24 339.87 | 22 259.06 | 31 385.86 | 33 445.69 | 27 731.11 |
| Sri Lanka | 650.56 | 824.72 | 825.28 | 1 080.68 | 1 385.02 | 1 844.24 | 1 992.52 | 2 189.56 | 4 819.50 | 6 636.24 |
| State of Palestine | 22.13 | 72.25 | 134.03 | 125.39 | 240.90 | 388.00 | 417.60 | 253.30 | 497.70 | 535.97 |
| Sudan | ... | ... | ... | ... | ... | ... | ... | ... | 22 842.91 | 25 784.66 |
| Sudan (former) | 478.85 | 1 124.53 | 2 192.85 | 2 342.99 | 5 099.78 | 4 529.07 | 4 662.41 | 11 606.40 | ... | ... |
| Suriname | 23.98 | 40.08 | 84.06 | 97.72 | 132.06 | 256.05 | 239.26 | 233.36 | 413.68 | 505.21 |
| Swaziland | 37.88 | 79.09 | 162.37 | 78.14 | 103.42 | 146.80 | 145.12 | 241.97 | 329.88 | 265.32 |
| Sweden | 1 884.48 | 4 313.15 | 5 472.54 | 4 483.40 | 8 059.08 | 6 471.09 | 4 369.02 | 3 905.88 | 6 974.79 | 5 779.48 |
| Switzerland | 596.44 | 1 562.06 | 2 982.19 | 2 552.81 | 5 445.30 | 5 135.89 | 3 138.46 | 3 520.20 | 4 081.34 | 4 422.43 |
| Syrian Arab Republic | 354.36 | 950.00 | 2 658.72 | 2 108.84 | 3 157.66 | 3 820.39 | 4 864.11 | 5 762.64 | 11 935.57 | 5 865.56 |
| Tajikistan | ... | ... | ... | ... | 797.29 | 415.65 | 216.21 | 490.03 | 1 105.12 | 1 719.50 |
| Thailand | 1 909.37 | 4 162.86 | 7 777.75 | 6 361.66 | 8 834.94 | 15 375.13 | 10 746.99 | 17 413.67 | 35 901.90 | 36 128.25 |
| The former Yugoslav Republic of Macedonia | ... | ... | ... | ... | 226.78 | 518.57 | 380.93 | 609.35 | 952.08 | 1 001.55 |
| Timor-Leste | ... | ... | ... | ... | 43.13 | 92.80 | 102.12 | 134.53 | 190.51 | 147.22 |
| Togo | 98.08 | 147.66 | 301.21 | 256.52 | 549.39 | 494.22 | 454.70 | 828.56 | 1 300.80 | 1 626.60 |
| Tonga | 6.98 | 18.00 | 31.76 | 23.31 | 47.51 | 39.67 | 37.63 | 46.58 | 61.33 | 70.80 |
| Trinidad and Tobago | 40.00 | 80.19 | 140.42 | 222.86 | 126.82 | 101.89 | 99.37 | 83.82 | 115.25 | 127.70 |
| Tunisia | 228.97 | 747.20 | 1 153.96 | 1 236.26 | 1 808.14 | 1 913.75 | 2 148.70 | 2 959.30 | 3 319.08 | 4 167.87 |
| Turkey | 6 510.75 | 15 170.18 | 17 281.83 | 12 720.90 | 25 302.21 | 25 532.00 | 26 896.46 | 45 184.85 | 61 704.57 | 54 706.45 |
| Turkmenistan | ... | ... | ... | ... | 1 011.81 | 353.24 | 1 131.92 | 2 628.01 | 3 176.79 | 4 913.78 |
| Turks and Caicos Islands | 0.13 | 0.24 | 0.44 | 0.80 | 1.45 | 2.57 | 4.62 | 6.64 | 4.20 | 4.78 |
| Tuvalu | 0.38 | 0.56 | 0.61 | 0.38 | 2.20 | 2.54 | 2.25 | 4.45 | 8.51 | 8.39 |
| Uganda | 616.05 | 1 208.17 | 1 408.98 | 2 153.65 | 1 868.47 | 2 665.09 | 2 009.00 | 2 978.02 | 4 800.10 | 5 958.55 |
| Ukraine | ... | ... | ... | ... | 22 086.84 | 6 693.50 | 4 516.90 | 7 920.22 | 10 452.59 | 10 803.67 |
| Union of Soviet Socialist Republics | 70 777.78 | 85 892.12 | 105 303.03 | 133 529.41 | 141 397.95 | ... | ... | ... | ... | ... |
| United Arab Emirates | 5.73 | 79.59 | 213.76 | 375.90 | 536.70 | 1 174.95 | 2 360.68 | 2 520.41 | 2 448.49 | 2 866.44 |
| United Kingdom of Great Britain and Northern Ireland | 2 838.04 | 5 267.58 | 9 183.52 | 6 258.52 | 14 389.05 | 17 139.89 | 12 727.50 | 14 396.41 | 15 964.66 | 16 550.42 |
| United Republic of Tanzania | 411.62 | 828.10 | 1 919.82 | 3 063.39 | 2 103.28 | 2 557.83 | 4 024.67 | 5 182.60 | 9 302.76 | 13 230.28 |
| United Republic of Tanzania: Zanzibar | ... | ... | ... | ... | 35.45 | 36.28 | 65.12 | 92.64 | 218.34 | 297.34 |

Annex table A.3
**Agriculture, hunting, forestry and fishing value added, 1970–2015** (*continued*)

Millions of current United States dollars

| Country/area | 1970 | 1975 | 1980 | 1985 | 1990 | 1995 | 2000 | 2005 | 2010 | 2015 |
|---|---|---|---|---|---|---|---|---|---|---|
| United States of America | 25 131.50 | 45 964.19 | 56 380.53 | 71 013.02 | 90 638.77 | 91 894.15 | 98 500.00 | 128 600.00 | 160 200.00 | 175 200.00 |
| Uruguay | 365.53 | 514.98 | 1 321.33 | 617.91 | 910.82 | 1 597.09 | 1 368.07 | 1 518.53 | 2 901.32 | 3 316.84 |
| Uzbekistan | … | … | … | … | 4 926.41 | 3 787.60 | 4 135.53 | 3 790.60 | 7 112.19 | 12 177.05 |
| Vanuatu | 11.38 | 24.05 | 37.17 | 45.31 | 39.81 | 78.62 | 63.46 | 87.98 | 145.24 | 184.63 |
| Venezuela (Bolivarian Republic of) | 802.09 | 1 541.15 | 3 190.14 | 3 789.86 | 2 763.60 | 4 255.14 | 4 607.36 | 5 377.01 | 21 168.21 | 17 154.25 |
| Viet Nam | 1 150.85 | 1 615.85 | 993.79 | 2 001.92 | 2 438.86 | 5 483.59 | 7 440.38 | 10 795.48 | 21 306.50 | 32 835.95 |
| Yemen | … | … | … | … | 857.42 | 1 017.58 | 1 307.69 | 1 807.68 | 3 715.36 | 4 252.34 |
| Yemen Arab Republic | 220.86 | 415.83 | 514.41 | 603.48 | 959.19 | … | … | … | … | … |
| Yemen (People's Democratic Republic of) | 33.28 | 28.81 | 52.15 | 73.01 | 109.59 | … | … | … | … | … |
| Yugoslavia | 2 368.96 | 4 817.30 | 8 158.90 | 8 438.01 | 9 521.79 | … | … | … | … | … |
| Zambia | 139.15 | 309.04 | 446.54 | 319.31 | 574.26 | 536.38 | 581.48 | 1 215.50 | 1 909.19 | 1 661.90 |
| Zimbabwe | 270.56 | 715.63 | 883.82 | 1 475.51 | 1 642.46 | 1 209.58 | 1 686.42 | 683.95 | 1 154.00 | 1 538.97 |

Source: UN/DESA, based on data from the Statistics Division. Available at http://data.un.org/Data.aspx?d=SNAAMA&f=grID%3a201%3bcurrID%3aUS-D%3bpcFlag%3a0.

Note: In general, data in constant prices (where the base year is relevant) are used to examine changes over time for individual countries versus comparisons across countries. To assess structural changes in economic activity of a country, the data in current prices should be used since the sum of value added is distorted when data are converted from differing base years to a common base year.

Three dots (…) indicate that data are not applicable or not available.

## Annex table A.4
## Industry value added, 1970–2015

Millions of current United States dollars

| Country/area | 1970 | 1975 | 1980 | 1985 | 1990 | 1995 | 2000 | 2005 | 2010 | 2015 |
|---|---|---|---|---|---|---|---|---|---|---|
| Afghanistan | 427.75 | 578.81 | 890.33 | 827.80 | 858.20 | 340.40 | 819.85 | 1 669.39 | 3 306.78 | 4 485.55 |
| Albania | 1 034.02 | 1 190.93 | 996.79 | 1 040.93 | 1 069.82 | 660.08 | 676.44 | 2 019.60 | 2 974.28 | 2 609.59 |
| Algeria | 1 769.45 | 7 261.92 | 22 730.35 | 28 796.57 | 28 545.33 | 19 241.68 | 29 843.92 | 59 167.68 | 81 402.27 | 59 024.88 |
| Andorra | 15.22 | 42.61 | 86.42 | 67.15 | 199.98 | 235.09 | 202.16 | 515.08 | 451.54 | 275.07 |
| Angola | 1 496.58 | 1 633.09 | 2 849.27 | 3 906.33 | 5 560.94 | 4 413.16 | 8 804.27 | 22 331.16 | 43 884.48 | 61 617.29 |
| Anguilla | 0.63 | 1.18 | 1.91 | 3.92 | 12.06 | 13.20 | 23.18 | 38.70 | 38.22 | 44.97 |
| Antigua and Barbuda | 4.60 | 10.76 | 16.14 | 26.27 | 63.91 | 73.29 | 114.79 | 148.52 | 186.00 | 218.49 |
| Argentina | 13 186.81 | 22 048.20 | 28 831.40 | 32 325.17 | 47 835.16 | 63 904.70 | 70 188.33 | 57 400.84 | 107 655.64 | 147 188.99 |
| Armenia | ... | ... | ... | ... | 1 140.77 | 369.15 | 689.66 | 2 056.09 | 3 067.87 | 2 707.85 |
| Aruba | 26.82 | 34.77 | 45.08 | 58.44 | 116.03 | 200.00 | 296.48 | 441.22 | 353.16 | 398.04 |
| Australia | 15 900.75 | 38 423.74 | 61 338.40 | 60 626.88 | 90 273.13 | 102 559.43 | 96 987.72 | 195 629.03 | 344 065.25 | 304 541.21 |
| Austria | 6 281.96 | 14 946.21 | 27 012.17 | 21 115.33 | 49 182.37 | 69 510.98 | 55 444.07 | 84 875.25 | 99 668.87 | 95 130.01 |
| Azerbaijan | ... | ... | ... | ... | 1 961.42 | 955.01 | 2 242.88 | 7 786.69 | 31 740.86 | 24 439.38 |
| Bahamas | 70.26 | 110.23 | 195.03 | 271.83 | 477.58 | 518.63 | 1 019.93 | 1 107.26 | 1 197.24 | 1 123.63 |
| Bahrain | 192.95 | 535.21 | 1 814.49 | 1 889.21 | 1 814.62 | 2 401.86 | 3 668.43 | 6 769.44 | 11 564.80 | 12 543.25 |
| Bangladesh | 732.62 | 1 184.48 | 3 659.57 | 3 964.84 | 5 800.45 | 8 929.12 | 11 093.30 | 15 048.95 | 28 577.10 | 52 177.94 |
| Barbados | 43.59 | 94.16 | 247.26 | 310.09 | 378.50 | 333.20 | 468.30 | 570.85 | 563.75 | 453.75 |
| Belarus | ... | ... | ... | ... | 9 067.21 | 4 896.74 | 3 789.21 | 11 431.12 | 20 348.92 | 18 917.36 |
| Belgium | 10 295.26 | 22 794.03 | 39 595.71 | 25 120.47 | 58 225.56 | 75 702.13 | 59 052.56 | 86 934.91 | 100 230.32 | 90 362.32 |
| Belize | 4.24 | 20.08 | 52.55 | 45.70 | 90.20 | 120.45 | 154.24 | 166.80 | 263.10 | 287.02 |
| Benin | 41.33 | 102.31 | 163.71 | 161.46 | 248.19 | 688.41 | 724.97 | 1 328.05 | 1 542.96 | 1 867.62 |
| Bermuda | 27.36 | 50.66 | 92.96 | 147.08 | 209.58 | 265.76 | 385.36 | 484.43 | 431.87 | 324.75 |
| Bhutan | 11.26 | 15.78 | 18.62 | 36.85 | 71.71 | 93.51 | 154.66 | 294.21 | 678.25 | 860.98 |
| Bolivia (Plurinational State of) | 347.73 | 727.79 | 1 230.71 | 1 190.36 | 1 552.01 | 1 957.15 | 2 161.53 | 2 508.48 | 5 923.20 | 8 316.85 |
| Bosnia and Herzegovina | ... | ... | ... | ... | 2 003.34 | 531.24 | 1 298.45 | 2 393.09 | 3 842.51 | 3 644.14 |
| Botswana | 17.17 | 71.34 | 330.24 | 386.40 | 1 896.16 | 2 076.40 | 2 680.03 | 4 256.01 | 4 073.98 | 4 343.75 |
| Brazil | 11 318.74 | 41 230.14 | 76 274.58 | 81 360.52 | 148 193.64 | 177 358.31 | 150 157.36 | 215 530.88 | 513 951.95 | 345 075.70 |
| British Virgin Islands | 4.15 | 3.67 | 4.89 | 11.25 | 15.54 | 53.47 | 91.41 | 104.33 | 90.00 | 102.14 |
| Brunei Darussalam | 207.84 | 1 434.54 | 5 785.33 | 3 475.37 | 2 466.09 | 2 799.44 | 4 411.82 | 7 787.82 | 9 410.39 | 7 934.39 |
| Bulgaria | 4 002.56 | 5 287.21 | 4 813.77 | 8 492.54 | 8 716.79 | 3 325.42 | 2 982.47 | 7 166.94 | 11 910.78 | 11 550.69 |
| Burkina Faso | 79.46 | 156.37 | 290.55 | 301.56 | 637.87 | 543.78 | 531.87 | 888.13 | 1 682.20 | 2 167.83 |
| Burundi | 21.20 | 42.33 | 121.57 | 194.34 | 235.80 | 167.74 | 118.62 | 189.16 | 312.67 | 396.85 |
| Cabo Verde | 13.99 | 25.76 | 31.22 | 35.43 | 111.74 | 172.37 | 151.61 | 229.34 | 302.05 | 277.62 |
| Cambodia | 106.44 | 99.82 | 99.37 | 147.31 | 202.25 | 409.85 | 801.40 | 1 572.72 | 2 458.53 | 4 996.15 |
| Cameroon | 227.29 | 604.88 | 2 470.32 | 2 577.79 | 3 447.25 | 2 490.13 | 3 093.11 | 4 907.74 | 6 545.16 | 7 432.33 |
| Canada | 29 257.42 | 59 475.00 | 98 281.30 | 120 680.07 | 172 566.08 | 172 094.55 | 228 907.41 | 352 337.05 | 431 006.64 | 416 174.03 |
| Cayman Islands | 2.56 | 7.74 | 18.59 | 41.87 | 96.90 | 130.85 | 229.98 | 303.60 | 270.46 | 295.65 |
| Central African Republic | 71.25 | 148.51 | 291.57 | 204.53 | 414.57 | 317.95 | 179.12 | 250.54 | 458.49 | 377.10 |
| Chad | 57.20 | 121.13 | 125.54 | 157.24 | 338.56 | 271.04 | 221.77 | 2 297.17 | 3 504.72 | 3 830.95 |
| Chile | 3 525.99 | 2 802.01 | 10 203.42 | 6 576.86 | 13 072.86 | 27 604.15 | 26 331.12 | 45 302.49 | 79 185.42 | 72 041.74 |
| China | 37 403.38 | 74 346.70 | 147 570.74 | 132 722.28 | 162 368.01 | 344 343.97 | 553 163.94 | 1 078 320.54 | 2 841 625.63 | 4 523 976.11 |

Annex table A.4
**Industry value added, 1970–2015** (*continued*)

Millions of current United States dollars

| Country/area | 1970 | 1975 | 1980 | 1985 | 1990 | 1995 | 2000 | 2005 | 2010 | 2015 |
|---|---|---|---|---|---|---|---|---|---|---|
| China, Hong Kong SAR | 1 041.16 | 2 746.96 | 7 906.29 | 9 036.21 | 16 894.70 | 19 956.34 | 20 772.76 | 15 369.54 | 15 638.23 | 21 568.48 |
| China, Macao SAR | 42.30 | 112.86 | 255.97 | 338.50 | 788.48 | 845.06 | 766.14 | 1 327.29 | 1 357.62 | 1 973.80 |
| Colombia | 2 363.42 | 4 644.92 | 12 859.21 | 14 863.83 | 17 539.93 | 32 166.24 | 27 271.85 | 43 982.46 | 91 903.40 | 90 773.09 |
| Comoros | 6.41 | 19.52 | 44.28 | 44.43 | 49.73 | 57.33 | 17.78 | 32.88 | 43.21 | 45.66 |
| Congo | 58.68 | 220.20 | 795.27 | 1 165.08 | 1 137.50 | 949.42 | 2 323.25 | 4 375.40 | 9 433.82 | 5 821.23 |
| Cook Islands | 2.25 | 1.81 | 2.08 | 2.49 | 5.76 | 8.68 | 7.85 | 18.25 | 22.63 | 27.23 |
| Costa Rica | 259.46 | 586.38 | 1 492.13 | 1 253.49 | 1 642.13 | 2 643.01 | 3 820.00 | 4 863.58 | 8 661.11 | 10 425.51 |
| Côte d'Ivoire | 319.60 | 836.19 | 2 035.81 | 1 474.86 | 2 835.48 | 2 283.89 | 2 807.68 | 3 898.24 | 5 576.19 | 8 087.76 |
| Croatia | ... | ... | ... | ... | 6 744.48 | 6 028.54 | 5 316.95 | 11 162.39 | 13 804.58 | 10 855.86 |
| Cuba | 964.15 | 2 206.26 | 3 376.30 | 3 934.39 | 4 972.16 | 5 465.24 | 7 182.30 | 6 761.40 | 10 925.85 | 14 829.49 |
| Curaçao | ... | ... | ... | ... | ... | ... | ... | 361.30 | 437.77 | 568.73 |
| Cyprus | 145.22 | 184.35 | 734.73 | 687.78 | 1 451.51 | 1 992.48 | 1 762.10 | 3 344.51 | 3 762.29 | 1 817.10 |
| Czechoslovakia | 6 777.07 | 12 225.94 | 20 362.70 | 18 627.20 | 22 844.80 | ... | ... | ... | ... | ... |
| Czech Republic | ... | ... | ... | ... | 15 914.62 | 21 135.23 | 20 883.03 | 46 427.42 | 69 004.28 | 62 883.20 |
| Democratic People's Republic of Korea | 2 389.46 | 3 918.73 | 4 790.70 | 5 855.53 | 8 017.71 | 2 038.96 | 3 939.01 | 5 575.14 | 6 722.92 | 7 517.48 |
| Democratic Republic of the Congo | 1 741.15 | 2 612.24 | 5 169.53 | 2 196.76 | 4 185.84 | 1 508.75 | 1 868.40 | 3 803.80 | 8 343.58 | 15 476.17 |
| Denmark | 4 666.82 | 10 344.17 | 16 750.14 | 14 352.18 | 31 002.08 | 40 872.90 | 38 827.71 | 58 816.29 | 63 448.83 | 59 960.10 |
| Djibouti | 9.73 | 27.16 | 49.49 | 67.70 | 87.03 | 67.65 | 73.90 | 102.17 | 200.45 | 334.00 |
| Dominica | 1.39 | 4.56 | 9.93 | 13.38 | 24.98 | 39.27 | 52.89 | 47.42 | 59.22 | 57.09 |
| Dominican Republic | 767.97 | 2 108.52 | 3 066.64 | 2 284.49 | 3 192.47 | 5 067.08 | 7 588.22 | 10 748.77 | 14 779.26 | 17 317.57 |
| Ecuador | 785.71 | 1 979.89 | 4 790.61 | 5 055.74 | 4 589.37 | 6 627.90 | 6 158.27 | 13 093.24 | 24 152.54 | 31 606.25 |
| Egypt | 1 970.47 | 2 950.85 | 6 989.53 | 7 175.22 | 9 897.49 | 20 550.79 | 29 902.54 | 33 103.28 | 76 801.92 | 116 119.57 |
| El Salvador | 78.95 | 146.58 | 242.76 | 413.02 | 1 283.40 | 2 602.60 | 3 877.70 | 4 717.44 | 5 310.38 | 6 371.78 |
| Equatorial Guinea | 3.80 | 6.33 | 10.21 | 17.74 | 24.01 | 69.37 | 1 045.15 | 6 916.38 | 12 182.27 | 10 184.04 |
| Eritrea | ... | ... | ... | ... | 40.74 | 96.50 | 151.08 | 224.76 | 472.33 | 1 085.09 |
| Estonia | ... | ... | ... | ... | 2 627.12 | 1 244.81 | 1 413.38 | 3 692.13 | 4 772.49 | 5 325.30 |
| Ethiopia | ... | ... | ... | ... | 1 042.76 | 704.53 | 953.82 | 1 475.69 | 2 544.35 | 8 996.19 |
| Ethiopia (former) | 345.14 | 592.28 | 824.11 | 1 034.47 | 1 285.19 | ... | ... | ... | ... | ... |
| Fiji | 41.31 | 146.23 | 253.48 | 190.28 | 246.66 | 360.50 | 297.60 | 496.01 | 560.18 | 649.95 |
| Finland | 3 880.30 | 10 459.30 | 18 263.98 | 17 278.21 | 41 330.04 | 39 568.61 | 39 707.91 | 59 903.99 | 64 953.75 | 53 704.34 |
| France | 42 806.99 | 102 450.65 | 192 756.81 | 140 364.71 | 307 620.47 | 353 563.57 | 286 670.13 | 425 814.56 | 467 557.59 | 421 774.77 |
| French Polynesia | 31.60 | 105.63 | 242.39 | 329.19 | 510.20 | 509.35 | 466.83 | 648.78 | 674.88 | 555.61 |
| Gabon | 177.74 | 1 470.84 | 2 767.42 | 2 460.84 | 2 682.86 | 2 794.16 | 3 126.29 | 5 739.95 | 6 723.95 | 7 082.12 |
| Gambia | 8.89 | 54.81 | 93.80 | 77.18 | 109.53 | 116.91 | 116.05 | 87.90 | 117.35 | 130.94 |
| Georgia | ... | ... | ... | ... | 2 909.84 | 366.40 | 642.11 | 1 523.14 | 2 248.09 | 2 961.10 |
| Germany | 94 459.25 | 189 707.67 | 356 919.78 | 263 129.77 | 605 860.66 | 772 781.66 | 543 652.61 | 761 183.65 | 927 470.61 | 922 980.90 |
| Ghana | 561.80 | 678.77 | 565.23 | 1 009.10 | 1 437.84 | 2 000.24 | 1 578.97 | 3 342.11 | 5 795.84 | 9 547.50 |
| Greece | 3 888.90 | 7 953.44 | 15 850.59 | 12 575.22 | 23 805.78 | 26 849.78 | 24 694.19 | 44 115.40 | 41 395.25 | 26 990.25 |
| Greenland | 9.90 | 30.07 | 67.79 | 58.79 | 145.11 | 172.15 | 152.11 | 242.96 | 389.58 | 317.97 |
| Grenada | 3.18 | 5.72 | 9.31 | 18.20 | 31.87 | 46.74 | 93.14 | 158.91 | 113.41 | 113.81 |
| Guatemala | 458.81 | 863.85 | 2 180.06 | 2 806.29 | 1 907.02 | 3 584.80 | 4 675.60 | 7 387.16 | 11 182.73 | 16 906.59 |
| Guinea | 262.27 | 428.04 | 684.21 | 981.97 | 1 437.73 | 1 535.91 | 1 340.97 | 1 378.80 | 2 214.43 | 2 612.48 |

Annex table A.4
**Industry value added, 1970–2015** (*continued*)

Millions of current United States dollars

| Country/area | 1970 | 1975 | 1980 | 1985 | 1990 | 1995 | 2000 | 2005 | 2010 | 2015 |
|---|---|---|---|---|---|---|---|---|---|---|
| Guinea-Bissau | 59.67 | 128.77 | 87.82 | 64.96 | 111.10 | 91.79 | 52.09 | 84.37 | 111.58 | 139.30 |
| Guyana | 188.18 | 376.68 | 420.40 | 212.38 | 169.86 | 303.92 | 338.85 | 346.85 | 704.95 | 944.60 |
| Haiti | 79.39 | 187.73 | 469.35 | 631.60 | 714.80 | 819.30 | 1 130.35 | 1 351.85 | 2 325.22 | 3 434.45 |
| Honduras | 185.59 | 329.14 | 736.83 | 1 005.14 | 926.81 | 1 329.22 | 2 111.71 | 2 560.25 | 4 052.84 | 4 958.60 |
| Hungary | 2 614.15 | 5 829.53 | 9 527.52 | 8 899.01 | 11 253.76 | 11 957.13 | 12 786.08 | 30 463.54 | 33 195.56 | 32 562.03 |
| Iceland | 178.72 | 437.88 | 1 047.53 | 911.10 | 1 779.34 | 1 828.82 | 2 031.31 | 3 493.86 | 2 914.55 | 3 522.84 |
| India | 13 249.88 | 23 121.13 | 46 526.09 | 62 087.67 | 93 098.22 | 108 260.12 | 129 917.24 | 249 957.00 | 497 046.74 | 568 937.86 |
| Indonesia | 1 689.82 | 10 372.57 | 31 758.74 | 32 750.16 | 47 523.57 | 90 352.18 | 73 588.53 | 129 637.48 | 322 998.07 | 344 901.22 |
| Iran (Islamic Republic of) | 4 454.44 | 29 594.43 | 33 612.97 | 23 300.63 | 31 607.10 | 45 105.82 | 44 171.94 | 104 328.44 | 191 576.45 | 157 195.46 |
| Iraq | 1 557.97 | 4 998.28 | 14 139.85 | 7 890.67 | 8 271.07 | 4 098.76 | 17 778.70 | 31 775.52 | 77 283.32 | 110 315.64 |
| Ireland | 1 141.65 | 2 531.97 | 6 514.05 | 5 931.44 | 13 174.02 | 19 991.69 | 31 453.89 | 63 658.66 | 52 432.45 | 109 401.62 |
| Israel | 2 116.23 | 4 377.04 | 6 207.79 | 6 841.15 | 14 513.96 | 23 087.95 | 29 256.62 | 29 273.59 | 47 573.26 | 56 860.02 |
| Italy | 39 116.39 | 80 108.56 | 163 632.07 | 139 412.01 | 332 199.73 | 307 873.53 | 277 667.10 | 431 579.47 | 465 914.78 | 384 901.61 |
| Jamaica | 547.46 | 961.68 | 966.36 | 685.34 | 1 671.71 | 1 785.22 | 2 031.88 | 2 462.49 | 2 376.76 | 2 785.80 |
| Japan | 90 333.14 | 201 851.08 | 423 231.14 | 522 148.01 | 1 168 032.04 | 1 778 799.05 | 1 512 705.86 | 1 329 022.11 | 1 556 939.34 | 1 149 540.01 |
| Jordan | 106.73 | 269.36 | 1 080.09 | 1 262.46 | 1 171.89 | 1 606.28 | 1 813.70 | 3 137.29 | 6 993.91 | 9 661.15 |
| Kazakhstan | ... | ... | ... | ... | 7 735.47 | 5 952.56 | 6 909.95 | 21 494.50 | 60 110.81 | 56 892.65 |
| Kenya | 639.77 | 1 247.93 | 2 869.67 | 2 217.70 | 2 975.10 | 2 603.37 | 2 671.19 | 4 319.42 | 7 419.88 | 11 272.15 |
| Kiribati | 8.88 | 40.32 | 3.99 | 2.70 | 4.79 | 4.88 | 9.71 | 9.74 | 15.71 | 21.74 |
| Kosovo | ... | ... | ... | ... | 1 341.40 | 1 509.40 | 371.47 | 824.23 | 1 386.74 | 1 531.81 |
| Kuwait | 1 951.60 | 9 450.67 | 21 161.87 | 12 219.32 | 9 634.09 | 14 200.14 | 22 314.47 | 50 458.90 | 76 247.37 | 64 082.42 |
| Kyrgyzstan | ... | ... | ... | ... | 974.75 | 306.32 | 402.85 | 494.03 | 1 259.25 | 1 555.68 |
| Lao People's Democratic Republic | 17.51 | 31.46 | 49.43 | 104.33 | 112.42 | 271.32 | 302.46 | 598.64 | 1 891.12 | 3 921.78 |
| Latvia | ... | ... | ... | ... | 4 274.59 | 1 453.68 | 1 884.80 | 3 440.94 | 5 071.84 | 5 523.93 |
| Lebanon | 404.17 | 906.81 | 1 127.90 | 505.23 | 655.12 | 3 331.57 | 4 184.05 | 3 215.26 | 5 406.97 | 9 356.76 |
| Lesotho | 4.56 | 11.56 | 58.70 | 28.99 | 94.23 | 212.15 | 221.06 | 416.31 | 620.76 | 561.04 |
| Liberia | 98.33 | 254.95 | 235.09 | 201.94 | 76.68 | 8.43 | 3.24 | 57.30 | 112.00 | 232.89 |
| Libya | 2 722.05 | 8 758.71 | 27 408.56 | 17 459.53 | 13 824.45 | 12 805.32 | 19 538.92 | 38 703.08 | 60 204.17 | 18 676.63 |
| Liechtenstein | 31.26 | 85.52 | 188.50 | 173.41 | 450.57 | 735.25 | 1 044.09 | 1 461.08 | 2 021.47 | 2 408.55 |
| Lithuania | ... | ... | ... | ... | 2 882.33 | 1 887.00 | 3 035.17 | 7 740.03 | 9 707.16 | 11 113.29 |
| Luxembourg | 586.45 | 983.07 | 1 726.10 | 1 237.96 | 3 159.87 | 4 093.30 | 3 517.14 | 5 482.55 | 6 041.83 | 6 193.01 |
| Madagascar | 165.64 | 329.43 | 588.32 | 339.06 | 401.11 | 442.43 | 563.73 | 859.20 | 1 590.58 | 1 694.06 |
| Malawi | 123.31 | 328.46 | 799.29 | 490.39 | 937.33 | 500.85 | 583.68 | 543.50 | 1 058.90 | 943.28 |
| Malaysia | 1 053.63 | 3 370.74 | 10 234.11 | 12 240.95 | 18 577.57 | 36 778.41 | 45 319.74 | 66 554.50 | 103 279.42 | 115 934.96 |
| Maldives | 3.02 | 4.25 | 9.44 | 15.61 | 26.98 | 57.57 | 99.12 | 152.05 | 331.58 | 670.18 |
| Mali | 39.30 | 89.56 | 223.85 | 207.29 | 457.73 | 551.26 | 650.66 | 1 475.86 | 2 501.58 | 2 358.25 |
| Malta | 77.38 | 176.43 | 442.39 | 377.26 | 749.11 | 938.34 | 1 054.07 | 1 288.60 | 1 443.36 | 1 260.55 |
| Marshall Islands | 0.98 | 1.94 | 3.11 | 5.10 | 8.99 | 16.05 | 11.93 | 11.73 | 18.26 | 18.28 |
| Mauritania | 95.29 | 184.52 | 248.77 | 269.47 | 375.39 | 395.70 | 339.12 | 669.22 | 1 692.31 | 1 952.50 |
| Mauritius | 40.32 | 141.70 | 310.85 | 311.22 | 772.09 | 1 122.49 | 1 211.79 | 1 516.06 | 2 291.13 | 2 313.51 |
| Mexico | 18 197.62 | 44 401.38 | 98 725.83 | 91 113.06 | 120 476.75 | 122 990.03 | 242 474.45 | 321 068.60 | 385 854.70 | 389 637.30 |
| Micronesia (Federated States of) | 1.51 | 3.51 | 4.88 | 7.75 | 11.33 | 15.30 | 19.23 | 13.16 | 21.41 | 19.22 |

**Annex table A.4**
**Industry value added, 1970–2015** (*continued*)

Millions of current United States dollars

| Country/area | 1970 | 1975 | 1980 | 1985 | 1990 | 1995 | 2000 | 2005 | 2010 | 2015 |
|---|---|---|---|---|---|---|---|---|---|---|
| Monaco | 37.01 | 89.95 | 174.80 | 137.94 | 316.85 | 400.04 | 340.73 | 521.66 | 693.05 | 838.79 |
| Mongolia | 65.73 | 118.62 | 229.26 | 446.79 | 724.01 | 596.37 | 316.27 | 996.81 | 2 386.49 | 3 688.51 |
| Montenegro | ... | ... | ... | ... | 485.30 | 274.73 | 219.15 | 412.81 | 709.74 | 581.76 |
| Montserrat | 1.44 | 2.71 | 4.71 | 7.00 | 23.86 | 7.48 | 5.51 | 7.29 | 6.77 | 6.66 |
| Morocco | 1 123.59 | 3 358.66 | 6 094.13 | 4 404.99 | 8 322.59 | 10 336.93 | 10 407.58 | 16 281.18 | 23 917.10 | 26 400.55 |
| Mozambique | 1 128.52 | 1 793.79 | 1 803.01 | 762.48 | 596.28 | 365.21 | 1 015.58 | 1 476.33 | 1 782.09 | 2 913.49 |
| Myanmar | 351.72 | 396.43 | 748.22 | 863.38 | 546.70 | 766.41 | 705.14 | 2 089.35 | 10 969.67 | 21 625.23 |
| Namibia | 285.84 | 528.72 | 1 244.29 | 633.44 | 917.70 | 1 012.97 | 995.27 | 1 801.43 | 3 149.71 | 3 256.26 |
| Nauru | 6.16 | 10.16 | 16.63 | 11.68 | 14.30 | 10.45 | 9.08 | -1.70 | 30.04 | 114.15 |
| Nepal | 84.44 | 104.66 | 177.49 | 302.65 | 449.27 | 773.28 | 961.78 | 1 359.98 | 2 312.01 | 2 842.47 |
| Netherlands | 13 452.86 | 32 506.82 | 60 339.09 | 44 980.28 | 87 445.10 | 114 643.96 | 91 490.62 | 144 895.04 | 166 453.67 | 135 020.01 |
| Netherlands Antilles | 43.84 | 91.56 | 191.50 | 221.43 | 330.17 | 454.09 | 429.73 | 445.16 | ... | ... |
| New Caledonia | 142.95 | 392.87 | 394.40 | 221.73 | 630.45 | 796.76 | 822.84 | 1 527.80 | 2 094.48 | 2 105.34 |
| New Zealand | 2 198.95 | 4 701.39 | 8 116.45 | 8 033.12 | 12 051.04 | 16 244.75 | 12 843.29 | 27 467.25 | 31 064.24 | 36 528.57 |
| Nicaragua | 264.24 | 641.16 | 712.28 | 1 145.56 | 691.09 | 825.52 | 1 029.85 | 1 325.36 | 1 925.84 | 3 076.96 |
| Niger | 68.14 | 142.06 | 576.54 | 301.61 | 448.83 | 249.77 | 208.44 | 370.08 | 893.07 | 1 258.95 |
| Nigeria | 4 926.13 | 17 198.08 | 46 873.47 | 29 593.59 | 13 972.74 | 10 786.58 | 20 768.51 | 42 642.76 | 91 993.45 | 99 711.73 |
| Norway | 8 364.84 | 19 336.20 | 25 945.45 | 21 559.13 | 37 921.47 | 43 774.29 | 62 496.01 | 117 273.11 | 149 071.34 | 119 154.78 |
| Oman | 188.59 | 1 553.94 | 4 555.16 | 6 700.16 | 6 651.96 | 6 797.22 | 11 539.96 | 19 748.12 | 37 581.23 | 37 669.70 |
| Pakistan | 2 064.64 | 2 470.66 | 5 816.69 | 6 033.06 | 9 119.30 | 12 684.69 | 12 879.17 | 23 313.03 | 34 412.06 | 47 719.17 |
| Palau | 1.77 | 2.83 | 4.53 | 7.80 | 14.92 | 12.17 | 23.23 | 28.85 | 17.00 | 18.35 |
| Panama | 300.30 | 576.19 | 938.39 | 1 390.38 | 1 044.02 | 1 710.61 | 2 093.90 | 2 420.20 | 5 762.22 | 13 902.50 |
| Papua New Guinea | 144.73 | 465.87 | 797.68 | 604.34 | 1 004.73 | 1 677.03 | 1 548.35 | 2 380.34 | 4 631.72 | 5 790.09 |
| Paraguay | 105.08 | 266.64 | 918.77 | 920.67 | 1 100.81 | 1 878.74 | 1 613.43 | 2 806.23 | 5 458.03 | 7 383.07 |
| Peru | 1 345.81 | 3 145.36 | 4 284.09 | 4 307.18 | 8 618.23 | 15 529.88 | 15 023.21 | 26 138.69 | 52 773.59 | 57 652.54 |
| Philippines | 2 556.84 | 6 255.18 | 15 124.95 | 13 039.85 | 18 406.98 | 28 723.59 | 27 918.32 | 34 873.32 | 65 003.34 | 89 991.52 |
| Poland | 14 584.20 | 25 247.86 | 30 458.02 | 37 406.67 | 35 687.35 | 45 831.76 | 49 373.81 | 85 757.51 | 139 851.42 | 144 494.23 |
| Portugal | 1 891.41 | 4 727.61 | 8 370.69 | 6 990.29 | 20 031.09 | 29 309.27 | 28 938.49 | 42 157.73 | 47 440.77 | 38 648.04 |
| Puerto Rico | 1 937.15 | 3 312.26 | 6 323.81 | 9 072.74 | 14 075.41 | 20 469.71 | 28 221.12 | 39 634.80 | 50 077.30 | 51 507.50 |
| Qatar | 419.99 | 1 977.15 | 5 959.19 | 3 514.16 | 4 120.65 | 4 286.75 | 12 460.19 | 33 001.47 | 85 010.37 | 96 318.96 |
| Republic of Korea | 2 204.64 | 5 723.12 | 20 467.98 | 33 483.04 | 99 927.46 | 199 111.59 | 192 060.03 | 303 915.68 | 379 076.76 | 476 023.28 |
| Republic of Moldova | ... | ... | ... | ... | 1 563.56 | 503.60 | 245.02 | 570.88 | 967.91 | 1 182.60 |
| Romania | 7 020.30 | 12 466.45 | 19 074.83 | 24 447.16 | 16 962.20 | 13 619.89 | 11 274.27 | 31 767.47 | 62 057.77 | 54 531.85 |
| Russian Federation | ... | ... | ... | ... | 263 459.87 | 144 024.96 | 90 249.82 | 249 292.55 | 457 468.73 | 373 004.15 |
| Rwanda | 21.95 | 63.76 | 144.11 | 255.49 | 436.90 | 139.98 | 220.68 | 299.38 | 735.68 | 1 152.61 |
| Saint Kitts and Nevis | 4.22 | 8.95 | 12.95 | 18.41 | 52.10 | 65.21 | 113.08 | 121.75 | 175.56 | 212.20 |
| Saint Lucia | 5.11 | 11.47 | 27.19 | 34.89 | 62.90 | 91.13 | 118.16 | 151.78 | 170.60 | 160.09 |
| Saint Vincent and the Grenadines | 3.62 | 6.50 | 13.91 | 23.13 | 39.56 | 56.81 | 67.76 | 90.23 | 112.27 | 107.98 |
| Samoa | 11.10 | 22.95 | 30.94 | 23.52 | 30.86 | 53.81 | 62.53 | 134.27 | 177.72 | 189.45 |
| San Marino | 33.39 | 67.06 | 140.54 | 133.17 | 347.87 | 426.00 | 480.73 | 724.34 | 701.64 | 480.60 |
| Sao Tome and Principe | 6.33 | 10.22 | 13.88 | 14.06 | 20.28 | 19.37 | 12.57 | 18.93 | 34.34 | 45.64 |
| Saudi Arabia | 3 116.13 | 33 490.76 | 117 215.62 | 42 710.55 | 56 545.75 | 69 053.32 | 101 033.95 | 203 151.19 | 306 926.60 | 299 813.73 |

Annex table A.4
**Industry value added, 1970–2015** (*continued*)

Millions of current United States dollars

| Country/area | 1970 | 1975 | 1980 | 1985 | 1990 | 1995 | 2000 | 2005 | 2010 | 2015 |
|---|---|---|---|---|---|---|---|---|---|---|
| Senegal | 146.00 | 354.49 | 559.96 | 558.17 | 1 304.98 | 1 081.00 | 957.57 | 1 789.29 | 2 643.99 | 2 878.71 |
| Serbia | ... | ... | ... | ... | 12 846.54 | 7 288.53 | 2 887.36 | 6 418.67 | 9 343.86 | 9 644.16 |
| Seychelles | 1.20 | 3.06 | 10.22 | 15.71 | 28.52 | 70.08 | 120.74 | 150.70 | 135.97 | 157.32 |
| Sierra Leone | 128.65 | 164.23 | 282.32 | 267.03 | 75.63 | 100.53 | 77.78 | 185.80 | 200.61 | 767.82 |
| Singapore | 516.17 | 1 806.60 | 4 213.42 | 5 971.55 | 11 997.35 | 27 668.19 | 31 112.90 | 39 388.01 | 61 687.85 | 72 665.68 |
| Sint Maarten | ... | ... | ... | ... | ... | ... | ... | 110.07 | 113.12 | 124.03 |
| Slovakia | ... | ... | ... | ... | 9 196.76 | 6 603.62 | 6 661.63 | 15 694.55 | 28 630.77 | 27 415.95 |
| Slovenia | ... | ... | ... | ... | 6 612.76 | 6 335.23 | 6 221.86 | 10 884.55 | 12 801.88 | 12 097.85 |
| Solomon Islands | 2.42 | 4.89 | 10.88 | 11.95 | 14.28 | 49.62 | 41.18 | 31.89 | 96.27 | 166.72 |
| Somalia | 41.56 | 75.19 | 43.23 | 59.34 | 60.71 | 85.48 | 136.72 | 149.50 | 69.28 | 100.82 |
| South Africa | 6 554.95 | 14 758.59 | 37 209.47 | 23 252.98 | 41 272.10 | 48 649.79 | 38 933.49 | 69 952.51 | 102 775.47 | 81 311.67 |
| South Sudan | ... | ... | ... | ... | ... | ... | ... | ... | 8 385.45 | 7 397.09 |
| Spain | 15 954.05 | 45 860.00 | 85 828.30 | 60 254.82 | 176 870.77 | 177 460.79 | 166 028.06 | 315 748.89 | 341 044.60 | 255 812.91 |
| Sri Lanka | 404.38 | 951.05 | 987.12 | 1 212.77 | 1 733.44 | 2 870.01 | 4 237.30 | 6 872.96 | 15 114.08 | 23 480.63 |
| State of Palestine | 51.20 | 167.14 | 310.15 | 290.89 | 567.35 | 969.20 | 927.10 | 1 121.20 | 1 803.20 | 2 624.41 |
| Sudan | ... | ... | ... | ... | ... | ... | ... | ... | 7 291.60 | 15 984.25 |
| Sudan (former) | 177.45 | 471.64 | 912.36 | 839.95 | 1 493.37 | 1 203.39 | 2 180.42 | 7 306.56 | ... | ... |
| Suriname | 119.47 | 205.04 | 357.33 | 322.78 | 178.29 | 236.08 | 313.08 | 770.01 | 1 535.89 | 1 211.71 |
| Swaziland | 41.60 | 96.62 | 242.04 | 133.73 | 493.51 | 769.17 | 661.95 | 1 230.06 | 1 814.58 | 1 689.84 |
| Sweden | 12 919.99 | 28 823.78 | 42 395.70 | 33 891.16 | 71 405.15 | 72 283.98 | 69 729.42 | 101 642.72 | 124 224.07 | 115 270.11 |
| Switzerland | 7 993.83 | 20 944.04 | 39 849.39 | 33 447.56 | 77 146.43 | 98 426.72 | 68 310.46 | 104 853.25 | 146 980.85 | 165 695.29 |
| Syrian Arab Republic | 451.54 | 1 316.15 | 3 063.33 | 2 199.41 | 2 696.06 | 2 452.80 | 6 552.43 | 8 856.24 | 18 543.08 | 8 526.39 |
| Tajikistan | ... | ... | ... | ... | 1 222.79 | 636.47 | 303.58 | 632.81 | 1 409.24 | 1 929.23 |
| Thailand | 1 867.54 | 3 994.75 | 9 597.76 | 12 813.44 | 32 838.23 | 63 524.42 | 46 562.47 | 73 131.76 | 136 485.24 | 141 143.33 |
| The former Yugoslav Republic of Macedonia | ... | ... | ... | ... | 900.48 | 1 023.43 | 807.60 | 1 274.38 | 1 979.50 | 2 337.43 |
| Timor-Leste | ... | ... | ... | ... | 105.37 | 228.41 | 136.95 | 1 406.05 | 3 498.05 | 2 282.08 |
| Togo | 52.21 | 158.88 | 267.48 | 165.15 | 366.84 | 290.42 | 237.10 | 363.59 | 513.20 | 701.84 |
| Tonga | 1.54 | 3.77 | 7.75 | 9.19 | 18.60 | 39.50 | 35.12 | 44.11 | 67.10 | 68.01 |
| Trinidad and Tobago | 337.50 | 1 442.99 | 3 823.75 | 3 237.14 | 2 288.24 | 2 187.03 | 3 669.96 | 9 049.05 | 11 340.98 | 10 956.29 |
| Tunisia | 293.53 | 1 073.76 | 2 591.38 | 2 977.52 | 3 684.04 | 5 388.01 | 5 756.24 | 8 530.66 | 12 765.44 | 11 249.65 |
| Turkey | 6 364.83 | 16 407.54 | 26 211.76 | 27 953.65 | 72 925.99 | 82 061.48 | 74 500.40 | 119 136.29 | 172 198.81 | 168 059.04 |
| Turkmenistan | ... | ... | ... | ... | 910.63 | 1 367.42 | 2 062.12 | 5 256.02 | 10 577.08 | 18 724.83 |
| Turks and Caicos Islands | 1.68 | 3.04 | 5.52 | 10.02 | 18.16 | 32.19 | 47.96 | 105.31 | 81.98 | 81.12 |
| Tuvalu | 0.43 | 0.63 | 0.70 | 0.48 | 1.25 | 1.48 | 0.90 | 1.76 | 1.77 | 2.45 |
| Uganda | 169.93 | 333.16 | 376.80 | 409.66 | 528.45 | 1 128.59 | 1 326.26 | 2 310.58 | 3 741.19 | 5 011.07 |
| Ukraine | ... | ... | ... | ... | 40 487.83 | 19 353.61 | 10 246.80 | 26 937.81 | 36 219.14 | 20 244.68 |
| Union of Soviet Socialist Republics | 198 111.11 | 321 576.76 | 432 878.79 | 382 823.53 | 293 997.26 | ... | ... | ... | ... | ... |
| United Arab Emirates | 748.23 | 10 892.59 | 31 680.47 | 24 870.70 | 30 059.14 | 31 892.39 | 54 765.66 | 100 502.24 | 157 018.75 | 176 746.18 |
| United Kingdom of Great Britain and Northern Ireland | 46 722.89 | 85 634.04 | 202 907.03 | 160 933.91 | 304 494.30 | 331 880.35 | 371 311.17 | 497 356.05 | 439 630.84 | 493 846.51 |

Annex table A.4
**Industry value added, 1970–2015** (*continued*)

Millions of current United States dollars

| Country/area | 1970 | 1975 | 1980 | 1985 | 1990 | 1995 | 2000 | 2005 | 2010 | 2015 |
|---|---|---|---|---|---|---|---|---|---|---|
| United Republic of Tanzania | 442.88 | 838.61 | 1 483.83 | 1 435.46 | 1 167.77 | 1 247.34 | 2 189.83 | 3 577.18 | 6 315.41 | 11 094.73 |
| United Republic of Tanzania: Zanzibar | ... | ... | ... | ... | 25.92 | 38.36 | 43.53 | 70.58 | 129.27 | 209.47 |
| United States of America | 341 892.92 | 510 261.62 | 880 898.27 | 1 229 257.31 | 1 544 400.19 | 1 862 843.24 | 2 334 500.00 | 2 820 300.00 | 3 016 400.00 | 3 559 600.00 |
| Uruguay | 629.13 | 1 100.20 | 3 173.45 | 1 516.85 | 2 409.30 | 5 128.24 | 5 031.40 | 4 128.08 | 9 881.28 | 13 598.92 |
| Uzbekistan | ... | ... | ... | ... | 5 436.46 | 3 724.93 | 2 783.50 | 3 744.68 | 11 984.16 | 20 844.22 |
| Vanuatu | 2.70 | 5.71 | 8.82 | 8.22 | 16.55 | 23.60 | 30.92 | 30.99 | 86.31 | 57.76 |
| Venezuela (Bolivarian Republic of) | 6 822.61 | 18 656.00 | 40 371.84 | 30 920.34 | 27 049.45 | 34 135.12 | 54 361.58 | 77 250.79 | 190 636.93 | 145 917.48 |
| Viet Nam | 517.61 | 726.76 | 446.79 | 895.37 | 1 223.07 | 5 007.33 | 9 680.81 | 18 357.33 | 37 251.05 | 64 252.83 |
| Yemen | ... | ... | ... | ... | 877.53 | 1 608.78 | 4 490.91 | 8 222.78 | 11 826.43 | 10 663.14 |
| Yemen Arab Republic | 38.03 | 91.80 | 243.59 | 405.98 | 632.93 | ... | ... | ... | ... | ... |
| Yemen (People's Democratic Republic of) | 47.65 | 25.94 | 86.50 | 128.46 | 143.65 | ... | ... | ... | ... | ... |
| Yugoslavia | 6 127.52 | 13 929.47 | 29 727.85 | 34 010.81 | 32 073.07 | ... | ... | ... | ... | ... |
| Zambia | 584.73 | 965.38 | 1 479.29 | 1 224.39 | 1 625.24 | 1 306.30 | 836.94 | 2 237.07 | 6 533.35 | 6 513.29 |
| Zimbabwe | 698.95 | 1 723.43 | 2 635.68 | 1 967.98 | 3 554.60 | 2 485.62 | 1 403.13 | 2 335.64 | 2 452.00 | 3 617.13 |

**Source:** UN/DESA, based on data from the Statistics Division. Available at http://data.un.org/Data.aspx?d=SNAAMA&f=grID%3a201%3bcurrID%3aUS-D%3bpcFlag%3a0.

**Note:** In general, data in constant prices (where the base year is relevant) are used to examine changes over time for individual countries versus comparisons across countries. To assess structural changes in economic activity of a country, the data in current prices should be used, since the sum of value added is distorted when data are converted from differing base years to a common base year.

Three dots (...) indicate that data are not applicable or not available.

Annex table A.5
## Balance-of-payments current account balance, 1970–2015

Millions of current United States dollars

| Country/area | 1970 | 1975 | 1980 | 1985 | 1990 | 1995 | 2000 | 2005 | 2010 | 2015 |
|---|---|---|---|---|---|---|---|---|---|---|
| Afghanistan | ... | ... | 54 | -243 | -296 | -119 | -148 | -21 | -1 650 | -3 652 |
| Albania | ... | ... | 16 | -36 | -118 | -12 | -156 | -571 | -1 353 | -1 277 |
| Algeria | ... | ... | 249 | 1 015 | 1 420 | -2 237 | 9 142 | 21 180 | 12 220 | -27 556 |
| Angola | ... | ... | 70 | 195 | -236 | -295 | 796 | 5 138 | 7 506 | -8 531 |
| Anguilla | ... | ... | ... | ... | -9 | -10 | -61 | -52 | -51 | -50 |
| Antigua and Barbuda | ... | ... | -19 | -23 | -31 | -1 | -67 | -171 | -167 | -178 |
| Argentina | ... | ... | -4 774 | -952 | 4 552 | -5 118 | -8 981 | 5 274 | -1 517 | -15 934 |
| Armenia | ... | ... | ... | ... | ... | -221 | -302 | -124 | -1 261 | -279 |
| Aruba | ... | ... | ... | ... | -158 | 0 | 207 | 105 | -460 | 96 |
| Australia | -903 | -1 058 | -4 447 | -9 172 | -15 948 | -19 277 | -14 763 | -43 343 | -44 714 | -58 434 |
| Austria | -78 | -744 | -3 865 | -158 | 1 166 | -7 014 | -1 339 | 6 245 | 11 479 | 9 621 |
| Azerbaijan | ... | ... | ... | ... | ... | -401 | -168 | 167 | 15 040 | -222 |
| Bahamas | ... | ... | -75 | -3 | -37 | -146 | -633 | -701 | -814 | -1 356 |
| Bahrain | ... | -203 | 184 | 39 | 70 | 237 | 830 | 1 474 | 770 | -888 |
| Bangladesh | ... | ... | -702 | -455 | -398 | -824 | -306 | 508 | 2 109 | 2 687 |
| Barbados | -42 | -41 | -17 | 60 | -8 | 10 | -213 | -466 | -218 | -231 |
| Belarus | ... | ... | ... | ... | ... | -458 | -459 | 459 | -8 280 | -2 074 |
| Belgium | ... | ... | -4 938 | 675 | 3 637 | 15 391 | 9 393 | 7 703 | 7 977 | -249 |
| Belize | ... | ... | -4 | 9 | 15 | -17 | -162 | -151 | -46 | -175 |
| Benin | ... | -53 | -36 | -39 | -18 | -167 | -81 | -226 | -530 | -955 |
| Bolivia (Plurinational State of) | ... | ... | -6 | -285 | -199 | -303 | -446 | 622 | 874 | -2 143 |
| Bosnia and Herzegovina | ... | ... | ... | ... | ... | -193 | -396 | -1 844 | -1 031 | -899 |
| Botswana | ... | -36 | -151 | 82 | -19 | 300 | 545 | 1 634 | -356 | 1 117 |
| Brazil | ... | -6 968 | -12 831 | -280 | -3 823 | -18 136 | -24 225 | 13 985 | -75 760 | -58 882 |
| Brunei Darussalam | ... | ... | ... | 3 298 | 2 531 | 1 595 | 2 998 | 4 033 | 5 016 | 2 071 |
| Bulgaria | ... | ... | 954 | -136 | -1 710 | -26 | -704 | -3 347 | 504 | 676 |
| Burkina Faso | ... | -54 | -49 | -63 | -77 | -92 | -319 | -634 | -181 | -1 145 |
| Burundi | ... | ... | -83 | -41 | -69 | 10 | -50 | -6 | -301 | -468 |
| Cabo Verde | ... | ... | 4 | -9 | -4 | -62 | -58 | -41 | -223 | -69 |
| Cambodia | ... | ... | ... | ... | -35 | -186 | -136 | -321 | -410 | -1 693 |
| Cameroon | ... | ... | -445 | -562 | -551 | 90 | -218 | -495 | -856 | -1 552 |
| Canada | 494 | -8 196 | -6 088 | -5 839 | -20 259 | -5 061 | 18 500 | 21 931 | -58 160 | -51 713 |
| Central African Republic | ... | ... | -43 | -49 | -89 | -91 | -13 | -88 | -202 | -140 |
| Chad | ... | ... | 12 | -87 | -46 | -170 | -214 | 70 | -956 | -1 351 |
| Chile | ... | -490 | -1 971 | -1 413 | -485 | -1 350 | -898 | 1 449 | 3 581 | -4 761 |
| China | ... | ... | 286 | -11 417 | 11 997 | 1 618 | 20 518 | 132 378 | 237 810 | 330 602 |
| China, Macao SAR | ... | ... | ... | ... | ... | ... | ... | 2 965 | 12 093 | 12 108 |
| Colombia | -293 | -172 | -206 | -1 809 | 542 | -4 516 | 833 | -1 892 | -8 663 | -18 925 |
| Comoros | ... | ... | -9 | -14 | -10 | -19 | -3 | -27 | -39 | 6 |
| Congo | ... | ... | -167 | -161 | -251 | -625 | 648 | 696 | 897 | -1 260 |
| Costa Rica | ... | ... | -664 | -126 | -424 | -358 | -707 | -981 | -1 179 | -2 203 |

Annex table A.5
**Balance-of-payments current account balance, 1970–2015** (*continued*)

Millions of current United States dollars

| Country/area | 1970 | 1975 | 1980 | 1985 | 1990 | 1995 | 2000 | 2005 | 2010 | 2015 |
|---|---|---|---|---|---|---|---|---|---|---|
| Côte d'Ivoire | ... | -379 | -1 826 | 68 | -1 214 | -492 | -241 | 40 | 465 | -340 |
| Croatia | ... | ... | ... | ... | ... | -1 442 | -503 | -2 479 | -894 | 2 529 |
| Cyprus | ... | ... | -258 | -180 | -154 | -205 | -488 | -971 | -2 728 | -713 |
| Czechoslovakia | ... | ... | ... | 691 | -1 227 | ... | ... | ... | ... | ... |
| Czech Republic | ... | ... | ... | ... | ... | -1 374 | -2 690 | -1 210 | -7 351 | 1 684 |
| Denmark | ... | -490 | -2 389 | -2 767 | 1 372 | 1 855 | 2 262 | 11 104 | 18 183 | 20 691 |
| Djibouti | ... | ... | ... | ... | -11 | 78 | 33 | 20 | 50 | -537 |
| Dominica | ... | ... | -14 | -6 | -44 | -40 | -60 | -76 | -80 | -85 |
| Dominican Republic | -102 | -73 | -720 | -108 | -280 | -183 | -1 027 | -473 | -4 006 | -1 307 |
| Ecuador | ... | ... | -642 | 76 | -360 | -1 000 | 1 113 | 474 | -1 586 | -2 201 |
| Egypt | ... | ... | -436 | -1 816 | 2 327 | -254 | -971 | 2 103 | -4 504 | -16 754 |
| El Salvador | ... | ... | 34 | -29 | -152 | -262 | -431 | -622 | -533 | -920 |
| Equatorial Guinea | ... | ... | -21 | -6 | -19 | -123 | -196 | -511 | -1 129 | -1 661 |
| Eritrea | ... | ... | ... | ... | ... | -31 | -105 | 4 | -119 | -250 |
| Estonia | ... | ... | ... | ... | ... | -158 | -299 | -1 386 | 344 | 484 |
| Ethiopia | ... | ... | -226 | 106 | -294 | 39 | 13 | -1 568 | -425 | -7 788 |
| Faroe Islands | ... | ... | ... | ... | ... | ... | 99 | 31 | 144 | ... |
| Fiji | ... | ... | -17 | 19 | -94 | -113 | -26 | -212 | -142 | -306 |
| Finland | ... | -2 140 | -1 403 | -806 | -6 962 | 5 231 | 10 526 | 7 788 | 3 168 | 315 |
| France | ... | 2 740 | -4 208 | -35 | -9 944 | 10 840 | 16 124 | -137 | -22 034 | -4 800 |
| Gabon | ... | ... | 384 | -162 | 168 | 515 | 1 001 | 1 983 | 1 239 | -411 |
| Gambia | ... | ... | -91 | 8 | 24 | -8 | -35 | -43 | 56 | -146 |
| Georgia | ... | ... | ... | ... | ... | -347 | -176 | -695 | -1 198 | -1 644 |
| Germany | ... | 3 097 | ... | ... | 46 456 | -32 186 | -33 786 | 131 661 | 193 034 | 285 370 |
| Ghana | ... | 18 | 30 | -134 | -223 | -144 | -386 | -1 105 | -2 747 | -2 809 |
| Greece | ... | ... | -2 209 | -3 276 | -3 537 | -2 864 | -9 820 | -18 233 | -30 275 | -119 |
| Grenada | ... | ... | 0 | 3 | -46 | -42 | -88 | -193 | -204 | -203 |
| Guatemala | ... | ... | -163 | -246 | -213 | -572 | -1 050 | -1 241 | -563 | -203 |
| Guinea | ... | ... | 54 | -41 | -203 | -216 | -140 | -160 | -327 | -962 |
| Guinea-Bissau | ... | ... | -61 | -76 | -45 | -35 | 32 | -10 | -71 | 20 |
| Guyana | ... | ... | -129 | -97 | -161 | -135 | -82 | -96 | -246 | -144 |
| Haiti | ... | -25 | -101 | -95 | -22 | -87 | -114 | 7 | -102 | -234 |
| Honduras | ... | -112 | -317 | -220 | -51 | -201 | -508 | -304 | -682 | -1 291 |
| Hungary | ... | ... | -1 102 | -455 | 379 | -1 577 | -3 996 | -7 883 | 346 | 5 035 |
| Iceland | ... | ... | -76 | -115 | -134 | -47 | -804 | -2 339 | -308 | 709 |
| India | ... | -148 | -1 785 | -4 141 | -7 036 | -5 563 | -4 601 | -10 284 | -54 516 | -22 456 |
| Indonesia | ... | ... | 2 900 | -1 923 | -2 988 | -6 431 | 7 992 | 278 | 5 144 | -17 696 |
| Iran (Islamic Republic of) | ... | ... | -2 438 | -476 | 327 | 3 358 | 12 481 | 15 393 | 27 330 | 9 016 |
| Iraq | ... | ... | 14 710 | -488 | 3 801 | -762 | 2 238 | -3 335 | 6 488 | -134 |
| Ireland | ... | -124 | -2 132 | -736 | -361 | 1 721 | -356 | -7 150 | 2 319 | 10 562 |
| Israel | -617 | -1 822 | -871 | 988 | 163 | -4 790 | -2 057 | 4 043 | 7 855 | 14 455 |
| Italy | 816 | -635 | -10 569 | -4 088 | -16 438 | 25 096 | -5 781 | -29 744 | -74 382 | 39 478 |
| Jamaica | ... | ... | -136 | -271 | -312 | -99 | -367 | -1 071 | -934 | -326 |

Annex table A.5
**Balance-of-payments current account balance, 1970–2015** (*continued*)

Millions of current United States dollars

| Country/area | 1970 | 1975 | 1980 | 1985 | 1990 | 1995 | 2000 | 2005 | 2010 | 2015 |
|---|---|---|---|---|---|---|---|---|---|---|
| Japan | ... | ... | -10 750 | 51 129 | 44 078 | 111 044 | 119 660 | 170 123 | 220 888 | 135 608 |
| Jordan | ... | 45 | 374 | -260 | -227 | -259 | 28 | -2 271 | -1 882 | -3 332 |
| Kazakhstan | ... | ... | ... | ... | ... | -213 | 366 | -1 036 | 1 386 | -5 823 |
| Kenya | ... | -220 | -876 | -115 | -527 | -1 578 | -199 | -252 | -2 369 | -4 038 |
| Kiribati | ... | ... | 11 | 6 | -6 | -6 | -2 | -40 | -25 | ... |
| Kuwait | ... | 5 930 | 15 302 | 4 798 | 3 886 | 5 016 | 14 672 | 30 071 | 36 989 | 8 584 |
| Kyrgyzstan | ... | ... | ... | ... | ... | -235 | -76 | -37 | -317 | -813 |
| Latvia | ... | ... | ... | ... | ... | -16 | -291 | -1 988 | 563 | -334 |
| Lebanon | ... | ... | -139 | -491 | -1 098 | -1 071 | -2 996 | -2 748 | -7 552 | -8 146 |
| Lesotho | ... | -1 | 56 | -12 | 65 | -323 | -76 | 166 | -158 | -197 |
| Liberia | ... | ... | 46 | 57 | ... | ... | -106 | -184 | -415 | -860 |
| Libya | ... | ... | 8 214 | 1 906 | 2 201 | 1 672 | 6 270 | 14 945 | 16 801 | -7 762 |
| Lithuania | ... | ... | ... | ... | ... | -614 | -675 | -1 878 | -119 | -719 |
| Luxembourg | ... | ... | ... | ... | ... | 2 426 | 2 562 | 4 107 | 3 665 | 3 194 |
| Madagascar | ... | -56 | -556 | -184 | -265 | -276 | -260 | -695 | -888 | -183 |
| Malawi | ... | ... | -260 | -126 | -86 | -78 | -73 | -507 | -969 | -867 |
| Malaysia | ... | -491 | -266 | -600 | -870 | -8 644 | 8 488 | 19 980 | 25 644 | 8 960 |
| Maldives | ... | ... | -22 | -6 | 10 | -18 | -51 | -273 | -196 | -296 |
| Mali | ... | -61 | -124 | -210 | -221 | -284 | -255 | -438 | -1 190 | -427 |
| Malta | ... | 59 | 39 | -26 | -56 | -380 | -480 | -418 | -420 | 959 |
| Mauritania | ... | -63 | -133 | -116 | -10 | 22 | -98 | -877 | -332 | -956 |
| Mauritius | ... | ... | -117 | -30 | -119 | -22 | -37 | -324 | -1 006 | -566 |
| Mexico | ... | ... | -10 422 | 800 | -7 451 | -1 576 | -18 752 | -9 037 | -5 194 | -31 725 |
| Mongolia | ... | ... | -346 | -814 | -640 | 39 | -70 | 84 | -887 | -648 |
| Montenegro | ... | ... | ... | ... | ... | ... | ... | ... | -952 | -532 |
| Montserrat | ... | ... | ... | ... | -23 | -2 | -8 | -16 | -19 | -18 |
| Morocco | ... | -504 | -1 407 | -891 | -196 | -1 186 | -475 | 1 041 | -3 925 | -1 923 |
| Mozambique | ... | ... | -367 | -301 | -415 | -445 | -764 | -761 | -1 450 | -6 155 |
| Myanmar | ... | ... | -350 | -205 | -431 | -258 | -210 | 582 | 1 574 | -4 619 |
| Namibia | ... | ... | ... | 442 | 28 | 176 | 192 | 333 | -390 | -1 460 |
| Nepal | ... | ... | -39 | -122 | -289 | -356 | -131 | 153 | -128 | 2 447 |
| Netherlands | 193 | 2 394 | -855 | 4 248 | 8 089 | 25 773 | 7 264 | 41 600 | 61 820 | 68 777 |
| Netherlands Antilles | ... | ... | 1 | 403 | -44 | 128 | -48 | -106 | -968 | ... |
| New Zealand | ... | -1 222 | -973 | -2 657 | -1 453 | -3 065 | -2 407 | -8 025 | -3 433 | -5 068 |
| Nicaragua | ... | ... | -411 | -771 | -305 | -722 | -936 | -784 | -791 | -1 045 |
| Niger | ... | -39 | -276 | -64 | -236 | -152 | -104 | -312 | -1 136 | -1 238 |
| Nigeria | ... | ... | 5 178 | 2 604 | 4 988 | -2 578 | 7 427 | 36 529 | 13 111 | -15 439 |
| Norway | ... | -2 478 | 1 079 | 3 030 | 3 985 | 5 233 | 25 079 | 49 968 | 50 258 | 35 344 |
| Oman | ... | 57 | 942 | -10 | 1 106 | -801 | 3 129 | 5 178 | 4 884 | -10 892 |
| Pakistan | ... | ... | -866 | -1 067 | -1 661 | -3 349 | -85 | -3 606 | -1 354 | -1 603 |
| Panama | ... | ... | -329 | 75 | 209 | -471 | -673 | -1 064 | -3 113 | -3 377 |
| Papua New Guinea | ... | ... | -289 | -122 | -76 | 674 | 351 | 539 | -633 | 4 854 |
| Paraguay | ... | -72 | -277 | -252 | 390 | -217 | -247 | -68 | -57 | 338 |
| Peru | ... | ... | -101 | 102 | -1 419 | -4 625 | -1 546 | 1 148 | -3 782 | -8 430 |

Annex table A.5
## Balance-of-payments current account balance, 1970–2015 (continued)

Millions of current United States dollars

| Country/area | 1970 | 1975 | 1980 | 1985 | 1990 | 1995 | 2000 | 2005 | 2010 | 2015 |
|---|---|---|---|---|---|---|---|---|---|---|
| Philippines | ... | ... | -1 904 | -36 | -2 695 | -1 980 | -2 228 | 1 990 | 7 179 | 8 396 |
| Poland | ... | ... | -3 417 | -982 | 3 067 | 854 | -10 343 | -7 981 | -25 875 | -1 137 |
| Portugal | ... | -755 | -1 064 | 380 | -181 | -132 | -12 848 | -19 538 | -24 202 | 903 |
| Republic of Korea | ... | ... | -6 845 | -2 079 | -2 404 | -9 752 | 10 444 | 12 655 | 28 850 | 105 871 |
| Republic of Moldova | ... | ... | ... | ... | ... | -85 | -98 | -226 | -437 | -464 |
| Romania | ... | -135 | -2 420 | 1 381 | -3 254 | -1 774 | -1 355 | -8 541 | -8 478 | -2 008 |
| Russian Federation | ... | ... | ... | ... | ... | 6 963 | 45 382 | 84 389 | 67 452 | 69 564 |
| Rwanda | ... | ... | -52 | -64 | -85 | 57 | -94 | -66 | -412 | -1 099 |
| Saint Kitts and Nevis | ... | ... | -3 | -7 | -47 | -45 | -66 | -65 | -139 | -77 |
| Saint Lucia | ... | ... | -33 | -13 | -57 | -36 | -95 | -129 | -203 | -153 |
| Saint Vincent and the Grenadines | ... | ... | -9 | 4 | -24 | -40 | -24 | -102 | -208 | -201 |
| Samoa | ... | ... | -13 | 2 | 9 | 9 | -4 | -48 | -44 | ... |
| Sao Tome and Principe | ... | 0 | 1 | -16 | -12 | -27 | -20 | -36 | -88 | -79 |
| Saudi Arabia | ... | 14 385 | 41 503 | -12 932 | -4 147 | -5 318 | 14 317 | 90 060 | 66 751 | -53 478 |
| Senegal | ... | -86 | -386 | -360 | -363 | -244 | -332 | -676 | -589 | -1 063 |
| Serbia | ... | ... | ... | ... | ... | ... | ... | ... | -2 692 | -1 751 |
| Seychelles | ... | ... | -16 | -19 | -13 | 1 | -43 | -174 | -214 | -244 |
| Sierra Leone | ... | ... | -165 | 3 | -69 | -118 | -112 | -105 | -585 | -1 611 |
| Singapore | ... | -584 | -1 563 | -4 | 3 122 | 14 445 | 10 358 | 28 133 | 56 292 | 57 922 |
| Slovakia | ... | ... | ... | ... | ... | 390 | -694 | -5 125 | -4 211 | -1 119 |
| Slovenia | ... | ... | ... | ... | ... | -75 | -548 | -681 | -55 | 3 133 |
| Solomon Islands | ... | -13 | -12 | -28 | -28 | 8 | -41 | -90 | -144 | -17 |
| Somalia | ... | ... | -136 | -103 | ... | ... | ... | ... | ... | ... |
| South Africa | -1 289 | -2 397 | 3 161 | 2 261 | 1 552 | -2 493 | -191 | -8 015 | -5 492 | -13 647 |
| Spain | ... | -3 893 | -5 580 | 2 785 | -18 009 | -1 967 | -26 364 | -87 006 | -56 363 | 16 658 |
| Sri Lanka | ... | -110 | -655 | -418 | -298 | -770 | -1 044 | -650 | -1 075 | -2 009 |
| State of Palestine | ... | ... | ... | ... | ... | -984 | -857 | -1 365 | -1 307 | -629 |
| Sudan | ... | ... | -316 | 154 | -372 | -500 | -518 | -2 473 | -1 725 | -5 933 |
| Suriname | ... | ... | 32 | -18 | 67 | 73 | 32 | -144 | 651 | -808 |
| Swaziland | ... | 52 | -130 | -38 | 51 | -30 | -46 | -103 | -388 | 30 |
| Sweden | -253 | -308 | -4 331 | -1 010 | -6 339 | 4 940 | 11 689 | 26 423 | 29 402 | 28 497 |
| Switzerland | ... | ... | -201 | 6 039 | 6 124 | 20 703 | 33 625 | 57 530 | 86 601 | 75 918 |
| Syrian Arab Republic | ... | ... | 251 | -958 | 1 762 | 263 | 1 061 | 299 | -367 | -2 955 |
| Tajikistan | ... | ... | ... | ... | ... | -102 | -16 | -19 | -370 | -470 |
| Thailand | ... | -606 | -2 076 | -1 537 | -7 281 | -13 582 | 9 313 | -7 647 | 9 945 | 31 604 |
| The former Yugoslav Republic of Macedonia | ... | ... | ... | ... | ... | -273 | -103 | -159 | -198 | -137 |
| Togo | ... | -75 | -95 | -27 | -84 | -122 | -140 | -204 | -200 | -237 |
| Tonga | ... | 0 | -7 | 2 | 6 | -18 | -12 | -21 | -80 | -26 |
| Trinidad and Tobago | ... | 340 | 357 | -48 | 459 | 294 | 544 | 3 881 | 4 172 | -1 285 |
| Tunisia | ... | ... | -353 | -581 | -463 | -774 | -821 | -299 | -2 104 | -3 875 |
| Turkey | ... | -1 648 | -3 408 | -1 013 | -2 625 | -2 338 | -9 920 | -20 980 | -44 616 | -32 136 |
| Turkmenistan | ... | ... | ... | ... | ... | 0 | 412 | 875 | -2 349 | -1 047 |
| Uganda | ... | ... | -83 | 5 | -263 | -281 | -359 | -13 | -1 659 | -2 305 |

Annex table A.5
## Balance-of-payments current account balance, 1970–2015 (*continued*)

Millions of current United States dollars

| Country/area | 1970 | 1975 | 1980 | 1985 | 1990 | 1995 | 2000 | 2005 | 2010 | 2015 |
|---|---|---|---|---|---|---|---|---|---|---|
| Ukraine | ... | ... | ... | ... | ... | -1 152 | 1 481 | 2 534 | -3 016 | -176 |
| United Kingdom of Great Britain and Northern Ireland | 1 970 | -3 465 | 6 862 | 3 314 | -38 811 | -13 436 | -34 547 | -30 054 | -67 601 | -146 920 |
| United Republic of Tanzania | ... | ... | -521 | -375 | -559 | -590 | -428 | -1 093 | -2 211 | -3 312 |
| United States of America | 2 620 | 17 880 | 2 127 | -124 455 | -78 952 | -113 561 | -410 762 | -745 445 | -441 963 | -484 082 |
| Uruguay | ... | ... | -709 | -98 | 186 | -213 | -566 | 42 | -731 | -1 947 |
| Vanuatu | ... | ... | 1 | -10 | -6 | -18 | 5 | -34 | -42 | -91 |
| Venezuela (Bolivarian Republic of) | -104 | 2 171 | 4 728 | 3 327 | 8 279 | 2 014 | 11 853 | 25 447 | 5 585 | -20 360 |
| Viet Nam | ... | ... | -565 | -943 | -259 | -2 648 | 1 106 | -560 | -4 276 | 906 |
| Yemen | ... | ... | ... | ... | 739 | 184 | 1 337 | 624 | -1 054 | -911 |
| Zambia | ... | ... | -516 | -395 | -594 | -145 | -662 | -232 | 1 525 | -1 655 |
| Zimbabwe | ... | ... | -149 | -64 | -140 | -369 | -20 | -626 | -1 507 | -1 891 |

Sources: UN/DESA, based on data from the Statistics Division (1970-1979); and United Nations Conference on Trade and Development (UNCTAD) (1980 onward). Statistics Division data are available at http://data.un.org/Data.aspx?d=IFS&f=SeriesCode%3A78. UNCTAD data are available at http://unctadstat.unctad.org/wds/TableViewer/tableView.aspx?ReportId=113.

Note: The range of the Statistics Division database was from 1948 to 2009 and that of the UNCTAD database, from 1980 to 2015. The aim of table A.5 is to provide a time series ranging from 1948 to 2015 by merging data from the two databases. However, the period 1948-1969 was eventually omitted owing to a dearth of data. Since the UNCTAD statistics database was a more updated resource, its start year of 1980 was used as the benchmark year for comparison across both databases in order to determine which countries and areas would be covered by the merged table. Countries and areas were omitted from the merged table if (a) they were not present in both databases and therefore could not be compared (i.e., Bermuda, Bhutan, British Virgin islands, Cayman Islands, Cuba, Curaçao, Democratic Republic of the Congo, Federal Republic of Germany, French Polynesia, Marshall Islands, Micronesia (Federated States of), New Caledonia, Palau, People's Democratic Republic of Yemen, Qatar, Serbia and Montenegro, Sint Maarten, South Sudan, Taiwan Province of China, Timor-Leste, Tuvalu, United Arab Emirates, Uzbekistan, Yemen Arab Republic and Yugoslavia); (b) the absolute percentage difference between their 1980 data from both databases was greater than 1 per cent (i.e., Barbados, Chad, Gambia, Grenada, Kiribati, Mali, Pakistan and Republic of Korea); or (c) there were no 1980 data in either database but a comparison of their data from subsequent years revealed great discrepancies (i.e., Lao People's Democratic Republic and China, Hong Kong SAR).

Three dots (…) indicate that data are not applicable or not available in each database in a given year.

Annex table A.6
**Merchandise exports, 1948–2015**

Millions of current United States dollars

| Country/area | 1948 | 1949 | 1950 | 1955 | 1960 | 1965 | 1970 | 1975 | 1980 | 1985 | 1990 | 1995 | 2000 | 2005 | 2010 | 2015 |
|---|---|---|---|---|---|---|---|---|---|---|---|---|---|---|---|---|
| Afghanistan | 49.00 | 47.00 | 53.00 | 60.00 | 50.00 | 73.93 | 85.57 | 217.38 | 670.23 | 566.83 | 235.10 | 166.06 | 137.31 | 384.00 | 388.48 | 571.40 |
| Albania | ... | ... | 6.00 | 13.00 | 49.00 | ... | ... | ... | ... | ... | 230.00 | 202.03 | 261.48 | 658.00 | 1 544.61 | 1 929.55 |
| Algeria | 417.71 | 334.52 | 333.24 | 463.14 | 394.16 | 637.22 | 1 008.70 | 4 700.20 | 13 871.00 | 12 841.00 | 12 880.00 | 10 258.20 | 22 031.29 | 46 002.40 | 57 052.59 | 37 787.00 |
| American Samoa | 1.00 | 1.00 | 1.00 | 3.71 | 7.57 | 15.00 | 125.00 | 50.00 | 127.00 | 201.00 | 311.00 | 272.00 | 346.30 | 373.80 | 320.00 | 215.00 |
| Andorra | ... | ... | ... | ... | ... | ... | ... | ... | ... | ... | ... | 47.80 | 45.33 | 142.74 | 92.32 | 88.73 |
| Angola | 60.00 | 70.00 | 75.00 | 98.00 | 124.00 | 200.00 | 423.00 | 1 012.00 | 1 883.00 | 2 245.00 | 3 910.00 | 3 642.00 | 7 921.00 | 24 109.00 | 50 594.90 | 33 164.50 |
| Anguilla | | | | | | | | | | | | 1.23 | 4.04 | 15.02 | 12.67 | 17.44 |
| Antigua and Barbuda | 1.41 | 1.67 | 3.11 | 2.87 | 2.19 | 1.44 | 10.92 | 19.82 | 26.28 | 16.68 | 20.66 | 53.00 | 52.00 | 83.00 | 45.72 | 55.00 |
| Argentina | 1 629.00 | 1 043.50 | 1 177.50 | 928.60 | 1 079.20 | 1 493.40 | 1 773.20 | 2 961.30 | 8 021.40 | 8 396.10 | 12 352.50 | 20 963.11 | 26 341.00 | 40 351.00 | 68 187.30 | 56 752.20 |
| Armenia | | | | | | | | | | | | 270.90 | 294.20 | 973.90 | 1 011.43 | 1 486.90 |
| Aruba | | | | | | | | | | | 155.48 | 1 347.21 | 2 523.52 | 4 416.20 | 264.64 | 334.08 |
| Australia | 1 649.40 | 1 592.04 | 1 667.68 | 1 787.41 | 2 049.82 | 3 005.30 | 4 769.52 | 11 948.40 | 21 944.30 | 22 603.60 | 39 752.40 | 53 111.30 | 63 870.40 | 106 097.17 | 212 634.22 | 188 445.00 |
| Austria | 198.00 | 285.98 | 325.57 | 698.81 | 1 120.35 | 1 600.00 | 2 856.62 | 7 519.39 | 17 489.00 | 17 238.70 | 41 134.60 | 57 739.53 | 67 543.28 | 125 182.14 | 152 559.59 | 152 335.02 |
| Azerbaijan | | | | | | | | | | | | 635.00 | 1 745.00 | 7 648.96 | 26 476.03 | 15 586.10 |
| Bahamas | 2.00 | 2.00 | 3.00 | 3.30 | 6.00 | 18.62 | 89.85 | 2 508.00 | 5 009.44 | 2 728.43 | 238.02 | 175.92 | 575.90 | 549.00 | 702.40 | 628.80 |
| Bahrain | 133.00 | 135.00 | 137.00 | 193.00 | 190.00 | 164.60 | 217.77 | 1 107.46 | 3 606.36 | 2 896.81 | 3 760.64 | 4 112.77 | 6 194.41 | 10 242.00 | 14 971.25 | 11 300.00 |
| Bangladesh | | | | | | | | 322.74 | 758.51 | 998.78 | 1 671.34 | 3 501.00 | 6 389.00 | 9 297.00 | 19 194.40 | 32 378.70 |
| Barbados | 12.28 | 17.33 | 16.13 | 22.66 | 23.87 | 37.49 | 39.57 | 107.32 | 227.69 | 356.72 | 215.08 | 238.88 | 272.35 | 359.45 | 428.98 | 482.75 |
| Belarus | | | | | | | | | | | | 4 803.20 | 7 326.40 | 15 979.00 | 25 283.50 | 26 676.10 |
| Belgium | 1 690.00 | 1 759.00 | 1 652.00 | 2 782.00 | 3 792.00 | 6 394.00 | 11 600.00 | 28 804.00 | 64 540.00 | 53 739.00 | 117 703.00 | 178 280.95 | 187 906.09 | 334 400.14 | 407 692.34 | 398 158.28 |
| Belize | 6.00 | 5.00 | 3.32 | 5.73 | 7.87 | 12.22 | 18.80 | 66.59 | 110.65 | 90.13 | 129.05 | 161.68 | 195.79 | 319.11 | 478.21 | 537.91 |
| Benin | 9.81 | 11.36 | 12.77 | 15.68 | 18.39 | 13.71 | 32.78 | 31.84 | 62.82 | 199.00 | 288.00 | 420.00 | 392.00 | 578.23 | 1 281.61 | 2 538.56 |
| Bermuda | ... | ... | 3.00 | 4.03 | 10.36 | 22.69 | 80.00 | 36.20 | 37.00 | 23.06 | 60.00 | 55.94 | 51.00 | 49.00 | 14.68 | 28.93 |
| Bhutan | | | | | | | | | 16.73 | 21.99 | 69.78 | 103.31 | 103.00 | 258.20 | 641.31 | 442.78 |
| Bolivia (Plurinational State of) | 113.00 | 89.00 | 75.00 | 86.00 | 51.00 | 129.00 | 190.20 | 444.10 | 942.20 | 623.40 | 926.08 | 1 100.70 | 1 229.50 | 2 826.72 | 6 401.89 | 8 260.74 |
| Bonaire, Sint Eustatius and Saba | ... | ... | ... | ... | | | | | | | | | ... | ... | ... | 1.42 |
| Bosnia and Herzegovina | ... | ... | ... | ... | | | | | | | | 152.00 | 1 069.00 | 2 400.00 | 4 803.11 | 5 099.12 |
| Botswana | ... | ... | 3.00 | 7.84 | 7.56 | 14.34 | 25.63 | 141.78 | 504.38 | 838.85 | 1 784.68 | 2 142.09 | 2 675.00 | 4 425.35 | 4 693.24 | 6 273.51 |
| Brazil | 1 183.00 | 1 100.00 | 1 359.00 | 1 423.00 | 1 268.00 | 1 596.00 | 2 739.00 | 8 670.00 | 20 132.00 | 25 639.00 | 31 413.80 | 46 506.30 | 55 118.90 | 118 529.00 | 201 915.00 | 191 134.40 |
| British Virgin Islands | ... | ... | ... | ... | ... | ... | ... | 1.00 | 2.00 | 3.00 | 19.20 | 27.00 | 35.00 | 37.80 | 30.00 |
| Brunei Darussalam | 24.00 | 26.00 | 69.00 | 99.00 | 83.00 | 65.00 | 95.00 | 1 049.00 | 4 581.00 | 2 972.00 | 2 213.00 | 2 402.00 | 3 902.80 | 6 249.00 | 8 907.47 | 6 352.66 |
| Bulgaria | 91.00 | ... | ... | 237.00 | 572.00 | 1 176.07 | 2 004.27 | 4 691.00 | 10 390.00 | 13 310.00 | 5 030.00 | 5 355.00 | 4 851.73 | 11 739.00 | 20 629.76 | 25 690.14 |

Annex table A.6
**Merchandise exports, 1948–2015** *(continued)*

Millions of current United States dollars

| Country/area | 1948 | 1949 | 1950 | 1955 | 1960 | 1965 | 1970 | 1975 | 1980 | 1985 | 1990 | 1995 | 2000 | 2005 | 2010 | 2015 |
|---|---|---|---|---|---|---|---|---|---|---|---|---|---|---|---|---|
| Burkina Faso | ... | ... | 3.00 | 5.37 | 4.34 | 15.02 | 18.29 | 43.53 | 90.05 | 70.52 | 151.62 | 276.47 | 209.00 | 468.00 | 1 591.03 | 1 868.63 |
| Burundi | ... | ... | 3.00 | 4.00 | 7.00 | 12.69 | 24.36 | 31.93 | 65.39 | 112.24 | 74.83 | 105.65 | 50.02 | 58.01 | 101.19 | 123.36 |
| Cabo Verde | 9.58 | 6.94 | 7.92 | 9.70 | 10.66 | 0.97 | 1.66 | 2.44 | 5.00 | 6.00 | 6.00 | 8.94 | 11.00 | 17.62 | 44.50 | 53.52 |
| Cambodia | ... | ... | 47.00 | 40.06 | 69.74 | 105.43 | 38.98 | 5.00 | 16.00 | 20.00 | 86.00 | 855.00 | 1 389.45 | 3 091.50 | 5 143.22 | 12 325.07 |
| Cameroon | 36.00 | 49.80 | 47.00 | 95.00 | 97.00 | 145.51 | 227.05 | 447.23 | 1 384.18 | 722.12 | 2 002.13 | 1 630.31 | 1 833.00 | 2 861.25 | 3 878.43 | 3 705.51 |
| Canada | 3 201.91 | 3 049.99 | 3 019.86 | 4 574.39 | 5 818.30 | 8 473.21 | 16 786.50 | 34 074.20 | 67 733.80 | 90 950.30 | 127 629.00 | 192 203.00 | 276 617.00 | 360 475.25 | 387 481.22 | 408 474.69 |
| Cayman Islands | ... | ... | ... | ... | ... | ... | ... | ... | 3.00 | 6.00 | 18.00 | 19.00 | 18.50 | 59.30 | 13.32 | 25.00 |
| Central African Republic | ... | ... | 16.00 | 16.00 | 13.97 | 26.55 | 30.51 | 47.29 | 115.68 | 91.74 | 120.36 | 170.89 | 161.00 | 128.00 | 140.00 | 190.97 |
| Chad | ... | ... | 19.00 | 20.00 | 13.34 | 27.43 | 29.68 | 47.76 | 70.99 | 61.84 | 188.00 | 243.00 | 183.00 | 3 080.95 | 3 600.00 | 3 200.00 |
| Chile | 327.00 | 293.80 | 281.40 | 472.40 | 488.10 | 637.40 | 1 248.60 | 1 552.10 | 4 705.30 | 3 804.10 | 8 372.70 | 16 024.20 | 19 210.30 | 41 266.90 | 71 108.53 | 63 362.19 |
| China | 520.00 | ... | 550.00 | 1 410.00 | 2 571.28 | 2 563.16 | 2 307.25 | 7 689.00 | 18 099.30 | 27 350.00 | 62 091.00 | 148 780.00 | 249 203.00 | 761 953.00 | 1 577 754.00 | 2 274 949.00 |
| China, Hong Kong SAR | 398.72 | 526.30 | 650.30 | 443.45 | 688.80 | 1 142.75 | 2 514.60 | 6 026.46 | 20 323.00 | 30 077.00 | 82 390.00 | 173 871.00 | 202 683.00 | 292 119.00 | 400 692.02 | 510 596.00 |
| China, Macao SAR | 10.00 | 2.00 | 3.00 | 6.92 | 10.78 | 21.38 | 42.26 | 133.41 | 613.00 | 906.00 | 1 701.00 | 1 997.00 | 2 539.00 | 2 476.00 | 869.79 | 1 339.02 |
| Colombia | 306.60 | 335.20 | 393.60 | 583.90 | 464.60 | 537.80 | 726.70 | 1 465.00 | 3 924.30 | 3 551.60 | 6 720.50 | 10 125.80 | 13 043.30 | 21 190.00 | 39 713.34 | 35 690.78 |
| Comoros | ... | ... | 2.00 | 2.03 | 3.26 | 3.73 | 4.62 | 9.50 | 11.19 | 16.36 | 17.93 | 11.00 | 13.60 | 12.03 | 20.61 | 24.27 |
| Congo | 50.00 | 41.00 | 43.00 | 77.00 | 18.07 | 47.15 | 30.99 | 178.34 | 910.64 | 1 087.37 | 981.03 | 1 172.60 | 2 489.00 | 4 745.00 | 9 400.00 | 5 519.16 |
| Cook Islands | ... | ... | ... | ... | ... | 2.77 | 3.02 | 2.87 | 4.00 | 3.00 | 4.88 | 4.56 | 9.08 | 5.23 | 5.16 | 16.00 |
| Costa Rica | 50.30 | 51.20 | 55.60 | 80.90 | 84.30 | 111.80 | 231.20 | 493.30 | 1 001.70 | 976.00 | 1 448.20 | 3 475.90 | 5 849.70 | 7 026.40 | 9 448.10 | 9 624.20 |
| Côte d'Ivoire | 42.00 | 42.00 | 78.64 | 146.18 | 158.28 | 279.19 | 470.95 | 1 180.63 | 3 134.98 | 2 969.45 | 3 072.12 | 3 734.96 | 3 888.00 | 7 697.34 | 11 410.18 | 11 158.00 |
| Croatia | ... | ... | ... | ... | ... | ... | ... | ... | ... | ... | ... | 4 517.25 | 4 431.60 | 8 773.00 | 11 805.68 | 12 902.60 |
| Cuba | 710.00 | 578.00 | 667.00 | 611.00 | 618.00 | 686.00 | 1 046.00 | 3 677.00 | 5 577.00 | 5 983.00 | 5 100.00 | 1 600.00 | 1 676.00 | 2 318.59 | 4 913.60 | 4 400.00 |
| Curaçao | ... | ... | ... | ... | ... | ... | ... | ... | ... | ... | ... | ... | ... | ... | ... | 605.43 |
| Cyprus | 22.89 | 30.68 | 30.97 | 51.91 | 53.85 | 70.81 | 106.56 | 150.07 | 531.50 | 475.65 | 957.28 | 1 229.11 | 951.05 | 1 464.84 | 1 402.16 | 1 829.34 |
| Czechoslovakia | 753.00 | 806.20 | 779.00 | 1 176.00 | 1 930.00 | 2 689.00 | 3 792.00 | 8 356.00 | 14 930.00 | 10 660.00 | 11 880.00 | ... | ... | ... | ... | ... |
| Czech Republic | ... | ... | ... | ... | ... | ... | ... | ... | ... | ... | ... | 21 686.10 | 29 093.89 | 78 110.30 | 132 981.64 | 158 163.55 |
| Democratic People's Republic of Korea | ... | ... | ... | ... | ... | ... | ... | ... | 900.00 | 1 325.00 | 1 857.00 | 959.00 | 708.00 | 1 338.00 | 2 555.00 | 3 810.00 |
| Democratic Republic of the Congo | 245.00 | 235.00 | 261.00 | 456.00 | 480.00 | 306.13 | 781.37 | 864.98 | 2 269.00 | 1 853.00 | 2 326.00 | 1 563.00 | 806.60 | 2 402.80 | 5 300.00 | 5 856.59 |
| Denmark | 569.08 | 685.27 | 664.82 | 1 057.31 | 1 493.67 | 2 319.77 | 3 356.13 | 8 712.25 | 16 749.00 | 17 090.20 | 36 870.00 | 50 911.25 | 51 165.79 | 85 120.85 | 96 440.24 | 95 292.63 |
| Djibouti | 9.00 | 12.00 | 6.00 | 12.70 | 20.90 | 27.92 | 9.82 | 14.85 | 13.00 | 14.00 | 25.00 | 13.60 | 31.60 | 39.50 | 85.13 | 130.20 |
| Dominica | ... | ... | 1.00 | 3.00 | 3.61 | 5.55 | 5.90 | 11.36 | 9.74 | 28.43 | 55.03 | 45.10 | 53.58 | 41.78 | 36.82 | 30.21 |
| Dominican Republic | 82.80 | 73.75 | 86.86 | 114.85 | 180.37 | 125.50 | 249.09 | 893.80 | 1 217.00 | 1 228.00 | 2 170.00 | 3 780.00 | 5 737.00 | 6 145.00 | 6 753.69 | 9 523.30 |
| Ecuador | 46.00 | 41.70 | 77.34 | 114.36 | 146.01 | 164.10 | 189.90 | 973.90 | 2 480.80 | 2 904.70 | 2 714.30 | 4 307.20 | 4 926.63 | 10 100.00 | 17 489.92 | 18 330.61 |

**Annex table A.6**
**Merchandise exports, 1948–2015** (*continued*)

Millions of current United States dollars

| Country/area | 1948 | 1949 | 1950 | 1955 | 1960 | 1965 | 1970 | 1975 | 1980 | 1985 | 1990 | 1995 | 2000 | 2005 | 2010 | 2015 |
|---|---|---|---|---|---|---|---|---|---|---|---|---|---|---|---|---|
| Egypt | 591.43 | 526.83 | 503.67 | 419.25 | 567.88 | 605.20 | 761.71 | 1 401.95 | 3 045.97 | 3 714.21 | 2 585.15 | 3 434.70 | 5 275.99 | 12 912.02 | 26 437.82 | 20 050.72 |
| El Salvador | 45.60 | 54.96 | 69.52 | 106.92 | 116.52 | 188.72 | 229.36 | 531.44 | 967.00 | 679.00 | 582.00 | 1 652.00 | 2 941.00 | 3 418.00 | 4 499.40 | 5 484.90 |
| Equatorial Guinea | 19.00 | 30.00 | 33.00 | 55.00 | 34.00 | 27.00 | 24.87 | 26.46 | 13.69 | 16.63 | 62.42 | 127.48 | 1 097.00 | 7 064.00 | 10 000.00 | 6 373.49 |
| Eritrea | ... | ... | ... | ... | ... | ... | ... | ... | ... | ... | ... | 86.00 | 37.00 | 11.32 | 13.00 | 499.90 |
| Estonia | ... | ... | ... | ... | ... | ... | ... | ... | ... | ... | ... | 1 840.38 | 3 829.70 | 7 715.75 | 11 590.60 | 12 905.59 |
| Ethiopia | 38.88 | 37.84 | 36.75 | 65.29 | 77.52 | 115.93 | 122.36 | 240.50 | 424.52 | 333.06 | 297.51 | 422.62 | 485.64 | 903.00 | 2 329.79 | 5 027.55 |
| Falkland Islands (Malvinas) | ... | ... | ... | ... | ... | ... | ... | ... | 7.64 | 11.45 | 16.69 | 30.06 | 87.00 | 150.00 | 170.00 | 189.43 |
| Faroe Islands | 16.60 | 15.10 | 10.70 | 11.30 | 14.00 | 25.70 | 33.50 | 80.50 | 178.00 | 179.00 | 418.00 | 362.00 | 474.00 | 599.00 | 838.96 | 1 201.86 |
| Fiji | 24.62 | 22.39 | 19.70 | 32.19 | 39.14 | 53.60 | 71.55 | 170.38 | 376.85 | 307.00 | 497.00 | 619.00 | 585.00 | 701.00 | 841.36 | 823.53 |
| Finland | 500.74 | 468.64 | 390.04 | 788.26 | 988.75 | 1 426.56 | 2 306.45 | 5 502.24 | 14 150.30 | 13 617.10 | 26 570.90 | 40 498.78 | 45 988.65 | 65 497.62 | 69 517.83 | 59 444.57 |
| France | 2 058.99 | 2 840.50 | 3 133.75 | 5 052.90 | 6 970.93 | 10 288.88 | 18 221.34 | 53 343.67 | 116 423.00 | 102 028.00 | 217 262.00 | 301 933.00 | 326 801.95 | 463 427.96 | 523 767.04 | 505 897.05 |
| French Polynesia | 9.00 | 9.00 | 8.00 | 12.45 | 12.53 | 10.25 | 18.22 | 25.27 | 30.00 | 40.00 | 111.00 | 193.00 | 221.00 | 217.06 | 153.19 | 130.19 |
| Gabon | ... | ... | 20.00 | 28.00 | 47.68 | 105.71 | 144.28 | 942.58 | 2 172.76 | 1 951.42 | 2 203.74 | 2 713.42 | 2 598.14 | 5 065.01 | 8 685.98 | 7 083.18 |
| Gambia | 8.90 | 7.10 | 6.40 | 7.38 | 7.79 | 13.68 | 16.86 | 44.24 | 31.16 | 43.22 | 30.79 | 16.36 | 16.13 | 7.46 | 68.29 | 108.22 |
| Georgia | ... | ... | ... | ... | ... | ... | ... | ... | ... | ... | ... | 151.00 | 323.00 | 865.00 | 1 677.00 | 2 204.00 |
| Germany | ... | ... | ... | ... | ... | ... | ... | ... | ... | ... | 421 100.00 | 523 501.62 | 550 447.22 | 970 914.50 | 1 258 923.74 | 1 329 469.03 |
| Germany (Federal Republic of) | 791.00 | 985.00 | 1 992.86 | 6 123.81 | 11 415.50 | 17 912.50 | 34 228.40 | 90 175.60 | 192 860.00 | 183 933.00 | | | | | | |
| German Democratic Republic | 320.00 | 330.00 | 406.00 | 1 278.00 | 2 207.00 | 3 070.00 | 4 581.00 | 10 088.00 | 18 590.00 | 15 200.00 | ... | ... | ... | ... | ... | ... |
| Ghana | 226.08 | 185.94 | 216.72 | 267.82 | 324.97 | 317.83 | 458.30 | 816.44 | 1 258.13 | 622.92 | 897.00 | 1 725.95 | 1 670.90 | 2 802.21 | 7 960.09 | 10 355.70 |
| Gibraltar | ... | ... | ... | ... | ... | ... | ... | 3.10 | 9.80 | 13.80 | 82.90 | 116.15 | 127.10 | 200.00 | 258.35 | 250.00 |
| Greece | 94.00 | 115.00 | 90.33 | 182.80 | 203.20 | 327.77 | 642.53 | 2 294.31 | 5 153.05 | 4 538.81 | 8 105.16 | 11 053.45 | 11 721.56 | 17 278.41 | 27 950.21 | 28 617.22 |
| Greenland | 4.00 | 3.00 | 5.00 | 5.00 | 8.00 | 13.00 | 14.00 | 87.40 | 186.00 | 174.00 | 452.00 | 371.00 | 273.00 | 402.40 | 380.07 | 474.99 |
| Grenada | 4.00 | 4.00 | 4.00 | 5.11 | 4.18 | 6.34 | 6.04 | 12.41 | 17.39 | 22.31 | 26.44 | 21.75 | 48.00 | 27.65 | 24.97 | 33.77 |
| Guam | 6.00 | 2.00 | 1.00 | 5.13 | 8.39 | 8.00 | 5.83 | 28.49 | 61.00 | 13.00 | 82.00 | 84.99 | 74.00 | 51.87 | 45.60 | 35.00 |
| Guatemala | 50.17 | 52.23 | 67.61 | 98.70 | 112.52 | 185.80 | 290.18 | 623.50 | 1 519.83 | 1 057.00 | 1 162.97 | 1 990.80 | 2 711.20 | 5 380.93 | 8 462.50 | 10 751.90 |
| Guinea | 10.00 | 10.00 | 11.00 | 29.00 | 50.63 | 53.95 | 56.26 | 160.74 | 400.96 | 492.00 | 671.00 | 701.86 | 666.00 | 852.69 | 1 471.17 | 2 059.26 |
| Guinea-Bissau | 5.00 | 5.00 | 4.00 | 5.00 | 4.38 | 4.30 | 3.70 | 7.07 | 10.96 | 11.56 | 19.26 | 24.00 | 62.22 | 89.48 | 126.60 | 174.68 |
| Guyana | 30.81 | 28.97 | 29.68 | 52.81 | 73.34 | 103.31 | 135.15 | 356.60 | 389.18 | 206.10 | 250.61 | 467.48 | 501.57 | 553.11 | 879.77 | 1 169.97 |
| Haiti | 29.90 | 35.36 | 38.64 | 36.04 | 33.14 | 36.74 | 40.36 | 79.76 | 226.20 | 168.40 | 160.26 | 110.29 | 317.67 | 470.15 | 579.06 | 1 028.96 |
| Honduras | 55.00 | 54.90 | 55.15 | 47.20 | 63.00 | 127.22 | 179.11 | 295.00 | 829.45 | 780.05 | 933.80 | 1 768.71 | 3 343.40 | 5 048.01 | 6 264.40 | 8 040.70 |
| Hungary | 253.00 | 387.00 | 329.00 | 601.00 | 874.00 | 1 510.00 | 1 726.17 | 4 519.30 | 8 610.00 | 8 470.00 | 10 000.00 | 12 865.00 | 28 192.45 | 62 936.38 | 95 482.57 | 98 577.97 |

Annex table A.6
**Merchandise exports, 1948–2015** (continued)

Millions of current United States dollars

| Country/area | 1948 | 1949 | 1950 | 1955 | 1960 | 1965 | 1970 | 1975 | 1980 | 1985 | 1990 | 1995 | 2000 | 2005 | 2010 | 2015 |
|---|---|---|---|---|---|---|---|---|---|---|---|---|---|---|---|---|
| Iceland | 61.63 | 31.05 | 25.78 | 52.18 | 73.11 | 129.30 | 146.59 | 305.64 | 918.30 | 814.93 | 1 591.50 | 1 802.00 | 1 901.00 | 3 091.00 | 4 604.36 | 4 745.33 |
| India | 1 295.44 | 1 197.21 | 1 144.92 | 1 263.36 | 1 331.61 | 1 686.72 | 2 026.40 | 4 355.12 | 8 585.54 | 9 139.56 | 17 969.10 | 30 630.00 | 42 379.30 | 99 616.00 | 226 351.40 | 267 147.08 |
| Indonesia | 394.00 | 527.00 | 800.00 | 946.00 | 841.00 | 708.00 | 1 108.00 | 7 102.00 | 21 909.00 | 18 590.00 | 25 673.90 | 45 417.00 | 65 403.00 | 86 996.06 | 158 074.49 | 150 282.40 |
| Iran (Islamic Republic of) | 490.80 | 588.12 | 701.12 | 539.54 | 636.30 | 1 304.78 | 2 402.80 | 7 963.06 | 12 338.00 | 14 175.00 | 19 305.00 | 18 360.00 | 28 739.00 | 56 252.00 | 101 316.00 | 63 100.00 |
| Iraq | 49.97 | 98.76 | 126.67 | 519.01 | 654.00 | 882.00 | 1 098.00 | 8 298.00 | 26 349.00 | 10 409.00 | 10 314.00 | 496.00 | 20 380.00 | 23 697.00 | 52 482.60 | 49 319.82 |
| Ireland | 198.68 | 225.58 | 202.72 | 308.84 | 426.72 | 618.24 | 1 120.08 | 3 192.43 | 8 398.35 | 10 357.40 | 23 746.50 | 44 710.86 | 77 222.03 | 109 657.45 | 116 496.53 | 120 439.11 |
| Israel | 6.20 | 28.50 | 35.10 | 89.10 | 216.60 | 429.60 | 778.70 | 1 940.70 | 5 537.50 | 6 260.40 | 12 080.00 | 19 046.10 | 31 404.20 | 42 770.40 | 58 413.03 | 64 062.22 |
| Italy | 1 077.00 | 1 121.43 | 1 205.55 | 1 856.00 | 3 656.90 | 7 198.40 | 13 204.80 | 34 987.70 | 78 104.00 | 76 717.00 | 170 304.00 | 233 766.00 | 240 517.68 | 373 134.72 | 447 300.93 | 459 067.61 |
| Jamaica | 45.90 | 45.19 | 42.62 | 93.32 | 158.66 | 214.40 | 341.80 | 759.25 | 962.73 | 565.94 | 1 158.15 | 1 426.96 | 1 294.87 | 1 531.50 | 1 327.60 | 1 261.12 |
| Japan | 257.92 | 510.00 | 825.26 | 2 010.56 | 4 054.72 | 8 451.11 | 19 317.50 | 55 819.10 | 130 441.00 | 177 164.00 | 287 580.00 | 443 116.00 | 479 296.00 | 594 940.87 | 769 773.83 | 624 938.68 |
| Jordan | 10.49 | 12.63 | 4.40 | 8.03 | 11.14 | 27.75 | 34.08 | 152.66 | 574.20 | 788.66 | 1 063.85 | 1 769.47 | 1 899.15 | 4 301.76 | 7 028.33 | 7 828.67 |
| Kazakhstan | ... | ... | ... | ... | ... | ... | ... | ... | ... | ... | ... | 5 250.20 | 8 812.20 | 27 849.00 | 59 970.80 | 45 725.60 |
| Kenya | 137.00 | 52.00 | 57.10 | 78.10 | 112.30 | 228.06 | 305.06 | 606.22 | 1 245.26 | 957.53 | 1 032.12 | 1 878.55 | 1 733.90 | 3 419.90 | 5 169.11 | 5 906.28 |
| Kiribati | ... | ... | 2.00 | 4.10 | 2.10 | 3.78 | 7.84 | 36.31 | 2.96 | 4.00 | 2.88 | 7.44 | 3.59 | 4.31 | 3.89 | 11.45 |
| Kuwait | ... | ... | 195.00 | 651.00 | 961.80 | 1 283.52 | 1 693.16 | 9 184.40 | 19 663.00 | 10 597.00 | 7 042.00 | 12 785.00 | 19 436.00 | 44 868.50 | 69 977.95 | 54 996.62 |
| Kyrgyzstan | ... | ... | ... | ... | ... | ... | ... | ... | ... | ... | ... | 408.94 | 510.90 | 672.00 | 1 755.90 | 1 676.00 |
| Lao People's Democratic Republic | ... | ... | 1.00 | 1.37 | 0.90 | 1.00 | 7.20 | 11.50 | 28.00 | 54.00 | 78.70 | 311.00 | 330.31 | 553.08 | 1 746.37 | 2 768.99 |
| Latvia | ... | ... | ... | ... | ... | ... | ... | ... | ... | ... | ... | 1 304.98 | 1 868.47 | 5 161.29 | 9 532.46 | 12 054.39 |
| Lebanon | ... | ... | 15.00 | 33.00 | 43.00 | 86.87 | 189.98 | 1 233.00 | 955.00 | 287.99 | 494.00 | 655.77 | 714.58 | 2 337.00 | 5 021.00 | 3 981.54 |
| Lesotho | ... | ... | 2.00 | 3.00 | 4.00 | 6.58 | 5.93 | 12.28 | 57.99 | 22.34 | 61.67 | 160.15 | 220.70 | 650.57 | 877.66 | 844.10 |
| Liberia | 16.00 | 16.00 | 28.00 | 42.84 | 82.60 | 135.40 | 213.73 | 393.83 | 600.40 | 435.60 | 868.00 | 820.00 | 329.00 | 131.30 | 222.00 | 259.50 |
| Libya | 9.27 | 7.82 | 10.64 | 12.04 | 8.96 | 789.60 | 2 357.04 | 6 833.96 | 21 910.00 | 12 314.00 | 13 225.00 | 8 975.00 | 12 725.40 | 31 358.00 | 48 672.63 | 10 057.91 |
| Lithuania | ... | ... | ... | ... | ... | ... | ... | ... | ... | ... | ... | 2 705.00 | 3 809.20 | 11 806.57 | 20 748.18 | 25 573.09 |
| Luxembourg | ... | ... | ... | ... | ... | ... | 855.00 | 1 787.47 | 3 005.44 | 2 830.54 | 6 304.88 | 7 750.28 | 8 357.20 | 18 797.18 | 19 748.44 | 17 297.77 |
| Madagascar | 49.00 | 54.00 | 69.44 | 81.54 | 74.88 | 91.71 | 144.84 | 301.12 | 401.49 | 274.20 | 319.00 | 507.00 | 824.00 | 854.64 | 1 149.47 | 2 296.05 |
| Malawi | 16.97 | 17.61 | 14.14 | 20.00 | 25.00 | 40.35 | 59.64 | 140.41 | 295.32 | 245.58 | 416.91 | 405.28 | 379.27 | 508.79 | 1 066.20 | 1 080.10 |
| Malaysia | 621.09 | 593.52 | 1 003.52 | 963.02 | 1 186.78 | 1 235.78 | 1 686.58 | 3 842.96 | 12 944.70 | 15 315.80 | 29 452.41 | 73 914.93 | 98 229.03 | 141 625.52 | 198 612.02 | 199 869.39 |
| Maldives | 2.00 | 2.00 | 2.00 | 1.33 | 2.07 | 2.49 | 3.87 | 2.54 | 7.78 | 23.02 | 78.00 | 85.00 | 108.70 | 161.60 | 197.50 | 239.71 |
| Mali | ... | ... | 8.00 | 10.00 | 13.00 | 8.63 | 34.92 | 53.22 | 205.29 | 123.67 | 358.77 | 441.00 | 545.00 | 1 100.92 | 1 996.26 | 2 532.42 |
| Malta | 5.07 | 3.86 | 4.65 | 7.48 | 10.71 | 24.23 | 38.56 | 165.88 | 482.73 | 399.51 | 1 130.31 | 1 914.26 | 2 452.98 | 2 398.88 | 3 585.93 | 2 575.93 |
| Marshall Islands | ... | ... | ... | ... | ... | ... | ... | ... | ... | ... | 2.79 | 23.07 | 9.12 | 25.36 | 32.30 | 46.84 |
| Mauritania | ... | ... | 1.00 | 2.00 | 2.00 | 57.61 | 88.87 | 175.54 | 194.18 | 374.32 | 447.00 | 488.27 | 354.57 | 625.10 | 2 073.50 | 1 388.56 |

Annex table A.6
**Merchandise exports, 1948–2015** *(continued)*

Millions of current United States dollars

| Country/area | 1948 | 1949 | 1950 | 1955 | 1960 | 1965 | 1970 | 1975 | 1980 | 1985 | 1990 | 1995 | 2000 | 2005 | 2010 | 2015 |
|---|---|---|---|---|---|---|---|---|---|---|---|---|---|---|---|---|
| Mauritius | 43.69 | 45.73 | 32.11 | 52.88 | 38.85 | 65.81 | 69.01 | 297.98 | 434.81 | 440.02 | 1 193.77 | 1 538.08 | 1 557.00 | 2 143.29 | 2 261.50 | 2 456.81 |
| Mexico | 555.30 | 428.44 | 532.02 | 784.56 | 763.76 | 1 145.36 | 1 402.00 | 2 903.84 | 18 031.00 | 26 757.30 | 40 710.80 | 79 541.60 | 166 368.00 | 214 207.00 | 298 305.08 | 380 772.02 |
| Micronesia (Federated States of) | ... | ... | ... | ... | ... | ... | ... | ... | ... | ... | 3.72 | 20.57 | 21.60 | 18.50 | 30.05 | 20.00 |
| Mongolia | ... | ... | ... | ... | ... | ... | ... | ... | 403.00 | 689.10 | 660.70 | 473.30 | 535.80 | 1 065.00 | 2 899.20 | 4 669.50 |
| Montenegro | ... | ... | ... | ... | ... | ... | ... | ... | ... | ... | ... | ... | ... | ... | 436.58 | 353.02 |
| Montserrat | ... | ... | 0.76 | 0.75 | 0.47 | 0.47 | 0.90 | 2.27 | 1.00 | 3.00 | 2.00 | 3.00 | 1.12 | 1.44 | 1.10 | 2.98 |
| Morocco | 143.50 | 192.98 | 189.77 | 327.71 | 353.72 | 430.20 | 488.29 | 1 543.14 | 2 441.25 | 2 165.03 | 4 265.07 | 6 881.29 | 7 431.84 | 11 189.79 | 17 770.68 | 21 886.23 |
| Mozambique | 40.00 | 37.00 | 37.00 | 53.00 | 75.00 | 108.00 | 156.00 | 198.00 | 281.00 | 77.00 | 126.00 | 168.00 | 364.00 | 1 783.00 | 3 000.00 | 3 196.08 |
| Myanmar | 228.24 | 153.57 | 138.77 | 225.96 | 223.76 | 225.16 | 107.73 | 173.41 | 476.55 | 305.97 | 324.91 | 851.21 | 1 620.17 | 3 776.45 | 8 661.08 | 11 106.10 |
| Namibia | ... | ... | ... | ... | ... | ... | ... | ... | 1 459.00 | 727.00 | 1 085.68 | 1 409.40 | 1 320.49 | 2 070.00 | 4 025.52 | 4 015.11 |
| Nauru | 2.00 | 4.00 | 4.00 | 5.00 | 6.32 | 8.00 | 32.28 | 46.00 | 65.00 | 63.00 | 60.20 | 28.26 | 29.00 | 3.00 | 50.00 | 24.00 |
| Nepal | ... | ... | 1.00 | 1.00 | 17.00 | 57.03 | 42.44 | 100.33 | 80.35 | 159.92 | 204.00 | 345.00 | 804.00 | 863.24 | 855.76 | 660.18 |
| Netherlands | 1 184.76 | 1 483.86 | 1 603.95 | 3 058.42 | 4 602.37 | 7 343.37 | 13 355.00 | 39 887.90 | 84 947.50 | 77 872.50 | 131 775.00 | 203 187.17 | 232 554.08 | 406 372.45 | 574 251.15 | 567 217.01 |
| Netherlands Antilles | 406.93 | 431.53 | 552.69 | 802.66 | 657.90 | 602.75 | 675.98 | 2 397.22 | 5 162.22 | 1 031.11 | 1 789.94 | 1 522.00 | 2 009.00 | 608.02 | 806.53 | ... |
| New Caledonia | 7.00 | 8.00 | 10.80 | 39.09 | 51.28 | 65.15 | 191.73 | 327.11 | 418.00 | 271.00 | 449.00 | 565.00 | 605.72 | 1 093.09 | 1 492.56 | 1 313.65 |
| New Zealand | 518.01 | 534.79 | 514.50 | 726.04 | 846.86 | 1 006.54 | 1 222.59 | 2 162.05 | 5 420.90 | 5 720.11 | 9 393.84 | 13 644.80 | 13 297.43 | 21 730.10 | 31 396.37 | 34 358.79 |
| Nicaragua | 93.75 | 23.66 | 34.64 | 80.02 | 62.87 | 148.94 | 178.62 | 375.17 | 450.63 | 301.50 | 330.60 | 465.98 | 880.60 | 1 654.13 | 3 250.90 | 4 839.35 |
| Niger | 6.00 | 4.24 | 3.03 | 11.70 | 12.68 | 25.50 | 31.82 | 90.80 | 565.71 | 259.40 | 282.59 | 288.09 | 283.02 | 489.00 | 1 150.00 | 1 153.95 |
| Nigeria | 251.67 | 301.71 | 252.56 | 370.86 | 462.00 | 748.58 | 1 239.84 | 7 834.31 | 25 968.00 | 12 548.00 | 13 596.30 | 12 342.00 | 20 975.00 | 50 467.00 | 84 000.00 | 51 300.00 |
| Niue | ... | ... | ... | ... | ... | ... | ... | ... | 0.00 | 0.00 | 0.05 | 0.34 | 0.29 | 0.20 | 0.02 | 0.02 |
| Northern Mariana Islands | ... | ... | ... | ... | ... | ... | ... | ... | ... | ... | ... | 432.48 | 1 017.00 | 691.00 | 5.00 | 59.54 |
| Norway | 415.29 | 387.81 | 390.46 | 633.92 | 880.74 | 1 443.26 | 2 456.86 | 7 231.50 | 18 542.60 | 19 985.20 | 34 047.20 | 41 991.90 | 60 057.70 | 103 759.24 | 130 656.79 | 105 372.28 |
| Oman | ... | ... | 2.00 | 2.00 | 2.00 | 2.24 | 142.72 | 1 044.03 | 3 748.00 | 4 972.00 | 5 508.00 | 6 068.14 | 11 318.60 | 18 691.80 | 36 601.30 | 34 733.90 |
| Pakistan | 493.88 | 447.03 | 488.74 | 384.51 | 400.16 | 550.46 | 448.53 | 1 052.52 | 2 618.43 | 2 739.77 | 5 588.73 | 7 991.57 | 9 028.03 | 16 051.00 | 21 409.50 | 22 188.00 |
| Palau | ... | ... | ... | ... | ... | ... | ... | ... | ... | ... | ... | 14.00 | 11.51 | 13.41 | 6.00 | 19.58 |
| Panama | 14.09 | 14.69 | 12.97 | 21.66 | 21.24 | 62.11 | 108.51 | 286.45 | 360.53 | 336.20 | 340.09 | 625.16 | 859.50 | 7 050.00 | 10 986.60 | 17 028.34 |
| Papua New Guinea | 11.11 | 14.25 | 15.47 | 29.28 | 38.38 | 59.09 | 103.96 | 440.61 | 1 031.29 | 912.20 | 1 144.12 | 2 653.47 | 2 069.89 | 3 273.48 | 5 741.65 | 8 650.72 |
| Paraguay | 28.16 | 33.01 | 34.64 | 29.95 | 28.01 | 56.19 | 62.96 | 176.29 | 310.23 | 303.91 | 958.68 | 2 019.21 | 2 200.09 | 3 152.57 | 6 504.82 | 8 361.17 |
| Peru | 162.44 | 154.51 | 193.59 | 270.86 | 432.98 | 667.30 | 1 047.86 | 1 290.86 | 3 898.30 | 2 978.50 | 3 279.81 | 5 491.42 | 6 954.91 | 17 367.70 | 35 803.08 | 34 156.92 |
| Philippines | 310.00 | 248.00 | 331.00 | 400.50 | 624.10 | 697.90 | 1 040.80 | 2 294.46 | 5 741.15 | 4 611.38 | 8 116.80 | 17 501.80 | 38 078.25 | 41 254.68 | 51 496.00 | 58 647.77 |
| Poland | 594.00 | 691.92 | 630.00 | 919.75 | 1 326.00 | 2 227.75 | 3 547.60 | 10 289.40 | 17 020.00 | 11 490.00 | 14 320.00 | 22 895.00 | 31 747.23 | 89 437.38 | 159 723.75 | 198 242.58 |
| Portugal | 172.39 | 156.92 | 185.53 | 284.00 | 325.91 | 583.62 | 945.77 | 1 939.32 | 4 639.54 | 5 685.14 | 16 421.80 | 22 787.10 | 24 303.26 | 38 149.95 | 49 406.06 | 55 270.74 |

Annex table A.6
Merchandise exports, 1948–2015 (continued)

Millions of current United States dollars

| Country/area | 1948 | 1949 | 1950 | 1955 | 1960 | 1965 | 1970 | 1975 | 1980 | 1985 | 1990 | 1995 | 2000 | 2005 | 2010 | 2015 |
|---|---|---|---|---|---|---|---|---|---|---|---|---|---|---|---|---|
| Qatar | 5.00 | 10.00 | 22.00 | 83.00 | 126.00 | 163.00 | 239.90 | 1 804.89 | 5 680.00 | 3 419.00 | 3 641.21 | 3 557.16 | 11 594.00 | 25 762.00 | 74 964.48 | 77 294.23 |
| Republic of Korea | 19.00 | 14.30 | 23.00 | 18.00 | 32.00 | 173.00 | 836.00 | 4 945.00 | 17 512.00 | 30 282.00 | 65 016.00 | 125 058.00 | 172 268.00 | 284 419.00 | 466 384.00 | 526 755.00 |
| Republic of Moldova | ... | ... | ... | ... | ... | ... | ... | ... | ... | ... | ... | 745.00 | 472.00 | 1 091.00 | 1 541.49 | 1 966.90 |
| Romania | 160.00 | ... | ... | 391.00 | 717.00 | 1 101.50 | 1 850.80 | 5 341.45 | 11 400.00 | 10 175.00 | 4 960.00 | 7 910.00 | 10 411.98 | 27 687.54 | 49 579.10 | 60 586.13 |
| Russian Federation | ... | ... | ... | ... | ... | ... | ... | ... | ... | ... | ... | 82 419.00 | 105 033.00 | 243 798.00 | 400 630.00 | 340 349.00 |
| Rwanda | ... | ... | 1.00 | 2.00 | 4.00 | 14.00 | 24.81 | 41.74 | 120.55 | 131.49 | 109.00 | 51.89 | 53.00 | 124.62 | 297.28 | 683.67 |
| Saint Helena | ... | ... | ... | ... | ... | ... | ... | ... | 1.15 | 5.57 | 6.88 | 4.58 | 8.97 | 20.10 | 30.85 | 58.38 |
| Saint Kitts and Nevis | ... | ... | 3.00 | 5.00 | 6.00 | 8.80 | 3.86 | 20.78 | 23.55 | 18.11 | 28.00 | 19.00 | 32.58 | 34.31 | 32.01 | 44.00 |
| Saint Lucia | ... | 0.69 | 0.93 | 3.63 | 5.05 | 10.52 | 12.96 | 22.47 | 70.30 | 61.56 | 134.04 | 109.00 | 43.00 | 64.22 | 214.52 | 179.25 |
| Saint Pierre and Miquelon | 2.00 | 3.00 | 0.82 | 1.31 | 1.81 | 1.33 | 2.70 | 6.30 | 5.73 | 7.00 | 25.53 | 10.00 | 5.50 | 6.79 | 5.73 | 0.48 |
| Saint Vincent and the Grenadines | 1.57 | 1.16 | 1.23 | 2.12 | 3.48 | 3.75 | 3.54 | 7.56 | 15.44 | 63.25 | 82.70 | 42.66 | 47.00 | 39.88 | 41.52 | 45.75 |
| Samoa | 4.00 | 5.00 | 4.00 | 7.03 | 6.77 | 5.79 | 4.70 | 7.12 | 17.22 | 16.19 | 8.87 | 8.81 | 65.00 | 87.17 | 70.25 | 52.80 |
| Sao Tome and Principe | 9.00 | 5.00 | 7.00 | 5.62 | 7.37 | 5.08 | 8.33 | 7.06 | 16.98 | 5.83 | 4.40 | 5.10 | 3.00 | 6.80 | 10.93 | 12.75 |
| Saudi Arabia | 330.00 | 338.00 | 340.00 | 541.98 | 891.11 | 1 395.56 | 2 371.11 | 29 673.30 | 109 083.00 | 27 481.00 | 44 417.00 | 50 040.00 | 77 583.00 | 180 711.00 | 251 143.03 | 202 237.00 |
| Senegal | 155.00 | 198.00 | 174.00 | 131.00 | 113.71 | 130.78 | 152.60 | 461.05 | 476.95 | 562.01 | 761.69 | 993.29 | 920.08 | 1 578.11 | 2 161.13 | 2 611.67 |
| Serbia | ... | ... | ... | ... | ... | ... | ... | ... | ... | ... | ... | ... | ... | ... | 9 794.52 | 13 354.90 |
| Serbia and Montenegro | ... | ... | ... | ... | ... | ... | ... | ... | ... | ... | ... | 1 531.00 | 1 723.00 | 5 065.00 | ... | ... |
| Seychelles | 2.00 | 2.00 | 2.00 | 1.30 | 1.70 | 1.54 | 2.14 | 6.35 | 21.15 | 27.90 | 57.03 | 53.23 | 194.00 | 339.72 | 400.21 | 428.94 |
| Sierra Leone | 21.52 | 25.95 | 19.46 | 28.62 | 82.96 | 88.44 | 100.99 | 117.66 | 223.66 | 130.28 | 137.64 | 42.28 | 13.03 | 158.50 | 341.23 | 511.67 |
| Singapore | 690.20 | 611.74 | 1 005.48 | 1 100.54 | 1 135.82 | 981.31 | 1 553.63 | 5 376.20 | 19 375.30 | 22 812.30 | 52 729.70 | 118 268.00 | 137 804.00 | 229 649.00 | 351 867.09 | 350 506.00 |
| Sint Maarten | ... | ... | ... | ... | ... | ... | ... | ... | ... | ... | ... | ... | ... | ... | ... | 128.89 |
| Slovakia | ... | ... | ... | ... | ... | ... | ... | ... | ... | ... | ... | 8 580.00 | 11 831.88 | 31 889.28 | 64 663.54 | 75 583.69 |
| Slovenia | ... | ... | ... | ... | ... | ... | ... | ... | ... | ... | ... | 8 316.41 | 8 769.77 | 19 247.72 | 29 200.11 | 31 949.38 |
| Solomon Islands | 1.00 | 1.63 | 1.92 | 4.51 | 4.16 | 5.42 | 7.98 | 15.51 | 74.18 | 70.09 | 70.42 | 168.37 | 69.00 | 103.43 | 223.74 | 402.10 |
| Somalia | 5.00 | 5.00 | 5.00 | 14.00 | 23.00 | 33.20 | 31.40 | 88.60 | 141.00 | 91.00 | 150.00 | 169.99 | 193.00 | 250.00 | 450.00 | 440.00 |
| South Africa | 1 170.31 | 1 155.83 | 1 150.80 | 1 545.04 | 1 984.92 | 2 546.74 | 3 344.18 | 8 788.52 | 25 525.00 | 16 293.00 | 23 549.00 | 27 853.00 | 29 983.00 | 51 625.70 | 91 347.29 | 81 672.97 |
| Spain | 373.00 | 403.00 | 389.00 | 446.00 | 725.00 | 935.17 | 2 388.43 | 7 690.49 | 20 720.10 | 24 246.90 | 55 521.40 | 97 858.96 | 114 966.25 | 192 644.44 | 254 417.59 | 281 835.75 |
| Sri Lanka | 305.62 | 297.71 | 328.23 | 407.40 | 384.51 | 409.29 | 341.55 | 569.20 | 1 061.90 | 1 333.32 | 1 912.16 | 3 797.79 | 5 430.17 | 6 346.79 | 8 602.10 | 10 505.00 |
| State of Palestine | ... | ... | ... | ... | ... | ... | ... | ... | ... | ... | ... | 394.18 | 400.86 | 335.44 | 575.51 | 824.98 |
| Sudan | 98.70 | 104.76 | 95.08 | 145.04 | 182.09 | 195.12 | 298.41 | 437.91 | 542.68 | 373.89 | 374.10 | 555.60 | 1 806.70 | 4 824.00 | 11 404.00 | 3 168.96 |
| Suriname | 14.32 | 18.03 | 16.44 | 26.51 | 44.03 | 58.36 | 144.30 | 277.31 | 514.29 | 328.85 | 472.27 | 476.59 | 396.24 | 997.00 | 2 025.57 | 1 665.75 |

Annex table A.6
**Merchandise exports, 1948–2015** (*continued*)

Millions of current United States dollars

| Country/area | 1948 | 1949 | 1950 | 1955 | 1960 | 1965 | 1970 | 1975 | 1980 | 1985 | 1990 | 1995 | 2000 | 2005 | 2010 | 2015 |
|---|---|---|---|---|---|---|---|---|---|---|---|---|---|---|---|---|
| Swaziland | ... | ... | 5.00 | 11.00 | 16.87 | 43.06 | 71.25 | 195.08 | 372.57 | 179.23 | 557.15 | 866.37 | 914.06 | 1 770.00 | 1 800.00 | 1 598.22 |
| Sweden | 1 107.12 | 1 150.83 | 1 103.47 | 1 726.78 | 2 566.30 | 3 970.84 | 6 794.62 | 17 383.50 | 30 905.50 | 30 460.60 | 57 537.70 | 80 448.15 | 86 917.31 | 130 961.94 | 158 549.37 | 139 888.87 |
| Switzerland | 785.51 | 790.54 | 894.36 | 1 285.63 | 1 859.39 | 2 941.04 | 5 062.94 | 12 952.60 | 29 632.00 | 27 433.00 | 63 784.00 | 81 641.11 | 80 500.00 | 130 929.63 | 195 609.28 | 289 873.57 |
| Syrian Arab Republic | 36.00 | 35.00 | 82.30 | 143.70 | 113.16 | 168.51 | 202.96 | 929.92 | 2 107.69 | 1 637.45 | 4 212.03 | 3 563.47 | 4 633.03 | 8 708.00 | 12 796.11 | 1 349.04 |
| Taiwan Province of China | 17.00 | 17.00 | 72.60 | 123.40 | 164.20 | 449.50 | 1 428.25 | 5 302.37 | 19 842.00 | 30 784.00 | 67 245.00 | 113 047.00 | 151 356.88 | 198 431.70 | 274 600.60 | 285 420.96 |
| Tajikistan | ... | ... | ... | ... | ... | ... | ... | ... | ... | ... | ... | 750.00 | 785.00 | 909.00 | 1 195.30 | 890.60 |
| Thailand | 223.00 | 274.00 | 304.00 | 335.00 | 406.70 | 622.16 | 710.19 | 2 208.46 | 6 505.41 | 7 120.57 | 23 068.30 | 56 439.40 | 68 962.50 | 110 936.42 | 193 305.55 | 214 375.14 |
| The former Yugoslav Republic of Macedonia | ... | ... | ... | ... | ... | ... | ... | ... | ... | ... | ... | 1 204.05 | 1 322.62 | 2 041.00 | 3 351.43 | 4 489.93 |
| Timor-Leste | ... | ... | ... | ... | ... | ... | ... | ... | ... | ... | ... | ... | ... | 8.09 | 16.40 | 16.19 |
| Togo | 10.00 | 6.00 | 9.00 | 22.19 | 14.63 | 27.26 | 54.89 | 126.46 | 337.70 | 190.05 | 267.91 | 378.25 | 364.33 | 660.14 | 976.22 | 1 227.15 |
| Tokelau | ... | ... | ... | ... | ... | ... | ... | ... | ... | ... | ... | ... | 0.23 | 0.08 | 0.13 | |
| Tonga | 3.00 | 0.20 | 0.20 | 2.18 | 3.80 | 2.81 | 2.99 | 5.83 | 7.24 | 5.03 | 11.24 | 14.07 | 8.77 | 9.98 | 8.26 | 16.00 |
| Trinidad and Tobago | 110.74 | 106.71 | 102.84 | 166.60 | 286.77 | 402.79 | 481.55 | 1 771.09 | 4 077.00 | 2 138.97 | 1 960.16 | 2 454.33 | 4 274.00 | 9 941.67 | 10 981.68 | 11 099.93 |
| Tunisia | 47.71 | 78.51 | 113.80 | 106.83 | 119.69 | 119.85 | 182.48 | 855.56 | 2 231.37 | 1 737.93 | 3 527.08 | 5 475.29 | 5 850.15 | 10 493.60 | 16 426.56 | 14 073.00 |
| Turkey | 196.80 | 247.90 | 263.60 | 313.20 | 320.73 | 463.74 | 588.48 | 1 401.08 | 2 910.12 | 7 958.00 | 12 959.30 | 21 599.30 | 27 774.90 | 73 476.00 | 113 883.22 | 143 882.63 |
| Turkmenistan | ... | ... | ... | ... | ... | ... | ... | ... | ... | ... | ... | 1 880.00 | 2 506.00 | 4 944.00 | 6 500.00 | 14 000.00 |
| Turks and Caicos Islands | ... | ... | ... | ... | ... | ... | ... | ... | ... | ... | ... | ... | 8.84 | 14.72 | 16.00 | 32.13 |
| Tuvalu | ... | ... | ... | ... | ... | ... | ... | ... | 0.00 | 0.00 | 0.15 | 0.16 | 0.01 | 0.06 | 0.30 | 0.30 |
| Uganda | 66.00 | 89.00 | 81.00 | 118.00 | 129.00 | 206.00 | 282.00 | 257.00 | 345.00 | 387.00 | 152.00 | 460.00 | 402.82 | 812.81 | 1 618.60 | 2 244.54 |
| Ukraine | ... | ... | ... | ... | ... | ... | ... | ... | ... | ... | ... | 13 128.00 | 14 572.50 | 34 228.40 | 51 478.00 | 37 859.20 |
| Union of Soviet Socialist Republics | 1 295.00 | 1 433.00 | 1 794.00 | 3 427.00 | 5 564.00 | 8 175.00 | 12 800.00 | 33 316.00 | 76 500.00 | 86 780.00 | 103 840.00 | ... | ... | ... | ... | ... |
| United Arab Emirates | ... | ... | 3.00 | 2.00 | 2.00 | 198.00 | 523.00 | 7 218.00 | 21 970.00 | 16 780.00 | 23 544.00 | 28 363.93 | 49 835.26 | 117 287.13 | 214 000.00 | 310 635.89 |
| United Kingdom of Great Britain and Northern Ireland | 6 605.17 | 6 875.45 | 6 325.20 | 8 467.20 | 10 609.20 | 13 809.60 | 19 430.40 | 43 422.90 | 110 137.00 | 101 355.00 | 185 107.00 | 237 969.55 | 284 720.46 | 384 477.07 | 415 958.98 | 460 445.72 |
| United Republic of Tanzania | 63.51 | 66.09 | 67.93 | 102.30 | 154.95 | 206.63 | 251.61 | 372.49 | 511.33 | 246.47 | 331.01 | 681.81 | 733.70 | 1 679.10 | 4 050.55 | 5 854.23 |
| United States of America | 12 653.00 | 12 051.00 | 9 993.00 | 14 291.00 | 19 626.00 | 26 699.00 | 43 225.00 | 108 856.00 | 225 566.00 | 218 815.00 | 393 592.00 | 584 743.00 | 781 918.00 | 901 082.00 | 1 278 495.00 | 1 504 914.35 |
| Uruguay | 177.70 | 191.60 | 254.28 | 183.68 | 129.40 | 191.17 | 232.71 | 383.85 | 1 058.55 | 909.00 | 1 692.90 | 2 106.00 | 2 294.70 | 3 421.89 | 6 724.16 | 7 675.45 |
| Uzbekistan | ... | ... | ... | ... | ... | ... | ... | ... | ... | ... | ... | 3 430.00 | 2 817.00 | 4 749.00 | 11 695.01 | 12 304.20 |
| Vanuatu | 5.34 | 3.93 | 3.97 | 3.99 | 4.78 | 9.13 | 11.50 | 11.54 | 35.87 | 30.67 | 18.81 | 28.30 | 26.00 | 37.75 | 48.76 | 61.94 |

Annex table A.6
**Merchandise exports, 1948–2015** (*continued*)

Millions of current United States dollars

| Country/area | 1948 | 1949 | 1950 | 1955 | 1960 | 1965 | 1970 | 1975 | 1980 | 1985 | 1990 | 1995 | 2000 | 2005 | 2010 | 2015 |
|---|---|---|---|---|---|---|---|---|---|---|---|---|---|---|---|---|
| Venezuela (Bolivarian Republic of) | 897.60 | 863.15 | 929.14 | 1 819.03 | 2 304.81 | 2 455.28 | 3 168.99 | 8 799.77 | 19 221.00 | 14 438.00 | 17 497.00 | 18 457.00 | 33 529.00 | 55 716.00 | 65 745.00 | 36 627.00 |
| Viet Nam | ... | ... | ... | ... | ... | ... | ... | ... | 338.00 | 698.00 | 2 404.04 | 5 449.00 | 14 483.00 | 32 442.00 | 72 236.67 | 162 106.57 |
| Wallis and Futuna Islands | ... | ... | ... | ... | ... | ... | ... | ... | ... | ... | ... | ... | 0.04 | 0.04 | 0.04 | 0.09 |
| Yemen | ... | ... | ... | ... | ... | ... | ... | ... | ... | ... | 692.38 | 1 945.04 | 4 079.00 | 5 607.67 | 8 100.00 | ... |
| Yemen Arab Republic | 6.00 | 7.00 | 8.00 | 10.00 | 11.00 | 4.80 | 2.90 | 10.90 | 22.60 | 13.14 | ... | ... | ... | ... | ... | ... |
| Yemen (People's Democratic Republic of) | 52.39 | 111.68 | 110.60 | 175.56 | 163.04 | 184.71 | 145.28 | 190.51 | 777.37 | 550.00 | ... | ... | ... | ... | ... | ... |
| Yugoslavia | 304.00 | 204.00 | 154.00 | 256.70 | 566.10 | 1 091.50 | 1 678.90 | 4 072.30 | 8 977.50 | 10 699.60 | 14 308.00 | ... | ... | ... | ... | ... |
| Zambia | 115.30 | 92.12 | 138.32 | 484.10 | 576.70 | 526.68 | 1 001.00 | 810.24 | 1 305.41 | 784.00 | 1 308.58 | 1 032.04 | 892.36 | 1 809.76 | 7 200.27 | 6 960.97 |
| Zimbabwe | 99.00 | 109.00 | 117.00 | 126.00 | 173.00 | 420.00 | 420.00 | 877.01 | 1 396.30 | 1 115.46 | 1 711.13 | 2 120.98 | 1 925.00 | 1 850.00 | 3 199.23 | 2 715.70 |

Source: UN/DESA, based on data from United Nations Conference on Trade and Development. Available at http://unctadstat.unctad.org/wds/ReportFolders/reportFolders.aspx.
Note: The data set was used in its entirety by UN/DESA. Data for the following countries were appended: Ethiopia, prior to 1992 and post-1992; Indonesia, prior to 2003 and post-2003; and the Sudan, prior to 2002 and post-2002.
Three dots (...) indicate that data are not applicable or not available.

Annex table A.7
**Merchandise imports, 1948–2015**

Millions of current United States dollars

| Country/area | 1948 | 1949 | 1950 | 1955 | 1960 | 1965 | 1970 | 1975 | 1980 | 1985 | 1990 | 1995 | 2000 | 2005 | 2010 | 2015 |
|---|---|---|---|---|---|---|---|---|---|---|---|---|---|---|---|---|
| Afghanistan | 58.00 | 52.00 | 60.00 | 65.00 | 87.00 | 121.00 | 114.00 | 350.00 | 840.90 | 1 194.20 | 936.40 | 387.00 | 1 175.90 | 2 470.74 | 5 154.25 | 7 722.87 |
| Albania | ... | ... | 22.00 | 43.00 | 81.00 | ... | ... | ... | ... | ... | 380.00 | 713.51 | 1 090.84 | 2 618.00 | 4 405.94 | 4 318.44 |
| Algeria | 482.00 | 456.90 | 434.12 | 696.29 | 1 264.11 | 671.45 | 1 256.82 | 5 497.52 | 10 558.00 | 9 841.00 | 9 770.00 | 10 100.00 | 9 171.00 | 20 357.00 | 40 473.00 | 51 501.00 |
| American Samoa | 1.00 | 1.00 | 1.00 | 2.01 | 5.04 | 10.00 | 18.00 | 53.00 | 95.00 | 296.00 | 360.30 | 415.70 | 506.00 | 506.20 | 360.90 | 402.24 |
| Andorra | ... | ... | ... | ... | ... | ... | ... | ... | ... | ... | ... | 1 025.48 | 1 011.96 | 1 801.93 | 1 540.51 | 1 258.19 |
| Angola | 49.00 | 50.90 | 58.00 | 93.00 | 128.00 | 195.00 | 368.00 | 429.00 | 1 328.00 | 1 401.00 | 1 578.00 | 1 468.00 | 3 040.00 | 8 353.00 | 16 666.87 | 21 163.73 |
| Anguilla | ... | ... | ... | ... | ... | ... | ... | ... | ... | ... | ... | 53.41 | 94.51 | 129.89 | 157.99 | 151.21 |
| Antigua and Barbuda | 3.59 | 2.75 | 3.74 | 6.03 | 9.12 | 18.91 | 36.32 | 66.89 | 87.50 | 166.35 | 254.70 | 345.71 | 407.00 | 506.00 | 501.23 | 456.92 |
| Argentina | 1 561.50 | 1 179.60 | 964.20 | 1 172.60 | 1 249.40 | 1 198.60 | 1 694.00 | 3 949.10 | 10 545.40 | 3 814.20 | 4 077.50 | 20 121.68 | 25 154.00 | 28 688.70 | 56 792.50 | 59 786.90 |
| Armenia | ... | ... | ... | ... | ... | ... | ... | ... | ... | ... | ... | 673.90 | 881.90 | 1 801.70 | 3 782.88 | 3 254.00 |
| Aruba | ... | ... | ... | ... | ... | ... | ... | ... | ... | ... | 580.84 | 1 596.76 | 2 581.56 | 4 287.71 | 1 394.25 | 1 253.63 |
| Australia | 1 341.18 | 1 492.13 | 1 572.03 | 2 139.09 | 2 662.24 | 3 762.42 | 5 056.46 | 10 696.90 | 22 398.70 | 25 889.50 | 41 984.90 | 61 282.70 | 71 528.70 | 125 281.00 | 201 639.00 | 208 419.00 |
| Austria | 490.00 | 592.00 | 477.00 | 887.23 | 1 415.88 | 2 100.54 | 3 548.69 | 9 393.87 | 24 444.00 | 20 985.80 | 49 087.70 | 66 242.18 | 72 215.39 | 127 327.13 | 159 009.06 | 155 235.36 |
| Azerbaijan | ... | ... | ... | ... | ... | ... | ... | ... | ... | ... | ... | 668.00 | 1 172.00 | 4 349.86 | 6 746.00 | 9 773.63 |
| Bahamas | 19.00 | 17.50 | 17.00 | 30.40 | 66.00 | 104.86 | 337.43 | 2 697.00 | 7 545.59 | 3 077.86 | 1 111.80 | 1 243.10 | 2 073.60 | 2 311.60 | 2 590.60 | 3 161.31 |
| Bahrain | 120.00 | 120.00 | 119.00 | 174.00 | 180.00 | 168.00 | 247.17 | 1 189.38 | 3 482.76 | 3 106.65 | 3 711.70 | 3 715.43 | 4 633.24 | 9 393.07 | 12 260.00 | 9 900.00 |
| Bangladesh | ... | ... | ... | ... | ... | ... | ... | 1 303.11 | 2 598.96 | 2 542.35 | 3 618.10 | 6 694.00 | 8 883.00 | 13 889.00 | 27 821.20 | 39 460.40 |
| Barbados | 25.58 | 26.30 | 22.58 | 32.23 | 48.59 | 67.82 | 117.50 | 216.52 | 524.55 | 610.79 | 703.96 | 770.61 | 1 156.05 | 1 604.45 | 1 569.42 | 1 617.85 |
| Belarus | ... | ... | ... | ... | ... | ... | ... | ... | ... | ... | ... | 5 563.60 | 8 646.20 | 16 708.00 | 34 884.40 | 30 311.70 |
| Belgium | 1 985.00 | 1 789.70 | 1 950.00 | 2 854.00 | 3 970.00 | 6 502.00 | 11 412.00 | 30 781.00 | 71 860.00 | 56 182.00 | 119 702.00 | 164 951.41 | 177 072.91 | 318 699.89 | 391 177.10 | 375 267.41 |
| Belize | 8.00 | 8.00 | 6.00 | 10.00 | 13.15 | 24.49 | 33.37 | 88.07 | 149.76 | 128.13 | 211.30 | 257.22 | 524.29 | 592.94 | 705.65 | 961.27 |
| Benin | 7.23 | 13.51 | 12.22 | 23.87 | 31.16 | 34.69 | 63.89 | 188.17 | 331.17 | 331.16 | 265.16 | 745.67 | 613.00 | 1 018.00 | 2 053.88 | 3 569.52 |
| Bermuda | ... | ... | 25.28 | 41.30 | 60.52 | 64.45 | 115.61 | 178.31 | 312.00 | 403.00 | 595.00 | 550.00 | 719.00 | 985.00 | 972.00 | 934.94 |
| Bhutan | ... | ... | ... | ... | ... | ... | ... | ... | 50.18 | 84.21 | 81.38 | 112.31 | 175.20 | 386.29 | 853.80 | 997.00 |
| Bolivia (Plurinational State of) | 68.70 | 78.40 | 64.00 | 82.39 | 71.48 | 133.85 | 159.18 | 557.90 | 665.40 | 690.90 | 687.20 | 1 423.80 | 1 829.70 | 2 430.82 | 5 590.25 | 9 602.21 |
| Bonaire, Sint Eustatius and Saba | | | | | | | | | | | | | | | | 74.53 |
| Bosnia and Herzegovina | ... | ... | ... | ... | ... | ... | ... | ... | ... | ... | ... | 1 082.00 | 3 180.78 | 7 070.00 | 9 222.97 | 8 993.87 |
| Botswana | ... | ... | 1.00 | 6.86 | 9.24 | 23.23 | 57.30 | 216.13 | 692.63 | 671.82 | 1 947.47 | 1 911.10 | 2 081.00 | 3 161.00 | 5 656.81 | 7 089.63 |
| Brazil | 1 127.00 | 1 156.00 | 1 090.00 | 1 307.00 | 1 462.00 | 1 096.00 | 2 849.00 | 13 592.00 | 24 961.00 | 14 332.00 | 22 522.20 | 54 137.40 | 58 643.20 | 77 627.80 | 191 537.00 | 178 798.40 |
| British Virgin Islands | ... | ... | ... | ... | ... | ... | ... | ... | 40.00 | 86.00 | 115.00 | 130.80 | 237.00 | 280.00 | 300.00 | 230.00 |
| Brunei Darussalam | 16.50 | 15.50 | 18.00 | 30.00 | 17.00 | 36.00 | 84.00 | 273.00 | 572.00 | 615.00 | 1 001.00 | 2 091.00 | 1 107.00 | 1 491.00 | 2 537.79 | 3 229.08 |
| Bulgaria | 124.00 | ... | ... | 250.00 | 633.00 | 1 177.78 | 1 830.77 | 5 949.00 | 9 670.00 | 13 630.00 | 5 100.00 | 5 660.00 | 6 543.61 | 18 163.00 | 25 513.22 | 29 297.68 |

**Annex table A.7**
**Merchandise imports, 1948–2015** (continued)

Millions of current United States dollars

| Country/area | 1948 | 1949 | 1950 | 1955 | 1960 | 1965 | 1970 | 1975 | 1980 | 1985 | 1990 | 1995 | 2000 | 2005 | 2010 | 2015 |
|---|---|---|---|---|---|---|---|---|---|---|---|---|---|---|---|---|
| Burkina Faso | ... | ... | 8.00 | 10.00 | 10.74 | 37.42 | 49.58 | 151.24 | 358.57 | 331.99 | 535.63 | 454.78 | 611.00 | 1 260.00 | 2 048.22 | 2 979.78 |
| Burundi | ... | ... | 5.00 | 7.00 | 21.00 | 19.00 | 22.34 | 61.55 | 167.99 | 186.10 | 230.70 | 234.21 | 147.91 | 269.24 | 508.80 | 723.80 |
| Cabo Verde | 16.27 | 9.79 | 8.55 | 11.70 | 12.13 | 5.73 | 16.33 | 39.82 | 67.80 | 81.25 | 135.59 | 252.36 | 229.90 | 438.21 | 742.36 | 606.30 |
| Cambodia | ... | ... | 10.00 | 45.51 | 94.92 | 102.94 | 54.20 | 60.00 | 180.00 | 120.00 | 164.00 | 1 186.80 | 1 935.73 | 3 927.00 | 6 790.73 | 13 810.36 |
| Cameroon | 42.00 | 65.30 | 60.00 | 104.00 | 84.00 | 134.70 | 243.28 | 599.16 | 1 602.37 | 1 151.34 | 1 399.92 | 1 199.00 | 1 483.63 | 2 735.00 | 5 133.28 | 6 441.07 |
| Canada | 2 740.27 | 2 878.63 | 3 107.54 | 4 996.26 | 6 073.08 | 8 621.63 | 14 286.00 | 36 106.50 | 62 544.20 | 80 639.80 | 123 244.00 | 168 041.00 | 244 778.00 | 322 411.00 | 402 690.00 | 436 372.00 |
| Cayman Islands | ... | ... | ... | ... | ... | ... | ... | ... | 101.00 | 147.00 | 288.00 | 402.00 | 665.00 | 1 213.80 | 828.48 | 1 100.00 |
| Central African Republic | ... | ... | 15.00 | 18.00 | 20.21 | 27.65 | 34.35 | 68.77 | 81.15 | 112.82 | 154.45 | 174.10 | 117.00 | 175.00 | 300.00 | 130.36 |
| Chad | ... | ... | 12.00 | 24.00 | 25.43 | 31.44 | 62.30 | 132.78 | 73.52 | 166.29 | 285.00 | 365.00 | 317.00 | 950.00 | 2 400.00 | 2 854.55 |
| Chile | 270.00 | 304.60 | 294.29 | 447.80 | 625.46 | 718.28 | 1 063.31 | 1 524.97 | 5 796.90 | 3 071.60 | 7 939.90 | 15 898.40 | 18 507.20 | 32 735.10 | 59 207.44 | 63 038.71 |
| China | 387.00 | ... | 580.00 | 1 730.00 | 2 648.46 | 2 246.32 | 2 278.81 | 7 925.58 | 19 941.30 | 42 252.00 | 53 345.00 | 132 079.00 | 225 024.00 | 659 953.00 | 1 396 247.00 | 1 681 951.00 |
| China, Hong Kong SAR | 523.40 | 624.12 | 662.90 | 650.82 | 1 026.20 | 1 568.87 | 2 905.16 | 6 766.03 | 22 994.00 | 31 195.00 | 84 725.00 | 196 072.00 | 214 042.00 | 300 160.00 | 441 369.20 | 559 427.00 |
| China, Macao SAR | 21.00 | 41.00 | 41.00 | 10.77 | 30.35 | 46.93 | 64.95 | 160.85 | 544.00 | 778.00 | 1 539.00 | 2 042.00 | 2 625.22 | 4 514.27 | 5 629.45 | 10 602.84 |
| Colombia | 337.00 | 264.60 | 364.90 | 669.30 | 517.40 | 453.80 | 843.00 | 1 494.80 | 4 738.60 | 4 140.90 | 5 588.90 | 13 852.90 | 11 538.50 | 21 204.40 | 40 485.56 | 54 057.58 |
| Comoros | ... | ... | 1.00 | 3.03 | 3.83 | 6.62 | 8.59 | 23.21 | 29.09 | 36.46 | 51.57 | 63.00 | 43.20 | 98.69 | 232.82 | 232.04 |
| Congo | 53.00 | 82.00 | 50.00 | 43.00 | 70.64 | 67.14 | 59.30 | 170.19 | 561.61 | 598.08 | 620.80 | 669.51 | 465.00 | 1 303.59 | 4 000.00 | 7 724.36 |
| Cook Islands | ... | ... | ... | ... | ... | 4.26 | 6.46 | 12.64 | 23.00 | 25.00 | 51.54 | 48.49 | 50.77 | 81.00 | 91.00 | 95.00 |
| Costa Rica | 42.30 | 43.40 | 46.00 | 87.50 | 110.40 | 178.20 | 316.70 | 694.00 | 1 540.40 | 1 098.20 | 1 989.70 | 4 090.00 | 6 388.50 | 9 824.00 | 13 569.60 | 15 502.72 |
| Côte d'Ivoire | ... | ... | 61.08 | 108.64 | 131.98 | 238.06 | 389.66 | 1 127.04 | 2 991.04 | 1 749.16 | 2 097.59 | 2 946.22 | 2 482.19 | 5 864.96 | 7 849.33 | 9 915.29 |
| Croatia | ... | ... | ... | ... | ... | ... | ... | ... | ... | ... | ... | 7 351.51 | 7 886.51 | 18 560.00 | 20 067.14 | 20 460.18 |
| Cuba | 527.00 | 451.00 | 563.00 | 575.00 | 638.00 | 866.00 | 1 311.00 | 3 883.00 | 6 505.00 | 7 983.00 | 4 600.00 | 2 825.00 | 4 843.24 | 8 084.34 | 11 496.17 | 15 089.80 |
| Curaçao | ... | ... | ... | ... | ... | ... | ... | ... | ... | ... | ... | ... | ... | ... | ... | 1 499.29 |
| Cyprus | 62.73 | 41.03 | 37.73 | 85.18 | 109.73 | 143.89 | 234.67 | 308.05 | 1 202.23 | 1 246.67 | 2 567.97 | 3 694.17 | 3 846.37 | 6 315.83 | 8 568.99 | 5 566.58 |
| Czechoslovakia | 681.00 | 718.00 | 639.00 | 1 053.00 | 1 816.00 | 2 673.00 | 3 695.00 | 9 081.00 | 15 180.00 | 10 325.00 | 12 460.00 | ... | ... | ... | ... | ... |
| Czech Republic | ... | ... | ... | ... | ... | ... | ... | ... | ... | ... | ... | 25 085.00 | 31 974.29 | 76 511.92 | 126 652.13 | 140 479.23 |
| Democratic People's Republic of Korea | ... | ... | ... | ... | ... | ... | ... | ... | 1 200.00 | 1 787.00 | 2 930.00 | 1 380.00 | 1 686.00 | 2 718.00 | 3 530.00 | 4 760.33 |
| Democratic Republic of the Congo | 192.00 | 228.00 | 188.00 | 379.00 | 235.00 | 97.37 | 178.53 | 300.27 | 1 519.00 | 1 247.00 | 1 739.00 | 871.00 | 682.80 | 2 690.40 | 4 500.00 | 5 138.53 |
| Denmark | 713.48 | 810.78 | 852.74 | 1 178.35 | 1 806.97 | 2 822.73 | 4 407.20 | 10 368.30 | 19 340.20 | 18 245.30 | 33 333.00 | 45 940.47 | 45 444.65 | 75 581.16 | 83 052.13 | 85 522.37 |
| Djibouti | 17.00 | 14.00 | 13.00 | 22.40 | 33.40 | 61.18 | 38.15 | 135.98 | 213.00 | 201.00 | 215.00 | 176.70 | 206.50 | 277.32 | 373.89 | 739.30 |
| Dominica | ... | ... | 2.00 | 4.00 | 5.81 | 10.03 | 15.76 | 20.76 | 47.68 | 55.32 | 117.92 | 112.86 | 148.50 | 165.34 | 223.78 | 217.76 |
| Dominican Republic | 74.48 | 52.45 | 49.66 | 113.80 | 100.05 | 97.15 | 304.15 | 888.61 | 1 964.00 | 1 787.00 | 3 006.00 | 5 170.00 | 9 479.00 | 9 869.00 | 15 489.10 | 16 863.40 |
| Ecuador | 59.64 | 55.32 | 49.56 | 114.00 | 114.34 | 165.47 | 273.85 | 987.02 | 2 253.30 | 1 766.60 | 1 861.90 | 4 193.29 | 3 721.12 | 10 286.90 | 20 590.85 | 21 517.97 |

Annex table A.7
**Merchandise imports, 1948–2015** (*continued*)

Millions of current United States dollars

| Country/area | 1948 | 1949 | 1950 | 1955 | 1960 | 1965 | 1970 | 1975 | 1980 | 1985 | 1990 | 1995 | 2000 | 2005 | 2010 | 2015 |
|---|---|---|---|---|---|---|---|---|---|---|---|---|---|---|---|---|
| Egypt | 714.60 | 680.30 | 619.40 | 537.84 | 667.64 | 933.57 | 786.60 | 3 933.77 | 4 859.85 | 11 104.00 | 9 215.50 | 11 738.80 | 14 578.36 | 22 449.03 | 52 922.83 | 60 528.43 |
| El Salvador | 41.56 | 40.80 | 48.68 | 91.88 | 123.04 | 200.56 | 214.36 | 614.04 | 966.12 | 961.36 | 1 262.50 | 3 329.00 | 4 947.00 | 6 690.00 | 8 416.00 | 10 415.60 |
| Equatorial Guinea | 51.00 | 50.00 | 50.00 | 44.00 | 16.00 | 26.00 | 23.76 | 19.58 | 26.25 | 19.71 | 60.92 | 121.00 | 451.00 | 1 310.00 | 5 200.00 | 5 954.66 |
| Eritrea | ... | ... | ... | ... | ... | ... | ... | ... | ... | ... | ... | 453.48 | 471.37 | 490.00 | 660.00 | 880.26 |
| Estonia | ... | ... | ... | ... | ... | ... | ... | ... | ... | ... | ... | 2 546.00 | 5 052.00 | 10 238.46 | 12 286.95 | 14 510.04 |
| Ethiopia | 49.91 | 47.94 | 42.46 | 67.62 | 88.27 | 150.28 | 171.64 | 313.00 | 722.08 | 993.43 | 1 081.40 | 1 145.20 | 1 260.42 | 4 094.78 | 8 601.77 | 25 815.26 |
| Falkland Islands (Malvinas) | ... | ... | ... | ... | ... | ... | ... | ... | 6.24 | 14.19 | 32.40 | 43.61 | 59.00 | 60.00 | 100.00 | 243.86 |
| Faroe Islands | 7.00 | 9.00 | 9.70 | 11.30 | 15.10 | 26.40 | 30.40 | 113.40 | 223.00 | 248.00 | 338.00 | 315.00 | 533.00 | 743.00 | 780.02 | 1 001.30 |
| Fiji | 21.58 | 22.87 | 17.56 | 36.25 | 41.38 | 73.36 | 103.95 | 268.21 | 562.15 | 442.00 | 754.00 | 892.00 | 830.00 | 1 607.00 | 1 808.46 | 2 589.64 |
| Finland | 488.24 | 399.88 | 385.71 | 769.13 | 1 064.06 | 1 645.62 | 2 637.64 | 7 628.43 | 15 634.60 | 13 231.70 | 27 001.10 | 29 471.49 | 34 357.86 | 58 765.77 | 68 803.05 | 60 089.41 |
| France | 3 504.43 | 2 862.78 | 3 141.74 | 4 910.01 | 6 437.56 | 10 678.86 | 19 611.27 | 55 075.01 | 137 531.95 | 110 678.30 | 240 802.64 | 296 725.00 | 338 102.67 | 504 124.43 | 611 069.80 | 572 661.32 |
| French Polynesia | 8.00 | 11.00 | 8.00 | 14.13 | 18.31 | 107.36 | 135.09 | 286.37 | 547.46 | 549.00 | 930.00 | 1 005.00 | 971.00 | 1 723.20 | 1 725.76 | 1 526.97 |
| Gabon | ... | ... | 16.00 | 20.00 | 31.93 | 62.94 | 80.45 | 469.22 | 673.56 | 854.73 | 918.22 | 881.90 | 950.47 | 1 471.03 | 2 982.51 | 3 735.37 |
| Gambia | 7.81 | 6.12 | 8.18 | 10.39 | 9.02 | 16.23 | 17.97 | 59.66 | 165.40 | 93.34 | 187.90 | 182.40 | 187.00 | 259.58 | 285.03 | 410.09 |
| Georgia | ... | ... | ... | ... | ... | ... | ... | ... | ... | ... | ... | 392.00 | 709.38 | 2 490.00 | 5 257.00 | 7 724.00 |
| Germany | ... | ... | ... | ... | ... | ... | ... | ... | ... | ... | 355 686.00 | 463 904.58 | 495 969.67 | 777 072.77 | 1 054 813.87 | 1 050 024.59 |
| Germany (Federal Republic of) | 1 400.00 | 2 089.00 | 2 710.38 | 5 826.19 | 10 172.10 | 17 612.00 | 29 947.30 | 74 930.50 | 188 002.00 | 158 488.00 | ... | | | | | |
| German Democratic Republic | 172.00 | 331.00 | 470.00 | 1 173.00 | 2 195.00 | 2 810.00 | 4 847.00 | 11 290.00 | 19 080.00 | 13 800.00 | ... | | | | | |
| Ghana | 126.54 | 169.00 | 134.82 | 246.12 | 363.07 | 448.37 | 410.84 | 790.70 | 1 128.73 | 865.68 | 1 205.00 | 1 908.67 | 2 975.94 | 5 347.31 | 10 922.11 | 13 465.10 |
| Gibraltar | ... | ... | ... | ... | ... | ... | ... | 40.90 | 109.50 | 91.52 | 362.00 | 408.26 | 480.99 | 502.37 | 627.65 | 700.00 |
| Greece | 362.95 | 407.97 | 428.20 | 382.16 | 701.99 | 1 133.73 | 1 958.33 | 5 356.91 | 10 548.00 | 10 134.40 | 19 777.00 | 25 900.38 | 33 397.20 | 54 435.99 | 66 913.28 | 48 417.36 |
| Greenland | 4.00 | 6.00 | 5.00 | 11.00 | 16.00 | 34.00 | 53.00 | 127.80 | 328.00 | 296.00 | 445.00 | 434.00 | 365.00 | 592.50 | 808.43 | 647.09 |
| Grenada | ... | ... | 4.00 | 6.03 | 8.65 | 11.13 | 22.32 | 24.13 | 50.21 | 69.26 | 105.11 | 123.65 | 238.78 | 328.14 | 318.01 | 353.24 |
| Guam | 10.00 | 11.00 | 14.00 | 22.29 | 26.45 | 40.00 | 96.40 | 266.25 | 200.00 | 290.00 | 460.00 | 440.00 | 420.00 | 900.00 | 950.00 | 785.32 |
| Guatemala | 68.35 | 67.98 | 71.22 | 104.32 | 121.25 | 229.32 | 284.32 | 732.68 | 1 598.23 | 1 174.80 | 1 648.80 | 3 292.50 | 5 171.40 | 10 498.70 | 13 838.30 | 17 636.20 |
| Guinea | ... | ... | 24.00 | 37.00 | 49.94 | 52.59 | 78.20 | 216.42 | 360.00 | 448.00 | 723.00 | 818.51 | 612.00 | 820.00 | 1 404.92 | 1 844.34 |
| Guinea-Bissau | 7.43 | 5.51 | 4.46 | 6.52 | 11.19 | 14.58 | 27.34 | 37.76 | 55.01 | 60.00 | 85.73 | 132.91 | 59.55 | 123.17 | 196.46 | 171.91 |
| Guyana | 39.80 | 31.36 | 32.73 | 55.14 | 86.21 | 104.33 | 134.12 | 342.16 | 396.24 | 225.51 | 310.88 | 527.59 | 573.00 | 788.29 | 1 397.10 | 1 474.89 |
| Haiti | 32.21 | 31.43 | 36.20 | 39.20 | 40.40 | 33.61 | 55.00 | 148.94 | 375.36 | 441.56 | 332.22 | 652.97 | 1 036.16 | 1 453.74 | 3 146.10 | 3 445.34 |
| Honduras | 43.00 | 50.00 | 34.00 | 72.00 | 71.80 | 121.95 | 220.67 | 400.08 | 1 008.69 | 888.10 | 937.70 | 1 879.41 | 3 987.80 | 6 544.59 | 8 907.00 | 11 097.00 |
| Hungary | 168.00 | 286.00 | 313.00 | 554.00 | 976.00 | 1 521.00 | 1 876.67 | 5 400.33 | 9 190.00 | 8 185.00 | 10 340.00 | 15 465.00 | 32 171.54 | 66 552.20 | 88 177.90 | 92 599.65 |

**Annex table A.7**
**Merchandise imports, 1948–2015** (continued)

Millions of current United States dollars

| Country/area | 1948 | 1949 | 1950 | 1955 | 1960 | 1965 | 1970 | 1975 | 1980 | 1985 | 1990 | 1995 | 2000 | 2005 | 2010 | 2015 |
|---|---|---|---|---|---|---|---|---|---|---|---|---|---|---|---|---|
| Iceland | 70.88 | 46.04 | 33.15 | 77.96 | 97.05 | 137.21 | 157.27 | 483.87 | 998.86 | 905.23 | 1 680.04 | 1 758.00 | 2 589.00 | 4 979.00 | 3 919.51 | 5 294.60 |
| India | 1 426.62 | 1 840.21 | 1 091.16 | 1 356.18 | 2 303.28 | 2 838.36 | 2 124.40 | 6 380.66 | 14 864.40 | 15 928.00 | 23 579.60 | 34 706.90 | 51 522.90 | 142 870.00 | 350 232.80 | 391 976.57 |
| Indonesia | 464.00 | 579.00 | 440.00 | 630.00 | 574.10 | 694.60 | 1 001.50 | 4 769.80 | 10 834.00 | 10 262.00 | 21 767.80 | 40 630.00 | 43 595.00 | 75 724.93 | 135 323.49 | 142 694.80 |
| Iran (Islamic Republic of) | 167.00 | 329.00 | 216.00 | 312.00 | 650.00 | 859.41 | 1 662.05 | 10 343.10 | 12 246.00 | 11 635.00 | 20 322.00 | 13 882.00 | 13 898.00 | 40 041.00 | 65 404.00 | 41 800.00 |
| Iraq | 185.38 | 150.76 | 105.28 | 272.16 | 389.00 | 455.00 | 509.00 | 4 214.84 | 13 941.60 | 10 556.00 | 6 526.00 | 665.00 | 13 210.00 | 23 532.00 | 43 915.30 | 52 000.00 |
| Ireland | 549.29 | 484.67 | 446.32 | 572.04 | 633.92 | 1 041.04 | 1 621.44 | 3 778.41 | 11 153.20 | 10 015.30 | 20 681.70 | 32 336.23 | 50 915.22 | 68 565.08 | 60 276.21 | 71 335.97 |
| Israel | 108.20 | 329.40 | 302.00 | 336.80 | 496.20 | 837.50 | 2 079.40 | 5 997.40 | 9 784.10 | 9 874.90 | 16 793.70 | 29 578.60 | 37 686.00 | 47 141.50 | 61 209.00 | 64 989.60 |
| Italy | 1 539.00 | 1 544.81 | 1 482.53 | 2 712.00 | 4 733.93 | 7 377.60 | 14 974.40 | 38 525.50 | 100 741.00 | 87 692.00 | 181 968.00 | 205 990.00 | 238 756.70 | 384 790.24 | 487 048.67 | 408 931.97 |
| Jamaica | 79.39 | 71.66 | 62.72 | 127.82 | 217.00 | 289.06 | 525.41 | 1 123.55 | 1 171.34 | 1 111.39 | 1 927.84 | 2 817.77 | 3 301.46 | 4 739.44 | 5 225.23 | 4 861.93 |
| Japan | 684.00 | 904.70 | 964.28 | 2 471.39 | 4 491.11 | 8 169.44 | 18 881.40 | 57 860.30 | 141 296.00 | 130 488.00 | 235 368.00 | 335 885.00 | 379 510.00 | 515 866.39 | 694 059.16 | 648 494.07 |
| Jordan | 42.72 | 47.50 | 30.16 | 75.77 | 120.20 | 157.00 | 184.35 | 732.41 | 2 402.15 | 2 732.92 | 2 600.23 | 3 697.50 | 4 597.18 | 10 497.69 | 15 563.56 | 20 332.40 |
| Kazakhstan | ... | ... | ... | ... | ... | ... | ... | ... | ... | ... | ... | 3 806.70 | 5 040.00 | 17 353.00 | 31 106.70 | 30 186.00 |
| Kenya | 182.00 | 194.00 | 95.30 | 200.20 | 196.10 | 282.10 | 442.26 | 945.06 | 2 124.70 | 1 436.07 | 2 222.81 | 2 990.85 | 3 105.47 | 5 846.17 | 12 092.93 | 16 093.16 |
| Kiribati | 1.00 | 1.00 | 1.00 | 2.30 | 2.90 | 4.09 | 4.39 | 7.09 | 17.00 | 15.00 | 26.90 | 35.28 | 39.55 | 74.05 | 73.09 | 121.07 |
| Kuwait | ... | ... | 80.00 | 94.36 | 241.92 | 377.16 | 625.24 | 2 388.48 | 6 530.00 | 6 005.00 | 3 972.00 | 7 790.00 | 7 157.00 | 15 801.18 | 22 674.71 | 31 905.79 |
| Kyrgyzstan | ... | ... | ... | ... | ... | ... | ... | ... | ... | ... | ... | 522.33 | 558.10 | 1 102.00 | 3 222.80 | 4 069.50 |
| Lao People's Democratic Republic | ... | ... | 19.00 | 18.94 | 18.55 | 32.83 | 113.92 | 45.10 | 92.00 | 193.00 | 185.00 | 588.80 | 535.28 | 881.97 | 2 060.43 | 5 232.80 |
| Latvia | ... | ... | ... | ... | ... | ... | ... | ... | ... | ... | ... | 1 818.08 | 3 201.59 | 8 697.12 | 11 691.05 | 14 312.00 |
| Lebanon | ... | ... | 84.00 | 218.00 | 255.32 | 548.04 | 658.77 | 2 047.68 | 3 650.40 | 2 203.20 | 2 525.10 | 7 278.00 | 6 230.00 | 9 633.00 | 18 460.00 | 18 438.00 |
| Lesotho | ... | ... | 6.00 | 10.00 | 17.00 | 24.50 | 32.06 | 164.01 | 427.46 | 339.41 | 672.53 | 1 107.00 | 809.24 | 1 410.10 | 2 300.00 | 1 984.01 |
| Liberia | ... | ... | 11.00 | 25.96 | 69.19 | 104.60 | 149.70 | 331.20 | 534.62 | 284.40 | 570.00 | 510.00 | 668.00 | 309.90 | 709.80 | 2 237.20 |
| Libya | 22.17 | 22.71 | 19.60 | 40.32 | 169.12 | 320.32 | 554.40 | 3 542.30 | 6 777.00 | 4 101.00 | 5 336.00 | 5 392.00 | 3 732.00 | 6 079.00 | 17 674.37 | 18 165.51 |
| Lithuania | ... | ... | ... | ... | ... | ... | ... | ... | ... | ... | ... | 3 650.00 | 5 455.95 | 15 548.33 | 23 402.77 | 28 277.83 |
| Luxembourg | ... | ... | ... | ... | ... | ... | 747.36 | 1 823.31 | 3 612.04 | 3 144.21 | 7 595.66 | 9 748.36 | 11 250.20 | 21 892.86 | 25 092.23 | 23 430.98 |
| Madagascar | 78.00 | 87.00 | 85.84 | 122.40 | 111.56 | 138.37 | 170.49 | 365.74 | 600.00 | 402.00 | 651.00 | 628.00 | 1 097.10 | 1 706.33 | 2 583.79 | 2 960.91 |
| Malawi | 20.00 | 21.00 | 21.00 | 28.00 | 40.00 | 64.60 | 99.10 | 253.14 | 439.00 | 294.05 | 575.44 | 474.72 | 532.33 | 1 165.19 | 2 173.04 | 2 311.61 |
| Malaysia | 457.47 | 453.30 | 537.69 | 675.55 | 910.10 | 1 096.29 | 1 400.75 | 3 565.84 | 10 779.30 | 12 252.90 | 29 257.62 | 77 690.64 | 81 962.86 | 114 324.42 | 164 622.12 | 175 961.21 |
| Maldives | 4.00 | 4.00 | 4.00 | 4.00 | 4.00 | 1.81 | 2.37 | 7.43 | 28.63 | 53.00 | 137.40 | 267.91 | 388.59 | 744.87 | 1 090.86 | 2 265.16 |
| Mali | ... | ... | 26.00 | 36.00 | 33.00 | 33.01 | 34.25 | 176.43 | 438.62 | 299.47 | 602.43 | 772.12 | 806.00 | 1 543.60 | 3 427.51 | 3 113.95 |
| Malta | 65.20 | 57.00 | 46.93 | 59.32 | 82.93 | 98.40 | 161.09 | 375.17 | 937.93 | 758.68 | 1 961.10 | 2 943.38 | 3 413.49 | 3 680.70 | 5 062.06 | 5 771.73 |
| Marshall Islands | ... | ... | ... | ... | ... | ... | ... | ... | ... | ... | 55.59 | 74.67 | 54.72 | 94.00 | 150.00 | 138.41 |
| Mauritania | ... | ... | 19.00 | 27.00 | 24.00 | 23.76 | 55.87 | 161.13 | 285.71 | 233.54 | 220.32 | 431.32 | 454.20 | 1 428.00 | 1 935.30 | 1 948.00 |
| Mauritius | 41.18 | 41.70 | 36.92 | 52.61 | 69.70 | 77.13 | 75.58 | 331.81 | 614.18 | 528.56 | 1 617.99 | 1 976.18 | 2 207.28 | 3 157.00 | 4 385.66 | 4 791.86 |

Annex table A.7
**Merchandise imports, 1948–2015** (continued)

Millions of current United States dollars

| Country/area | 1948 | 1949 | 1950 | 1955 | 1960 | 1965 | 1970 | 1975 | 1980 | 1985 | 1990 | 1995 | 2000 | 2005 | 2010 | 2015 |
|---|---|---|---|---|---|---|---|---|---|---|---|---|---|---|---|---|
| Mexico | 643.05 | 439.77 | 549.42 | 873.58 | 1 186.48 | 1 559.76 | 2 460.80 | 6 580.16 | 22 143.80 | 19 116.00 | 43 548.40 | 74 427.47 | 179 464.22 | 228 240.23 | 310 205.06 | 405 280.49 |
| Micronesia (Federated States of) | ... | ... | ... | ... | ... | ... | ... | ... | ... | ... | 83.88 | 89.27 | 106.76 | 130.21 | 167.89 | 179.45 |
| Mongolia | ... | ... | ... | ... | ... | ... | ... | ... | 547.80 | 1 095.50 | 924.00 | 415.30 | 614.50 | 1 184.30 | 3 278.00 | 3 797.20 |
| Montenegro | ... | ... | ... | ... | ... | ... | ... | ... | ... | ... | ... | ... | ... | ... | 2 181.94 | 2 049.08 |
| Montserrat | ... | ... | 1.24 | 2.00 | 3.39 | 8.38 | 17.60 | 35.74 | 12.00 | 18.00 | 44.00 | 30.00 | 21.61 | 29.76 | 29.35 | 38.63 |
| Morocco | 281.37 | 365.38 | 328.38 | 496.86 | 413.00 | 452.72 | 684.32 | 2 567.58 | 4 255.08 | 3 849.53 | 6 921.89 | 10 022.90 | 11 533.60 | 20 790.09 | 35 381.50 | 37 513.72 |
| Mozambique | 71.00 | 68.00 | 58.00 | 90.00 | 127.00 | 173.00 | 324.00 | 411.00 | 800.00 | 424.00 | 878.00 | 704.00 | 1 158.00 | 2 408.20 | 4 600.00 | 8 357.00 |
| Myanmar | 175.89 | 78.18 | 90.78 | 180.64 | 262.06 | 247.40 | 154.98 | 195.47 | 356.60 | 285.52 | 270.00 | 1 334.59 | 2 370.89 | 1 908.13 | 4 759.66 | 17 505.14 |
| Namibia | ... | ... | ... | ... | ... | ... | ... | ... | 1 156.00 | 581.00 | 1 163.37 | 1 615.62 | 1 549.75 | 2 577.47 | 5 570.00 | 7 605.78 |
| Nauru | 2.00 | 2.00 | 2.00 | 2.00 | 3.01 | 6.00 | 5.04 | 11.00 | 12.00 | 19.00 | 34.30 | 28.15 | 26.00 | 25.00 | 20.00 | 62.80 |
| Nepal | ... | ... | 19.00 | 24.00 | 38.00 | 107.55 | 75.48 | 171.93 | 342.28 | 453.36 | 672.00 | 1 333.00 | 1 573.00 | 2 283.26 | 5 133.42 | 6 510.74 |
| Netherlands | 2 147.50 | 2 073.04 | 2 433.68 | 3 787.89 | 5 361.05 | 8 925.14 | 15 688.10 | 40 897.00 | 88 419.20 | 73 122.80 | 126 475.00 | 185 240.04 | 217 727.99 | 363 822.41 | 516 408.79 | 505 805.85 |
| Netherlands Antilles | 542.83 | 609.38 | 705.89 | 996.47 | 824.29 | 720.68 | 797.52 | 2 826.67 | 5 675.56 | 1 387.78 | 2 141.34 | 1 841.00 | 2 862.00 | 1 950.13 | 2 622.02 | ... |
| New Caledonia | 11.00 | 14.00 | 15.17 | 32.99 | 38.33 | 76.70 | 230.44 | 347.09 | 456.00 | 348.00 | 883.00 | 950.84 | 922.42 | 1 774.00 | 3 312.41 | 2 715.44 |
| New Zealand | 450.54 | 435.85 | 442.26 | 804.02 | 786.24 | 1 052.15 | 1 245.44 | 3 155.21 | 5 472.48 | 5 991.68 | 9 501.05 | 13 957.00 | 13 904.40 | 26 219.36 | 30 616.82 | 36 563.24 |
| Nicaragua | 24.13 | 21.33 | 24.70 | 69.65 | 71.71 | 160.29 | 198.75 | 516.86 | 887.21 | 964.30 | 637.46 | 975.18 | 1 801.50 | 2 956.10 | 4 792.20 | 6 902.64 |
| Niger | ... | 3.96 | 4.32 | 7.88 | 13.08 | 37.95 | 58.68 | 100.85 | 593.65 | 369.35 | 388.78 | 373.64 | 395.24 | 943.00 | 2 475.87 | 2 586.07 |
| Nigeria | 169.06 | 216.84 | 173.18 | 381.08 | 604.38 | 770.42 | 1 059.10 | 6 041.28 | 16 660.00 | 8 877.00 | 5 626.65 | 8 221.50 | 8 721.30 | 20 754.00 | 44 235.27 | 48 000.00 |
| Niue | ... | ... | ... | ... | ... | ... | ... | ... | 3.00 | 2.00 | 4.18 | 3.82 | 1.91 | 10.00 | 6.00 | 12.00 |
| Northern Mariana Islands | ... | ... | ... | ... | ... | ... | ... | ... | ... | ... | ... | 240.34 | 607.20 | 591.00 | 90.00 | 129.68 |
| Norway | 749.98 | 766.37 | 678.44 | 1 089.62 | 1 462.44 | 2 210.18 | 3 702.02 | 9 704.54 | 16 926.20 | 15 555.70 | 27 230.80 | 32 968.40 | 34 391.10 | 55 488.26 | 77 330.17 | 76 228.06 |
| Oman | 5.00 | 5.00 | 6.00 | 8.00 | 20.00 | 8.96 | 18.24 | 765.20 | 1 731.91 | 3 364.00 | 2 798.00 | 4 379.00 | 5 131.00 | 8 970.87 | 19 972.69 | 29 007.05 |
| Pakistan | 312.22 | 515.03 | 402.60 | 277.71 | 826.93 | 968.25 | 775.28 | 2 212.95 | 5 350.30 | 5 889.93 | 7 375.89 | 11 460.70 | 10 864.10 | 25 357.30 | 37 806.88 | 44 219.00 |
| Palau | ... | ... | ... | ... | ... | ... | ... | ... | ... | ... | ... | 52.00 | 127.10 | 105.18 | 107.19 | 150.32 |
| Panama | 71.00 | 65.00 | 67.23 | 82.00 | 119.52 | 208.47 | 357.03 | 892.04 | 1 449.22 | 1 391.75 | 1 538.57 | 2 510.70 | 3 378.70 | 9 600.00 | 16 737.10 | 18 922.32 |
| Papua New Guinea | 21.07 | 25.39 | 22.74 | 44.93 | 60.11 | 123.11 | 300.25 | 630.56 | 1 176.07 | 1 007.58 | 1 117.67 | 1 451.28 | 1 151.00 | 1 728.79 | 3 950.00 | 2 664.59 |
| Paraguay | 27.83 | 32.36 | 20.00 | 38.74 | 38.24 | 55.38 | 76.20 | 205.57 | 614.70 | 501.53 | 1 352.04 | 3 144.00 | 2 260.22 | 3 714.93 | 10 033.47 | 10 291.21 |
| Peru | 167.79 | 167.09 | 191.80 | 303.31 | 378.60 | 729.68 | 622.92 | 2 550.01 | 2 573.00 | 1 767.00 | 2 633.97 | 7 584.04 | 7 415.02 | 12 501.83 | 30 030.47 | 37 850.00 |
| Philippines | 644.00 | 644.50 | 376.00 | 607.00 | 714.81 | 893.55 | 1 236.25 | 3 755.70 | 8 291.41 | 5 454.72 | 13 003.70 | 28 340.50 | 37 027.30 | 49 487.42 | 58 467.80 | 70 153.47 |
| Poland | 519.00 | 632.00 | 663.00 | 932.00 | 1 495.00 | 2 340.00 | 3 608.00 | 11 155.00 | 19 120.00 | 10 840.00 | 11 570.00 | 29 050.00 | 49 028.96 | 101 638.83 | 178 049.07 | 192 601.21 |
| Portugal | 415.45 | 346.94 | 274.05 | 398.37 | 544.42 | 897.04 | 1 555.65 | 3 838.64 | 9 309.28 | 7 652.36 | 25 264.30 | 32 610.93 | 39 853.68 | 61 183.73 | 77 748.85 | 66 700.70 |
| Qatar | 5.00 | 6.00 | 7.00 | 17.00 | 32.00 | 70.00 | 64.16 | 412.97 | 1 423.00 | 1 139.00 | 1 695.00 | 3 398.00 | 3 252.00 | 10 061.00 | 23 239.84 | 32 610.46 |
| Republic of Korea | 205.70 | 138.80 | 54.00 | 341.00 | 344.00 | 463.00 | 1 984.00 | 7 274.00 | 22 292.00 | 31 136.00 | 69 844.00 | 135 119.00 | 160 481.00 | 261 238.00 | 425 212.00 | 436 499.00 |

**Annex table A.7**
**Merchandise imports, 1948–2015** (*continued*)

Millions of current United States dollars

| Country/area | 1948 | 1949 | 1950 | 1955 | 1960 | 1965 | 1970 | 1975 | 1980 | 1985 | 1990 | 1995 | 2000 | 2005 | 2010 | 2015 |
|---|---|---|---|---|---|---|---|---|---|---|---|---|---|---|---|---|
| Republic of Moldova | ... | ... | ... | ... | ... | ... | ... | ... | ... | ... | ... | 840.00 | 777.00 | 2 292.00 | 3 855.29 | 3 986.80 |
| Romania | 96.00 | ... | ... | 384.00 | 699.70 | 1 163.30 | 2 117.00 | 5 768.98 | 13 200.00 | 8 400.00 | 7 600.00 | 10 277.90 | 13 147.83 | 40 518.48 | 62 108.64 | 69 867.43 |
| Russian Federation | | | | | | | | | | | | 62 603.00 | 44 862.00 | 125 434.00 | 248 634.00 | 194 087.00 |
| Rwanda | ... | ... | 1.00 | 2.00 | 14.00 | 18.00 | 29.10 | 99.29 | 262.22 | 298.49 | 286.67 | 237.70 | 213.21 | 430.37 | 1 431.04 | 2 247.69 |
| Saint Helena | ... | ... | ... | ... | ... | ... | ... | | 13.24 | 17.47 | 19.33 | 22.97 | 38.61 | 55.77 | 61.38 | 43.18 |
| Saint Kitts and Nevis | ... | ... | 4.00 | 5.00 | 7.00 | 9.00 | 12.00 | 23.67 | 45.00 | 51.00 | 110.00 | 133.00 | 196.00 | 210.47 | 269.82 | 280.00 |
| Saint Lucia | ... | 4.02 | 3.64 | 5.62 | 11.19 | 20.23 | 36.85 | 57.46 | 124.00 | 125.00 | 271.00 | 307.00 | 355.00 | 485.78 | 662.49 | 569.98 |
| Saint Pierre and Miquelon | 2.00 | 3.00 | 1.99 | 3.34 | 4.42 | 5.54 | 11.73 | 23.80 | 41.98 | 40.21 | 86.31 | 74.00 | 70.00 | 84.82 | 98.89 | 90.00 |
| Saint Vincent and the Grenadines | 2.51 | 1.84 | 2.33 | 3.68 | 7.57 | 8.64 | 15.26 | 24.84 | 57.11 | 79.22 | 136.07 | 135.81 | 163.00 | 240.43 | 337.97 | 333.71 |
| Samoa | 3.00 | 3.00 | 3.00 | 5.31 | 7.41 | 9.15 | 13.58 | 37.00 | 62.53 | 51.33 | 80.68 | 94.95 | 90.13 | 238.65 | 309.85 | 333.91 |
| Sao Tome and Principe | 4.00 | 5.00 | 4.00 | 4.00 | 5.00 | 5.05 | 9.06 | 11.30 | 18.88 | 9.88 | 21.30 | 29.30 | 29.77 | 49.73 | 112.15 | 141.85 |
| Saudi Arabia | 127.00 | 130.00 | 115.00 | 245.07 | 234.00 | 506.00 | 692.89 | 4 213.22 | 30 166.00 | 23 622.00 | 24 069.00 | 28 091.00 | 30 238.00 | 59 458.70 | 106 862.97 | 169 968.00 |
| Senegal | 177.00 | 247.00 | 237.00 | 243.00 | 173.25 | 164.04 | 194.86 | 583.33 | 1 051.97 | 825.73 | 1 219.84 | 1 412.21 | 1 552.78 | 3 497.70 | 4 782.24 | 5 595.35 |
| Serbia | ... | ... | ... | ... | ... | ... | ... | ... | ... | ... | ... | ... | ... | ... | ... | 18 172.90 |
| Serbia and Montenegro | ... | ... | ... | ... | ... | ... | ... | ... | ... | ... | ... | 2 666.00 | 3 711.00 | 11 635.00 | ... | ... |
| Seychelles | 1.00 | 1.00 | 1.00 | 1.90 | 2.30 | 2.39 | 10.07 | 31.75 | 98.79 | 99.32 | 186.88 | 232.79 | 342.00 | 674.90 | 984.30 | 991.28 |
| Sierra Leone | 20.07 | 21.63 | 18.89 | 47.92 | 73.75 | 107.76 | 116.29 | 185.17 | 426.71 | 151.16 | 148.65 | 133.48 | 149.40 | 344.69 | 770.04 | 1 510.66 |
| Singapore | 845.83 | 787.55 | 1 069.51 | 1 261.92 | 1 332.80 | 1 243.30 | 2 461.44 | 8 133.10 | 24 007.30 | 26 285.20 | 60 899.10 | 124 507.00 | 134 545.00 | 200 047.00 | 310 791.00 | 296 745.00 |
| Sint Maarten | | | | | | | | | | | | | | | | 887.95 |
| Slovakia | | | | | | | | | | | | 8 770.00 | 12 759.82 | 34 649.34 | 65 026.07 | 73 509.26 |
| Slovenia | | | | | | | | | | | | 9 491.61 | 10 147.19 | 20 336.66 | 30 093.51 | 29 705.98 |
| Solomon Islands | 1.00 | 1.45 | 1.60 | 3.33 | 4.77 | 8.47 | 12.91 | 32.79 | 89.30 | 83.11 | 91.46 | 154.00 | 92.00 | 185.03 | 404.35 | 417.82 |
| Somalia | ... | ... | 13.00 | 22.00 | 30.30 | 49.50 | 45.10 | 154.70 | 435.31 | 112.00 | 95.00 | 267.95 | 342.99 | 626.00 | 840.00 | 1 100.00 |
| South Africa | 1 551.75 | 1 267.88 | 921.20 | 1 420.86 | 1 628.76 | 2 562.98 | 3 843.14 | 8 293.15 | 19 598.00 | 11 319.00 | 18 399.00 | 30 546.00 | 29 695.00 | 62 304.30 | 96 835.45 | 90 357.00 |
| Spain | 482.00 | 466.00 | 389.00 | 617.00 | 721.67 | 3 040.33 | 4 747.14 | 16 264.60 | 34 078.40 | 29 963.30 | 87 554.20 | 113 543.08 | 155 757.02 | 288 785.76 | 327 015.57 | 309 291.77 |
| Sri Lanka | 300.48 | 287.91 | 245.07 | 306.60 | 412.86 | 309.54 | 385.56 | 815.93 | 2 036.98 | 1 843.37 | 2 685.01 | 5 185.21 | 6 281.24 | 8 833.67 | 13 511.50 | 18 934.60 |
| State of Palestine | | | | | | | | | | | | 1 658.19 | 2 382.81 | 2 666.77 | 3 958.51 | 6 157.87 |
| Sudan | 91.55 | 91.13 | 78.31 | 140.13 | 183.06 | 207.56 | 287.50 | 887.19 | 1 576.38 | 770.73 | 618.50 | 1 218.80 | 1 552.70 | 6 756.80 | 10 044.77 | 8 584.56 |
| Suriname | 19.20 | 20.04 | 20.79 | 27.41 | 54.06 | 93.42 | 115.28 | 261.57 | 504.00 | 299.00 | 472.00 | 585.00 | 526.45 | 1 049.93 | 1 397.50 | 1 972.62 |
| Swaziland | ... | ... | 5.00 | 9.00 | 17.00 | 36.55 | 59.85 | 177.70 | 624.67 | 316.43 | 663.68 | 1 008.36 | 1 051.52 | 1 900.00 | 1 960.00 | 1 429.30 |
| Sweden | 1 377.57 | 1 175.47 | 1 182.54 | 1 998.18 | 2 900.71 | 4 377.17 | 7 007.45 | 17 450.30 | 33 438.20 | 28 547.50 | 54 244.60 | 65 038.73 | 72 699.81 | 111 696.84 | 148 945.62 | 137 624.71 |
| Switzerland | 1 143.16 | 866.92 | 1 037.29 | 1 463.77 | 2 206.29 | 3 642.62 | 6 374.19 | 13 303.40 | 36 341.00 | 30 696.00 | 69 681.00 | 80 152.00 | 82 521.00 | 126 573.68 | 176 280.63 | 251 873.08 |

Annex table A.7
**Merchandise imports, 1948–2015** (continued)

Millions of current United States dollars

| Country/area | 1948 | 1949 | 1950 | 1955 | 1960 | 1965 | 1970 | 1975 | 1980 | 1985 | 1990 | 1995 | 2000 | 2005 | 2010 | 2015 |
|---|---|---|---|---|---|---|---|---|---|---|---|---|---|---|---|---|
| Syrian Arab Republic | 213.50 | 216.70 | 211.30 | 179.10 | 239.39 | 213.35 | 360.47 | 1 685.41 | 4 124.08 | 3 966.88 | 2 400.00 | 4 709.13 | 3 815.43 | 10 862.22 | 17 561.58 | 4 767.95 |
| Taiwan Province of China | 5.00 | 58.80 | 110.20 | 201.20 | 271.86 | 557.25 | 1 527.75 | 5 959.47 | 19 754.00 | 20 122.00 | 54 782.00 | 103 558.00 | 140 641.91 | 182 614.40 | 251 236.40 | 237 548.85 |
| Tajikistan | ... | ... | ... | ... | ... | ... | ... | ... | ... | ... | ... | 810.00 | 675.00 | 1 330.00 | 2 656.90 | 3 885.46 |
| Thailand | 144.00 | 193.00 | 209.00 | 338.00 | 454.26 | 741.97 | 1 298.51 | 3 279.60 | 9 213.59 | 9 242.01 | 33 045.20 | 70 786.40 | 61 923.40 | 118 177.58 | 182 920.96 | 202 654.15 |
| The former Yugoslav Republic of Macedonia | | | | | | | | | | | | 1 718.90 | 2 093.87 | 3 228.00 | 5 474.49 | 6 399.87 |
| Timor-Leste | | | | | | | | | | | | | | 109.11 | 246.31 | 734.31 |
| Togo | 7.00 | 11.00 | 9.00 | 17.97 | 26.31 | 45.30 | 64.86 | 174.19 | 550.61 | 288.04 | 581.37 | 593.50 | 562.24 | 1 060.21 | 1 682.69 | 2 126.64 |
| Tokelau | | | | | | | | | | | | | 0.75 | 0.44 | 0.04 | 0.04 |
| Tonga | 2.20 | 1.90 | 2.00 | 1.48 | 3.70 | 3.81 | 6.20 | 17.06 | 37.68 | 41.16 | 61.86 | 77.17 | 69.44 | 120.69 | 158.78 | 205.00 |
| Trinidad and Tobago | 109.99 | 119.28 | 98.23 | 171.73 | 294.00 | 471.45 | 543.50 | 1 469.09 | 3 177.67 | 1 534.29 | 1 108.78 | 1 714.20 | 3 308.00 | 5 693.91 | 6 479.60 | 7 900.00 |
| Tunisia | 179.00 | 121.40 | 147.23 | 180.80 | 190.69 | 245.83 | 305.52 | 1 423.79 | 3 525.65 | 2 756.51 | 5 512.58 | 7 902.98 | 8 566.88 | 13 177.00 | 22 215.36 | 20 221.00 |
| Turkey | 347.50 | 345.80 | 311.40 | 497.60 | 468.20 | 572.00 | 947.60 | 4 738.70 | 7 909.60 | 11 343.50 | 22 303.10 | 35 710.20 | 54 502.80 | 116 774.00 | 185 544.33 | 207 199.14 |
| Turkmenistan | | | | | | | | | | | | 1 365.00 | 1 786.00 | 2 947.00 | 5 700.00 | 7 800.00 |
| Turks and Caicos Islands | | | | | | | | | | | | 148.67 | 303.72 | 302.00 | 224.66 | |
| Tuvalu | | | | | | | | 4.00 | | 3.00 | 5.00 | 5.71 | 5.17 | 12.92 | 16.00 | 11.00 |
| Uganda | | 47.00 | 43.12 | 95.06 | 91.42 | 161.14 | 172.06 | 207.15 | 293.00 | 327.00 | 288.00 | 1 056.00 | 1 536.00 | 2 054.14 | 4 664.34 | 5 780.22 |
| Ukraine | | | | | | | | | | | | 15 484.00 | 13 956.00 | 36 136.30 | 60 911.00 | 36 317.20 |
| Union of Soviet Socialist Republics | 1 212.00 | 1 474.00 | 1 456.00 | 3 061.00 | 5 630.00 | 8 058.00 | 11 732.00 | 36 971.00 | 68 515.00 | 82 915.00 | 120 880.00 | ... | | | | |
| United Arab Emirates | | | 72.00 | 120.00 | 160.00 | 225.00 | 267.00 | 2 669.00 | 8 746.00 | 6 549.00 | 11 199.00 | 23 777.72 | 35 008.85 | 84 654.00 | 165 000.00 | 197 690.14 |
| United Kingdom of Great Britain and Northern Ireland | 8 370.31 | 8 479.84 | 7 305.20 | 10 875.20 | 13 034.00 | 16 128.00 | 21 871.20 | 53 340.90 | 115 545.00 | 109 505.00 | 224 416.00 | 267 270.99 | 347 198.09 | 513 672.66 | 591 094.91 | 625 806.04 |
| United Republic of Tanzania | 80.80 | 92.60 | 67.20 | 121.90 | 111.10 | 197.40 | 318.36 | 777.72 | 1 257.64 | 844.50 | 1 363.63 | 1 674.54 | 1 523.52 | 3 287.06 | 7 874.20 | 10 788.90 |
| United States of America | 8 081.00 | 7 544.00 | 9 631.00 | 12 489.00 | 16 371.00 | 23 188.00 | 42 428.00 | 105 881.00 | 256 985.00 | 352 463.00 | 516 987.00 | 770 852.00 | 1 259 300.00 | 1 732 706.00 | 1 969 183.90 | 2 307 945.63 |
| Uruguay | 199.70 | 180.60 | 212.15 | 237.57 | 217.54 | 150.75 | 230.92 | 556.47 | 1 680.30 | 707.70 | 1 342.90 | 2 866.90 | 3 465.80 | 3 879.00 | 8 621.76 | 9 489.42 |
| Uzbekistan | | | | | | | | | | | | 2 750.00 | 2 697.00 | 3 666.00 | 8 689.48 | 10 263.58 |
| Vanuatu | 1.85 | 2.33 | 1.48 | 3.75 | 6.64 | 7.21 | 12.98 | 39.77 | 73.00 | 70.00 | 96.00 | 95.00 | 87.00 | 149.16 | 285.06 | 387.82 |
| Venezuela (Bolivarian Republic of) | 838.96 | 800.76 | 597.00 | 1 098.48 | 1 188.36 | 1 420.52 | 1 869.04 | 6 000.06 | 11 827.00 | 8 106.00 | 7 335.00 | 12 649.00 | 16 213.00 | 24 027.30 | 39 000.00 | 32 740.00 |
| Viet Nam | | | | | | | | | 1 314.00 | 1 857.00 | 2 752.41 | 8 155.40 | 15 638.00 | 36 761.00 | 84 838.55 | 166 103.04 |
| Wallis and Futuna Islands | | | | | | | | | | | | | 36.79 | 50.78 | 60.20 | 65.04 |
| Yemen | | | | | | | | | | | 1 570.94 | 1 582.00 | 2 324.00 | 5 377.72 | 9 255.37 | ... |

Annex table A.7
**Merchandise imports, 1948–2015** (*continued*)

Millions of current United States dollars

| Country/area | 1948 | 1949 | 1950 | 1955 | 1960 | 1965 | 1970 | 1975 | 1980 | 1985 | 1990 | 1995 | 2000 | 2005 | 2010 | 2015 |
|---|---|---|---|---|---|---|---|---|---|---|---|---|---|---|---|---|
| Yemen Arab Republic | 8.00 | 9.00 | 10.00 | 14.00 | 16.00 | 18.90 | 32.75 | 294.01 | 1 853.00 | 1 313.45 | ... | ... | ... | ... | ... | ... |
| Yemen (People's Democratic Republic of) | 110.83 | 122.10 | 117.32 | 210.00 | 217.00 | 301.00 | 199.92 | 322.82 | 1 526.95 | 1 310.46 | ... | ... | ... | ... | ... | ... |
| Yugoslavia | 315.70 | 297.60 | 230.00 | 441.00 | 826.00 | 1 288.00 | 2 874.00 | 7 697.00 | 15 076.00 | 12 207.00 | 18 871.00 | ... | ... | ... | ... | ... |
| Zambia | 51.18 | 43.82 | 41.86 | 441.00 | 495.00 | 298.66 | 477.19 | 929.05 | 1 088.40 | 721.67 | 1 255.46 | 691.63 | 887.96 | 2 558.01 | 5 320.83 | 8 451.26 |
| Zimbabwe | 171.00 | 200.40 | 184.40 | 229.00 | 252.00 | 420.00 | 420.00 | 877.01 | 1 396.30 | 867.58 | 1 833.35 | 2 651.23 | 1 863.00 | 2 350.00 | 3 800.00 | 4 115.59 |

Source: UN/DESA, based on data from United Nations Conference on Trade and Development. Available at http://unctadstat.unctad.org/wds/ReportFolders/reportFolders.aspx.

Note: The data set was used in its entirety by UN/DESA. Data were appended for the following countries: Ethiopia, prior to 1992 and post-1992; Indonesia, prior to 2003 and post-2003; and the Sudan, prior to 2002 and post-2002.

Three dots (...) indicate that data are not applicable or not available.

# Bibliography

Alesina, Alberto (2010). Fiscal adjustments: lessons from history. Harvard University. Paper prepared for the Ecofin meeting, Madrid, 15 April. Available at https://scholar.harvard.edu/alesina/publications/fiscal-adjustments-lessons-recent-history.

_____, and Silvia Ardagna (2010). Large changes in fiscal policy: taxes versus spending. In *Tax Policy and the Economy*, Jeffrey R. Brown, ed. Chicago, Illinois: University of Chicago Press. Pp. 35–68.

Autor, David H. (2014). Skills, education, and the rise of earnings inequality among the "other 99 percent". *Science*, vol. 344, No. 6186 ( May).

Bagchi, Amiya Kumar (2017). The 1990s: the fall of the Berlin Wall, globalization and crises. Background paper prepared for *World Economic and Social Survey 2017*.

Bluwstein, Kristina, and Fabio Canova (2016). Beggar-thy-neighbor? the international effects of ECB unconventional monetary policy measures. *International Journal of Central Banking*, vol. 12, No. 3 (September).

Blyth, Mark (2013). *Austerity: The History of a Dangerous Idea*. New York: Oxford University Press.

Bordo, Michael (1993). The Bretton Woods international monetary system: a historical overview. In *A Retrospective on the Bretton Woods System: Lessons for International Monetary Reform*, Michael D. Bordo and Barry Eichengreen, eds. Chicago, Illinois: University of Chicago Press. Pp. 3-108.

Braga de Macedo, Jorge, and Barry Eichengreen (2001). The European Payments Union: history and implications for the evolution of the international financial architecture. March. Available at http://www.jbmacedo.com/oecd/triffin.html. Accessed 16 January 2017.

Chowdhury, Anis, and Iyanatul Islam (2012). The debate on expansionary fiscal consolidation: how robust is the evidence? *Economic and Labour Relations Review*, vol. 23, No. 3 (September).

Chudik, Alexander, and others (2015).Is there a debt-threshold effect on output growth? IMF Working Paper, No. 15/197. Washington, D.C.: International Monetary Fund. September.

Cornia, Giovanni Andrea (2011). Economic integration, inequality and growth: Latin America vs. the European economies in transition. DESA Working Paper, No. 101. ST/ESA/2011/DWP/101. January. Available at http://www.un.org/esa/desa/papers/2011/wp101_2011.pdf.

_____ (2014). Recent distributive changes in Latin America: an overview. In *Falling Inequality in Latin America: Policy Changes and Lessons*, Giovanni Andrea Cornia, ed. WIDER Studies in Development Economics, Oxford: New York: Oxford University Press. Part I, chap. 1.

_____, Richard Jolly and Frances Stewart (1987). *Adjustment with a Human Face*, vol. I, *Protecting the Vulnerable and Promoting Growth*. Oxford: Clarendon Press.

De Janvry, Alain, and Élisabeth Sadoulet (2013). Soixante ans d'économie du développement: qu'avons-nous appris pour le développement économique? In *L'économie du développement vingt ans après*, vol. 1. *Revue d'économie du développement*, 2013/2-3 (vol. 21), pp. 9-21. Paris : De Boeck Supérieur. Available at www.cairn.info/revue-d-economie-du-developpement-2013-2-page-9.htm.

de Larosière, Jacques (1986). Statement made by the Managing Director of the International Monetary Fund to the Economic and Social Council, Geneva, 4 July 1986. Available at http://archive.unu.edu/unupress/food/8F091E0c.htm.

De Long, J. Bradford, and Barry Eichengreen (1991). The Marshall Plan: history's most successful structural adjustment program. *NBER Working Paper*, No. 3899. Cambridge, Massachusetts; National Bureau of Economic Research.

De Vries, Margaret Garritsen (1987). Balance of Payments Adjustment, 1945 to 1986: The IMF Experience. Washington, D.C.: International Monetary Fund.

Farrell, Henry, and John Quiggin (2011), Consensus, dissensus and economic ideas: the rise, fall and partial resurrection of Keynesianism during the economic crisis. Risk and Sustainable Management Group (RSMG) Working Paper P11_2. Brisbane, Australia: University of Queensland, Schools of Economics and Political Science. Available at https://ideas.repec.org/p/ags/uqsers/151527.html.

Galbraith, James K. (2012). *Inequality and Instability: A Study of the World Economy Just Before the Great Crisis*. New York: Oxford University Press.

Ghosh, Jayati (2017). The 2000s and beyond: development issues in a rapidly changing world. Background paper prepared for *World Economic and Social Survey 2017*.

Glyn, Andrew, and others (1990). The rise and fall of the Golden Age. In *The Golden Age of Capitalism: Reinterpreting the Postwar Experience,* Stephen A. Marglin and Juliet B. Schor, eds. UNU-WIDER Studies in Development Economics. Oxford: Clarendon Press.

Hausmann, Ricardo, Dani Rodrik and Andrés Velasco (2005). Growth diagnostics. March. Available at http://www6.iadb.org/WMSFiles/products/research/files/pubS-852.pdf.

Helleiner, G. K.(1983). *The IMF and Africa in the 1980s. Essays in International Finance*, No. 152, July 1983 .Princeton, New Jersey: Princeton University, Department of Economics, International Finance Section.

Herndon, T., M. Ash and R. Pollin (2014). Does high public debt consistently stifle economic growth? a critique of Reinhart and Rogoff. *Cambridge Journal of Economics*, vol. 38, No. 2 (March), pp. 257-279.

Ilzetzki, Ethan, Carmen M. Reinhart and Kenneth S. Rogoff (2010). Exchange rate arrangements entering the 21st century: which anchor will hold? Available at http://personal.lse.ac.uk/ilzetzki/index.htm/Data.htm.

Intergovernmental Panel on Climate Change (2014). Summary for Policymakers. In *Climate Change 2014: Impacts,Adaptation, and Vulnerability. Part A: Global and Sectoral Aspects.* Working Group II Contribution to the Fifth Assessment Report of the Intergovernmental Panel on Climate Change, C.B. Field and others, eds. Cambridge, United Kingdom: Cambridge University Press.

International Institute for Labour Studies (2008). *World of Work Report 2008: Income Inequalities in the Age of Financial Globalization.* Geneva: International Labour Office.

International Labour Organization (2016a). *World Employment and Social Outlook: Trends 2016.* Geneva: International Labour Office.

_____ (2016b). *World Employment and Social Outlook: Trends for Youth 2016.* Geneva: International Labour Office.

_____ (2017). *World Employment and Social Outlook: Trends 2017.* Geneva: International Labour Office.

International Monetary Fund (1979). Annual Report 1979. Washington, D.C.

_____ (2007). *World Economic Outlook, October 2007: Globalization and Inequality.* Washington, D.C. October.

_____ (2010). *Fiscal Monitor: Navigating the Fiscal Challenges Ahead.* 14 May. Washington, D.C.Jolly, Richard (1991). Adjustment with a human face: a UNICEF record and perspective on the 1980s. *World Development*, vol. 19, No. 12 (December), pp. 1807-1821.

Jolly, Richard (1991). Adjustment with a human face: a UNICEF record and perspective on the 1980s. *World Development*, vol. 19, No. 12 (December), pp. 1807-1821.

Julca, Alex, Nicole Hunt and Diana Alarcón (2015). Income convergence or persistent inequalities among countries? Development Issues, No. 5. 26 October. New York: UN/DESA, Development Policy and Analysis Division, Development Strategy and Policy Analysis Unit. Available at http://bit.ly/Devissues.

Krueger Anne O. (1978). *Foreign Trade Regimes and Economic Development: Liberalization Attempts and Consequences.* Cambridge, Massachusetts: Ballinger Press for the National Bureau of Economic Research.

LaFleur, Marcelo, Pingfan Hong and Hiroshi Kawamura (2015). Global partnership for promoting post-2015 sustainable development goals: lessons from the MDG period. Background paper prepared for *World Economic and Social Survey 2014/2015.* March.

LaFleur, Marcelo, and Ingo Pitterle (2017). Low growth with limited policy options? secular stagnation: causes, consequences and cures. Development Issues, No. 9. 2 March. New York: UN/DESA, Development Policy and Analysis Division, Development Strategy and Policy Analysis Unit. Available at http://bit.ly/DevIssues.

Lim, Mah-Hui (2014). Globalization, export-led growth and inequality: the East Asian story. South Centre Research Paper, No. 57. November. Geneva: South Centre.

Loxley, John (1986). *Debt and Disorder: External Financing for Development.* Boulder, Colorado: Westview Press.

_____ (2017). The 1970s: Shocks, stagflation and the Second UN Decade of Development. Background paper prepared for *World Economic and Social Survey 2017.*

Maddison, Angus (2001). *The World Economy: A Millennial Perspective.* Paris: OECD.

Marglin, Stephen A. (1990). Lessons of the Golden Age: an overview. In *The Golden Age of Capitalism: Reinterpreting the Postwar Experience*, Stephen A. Marglin and Juliet B. Schor, eds. Oxford: Clarendon Press.

Milanovic, Branko (2007) *Worlds Apart: Measuring International and Global Inequality.* Princeton, New Jersey: Princeton University Press.

_____ (2012a). Global income inequality by the numbers: in history and now - an overview. World Bank Policy Research Working Paper, No. 6259. Washington, D.C. November.

_____ (2012b). *The Haves and the Have-Nots: A Brief and Idiosyncratic History of Global Inequality.* New York: Basic Books.

Ocampo, José Antonio (2013). The Latin American debt crisis in historical perspective. New York: Columbia University, Initiative for Policy Dialogue. Available at http://policydialogue.org/publications/network_papers/the_latin_american_debt_crisis_in_historical_perspective/.

_____ (2016). From Reconstruction to the postwar boom. Background paper prepared for *World Economic and Social Survey 2017.* December.

_____, and Mariángela Parra-Lancourt (2010). The terms of trade for commodities since the mid-19th century. *Revista de Historia Económica - Journal of Iberian and Latin American Economic History*, vol. 28, No. 1, pp. 11-43.

Ocampo, José Antonio, and others (2014). *La crisis latinoamericana de la deuda desde la perspectiva histórica.* . Santiago: Economic Commission for Latin America and the Caribbean. Sales No. S.14.II.G.12.

Organization for Economic Cooperation and Development (2008). *Growing Unequal? Income Distribution and Poverty in OECD Countries.* Paris.

Park, Y. S. (1973). The link between special drawing rights and development finance., *Essays in International Finance*, No. 100. Princeton, New Jersey: Princeton University, Department of Economics, International Finance Section. September). Available at https//www.princeton.edu/~ies/IES_Essasys/E100.

Pescatori, Andrea, Damiano Sandri and John Simon (2014). "Debt and growth: is there a magic threshold? IMF Working Paper, No. 14/34. Washington, D.C.: International Monetary Fund. February.

Piketty, Thomas (2014). *Capital in the Twenty-First Century.* Cambridge Massachusetts: Belknap Press.

Punzi, Maria Teresa, and Pornpinun Chantapacdepong (2017). Spillover effects of unconventional monetary policy in Asia and the Pacific. ADBI Working Paper, No. 630. Tokyo: Asian Development Bank Institute. January. Available at https://www.adb.org/publications/spillover-effects-unconventional-monetary-policy-asia-pacific.

Quiggin, John (2017). Global financial crisis: analysis of economic policy, 2008-2016. Background paper prepared for *World Economic and Social Survey 2017*. January.

Rahman, Mahfuzur (2002). *World Economic Issues at the United Nations: Half a Century of Debate*. Norwell, Massachusetts: Kluwer Academic Publishers.

Reinhart, Carmen M., and Kenneth S. Rogoff (2009). *This Time is Different: Eight Centuries of Financial Folly*. Princeton, New Jersey: Princeton University Press.

_____ (2010) Growth in a time of debt. *American Economic Review*, vol. 100, No. 2 (May), pp. 573-578.

Stallings, Barbara (2014). La economía política de las negociaciones de la deuda: América Latina en la década de los ochenta. In José Antonio Ocampo and others, *La crisis latinoamericana de la deuda desde la perspectiva histórica*. Santiago: Economic Commission for Latin America and the Caribbean. Sales No. S.14.II.G.12. Chap. II, pp. 53-82.

_____ (2017). The 1980s: Debt crisis and development setbacks. Background paper prepared for *World Economic and Social Survey 2017*.

Stiglitz, Joseph E. (2016). *The State, the Market, and Development. WIDER Working Paper*, No. 2016/1. Helsinki: United Nations University World Institute for Development Economics Research. January.

Tillmann, Peter (2016). Unconventional monetary policy and the spillovers to emerging markets. *Journal of International Money and Finance*, vol. 66 (September), pp. 136-156.

United Nations (1996). *Report of the World Summit for Social Development, Copenhagen, 6-12 March 1995*. Sales No. E.96.IV.8. Chap. I, resolution 1, annex I.

_____ (2002). *Report of the International Conference on Financing for Development, Monterrey, Mexico, 18-22 March 2002*. Sales No. E.02. II.A.7. Chapter I, resolution 1, annex.

_____ (2005). *Report on the World Social Situation 2005: The Inequality Predicament*. ST/ESA/299. Sales No. E.05.IV.5.

_____ (2007). *United Nations Development Agenda: Development for All*. ST/ESA/316. Sales No. E.07.1.17. Available at http://www.un.org/ esa/devagenda/UNDA_BW5_Final.pdf . See this publication for a comprehensive discussion of the outcomes of the conferences and summits organized by the United Nations that are mentioned in *World Economic and Social Survey 2017*.

_____ (2013). *Report on the World Social Situation 2013: Inequality Matters*. ST/ESA/345. Sales No. 13.IV.2.

_____ (2016). *Report on the World Social Situation 2016: Leaving No One Behind – The Imperative of Inclusive Development*. ST/ESA/362. Sales No. E.16.IV.1.

_____, Economic and Social Council (2016). Report of the Committee for Development Policy on the eighteenth session (14-18 March 2016). *Official Records of the Economic and Social Council, 2016, Supplement No. 13*. E/2016/33.

_____ (2017). Report of the Committee for Development Policy on the nineteenth session (20-24 March 2017). *Official Records of the Economic and Social Council, 2017, Supplement No. 13*. E/2017/33.

United Nations, General Assembly and Economic and Social Council (1984). Review and appraisal of the International Development Strategy for the Third United Nations Development Decade. Report of the Secretary-General. 29 March. A/39/115-E/1984/49 and Corr.1 and 2.

United Nations Children's Fund and UN-Women (2013). Addressing inequalities: synthesis report of the global thematic public consultation on the post-2015 development agenda. February.

Vieira, Sergio (2013). Inequalities on the rise? an assessment of current available data on income inequality, at global, international and national levels. Background paper prepared for *World Economic and Social Survey 2013*.

_____, and Diana Alarcón (2017). Global context for achieving the 2030 Agenda for Sustainable Development: sustained global economic growth. Development Issues, No. 8. 28 February. New York: UN/DESA, Development Policy and Analysis Division, Development Strategy and Policy Analysis Unit. Available at http://bit.ly/DevIssues.

Vos, Rob (2017). The world economy in 1999-2007: bubble, bubble, toil and trouble. Background paper prepared for *World Economic and Social Survey 2017*.

Wangwe, Samuel (2016). 1960s: decolonization and the First Development Decade. Background paper prepared for *World Economic and Social Survey 2017*. February.

Williamson, John, ed. (1990). *Latin American Adjustment: How Much Has Happened?* Washington D.C.: Institute for International Economics.

Wolf, Martin (2017). Trump's bilateral trade policy is insane: economic nationalism and protectionism didn't work in the 1930s — it won't work now. *Irish Times*, 15 March. Available at http://www.irishtimes.com/business/economy/martin-wolf-trump-s-bilateral-trade-policy-is-insane-1.3011357.

World Bank (1990). *World Development Report 1990: Poverty*. New York: Oxford University Press.

_____ (2005). *World Development Report 2006: Equity and Development*. New York: Oxford University Press; and Washington, D.C.: World Bank.

# Editions of the *World Economic and Social Survey* and *World Economic Situation and Prospects* cited in *World Economic and Social Survey 2017*

## World Economic and Social Survey

*Economic Report: Salient Features of the World Economic Situation, 1945-47.* Lake Success, New York. Issued in January 1948

*World Economic Report 1948.* Lake Success, New York. Sales No. 1949.II.C.3. Issued in June 1949

*World Economic Report 1949-50.* E/1910/Rev.1-ST/ECA/9. Sales No. 1951.II.C.1. Issued on 16 March 1951

*World Economic Report 1950-51.* E/2193/Rev.1 -ST/ECA/14 and Corr.1. Sales No. 1952.II.C.4. Issued in April 1952

*World Economic Report 1951-52.* E/2353/Rev.1-ST/ECA/19. Sales No. 1953.II.C.2. Issued in April 1953

*World Economic Report 1953-54.* E/2729-ST/ECA/30. Sales No. 1955.II.C.1. Issued on 15 April 1955

*World Economic Survey 1955.* E/2864-ST/ECA/38. Sales No. 1956.II.C.1. Issued on 27 April 1956

*World Economic Survey 1956.* E/2982-ST/ECA/44. Sales No. 1957.II.C.1. Issued on 20 May 1957

*World Economic Survey 1957.* E/3110-ST/ECA/53. Sales No. 58.II.C.1. Issued in 1958

*World Economic Survey 1958.* E/3244-ST/ECA/60. Sales No. 59.II.C.1. Issued in 1959

*World Economic Survey 1959.* E/3361-ST/ECA/63. Sales No. 60.II.C.1. Issued in 1960

*World Economic Survey 1960.* E/3501/Rev.1-ST/ECA/68. Sales No. 61.II.C.1. Issued in 1961

*World Economic Survey 1961.* E/3624/Rev.1-ST/ECA/71. Sales No. 62.II.C.1. Issued in 1962

*World Economic Survey 1962.* Part I. *The Developing Countries in World Trade.* E/3774-ST/ECA/79. Sales No. 63.II.C.1. Issued in 1963

*World Economic Survey 1962.* Part II. *Current Economic Developments.* E/3761/Rev.1-ST/ECA/78. Sales No. 63.II.C.2. Issued in 1963

*World Economic Survey 1963.* Part I. *Trade and Development: Trends, Needs and Policies.* E/3908-ST/ECA/84. Sales No. 64.II.C.1. Issued in 1964

*World Economic Survey 1963.* Part II. *Current Economic Developments.* E/3902/Rev.1-ST/ECA/83. Sales No. 64.II.C.3. Issued in 1964

*World Economic Survey 1964.* Part I. *Development Plans: Appraisal of Targets and Progress in Developing Countries.* E/4046/Rev.1-ST/ECA/87. Sales No. 65.II.C.1. Issued in 1965

*World Economic Survey 1964.* Part II. *Current Economic Developments.* E/4047/Rev.1-ST/ECA/88. Sales No. 65.II.C.2. Issued in 1965

*World Economic Survey 1965.* Part I. *The Financing of Economic Development.* E/4187/Rev.1-ST/ECA/91. Sales No. 66.II.C.1. Issued in 1966

*World Economic Survey 1965.* Part II. *Current Economic Developments.* E/4221/Rev.1-ST/ECA/92. Sales No. 66.II.C.2. Issued in 1966

*World Economic Survey 1967.* Part One. *The Problems and Policies of Economic Development: An Appraisal of Recent Experience.* E/4488/Rev.1-ST/ECA/104. Issued in 1968

*World Economic Survey 1967.* Part Two. *Current Economic Developments.* E/4489/Rev.1-ST/ECA/105. Issued in 1968

*World Economic Survey 1968.* Part One. *Some Issues of Development Policy in the Coming Decade.* E/4687/Rev.1-ST/ECA/118. Issued in 1969

*World Economic Survey 1968.* Part Two. *Current Economic Developments.* E/4688-ST/ECA/119. Issued in 1970

*World Economic Survey 1969-1970: The Developing Countries in the 1960s – The Problem of Appraising Progress.* E/4942-ST/ECA/141. Sales No. E.71.II.C.1. Issued in 1971

*World Economic Survey, 1971: Current Economic Developments.* E/5144-ST/ECA/159. Sales No. E.72.II.C.2. Issued in 1972

*World Economic Survey, 1972: Current Economic Developments.* E/5310-ST/ECA/182. Sales No. E.73.II.C.1. Issued in 1973

*World Economic Survey, 1974.* Part One. *Mid-term Review and Appraisal of Progress in the Implementation of the International Development Strategy.* E/5665-ST/ESA/26. Sales No. E.75.II.C.1. Issued in 1975

*World Economic Survey, 1974.* Part Two. *Current Economic Developments.* E/5681/Rev.1-ST/ESA/26. Sales No. E.75.II.C.3. Issued in 1975

*World Economic Survey, 1975: Fluctuations and Development in the World Economy.* E/5790/Rev.1-ST/ESA/49. Sales No. E.76.II.C.1. Issued in 1976

*Supplement to World Economic Survey, 1975: Fluctuations and Development in the World Economy.* E/5873/Rev.1-ST/ESA/59. Sales No. E.77.II.C.2. Issued in 1977

*World Economic Survey, 1977.* E/1978/70/Rev.1-ST/ESA/82. Sales No. E.78.II.C.1. Issued in 1978

*World Economic Survey 1979-1980: Current Trends in the World Economy.* E/1980/38-ST/ESA/106. Sales No. E.80.II.C.2

*World Economic Survey 1980-1981.* E/1981/42-ST/ESA/115. Sales No. E.81.II.C.2

*World Economic Survey 1981-1982: Current Trends in the World Economy.* E/1982/46-ST/ESA/124. Sales No. E.82.II.C.1

*World Economic Survey 1983: Current Trends and Policies in the World Economy.* E/1983/42-ST/ESA/131. Sales No. E.83.II.C.1

*World Economic Survey 1986: Current Trends and Policies in the World Economy.* E/1986/59-ST/ESA/183. Sales No. E.86.II.C.1

*World Economic Survey 1988: Current Trends and Policies in the World Economy.* E/1988/50-ST/ESA/205. Sales No. E.88.II.C.1

*World Economic Survey 1989: Current Trends and Policies in the World Economy.* E/1989/45-ST/ESA/211. Sales No. E.89.II.C.1

*World Economic Survey 1990: Current Trends and Policies in the World Economy.* E/1990/55-ST/ESA/218 and Corr.1 and 2. Sales No. E.90.II.C.1

*World Economic Survey 1991: Current Trends and Policies in the World Economy.* E/1991/75-ST/ESA/222. Sales No. E.91.II.C.1

*World Economic and Social Survey 1995: Current Trends and Policies in the World Economy.* E/1995/50-ST/ESA/243. Sales No. E.95.II.C.1

*World Economic and Social Survey 1999: Trends and Policies in the World Economy.* E/1999/50/Rev.1-ST/ESA/268. Sales No. E.99.II.C.1

*World Economic and Social Survey 2000: Current Trends and Policies in the World Economy.* E/2000/50/Rev.1-ST/ESA/273. Sales No. E.00.II.C.1

*World Economic and Social Survey 2001: Trends and Policies in the World Economy.* E/2001/50/Rev.1-ST/ESA/276. Sales No. E.01.II.C.1

*World Economic and Social Survey 2003: Trends and Policies in the World Economy.* E/2003/70/Rev.1-ST/ESA/283. Sales No. E.03.II.C.1

*World Economic and Social Survey 2005: Financing for Development.* E/2005/51/Rev.1-ST/ESA/298. Sales No. E.05.II.C.1

*World Economic and Social Survey 2006: Diverging Growth and Development.* E/2006/50/Rev.1-ST/ESA/306. Sales No. E.06.II.C.1

*World Economic and Social Survey 2008: Overcoming Economic Insecurity.* E/2008/50/Rev.1-ST/ESA/317. Sales No. E.08.II.C.1

*World Economic and Social Survey 2009: Promoting Development, Saving the Planet.* E/2009/50/Rev.1-ST/ESA/319. Sales No. E.09.II.C.1

*World Economic and Social Survey 2010: Retooling Global Development.* E/2010/50/Rev.1- ST/ESA/330. Sales No. E.10.II.C.1

*World Economic and Social Survey 2011: The Great Green Technological Transformation.* E/2011/50/Rev.1-ST/ESA/333. Sales No. E.11.II.C.1

*World Economic and Social Survey 2012: In Search of New Development Finance.* E/2012/50/Rev.1-ST/ESA/341. Sales No. E.12.II.C.1

*World Economic and Social Survey 2013: Sustainable Development Challenges.* E/2013/50/Rev.1-ST/ESA/344. Sales No. E.13.II.C.1

*World Economic and Social Survey 2014/2015: Learning from National Policies Supporting MDG Implementation.* E/2015/50/Rev.1-ST/ESA/360. Sales No. E.15.II.C.1. Issued in 2016

*World Economic and Social Survey 2016: Climate Change Resilience – An Opportunity for Reducing Inequalities.* E/2016/50/Rev.1-ST/ESA/363. Sales No. E.16.II.C.1

# World Economic Situation and Prospects

*World Economic Situation and Prospects for 1999.* Available at https://www.un.org/development/desa/dpad/publication/world-economic-situation-and-prospects-for-1999/

*World Economic Situation and Prospects 2005.* Sales No. E.05.II.C.2

*World Economic Situation and Prospects 2006.* Sales No. E.06.II.C.2

*World Economic Situation and Prospects 2007.* Sales No. E.07.II.C.2

*World Economic Situation and Prospects 2008.* Sales No. E.08.II.C.2

*World Economic Situation and Prospects 2009.* Sales No. E.09.II.C.2

*World Economic Situation and Prospects 2009 as of mid-2009.* E/2009/73.

*World Economic Situation and Prospects 2010.* Sales No. E.10.II.C.2

*World Economic Situation and Prospects 2011.* Sales No. E.11.II.C.2

*World Economic Situation and Prospects 2012.* Sales No. E.12.II.C.2

*World Economic Situation and Prospects 2014.* Sales No. E.14.II.C.2

*World Economic Situation and Prospects 2015.* Sales No. E.15.II.C.2

*World Economic Situation and Prospects 2017.* Sales No. E.17.II.C.2

**DATE DUE**

| | | | |
|---|---|---|---|
| | | | |
| | | | |
| | | | |
| | | | |
| | | | |
| | | | |
| | | | |
| | | | |
| | | | |
| | | | |
| | | | |
| | | | |
| | | | |
| | | | |
| | | | |
| | | | |
| | | | |
| | | | |
| | | | |
| GAYLORD | | | PRINTED IN U.S.A. |

United Nations publication
ISBN: 978-92-1-109176-2
eISBN: 978-92-1-060598-4